HANDY ROAD ATLAS
GREAT BRITAIN

CONTENTS

first²
[europe] ltd

Supplied to

Fir st 2 Europe Ltd.
MK
23
Le
LE

D0316676

English	French	German
MOTORWAY	Autoroute	Autobahn
MOTORWAY UNDER CONSTRUCTION	Autoroute en construction	Autobahn im Bau
MOTORWAY PROPOSED	Autoroute prévue	Geplante Autobahn
MOTORWAY JUNCTIONS WITH NUMBERS — Unlimited interchange — Limited interchange	Echangeur numéroté — Echangeur non limité — Echangeur limité	Autobahnanschlußstelle mit Nummer — Unbeschränkter Fahrtrichtungswechsel — Beschränkter Fahrtrichtungswechsel
MOTORWAY SERVICE AREA — with access from one carriageway only	Aire de services d'autoroute — à sens unique	Rastplatz oder Raststätte — Einbahn
MAJOR ROAD SERVICE AREAS with 24 hour Facilities — Primary Route — Class A Road	Aire de services de route prioriataire Ouverte 24h sur 24 — Route à grande circulation — Route de type A	Raststätte Durchgehend geöffnet — Hauptverkehrsstraße — A-Straße
PRIMARY ROUTE	Route à grande circulation	Hauptverkehrsstraße
PRIMARY ROUTE JUNCTION WITH NUMBER	Echangeur numéroté	Hauptverkehrsstraßenkreuzung mit Nummer
PRIMARY ROUTE DESTINATION	Route prioritaire, direction	Hauptverkehrsstraße Richtung
DUAL CARRIAGEWAYS (A & B Roads)	Route à deux chaussées séparées (route A & B)	Zweispurige Schnellstraße (A- und B-Straßen)
CLASS A ROAD	Route de type A	A-Straße
CLASS B ROAD	Route de type B	B-Straße
NARROW MAJOR ROAD (Passing Places)	Route prioritaire étroite (possibilité de dépassement)	Schmale Hauptverkehrsstaße (mit Überholmöglichkeit)
MAJOR ROADS UNDER CONSTRUCTION	Route prioritaire en construction	Hauptverkehrsstaße im Bau
MAJOR ROADS PROPOSED	Route prioritaire prévue	Geplante Hauptverkehrsstaße
GRADIENT 1:5(20%) & STEEPER (Ascent in direction of arrow)	Pente égale et supérieure à 20% (dans le sens de la montée)	20% Steigung und steiler (in Pfeilrichtung)
TOLL	Péage	Gebührenpflichtig
MILEAGE BETWEEN MARKERS	Distance en milles entre les flèches	Strecke zwischen Markierungen in Meilen
RAILWAY AND STATION	Voie ferrée et gare	Eisenbahnlinie und Bahnhof
LEVEL CROSSING AND TUNNEL	Passage à niveau et tunnel	Bahnübergang und Tunnel
RIVER OR CANAL	Rivière ou canal	Fluß oder Kanal
COUNTY OR UNITARY AUTHORITY BOUNDARY	Limite des comté ou de division administrative	Grafschafts- oder Verwaltungsbezirksgrenze
NATIONAL BOUNDARY	Frontière nationale	Landesgrenze
BUILT-UP AREA	Agglomération	Geschlossene Ortschaft
VILLAGE OR HAMLET	Village ou hameau	Dorf oder Weiler
WOODED AREA	Zone boisée	Waldgebiet
SPOT HEIGHT IN FEET · 813	Altitude (en pieds) · 813	Höhe in Fuß · 813
HEIGHT ABOVE SEA LEVEL 400' - 1,000' 122m - 305m / 1,000' - 1,400' 305m - 427m / 1,400' - 2,000' 427m - 610m / 2,000'+ 610m +	Altitude par rapport au niveau de la mer 400' - 1,000' 122m - 305m / 1,000' - 1,400' 305m - 427m / 1,400' - 2,000' 427m - 610m / 2,000'+ 610m +	Höhe über Meeresspiegel 400' - 1,000' 122m - 305m / 1,000' - 1,400' 305m - 427m / 1,400' - 2,000' 427m - 610m / 2,000'+ 610m +
NATIONAL GRID REFERENCE (Kilometres) 100	Coordonnées géographiques nationales (Kilometres) 100	Nationale geographische Koordinaten (Kilometer) 100
PAGE CONTINUATION 48	Suite à la page indiquée 48	Seitenfortsetzung 48

Scale bar:
0 1 2 3 4 5 10 15 20 Miles
0 1 2 3 4 5 10 15 20 25 30 Kilometres

Tourist Information — Information — Touristeninformationen

AIRPORT		✈	Aéroport		✈	Flughafen		✈
AIRFIELD		+	Terrain d' aviation		+	Flugplatz		+
HELIPORT		⚙	Héliport		⚙	Hubschrauberlandeplatz		⚙
BATTLE SITE AND DATE		⚔ 1066	Champ de bataille avec date		⚔ 1066	Schlachtfeld mit Datum		⚔ 1066
CASTLE (Open to Public)		▦	Château (ouvert au public)		▦	Schloss / Burg (für die Öffentlichkeit zugänglich)		▦
CASTLE WITH GARDEN (Open to Public)		⊞	Château et parc (ouvert au public)		⊞	Schloß mit Garten (für die Öffentlichkeit zugänglich)		⊞
CATHEDRAL, ABBEY, CHURCH, FRIARY, PRIORY		✝	Cathédrale, abbaye, église, monastère, prieuré		✝	Kathedrale, Abtel, Kirche, Mönchskloster, Kloster		✝
COUNTRY PARK		⛺	Parc régonal		⛺	Landschaftspark		⛺
FERRY	(Vehicular, sea)	⛴	Bac	(véhicules, mer)	⛴	Fähre	(Autos, meer)	⛴
	(Vehicular, river)	⛴		(véhicules, rivière)	⛴		(Autos, fluß)	⛴
	(Foot only)	👥		(Piétons)	👥		(nur für Personen)	👥
GARDEN (Open to Public)		❀	Jardin ouvert au public		❀	Garten (für die Öffentlichkeit zugänglich)		❀
GOLF COURSE	(9 Hole)	⛳	Terrain de golf	(9 trous)	⛳	Golfplatz	(9 Löcher)	⛳
	(18 Hole)	⛳		(18 trous)	⛳		(18 Löcher)	⛳
HISTORIC BUILDING (Open to Public)		⌂	Monument historique (ouvert au public)		⌂	Historisches Gebäude (für die Öffentlichkeit zugänglich)		⌂
HISTORIC BUILDING WITH GARDEN (Open to Public)		⌂	Monument historique avec jardin (ouvert au public)		⌂	Historisches Gebäude mit Garten (für die Öffentlichkeit zugänglich)		⌂
HORSE RACECOURSE		🐎	Hippodrome		🐎	Pferderennbahn		🐎
INFORMATION CENTRE		ℹ	Syndicat d'initiative		ℹ	Information		ℹ
LIGHTHOUSE		⚑	Phare		⚑	Leuchtturm		⚑
MOTOR RACING CIRCUIT		⚙	Circuit automobile		⚙	Automobilrennbahn		⚙
MUSEUM, ART GALLERY		▣	Musée		▣	Museum, Galerie		▣
NATIONAL PARK OR FOREST PARK		▬	Parc national ou forêt domaniale		▬	National- oder Waldpark		▬
NATIONAL TRUST PROPERTY	(Open)	NT	National Trust Property	(ouvert)	NT	National Trust-Eigentum	(geöffnet)	NT
	(Restricted Opening)	NT		(heures d'ouverture)	NT		(beschränkte Öffnungszeit)	NT
	(National Trust of Scotland)	NTS		(National Trust of Scotland)	NTS		(National Trust of Scotland)	NTS
NATURE RESERVE OR BIRD SANCTUARY		⚘	Réserve naturelle botanique ou ornithologique		⚘	Natur- oder Vogelschutzgebiet		⚘
NATURE TRAIL OR FOREST WALK		♣	Chemin forestier, piste verte		♣	Naturpfad oder Waldweg		♣
PLACE OF INTEREST	Monument •		Site, curiosité	Monument •		Sehenswürdigkeit	Monument •	
PICNIC SITE		⊼	Lieu pour pique-nique		⊼	Picknickplatz		⊼
RAILWAY, STEAM OR NARROW GAUGE		🚂	Chemin de fer, à vapeur ou à voie étroite		🚂	Eisenbahn, Dampf- oder Schmalspurbahn		🚂
THEME PARK		⚒	Centre de loisir		⚒	Vergnügungspark		⚒
VIEWPOINT	(360 degrees)	✳	Vue panoramique	(360 degré)	✳	Aussichtspunkt	(360 grade)	✳
	(180 degrees)	✲		(180 degré)	✲		(180 grade)	✲
WILDLIFE PARK		ⱽ	Réserve de faune		ⱽ	Wildpark		ⱽ
WINDMILL		⚒	Moulin à vent		⚒	Windmühle		⚒
ZOO OR SAFARI PARK		🐾	Parc ou réserve zoologique		🐾	Zoo oder Safari-Park		🐾

4

80   90   '00   60

20

1

Round Island
St. Helen's
White Island
Piper's Hole
Middle Town
King Charles's Castle
Cromwell's Castle
Toan
Day Mark
BRYHER
Old Grimsby
Town
ST. MARTIN'S
Gweal
Lower
Old Blockhouse
Higher Town
New Grimsby
Pool Grimsby
Maiden Bower
Valhalla
Figureheads
TRESCO
Tresco Abbey
EASTERN ISLES
Mincarlo
Samson
Halangy Down
Innisidgen
Bant's Carn
Burial
ISLES OF SCILLY
The Road
Maypole
Porth Hellick Down
Burial Chamber
Star Castle
ST. MARY'S
Hugh Town
ISLES OF SCILLY
°10   °10   °50
Crim Rocks
Garrison Walls
Old Town (St. Mary's)
Nags' Head
Giant's Castle
Annet
Troy Town
Gugh
Maze
Punch Bowl
Western Rocks
ST. AGNES
Bishop Rock

Hugh Town to
Penzance 2hrs. 40mins.

90

The Isles of Scilly lie 28 miles S.W. of Land's End

30   40   '50   60

6

Portreath
Nan
Godrevy
Navax Point
Crane Islands
B3301
40
Godrevy Island
NT
Godrevy
Corne
Tehidy
Bottol
The Carracks
Barbara Hepworth Tate
St. Ives Bay
Gwithian
Kehelland
A30
CAMBORN
Gurnard's Head
Wayside
Hellesveor
St. Ives
Carbis Bay
Phillack
Treswithian
Brea
Shire Horse
Treen
Zennor
Towednack
Halsetown
The Towans
Connor Downs
Penponds
Pendeen Watch
Porthmeor
Cripplesease
Phillack
Copperhouse
Barripper
Penzarty
Carnhell Green
Morvah
Nancledra
Hayle
Gwinear
Wall
3
·828
Men-An-Tol
Chysauster Ancient Village
O Lelant
Paradise Park
Praze-an-Beeble
Levant Beam Engine
Lanyon
Quoit NT.
Canonstown
St. Erth
Tremelon
Fraddam
Leedstown
Pendeen
B3306
Bojewyan
New Mill
A30
St. Erth
Townshend
Crowan
Geevor Tin Mine
Chun Castle (Fort)
Great Bosullow
Boswarthen
Reawla
Trewellard
Carnyorth
Ludgvan
Relubbus
Godolphin House
Nancegollan
Botallack
Trengwainton
NT
Trevarrack
B3280
Godolphin Cross
Crowntown
Cape Cornwall
Kenidjack
Madron
Gulval
St. Hilary
Trescowe
Carleen
The Brisons
St. Just
Newbridge
Heamoor
Longrock
Chyandour
Goldsithney
Rosudgeon
Germoe
Trew
Breage
Lowertown
Kelynack
PENZANCE
Marazion
C O R N W A
Helston
736
Sancreed
Egyptian House NT
St. Michael's Mount
Perranuthnoe
Kenneggy Downs
Ashton
Pirsey
A394
Brane
Carn Euny Ancient Vill
Newlyn
Cudden Point
Praa Sands
Trewavas Head
Porthleven
Whitesand Bay
Escalls
A30
Drift
Newlyn
Longships
Sennen Cove
Crows-an-wra
Kerris
Paul
St. Clement's Isle
4
Longships
Sennen
Land's End
St. Buryan
Trewoofe
The Pipers (AM)
Mousehole
Loe Bar
Trevescan
B3315
Burial Chamber
Lamorna
Kemyel Crease
M O U N T ' S   B A Y
Berep
LAND'S END
Trevilley
B3283
Penberth
Tater-du
Porthcurno
St. Levan
Treen
NT
Cribba Head
Penzance to
Hugh Town 2hrs. 40mins.
NT
Porthgwarra
Minack Open-Air Theatre
Logan Rock
NT
Poldhu Point
Gwennap Head
Marconi Monument
Trenance
Runnel Stone
Mullion Island
Lwr. Predannack Cliffs

20

Vellan Head

Kynan

5

10

Wolf Rock
Wolf Rock

30   40   '50   60

56

10   20   30   40

A   B   68   C   D

300

1

90

2

80

C A R D I G A N   B A Y

3

(B A E   C E R E D I G I O N)

70

4

60

Sea Aquarium
Aberaeron
Honey Bee
Ffos-y-ffin
New Quay
(Ceinewydd)
Llwyncelyn
Cwmtudu   NT   Maen-y-groes
Gilfachreda
Bird & Wildlife Hospital   Oakford (Derwen G)
Cross Inn   Geneva
Nantemis
Honey Farm   Pen-cae
Llanarth
Ynys-Lochtyn   Caerwedros
NT   Honey Farm   Geneva
Llwyndafydd   Mydr
5   Blaen Celyn
Llangranog   Synod Inn or Post-mawr
Morfa   Pontgarreg
Penbryn   A487   Plwmp
Brynhoffnant   Pentregat   Talgarreg
Cardigan Island   Samau   C
Bird Sanctuary   NT   Rainforest & Butterfly Centre   Parclyn   Tresaith
Penpych   **Aberporth**   Countryside Collection
Cemaes Head   Gwbert   Farm Park   Capel Cynon
250   44   Blaenannerch   Glynarthen   Bwlch-y-fadfa
Allt-y-goed   Penffordd   **Castell**   Tan-y-groes   40   Castell Howell
A   Y Ferwig   Gwythian   15   B   Blaenporth   C   Rhydlewis   D   Flostrasol   Pont-sian
Pwllygranant   Cippyn   A487   Tremain
10   Penparc   Noyadd   Beulah   **Bettws**   Brithdir   Penrhiw-pal
Cardigan   Trefawr   **Ifan**   Felin   Hawen
St. Dogmaels   (Aberteifi)   Pantgwyn   **Troedyraur**   Penrhiw-pal

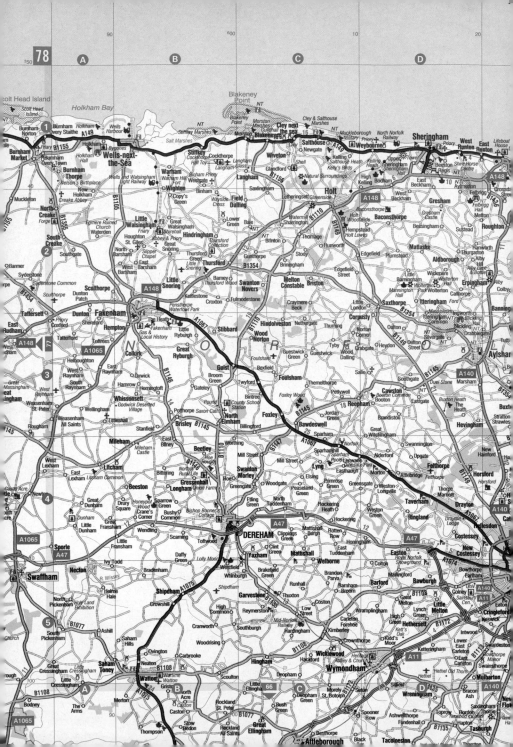

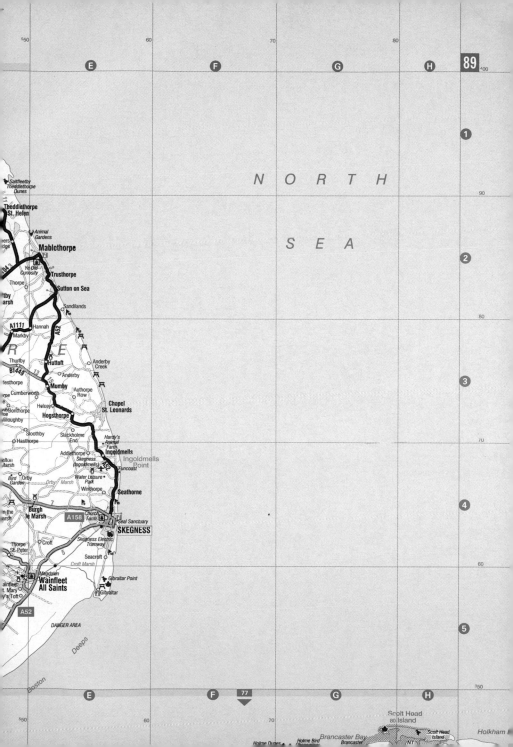

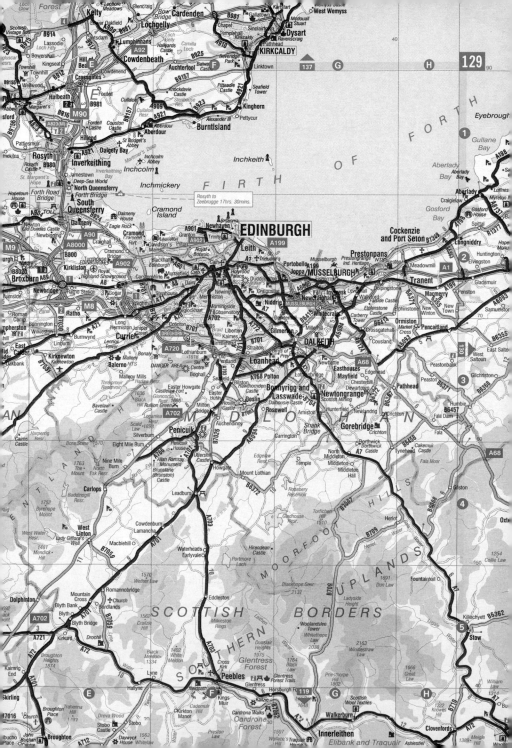

NORTH SEA

NORTHUMBERLAND

Fast Castle
Head
Fast Castle
Telegraph
Hill
Lumsdaine
Cross Law ·744
Coldingham Moor
ST. ABB'S HEAD
NTS
Houndwood
St. Abbs
Lifeboat
Station
Coldingham
Priory
Coldingham
Bay
Press
Lifeboat Station
Buss Craig
Eyemouth
A1107
Gunsgreenhill
Water
Horsley
Hill
Reston
Auchencraw
Ayton
Burnmouth
Ross
Chirnside
Edrom
Chirnside
bridge
Whiteadder
Water
Hutton
Foulden
Lamberton
Old Toll House
Marshall
Meadows
Tithe Barn
Clappers
Halidon
Hill
A1
Highfields
Scottish Borderers
BERWICK-
UPON-TWEED
Allanton
Hutton
Paxton
Tweedmouth
Whitsome
Church
Fishwick
Spittal
Horncliffe
East
Ord
Redshin
Cove
Horndean
Church
Murton
Thornton
Scremerston
Ladykirk
Norham
Railway
Shoreswood
Shoresdean
West
Allerdean
Cheswick
Swinton
Simprim
Upsettlington
Grindon
Felkington
Berrington Law
Ancroft
Berrington
Goswick
Haggerston
LINDISFARNE
HOLY ISLAND
Keel
Head
Twizel
Bridge
Chapel
Duddo
Duddo Tower
Bowsden
Beal
Holy
Island
Castle
Heaton
Melkington
NORTHUMBERLAND
Barmoor
West
Kyloe
East
Kyloe
Fenham
Castle Point
NT Lindisfarne
Priory
Burrows
Hole
Cornhill-
on-Tweed
stream
Pallinsburn
House
Etal
Etal
Manor
Waterford
Hall
Lowick
Buckton
Kyloe
Hills
Bareless
Crookham
Mill
Ford
FARNE
ISLANDS
Staple
Sound
West
Learmouth
Bronxton
Elwick
Ross
Budle
Bay
Bamburgh
East
Learmouth
Flodden
Field
Flodden
Detchant
St. Cuthbert's
Cave
Holburn

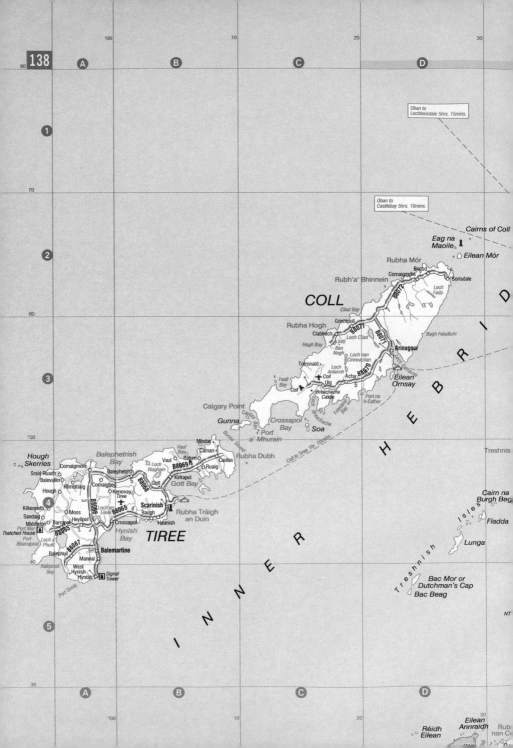

500

10

20

30

80

A   B   C   D

1

70

Oban to
Lochboisdale 5hrs. 15mins.

2

Oban to
Castlebay 5hrs. 10mins.

Cairns of Coll

Eag na
Maoile

Eilean Mór

Rubha Mór

Bousd

Cornaigmore

Sorisdale

60

Rubh'a' Bhinnein

Loch
Fada

COLL

Clad Bay

Rubha Hogh

Grishipoll

B8071

Clabhach

Loch Clad

Bagh Feisdlum

B8070

Hogh Bay

340
Ben
Nogh

Loch nan
Cinneachan

Arinagour

Totronald

Loch
Antlaimh

Loch
Antlaimh

3

Feall
Bay

Coll

Uig

Breachacha
Castle

Acha

5

Eilean
Ornsay

Coll

Port na
h-Eathar

Breachacha

Calgary Point

Gunna

Port
a' Mhurain

Crossapol
Bay

Soa

Freasdal
Bay

Treshnis

Gunna

50

Gunna Sound

Coll to Tiree 1hr. 10mins.

INNER HEBRIDES

Hough
Skerries

Balephetrish
Bay

Vaul
Bay

Miodar

Carnan

Rubha Dubh

Cornaigmore

Sraid Ruadh

Balevullin

Vaul

B8069

Saltum

Caolas

Balephetrish

Loch
Riaghain

Ruaig

Cairn na
Burgh Beg

Kilmoluaig

Cornaigbeg

B8068

Gott

Kirkapol

Treshnish Isles

Fladda

Hough

Kenovay
Tiree

Gott Bay

4

Kilkenneth

Moss

Loch
an Eilein

Scarinish

Rubha Tràigh
an Duin

Lunga

Sandaig

Heylipol

Crossapol

Baugh

Middleton

Barrapol

B8065

Hianish

Port Mor
Thatched House

Hynish
Bay

Port
Bharrapol

B8067

TIREE

Bac Mor or
Dutchman's Cap

Balephuil

Balemartine

Bac Beag

Loch a'
Phuill

Mannal

Balephuil
Bay

West
Hynish

Hynish

Signal
Tower

Réidh
Eilean

Port Spoig

Eilean
Annraidh

5

INNER

30

A   B   C   D

500

10

20

30

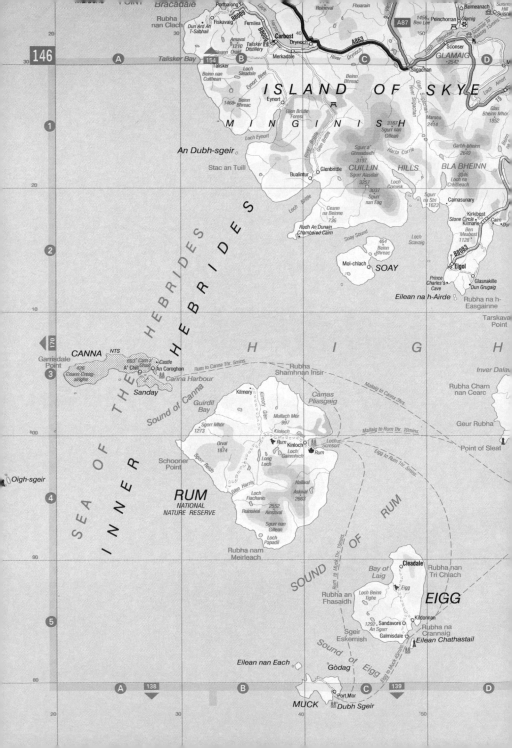

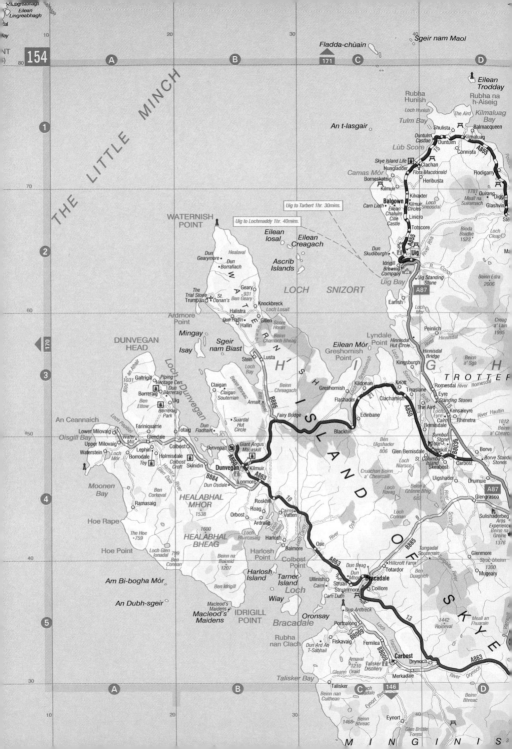

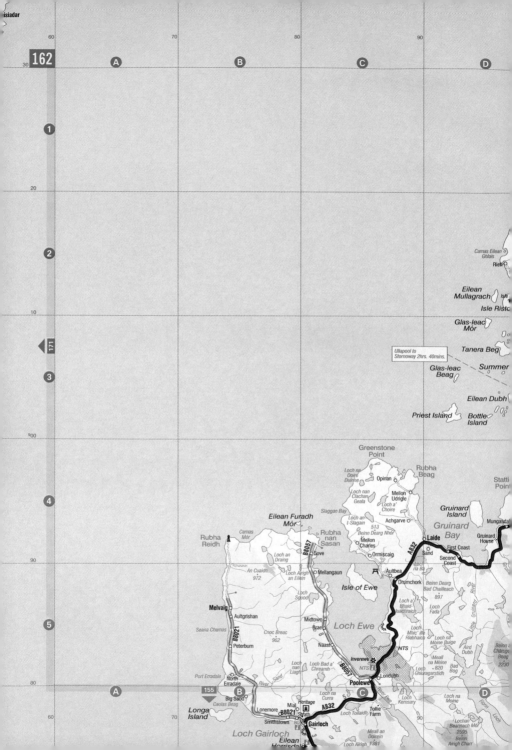

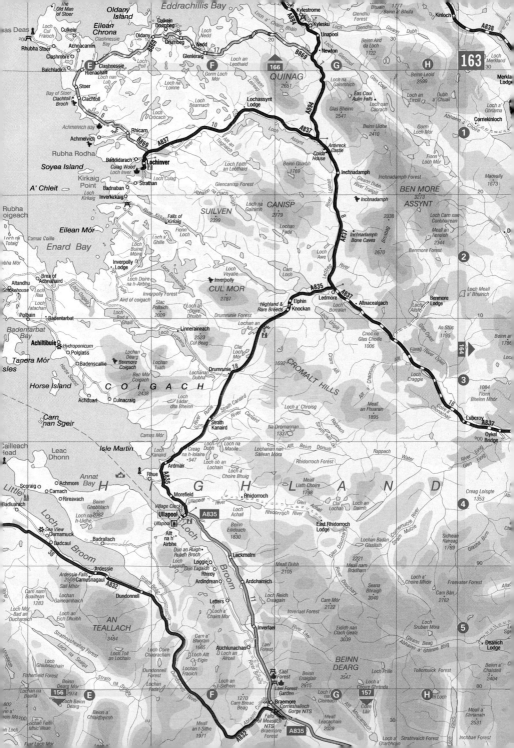

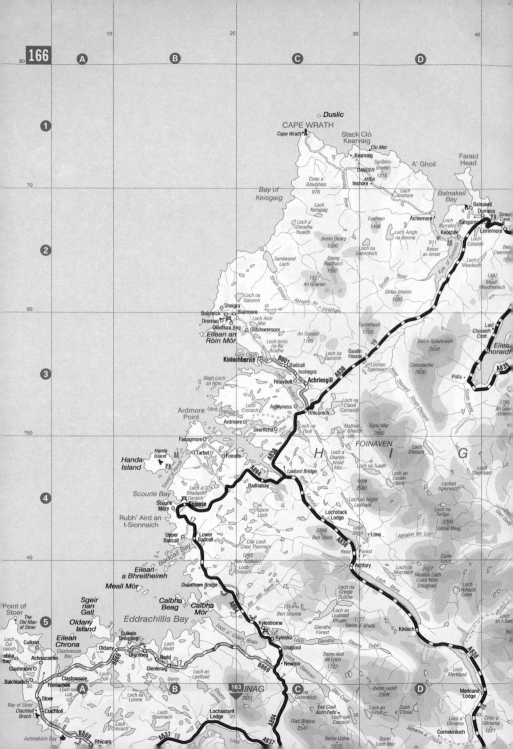

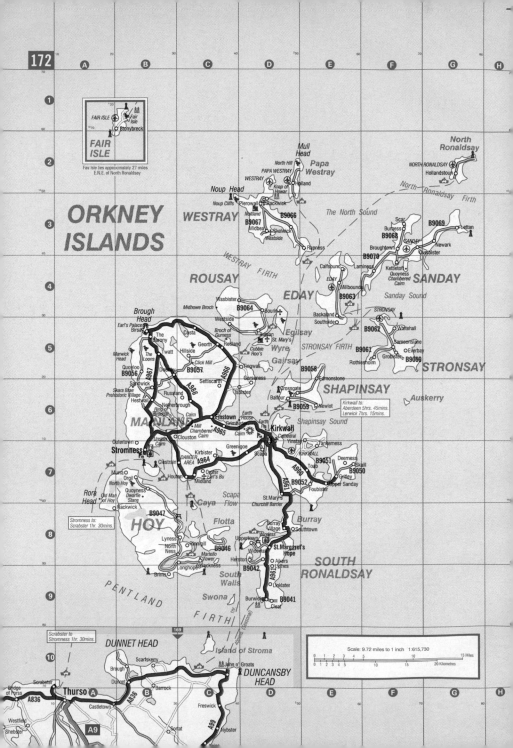

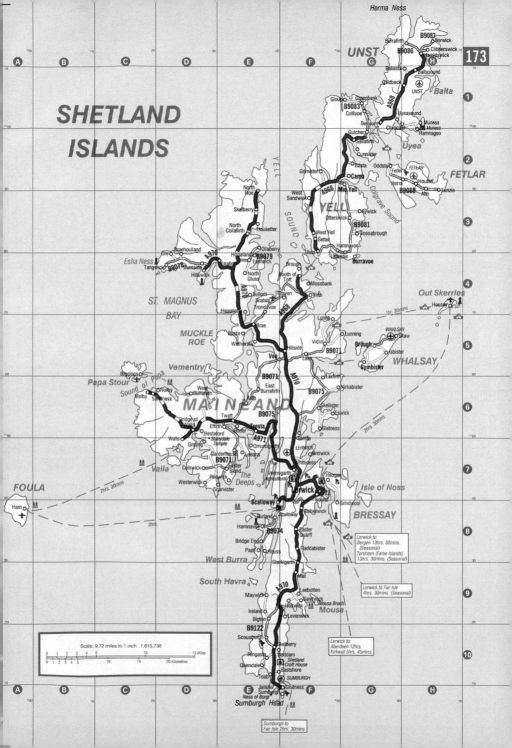

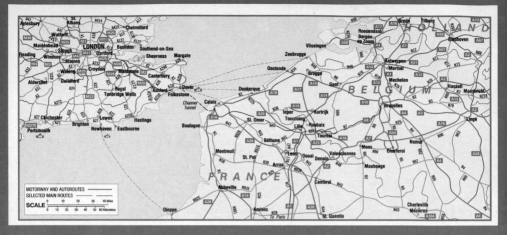

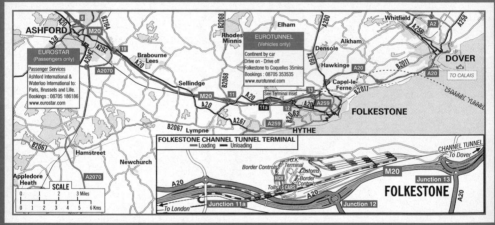

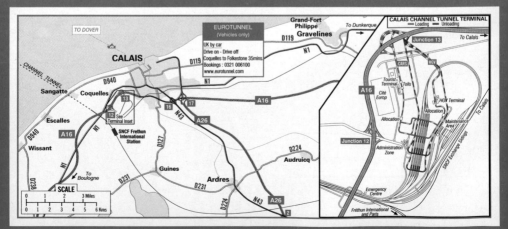

Mileage Chart

The distances for the mileage chart have been compiled by using a combination of Primary Routes and Motorways between any two towns shown.

To find the distance between any two towns shown, follow the horizontal line of one town and the vertical line of the other; at the intersection read off the mileage.

ie · Horizontal - LONDON
Intersection 216 miles
Vertical - Liverpool

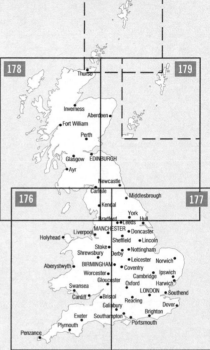

Key to Route Planning Map Pages

PRIMARY ROUTES, shown in green throughout this Atlas, are a national network of recommended through routes which complement the motorway system. Selected places of major traffic importance are known as Primary Route Destinations and, on road signs, have a green background.

```
ABERDEEN
449 ABERYSTWYTH
181 324 AYR
400 114 272 BIRMINGHAM
330 159 196 124 BRADFORD
562 258 441 169 263 BRIGHTON
503 122 375 88 215 129 BRISTOL
447 198 366 102 156 117 167 CAMBRIDGE
505 106 377 106 233 168 42 201 CARDIFF
217 232 89 183 107 345 286 256 288 CARLISLE
437 134 297 18 124 157 102 84 129 200 COVENTRY
397 137 269 41 88 138 134 99 159 180 43 DERBY
340 192 239 95 40 232 184 117 210 150 94 57 DONCASTER
558 315 477 195 284 81 194 118 233 393 180 208 244 DOVER
125 340 75 284 198 486 377 326 379 91 303 266 212 444 EDINBURGH
553 199 425 161 282 170 75 232 107 336 166 213 257 244 439 EXETER
148 430 136 391 305 568 478 456 486 198 415 387 345 591 131 549 FORT WILLIAM
148 322 36 291 203 468 378 355 384 96 313 282 245 491 46 449 100 GLASGOW
445 109 317 53 171 152 35 132 53 228 59 93 149 189 331 107 435 324 GLOUCESTER
520 258 411 170 224 130 203 64 234 323 152 167 185 129 397 262 524 419 171 HARWICH
443 96 315 151 158 330 204 252 209 226 167 156 169 358 316 279 423 323 189 331 HOLYHEAD
357 235 255 139 68 243 228 134 239 165 123 94 37 254 230 290 367 255 195 204 218 HULL
107 492 198 449 353 620 536 490 558 260 458 421 369 601 157 607 63 162 496 554 481 387 INVERNESS
505 268 420 156 210 125 206 54 240 311 138 155 171 127 381 264 510 409 177 21 307 189 538 IPSWICH
269 182 139 151 62 324 235 215 232 50 170 136 99 344 141 307 248 146 200 279 180 127 310 268 KENDAL
316 171 198 119 9 256 209 144 226 111 117 74 32 275 190 279 309 208 167 217 162 60 345 197 72 LEEDS
407 155 294 43 99 163 118 70 140 214 24 30 73 183 282 189 412 312 83 146 182 98 431 125 166 97 LEICESTER
376 208 249 87 80 207 170 88 192 178 76 53 41 206 247 241 376 274 135 152 204 46 402 124 140 72 52 LINCOLN
327 120 199 99 67 267 180 179 169 110 113 90 89 294 201 240 308 213 142 265 95 126 370 236 75 73 110 118 LIVERPOOL
321 128 204 87 37 252 167 159 188 117 99 58 51 273 208 239 315 215 132 230 120 96 363 211 72 42 95 87 34 MANCHESTER
273 233 181 174 69 316 265 196 287 92 175 130 84 316 147 337 279 192 230 266 226 88 306 253 77 64 154 127 134 106 MIDDLESBROUGH
230 266 146 209 98 345 300 232 312 58 209 165 115 350 104 369 231 153 263 297 257 130 263 287 88 96 188 153 167 136 40 NEWCASTLE
476 270 348 163 185 174 234 62 256 280 142 146 142 169 351 284 478 378 193 72 289 145 505 44 249 178 112 103 222 177 221 252 NORWICH
381 155 267 54 78 191 140 84 165 188 52 15 48 210 256 218 386 286 108 165 177 92 410 140 141 72 27 37 107 68 128 159 118 NOTTINGHAM
485 151 335 68 167 106 73 92 106 267 57 101 138 142 358 151 465 365 47 134 208 175 515 128 223 162 76 123 168 157 218 253 159 104 OXFORD
680 301 552 269 394 279 184 343 218 463 278 316 369 355 551 109 663 561 217 374 388 412 715 375 419 391 310 359 353 344 449 481 393 323 261 PENZANCE
87 366 85 336 245 509 412 370 422 134 346 309 254 485 43 487 103 59 362 439 360 273 113 424 184 233 326 290 244 254 191 148 394 299 404 598 PERTH
589 232 461 203 325 206 111 274 159 372 209 254 300 286 485 43 592 490 150 305 322 376 648 305 348 323 231 284 299 281 379 412 327 255 193 75 529 PLYMOUTH
575 231 440 147 274 50 95 132 138 357 132 184 231 137 448 127 555 455 114 161 303 268 603 158 308 245 166 209 254 237 315 360 200 191 83 235 486 170 PORTSMOUTH
526 180 399 103 213 79 77 90 112 309 90 138 184 115 402 66 479 406 75 129 264 209 554 126 263 207 113 168 193 197 264 295 75 251 445 184 60 READING
529 178 383 121 245 82 53 140 101 312 113 159 207 158 400 91 510 408 73 177 262 251 569 177 265 230 132 187 213 208 287 318 200 162 65 201 443 132 43 57 SALISBURY
355 173 235 79 40 225 163 121 193 154 75 35 21 268 230 245 352 250 139 185 164 66 387 176 102 33 68 46 74 40 102 133 144 37 137 361 273 293 228 160 203 SHEFFIELD
388 73 260 47 100 216 116 140 107 171 64 67 114 249 262 175 369 267 77 215 104 163 424 195 125 102 79 123 59 67 166 203 196 86 105 286 309 218 195 147 150 85 SHREWSBURY
547 213 401 128 235 64 75 129 122 330 114 167 201 150 433 106 528 426 98 157 287 249 590 162 276 230 136 189 235 215 288 320 160 162 66 217 476 149 20 47 23 206 175 SOUTHAMPTON
520 258 431 152 220 85 177 64 211 342 129 168 185 89 395 226 548 438 152 57 303 200 549 57 283 213 139 156 255 225 262 299 99 160 105 337 439 269 117 98 132 197 173 126 SOUTHEND
374 108 243 47 75 217 127 137 140 150 64 36 74 236 241 202 348 248 95 201 122 117 410 179 121 78 55 87 56 36 142 173 171 55 118 311 287 241 201 147 168 50 35 183 199 STOKE
496 76 368 124 220 209 80 236 41 279 150 184 244 264 370 154 477 375 91 279 172 262 578 279 249 229 174 226 168 187 293 323 286 178 144 266 446 196 175 114 136 202 124 159 245 159 SWANSEA
213 584 304 557 461 728 644 589 660 327 577 550 503 720 306 750 75 161 635 683 581 431 71 709 419 454 506 523 682 659 502 631 718 542 649 926 229 789 715 765 716 512 627 739 709 581 763 THURSO
437 96 309 29 135 162 62 119 73 220 46 68 124 197 306 136 418 311 28 168 151 166 480 174 169 146 72 118 108 101 203 229 180 85 57 244 350 177 146 95 101 103 49 124 150 65 97 572 WORCESTER
312 193 201 129 34 269 227 151 237 116 129 84 33 269 187 289 314 214 181 232 185 38 344 200 81 24 108 76 96 65 48 83 176 84 174 400 230 331 257 217 244 54 132 244 114 268 450 164 YORK
501 206 390 118 203 53 118 58 150 305 97 128 165 76 373 171 503 403 101 79 264 188 577 76 264 196 107 143 216 200 246 278 114 120 66 282 416 211 74 30 84 161 160 70 43 160 187 636 110 203 LONDON
```

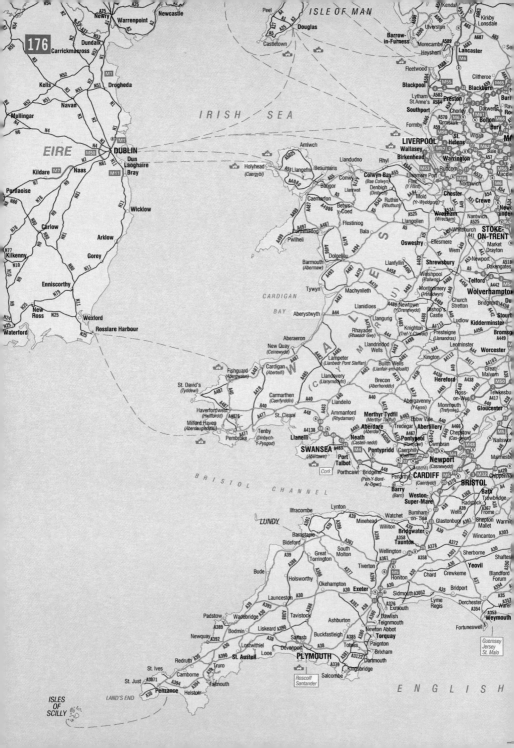

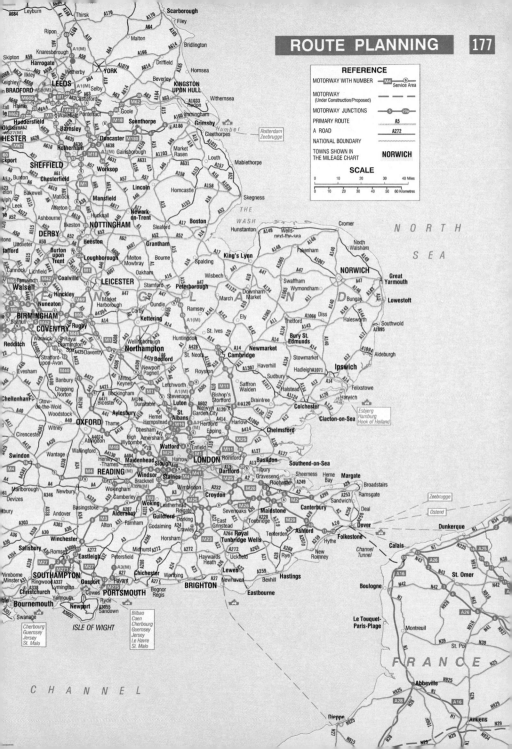

REFERENCE

MOTORWAY WITH NUMBER — M4 — S Service Area

MOTORWAY
(Under Construction/Proposed)

MOTORWAY JUNCTIONS

PRIMARY ROUTE   A5

A ROAD   A272

NATIONAL BOUNDARY

TOWNS SHOWN IN
THE MILEAGE CHART   **NORWICH**

SCALE

0   10   20   30   40 Miles

0   10   20   30   40   50   60 Kilometres

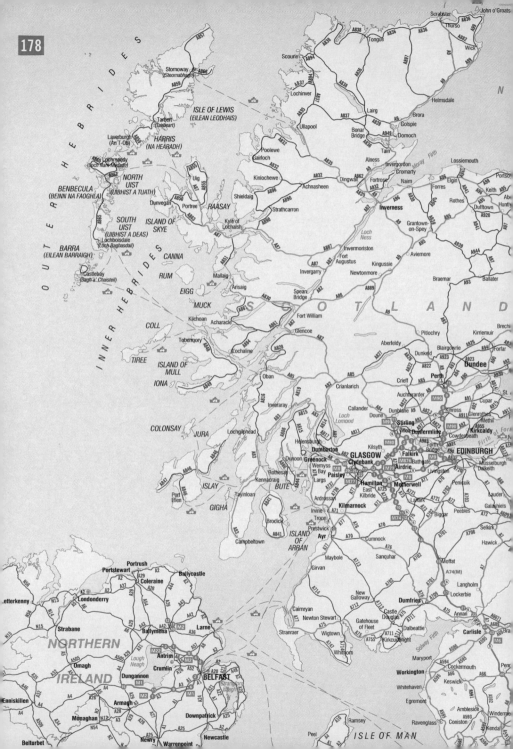

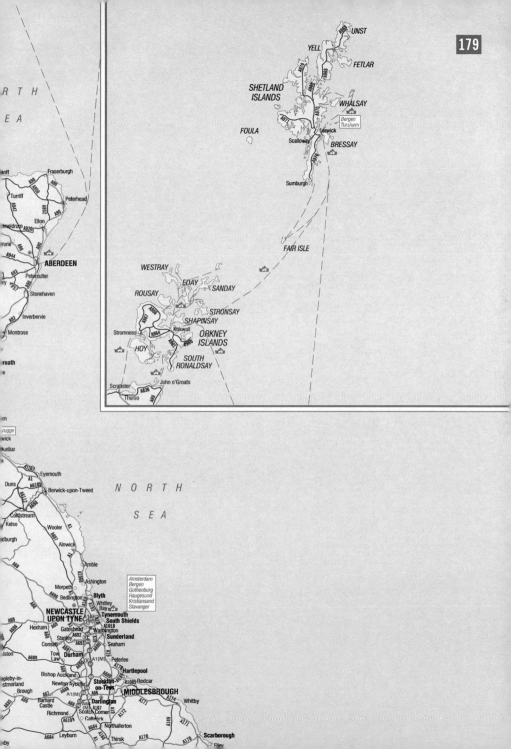

INDEX TO CITIES, TOWNS, VILLAGES, HAMLETS & LOCATIONS

(1) A strict alphabetical order is used e.g Abbotstone follows Abbot's Salford but precedes Abbots Worthy.

(2) The map reference given refers to the actual map square in which the town spot or built-up area is located and not to the place name.

(3) Where two or more places of the same name occur in the same County or Unitary Authority, the nearest large town is also given; e.g. Achiemore. *High* —2D **166** (nr. Durness) indicates that Achiemore is located in square 2D on page **166** and is situated near Durness in the Unitary Authority of Highland.

(4) Only one reference is given although due to page overlaps the place may appear on more than one page.

COUNTIES and UNITARY AUTHORITIES with the abbreviations used in this index

Aberdeen (City) : *Aber C*
Aberdeenshire : *Aber*
Angus : *Ang*
Argyll & Bute : *Arg*
Bath & N E Somerset : *Bath*
Bedfordshire : *Beds*
Blackburn with Darwen : *Bkbn*
Blackpool : *Bkpl*
Blaenau Gwent : *Blae*
Bournemouth : *Bour*
Bracknell Forest : *Brac*
Bridgend : *B'end*
Brighton & Hove (City) : *Brig*
Bristol (City) : *Bris*
Buckinghamshire : *Buck*
Caerphilly : *Cphy*
Cambridgeshire : *Cambs*
Cardiff : *Card*
Carmarthenshire : *Carm*
Ceredigion : *Cdgn*
Cheshire : *Ches*
Clackmannanshire : *Clac*
Conwy : *Cnwy*
Cornwall : *Corn*
Cumbria : *Cumb*
Darlington : *Darl*
Denbighshire : *Den*
Derby (City) : *Dby C*
Derbyshire : *Derbs*

Devon : *Devn*
Dorset : *Dors*
Dumfries & Galloway : *Dum*
Dundee : *D'dee*
Durham : *Dur*
East Ayrshire : *E Ayr*
East Dunbartonshire : *E Dun*
East Lothian : *E Lot*
East Renfrewshire : *E Ren*
East Riding of Yorkshire : *E Yor*
East Sussex : *E Sus*
Edinburgh : *Edin*
Essex : *Essx*
Falkirk : *Falk*
Fife : *Fife*
Flintshire : *Flin*
Glasgow : *Glas*
Gloucestershire : *Glos*
Greater London : *G Lon*
Greater Manchester : *G Man*
Gwynedd : *Gwyn*
Halton : *Hal*
Hampshire : *Hants*
Hartlepool : *Hart*
Herefordshire : *Here*
Hertfordshire : *Herts*
Highland : *High*
Inverclyde : *Inv*
Isle of Anglesey : *IOA*

Isle of Man : *IOM*
Isle of Wight : *IOW*
Isles of Scilly : *IOS*
Kent : *Kent*
Kingston upon Hull : *Hull*
Lancashire : *Lanc*
Leicester (City) : *Leic C*
Leicestershire : *Leics*
Lincolnshire : *Linc*
Luton : *Lutn*
Medway : *Medw*
Merseyside : *Mers*
Merthyr Tydfil : *Mer T*
Middlesbrough : *Midd*
Midlothian : *Midl*
Milton Keynes : *Mil*
Monmouthshire : *Mon*
Moray : *Mor*
Neath Port Talbot : *Neat*
Newport : *Newp*
Norfolk : *Norf*
Northamptonshire : *Nptn*
North Ayrshire : *N Ayr*
North East Lincolnshire : *NE Lin*
North Lanarkshire : *N Lan*
North Lincolnshire : *N Lin*
North Somerset : *N Som*
Northumberland : *Nmbd*
North Yorkshire : *N Yor*

Nottingham (City) : *Not C*
Nottinghamshire : *Notts*
Orkney : *Orkn*
Oxfordshire : *Oxon*
Pembrokeshire : *Pemb*
Perth & Kinross : *Per*
Peterborough : *Pet*
Plymouth : *Plym*
Poole : *Pool*
Portsmouth : *Port*
Powys : *Powy*
Reading : *Read*
Redcar & Cleveland : *Red C*
Renfrewshire : *Ren*
Rhondda Cynon Taff : *Rhon*
Rutland : *Rut*
Scottish Borders : *Scot*
Shetland : *Shet*
Shropshire : *Shrp*
Slough : *Slo*
Somerset : *Som*
Southampton : *Sotn*
South Ayrshire : *S Ayr*
Southend-on-Sea : *S'end*
South Gloucestershire : *S Glo*
South Lanarkshire : *S Lan*
South Yorkshire : *S Yor*
Staffordshire : *Staf*
Stirling : *Stir*

Stockton-on-Tees : *Stoc T*
Stoke-on-Trent : *Stoke*
Suffolk : *Suff*
Surrey : *Surr*
Swansea : *Swan*
Swindon : *Swin*
Telford & Wrekin : *Telf*
Thurrock : *Thur*
Torbay : *Torb*
Torfaen : *Torf*
Tyne & Wear : *Tyne*
Vale of Glamorgan, The : *V Glam*
Warrington : *Warr*
Warwickshire : *Warw*
West Berkshire : *W Ber*
West Dunbartonshire : *W Dun*
Western Isles : *W Isl*
West Lothian : *W Lot*
West Midlands : *W Mid*
West Sussex : *W Sus*
West Yorkshire : *W Yor*
Wiltshire : *Wilts*
Windsor & Maidenhead : *Wind*
Wokingham : *Wok*
Worcestershire : *Worc*
Wrexham : *Wrex*
York (City) : *York*

INDEX

Abbas Combe. *Som* —4C **22**
Abberley. *Worc* —4B **60**
Abberley Common. *Worc* —4B **60**
Abberton. *Essx* —4D **54**
Abberton. *Worc* —5D **61**
Abberwick. *Nmbd* —3F **121**
Abbess Roding. *Essx* —4F **53**
Abbey. *Devn* —1E **13**
Abbey-cwm-hir. *Powy* —3C **58**
Abbeydale. *S Yor* —2H **85**
Abbeydale Park. *S Yor* —2H **85**
Abbey Dore. *Here* —2G **47**
Abbey Hulton. *Stoke* —1D **72**
Abbey St Bathans. *Scot* —3D **130**
Abbeystead. *Lanc* —4E **97**
Abbeytown. *Cumb* —4C **112**
Abbey Village. *Lanc* —2E **91**
Abbey Wood. *G Lon* —3F **39**
Abbots Ann. *Hants* —2B **24**
Abbots Bickington. *Devn* —1D **11**
Abbots Bromley. *Staf* —3E **73**
Abbotsbury. *Dors* —4A **14**
Abbotsham. *Devn* —4E **19**
Abbotskerswell. *Devn* —2E **9**
Abbots Langley. *Herts* —5A **52**
Abbots Leigh. *N Som* —4A **34**
Abbotsley. *Cambs* —5B **64**
Abbots Morton. *Worc* —5E **61**
Abbots Ripton. *Cambs* —3B **64**
Abbot's Salford. *Warw* —5E **61**
Abbotstone. *Hants* —3D **24**
Abbots Worthy. *Hants* —3C **24**
Abcott. *Shrp* —3F **59**
Abdon. *Shrp* —2H **59**
Abenhall. *Glos* —4B **48**
Aber. *Cdgn* —1E **45**
Aberaeron. *Cdgn* —4D **56**
Aberafan. *Neat* —3A **32**
Aberaman. *Rhon* —5D **46**
Aberangell. *Powy* —4H **69**

Aberarad. *Carm* —1H **43**
Aberarder. *High* —1A **150**
Aberargie. *Per* —2D **136**
Aberarth. *Cdgn* —4D **57**
Aberavon. *Neat* —3A **32**
Aber-banc. *Cdgn* —1D **44**
Aberbargoed. *Cphy* —2E **33**
Aberbechan. *Powy* —1D **58**
Aberbeeg. *Blae* —5F **47**
Aberbowlan. *Carm* —2G **45**
Aberbran. *Powy* —3C **46**
Abercanaid. *Mer T* —5D **46**
Abercarn. *Cphy* —2F **33**
Abercastle. *Pemb* —1C **42**
Abercegir. *Powy* —5H **69**
Aberchalder. *High* —3F **149**
Aberchirder. *Aber* —3D **160**
Abercorn. *W Lot* —2D **129**
Abercraf. *Powy* —4B **46**
Abercregan. *Neat* —2B **32**
Abercrombie. *Fife* —3H **137**
Abercwmboi. *Rhon* —2D **32**
Abercych. *Pemb* —1C **44**
Abercynon. *Rhon* —2D **32**
Aber-Cywarch. *Gwyn* —4A **70**
Aberdalgie. *Per* —1C **136**
Aberdar. *Rhon* —5C **46**
Aberdare. *Rhon* —5C **46**
Aberdaron. *Gwyn* —3A **68**
Aberdaugleddau. *Pemb* —4D **42**
Aberdeen. *Aber C* —3G **153**
Aberdeen Airport. *Aber C* —2F **153**
Aberdesach. *Gwyn* —5D **80**
Aberdour. *Fife* —1E **129**
Aberdovey. *Gwyn* —1F **57**
Aberdulais. *Neat* —5A **46**
Aberdyfi. *Gwyn* —1F **57**
Aberedw. *Powy* —1D **46**
Abereiddy. *Pemb* —1B **42**
Abererch. *Gwyn* —2C **68**

Aberfan. *Mer T* —5D **46**
Aberfeldy. *Per* —4F **143**
Aberffraw. *IOA* —4C **80**
Aberffrwd. *Cdgn* —3F **57**
Aberford. *W Yor* —1E **93**
Aberfoyle. *Stir* —3E **135**
Abergarw. *B'End* —3C **32**
Abergarwed. *Neat* —5B **46**
Abergavenny. *Mon* —4G **47**
Abergele. *Cnwy* —3B **82**
Aber-Giar. *Carm* —1F **45**
Abergorlech. *Carm* —2F **45**
Abergwaun. *Pemb* —1D **42**
Abergwesyn. *Powy* —5A **58**
Abergwili. *Carm* —3E **45**
Abergwynfi. *Neat* —2B **32**
Abergwyngregyn. *Gwyn* —3F **81**
Abergynolwyn. *Gwyn* —5F **69**
Aberhafesp. *Powy* —1C **58**
Aberhonddu. *Powy* —3D **46**
Aberhosan. *Powy* —1H **57**
Aberkenfig. *B'End* —3B **32**
Aberlady. *E Lot* —2A **130**
Aberlemno. *Ang* —3E **145**
Aberllefenni. *Cdgn* —5G **69**
Abermaw. *Gwyn* —4F **69**
Abermeurig. *Cdgn* —5E **57**
Aber-miwl. *Powy* —1D **58**
Abermule. *Powy* —1D **58**
Abernant. *Carm* —2H **43**
Abernant. *Rhon* —5D **46**
Abernethy. *Per* —2D **136**
Abernyte. *Per* —5B **144**
Aber-oer. *Wrex* —1E **71**
Aberpennar. *Rhon* —2D **32**
Aberporth. *Cdgn* —5B **56**
Aberriw. *Powy* —5D **70**
Abersoch. *Gwyn* —3C **68**
Abersychan. *Torf* —5F **47**
Abertawe. *Swan* —3F **31**

Aberteifi. *Cdgn* —1B **44**
Aberthin. *V Glam* —4D **32**
Abertillery. *Blae* —5F **47**
Abertridwr. *Cphy* —3E **32**
Abertridwr. *Powy* —4C **70**
Abertyleri. *Blae* —5F **47**
Abertysswg. *Cphy* —5E **47**
Aberuthven. *Per* —2B **136**
Aber Village. *Powy* —3E **46**
Aberyscir. *Powy* —3D **46**
Aberystwyth. *Cdgn* —2E **57**
Abhainn Suidhe. *W Isl* —7C **171**
Abingdon. *Oxon* —2C **36**
Abinger Common. *Surr* —1C **26**
Abinger Hammer. *Surr* —1B **26**
Abington. *S Lan* —2B **118**
Abington Pigotts. *Cambs* —1D **52**
Ab Kettleby. *Leics* —3E **74**
Ab Lench. *Worc* —5E **61**
Ablington. *Glos* —5G **49**
Ablington. *Wilts* —2G **23**
Abney. *Derbs* —3F **85**
Aboyne. *Aber* —4C **152**
Abram. *G Man* —4E **90**
Abriachan. *High* —5H **157**
Abridge. *Essx* —1F **39**
Abronhill. *N Lan* —2A **128**
Abson. *S Glo* —4C **34**
Abthorpe. *Nptn* —1E **51**
Aby. *Linc* —3D **88**
Acairseid Mhor. *W Isl* —8C **170**
Acaster Malbis. *York* —5H **99**
Acaster Selby. *N Yor* —5H **99**
Accott. *Devn* —3G **19**
Accrington. *Lanc* —2F **91**
Acha. *Arg* —3C **138**
Achachork. *High* —4D **155**
Achahoish. *Arg* —2F **125**
Achaleven. *Arg* —5D **140**
Achallader. *Arg* —4H **141**

Acha Mor. *W Isl* —5F **171**
Achanalt. *High* —2E **157**
Achandunie. *High* —1A **158**
Ach'an Todhair. *High* —1E **141**
Achany. *High* —3C **164**
Achaphubuil. *High* —1E **141**
Acharacle. *High* —2A **140**
Acharn. *Ang* —1B **144**
Acharn. *Per* —4E **143**
Acharole. *High* —3E **169**
Achateny. *High* —2G **139**
Achavanich. *High* —4D **169**
Achdalieu. *High* —1E **141**
Achduart. *High* —3E **163**
Achentoul. *High* —5A **168**
Achfary. *High* —5C **166**
Achfrish. *High* —2C **164**
Achgarve. *High* —4C **162**
Achiemore. *High* —2D **166**
  (nr. Durness)
Achiemore. *High* —3A **168**
  (nr. Thurso)
A'Chill. *High* —3A **146**
Achiltibuie. *High* —3E **163**
Achina. *High* —2H **167**
Achinahuagh. *High* —2F **167**
Achindarroch. *High* —3E **141**
Achinduich. *High* —3C **164**
Achinduin. *Arg* —5C **140**
Achininver. *High* —2F **167**
Achintee. *High* —4B **156**
Achintraid. *High* —5H **155**
Achleck. *Arg* —4F **139**
Achlorachan. *High* —3F **157**
Achluachrach. *High* —5E **149**
Achlyness. *High* —3C **166**
Achmelvich. *High* —1E **163**
Achmony. *High* —5H **157**
Achmore. *High* —5A **156**
  (nr. Stromeferry)

Achmore. *High* —4E 163
(nr. Ullapool)
Achnacarnin. *High* —1E 163
Achnacarry. *High* —5D 148
Achnaclerach. *High* —2G 157
Achnacloich. *High* —3D 147
Achnaconeran. *High* —2G 149
Achnacroish. *Arg* —4C 140
Achnafalnich. *Arg* —1B 134
Achnagarron. *High* —2A 158
Achnaha. *High* —2F 139
Achnahanat. *High* —4C 164
Achnahannet. *High* —1D 151
Achnairn. *High* —2C 164
Achnaluachrach. *High* —3D 164
Achnamara. *Arg* —1F 125
Achnanellan. *High* —5C 148
Achnangoul. *Arg* —3H 133
Achnasheen. *High* —3D 156
Achnashellach. *High* —4C 156
Achosnich. *High* —2F 139
Achow. *High* —5E 169
Achranich. *High* —4B 140
Achreamie. *High* —2C 168
Achriabhach. *High* 2F 141
Achriesgill. *High* —3C 166
Achrimsdale. *High* —3G 165
Achscrabster. *High* —2C 168
Achtoty. *High* —2G 167
Achurch. *Nptn* —2H 63
Achuvoldrach. *High* —3F 167
Achvaich. *High* —4E 164
Achvoan. *High* —3E 165
Ackergill. *High* —3F 169
Ackergillshore. *High* —3F 169
Acklam. *Midd* —3B 106
Acklam. *N Yor* —3B 100
Ackleton. *Shrp* —1B 60
Acklington. *Nmbd* —4G 121
Ackton. *W Yor* —2E 93
Ackworth Moor Top. *W Yor* —3E 93
Acle. *Norf* —4G 79
Acock's Green. *W Mid* —2F 61
Acol. *Kent* —4H 41
Acomb. *Nmbd* —3C 114
Acomb. *York* —4H 99
Aconbury. *Here* —2A 48
Acre. *G Man* —4H 91
Acre. *Lanc* —2F 91
Acrefair. *Wrex* —1E 71
Acrise. *Kent* —1F 29
Acton. *Ches* —5A 84
Acton. *Dors* —5E 15
Acton. *G Lon* —2C 38
Acton. *Shrp* —2F 59
Acton. *Staf* —1C 72
Acton. *Suff* —1B 54
Acton. *Worc* —4C 60
Acton. *Wrex* —5F 83
Acton Beauchamp. *Here* —5A 60
Acton Bridge. *Ches* —3H 83
Acton Burnell. *Shrp* —5H 71
Acton Green. *Here* —5A 60
Acton Pigott. *Shrp* —5H 71
Acton Round. *Shrp* —1A 60
Acton Scott. *Shrp* —2G 59
Acton Trussell. *Staf* —4D 72
Acton Turville. *S Glo* —3D 34
Adabroc. *W Isl* —1H 171
Adam's Hill. *Worc* —3D 60
Adbaston. *Staf* —3B 72
Adber. *Dors* —4B 22
Adderbury. *Oxon* —2C 50
Adderley. *Shrp* —2A 72
Adderstone. *Nmbd* —1F 121
Addiewell. *W Lot* —3C 128
Addingham. *W Yor* —5C 98
Addington. *Buck* —3F 51
Addington. *G Lon* —4E 39
Addington. *Kent* —5A 40
Addinston. *Scot* —4B 130
Addiscombe. *G Lon* —4E 39
Addlestone. *Surr* —4B 38

Addlethorpe. *Linc* —4E 89
Adeney. *Telf* —4B 72
Adfa. *Powy* —5C 70
Adforton. *Here* —3G 59
Adgestone. *IOW* —4D 16
Adisham. *Kent* —5G 41
Adlestrop. *Glos* —3H 49
Adlingfleet. *E Yor* —2B 94
Adlington. *Ches* —2D 84
Adlington. *Lanc* —3E 90
Admaston. *Staf* 3E 73
Admaston. *Telf* —4A 72
Admington. *Warw* —1G 49
Adpar. *Cdgn* —1D 44
Adsborough. *Som* —4F 21
Adstock. *Buck* —2F 51
Adstone. *Nptn* —5C 62
Adversane. *W Sus* —3B 26
Advie. *High* —5F 159
Adwalton. *W Yor* —2C 92
Adwell. *Oxon* —2E 37
Adwick le Street. *S Yor* —4F 93
Adwick upon Dearne. *S Yor* —4E 93
Adziel. *Aber* —3G 161
Ac. *Dum* —1A 112
Affleck. *Aber* —1F 153
Affpuddle. *Dors* —3D 14
Affric Lodge. *High* —1D 148
Afon-wen. *Flin* —3D 82
Afton Bridgend. *E Ayr* —3F 117
Agglethorpe. *N Yor* —1C 98
Aglionby. *Cumb* —4F 113
Aigburth. *Mers* —2F 83
Aike. *E Yor* —5E 101
Aikers. *Orkn* —8D 172
Aiketgate. *Cumb* —5F 113
Aikhead. *Cumb* —5D 112
Aikton. *Cumb* —4D 112
Ailey. *Here* —1G 47
Ailsworth. *Pet* —1A 64
Ainderby Quernhow. *N Yor* —1F 99
Ainderby Steeple. *N Yor* —5A 106
Aingers Green. *Essx* —3E 54
Ainsdale. *Mers* —3B 90
Ainsdale-on-Sea. *Mers* —3A 90
Ainstable. *Cumb* —5G 113
Ainsworth. *G Man* —3F 91
Ainthorpe. *N Yor* —4E 107
Aintree. *Mers* —1F 83
Aird. *Arg* —3E 133
Aird. *Dum* —3F 109
Aird. *High* —1G 155
Aird. *W Isl* —3C 170
(on Benbecula)
Aird. *W Isl* —4H 171
(on Lewis)
Aird a Mhachair. *W Isl* —4C 170
Aird a Mhulaidh. *W Isl* —6D 171
Airdens. *High* —4D 164
Airdeny. *Arg* —1G 133
Aird Mhidhinis. *W Isl* —8C 170
Aird Mhighe. *W Isl* —8D 171
(nr. Ceann a Bhaigh)
Aird Mhighe. *W Isl* —9C 171
(nr. Fionnsbhagh)
Aird Mhor. *W Isl* —8C 170
(on Barra)
Aird Mhor. *W Isl* —4D 170
(on South Uist)
Aird of Sleat. *High* —3D 147
Airdrie. *N Lan* —3A 128
Aird Shleibhe. *W Isl* —9D 171
Aird, The. *High* —3D 154
Aird Thunga. *W Isl* —4G 171
Aird Uig. *W Isl* —4C 171
Airedale. *W Yor* —2E 93
Airidh a Bhruaich. *W Isl* —6E 171
Airies. *Dum* —3E 109
Airmyn. *E Yor* —2H 93
Airntully. *Per* —5H 143
Airor. *High* —3F 147
Airth. *Falk* —1C 128
Airton. *N Yor* —4B 98

Aisby. *Linc* —1F 87
(nr. Gainsborough)
Aisby. *Linc* —2H 75
(nr. Grantham)
Aisgernis. *W Isl* —6C 170
Aish. *Devn* —2C 8
(nr. Buckfastleigh)
Aish. *Devn* —3E 9
(nr. Totnes)
Aisholt. *Som* —3E 21
Aiskew. *N Yor* —1E 99
Aislaby. *N Yor* —1B 100
(nr. Pickering)
Aislaby. *N Yor* —4F 107
(nr. Whitby)
Aislaby. *Stoc T* —3B 106
Aisthorpe. *Linc* —3G 87
Aith. *Shet* —2H 173
(on Fetlar)
Aith. *Shet* —6E 173
(on Mainland)
Akeld. *Nmbd* —2D 120
Akeley. *Buck* —2F 51
Akenham. *Suff* —1E 55
Albaston. *Corn* —5E 11
Alberbury. *Shrp* —4F 71
Albert Town. *Pemb* —3D 42
Albert Village. *Leics* —4H 73
Albourne. *W Sus* —4D 26
Albrighton. *Shrp* —4G 71
(nr. Shrewsbury)
Albrighton. *Shrp* —5C 72
(nr. Telford)
Alburgh. *Norf* —2E 67
Albury. *Herts* —3E 53
Albury. *Surr* —1B 26
Albyfield. *Cumb* —4G 113
Alby Hill. *Norf* —2D 78
Alcaig. *High* —3H 157
Alcaston. *Shrp* —2G 59
Alcester. *Warw* —5E 61
Alciston. *E Sus* —5G 27
Alcombe. *Som* —2C 20
Alconbury. *Cambs* —3A 64
Alconbury Weston. *Cambs* —3A 64
Aldborough. *Norf* —2D 78
Aldborough. *N Yor* —3G 99
Aldbourne. *Wilts* —4A 36
Aldbrough. *E Yor* —1F 95
Aldbrough St John. *N Yor* —3F 105
Aldbury. *Herts* —4H 51
Aldcliffe. *Lanc* —3D 96
Aldclune. *Per* —2G 143
Aldeburgh. *Suff* —5G 67
Aldeby. *Norf* —1G 67
Aldenham. *Herts* —1C 38
Alderbury. *Wilts* —4G 23
Aldercar. *Derbs* —1B 74
Alderford. *Norf* —4D 78
Alderholt. *Dors* —1G 15
Alderley. *Glos* —2C 34
Alderley Edge. *Ches* —3C 84
Aldermaston. *W Ber* —5D 36
Aldermaston Stoke. *W Ber* —5E 36
Aldermaston Wharf. *W Ber* —5E 36
Alderminster. *Warw* —1H 49
Alder Moor. *Staf* —3G 73
Aldersey Green. *Ches* —5G 83
Aldershot. *Hants* —1G 25
Alderton. *Glos* —2E 49
Alderton. *Nptn* —1F 51
Alderton. *Shrp* —3G 71
Alderton. *Suff* —1G 55
Alderton. *Wilts* —3D 34
Alderton Fields. *Glos* —2F 49
Alderwasley. *Derbs* —5H 85
Aldfield. *N Yor* —3E 99
Aldford. *Ches* —5G 83
Aldgate. *Rut* —5G 75
Aldham. *Essx* —3C 54
Aldham. *Suff* —1D 54
Aldingbourne. *W Sus* —5A 26
Aldingham. *Cumb* —2B 96

Aldington. *Kent* —2E 29
Aldington. *Worc* —1F 49
Aldochlay. *Arg* —4C 134
Aldon. *Shrp* —3G 59
Aldoth. *Cumb* —5C 112
Aldreth. *Cambs* —3D 64
Aldridge. *W Mid* —5E 73
Aldringham. *Suff* —4G 67
Aldsworth. *Glos* —4G 49
Aldsworth. *W Sus* —2F 17
Aldwark. *Derbs* —5G 85
Aldwark. *N Yor* —3G 99
Aldwick. *W Sus* —3H 17
Aldwincle. *Nptn* —2H 63
Aldworth. *W Ber* —4D 36
Alexandria. *W Dun* —1E 127
Aley. *Som* —3E 21
Aley Green. *Beds* —4A 52
Alfardisworthy. *Devn* —1C 10
Alfington. *Devn* —3E 12
Alfold. *Surr* —2B 26
Alfold Bars. *W Sus* —2B 26
Alfold Crossways. *Surr* —2B 26
Alford. *Aber* —2C 152
Alford. *Linc* —3D 88
Alford. *Som* —3B 22
Alfreton. *Derbs* —5B 86
Alfrick. *Worc* —5B 60
Alfrick Pound. *Worc* —5B 60
Alfriston. *E Sus* —5G 27
Algarkirk. *Linc* —2B 76
Alhampton. *Som* —3B 22
Aline Lodge. *W Isl* —6D 171
Alkborough. *N Lin* —2B 94
Alkerton. *Oxon* —1B 50
Alkham. *Kent* —1G 29
Alkington. *Shrp* —2H 71
Alkmonton. *Derbs* —2F 73
Alladale Lodge. *High* —5B 164
Allaleigh. *Devn* —3E 9
Allanton. *N Lan* —4B 128
Allanton. *Scot* —4E 131
Allaston. *Glos* —5B 48
Allbrook. *Hants* —4C 24
All Cannings. *Wilts* —5F 35
Allendale Town. *Nmbd* —4B 114
Allen End. *Warw* —1F 61
Allenheads. *Nmbd* —5B 114
Allensford. *Dur* —5D 115
Allen's Green. *Herts* —4E 53
Allensmore. *Here* —2H 47
Allenton. *Dby C* —2A 74
Aller. *Som* —4H 21
Allerby. *Cumb* —1B 102
Allercombe. *Devn* —3D 12
Allerford. *Som* —2C 20
Allerston. *N Yor* —1C 100
Allerthorpe. *E Yor* —5B 100
Allerton. *Mers* —2G 83
Allerton. *W Yor* —1B 92
Allerton Bywater. *W Yor* —2E 93
Allerton Mauleverer. *N Yor* —4G 99
Allesley. *W Mid* —2G 61
Allestree. *Dby C* —2H 73
Allet. *Corn* —4B 6
Allexton. *Leics* —5F 75
Allgreave. *Ches* —4D 84
Allhallows. *Medw* —3C 40
Allhallows-on-Sea. *Medw* —3C 40
Alligin Shuas. *High* —3H 155
Allimore Green. *Staf* —4C 72
Allington. *Kent* —5B 40
Allington. *Linc* —1F 75
Allington. *Wilts* —3H 23
(nr. Amesbury)
Allington. *Wilts* —5F 35
(nr. Devizes)
Allithwaite. *Cumb* —2C 96
Alloa. *Clac* —4A 136
Allonby. *Cumb* —5B 112
Alloway. *S Ayr* —3C 116
Allowenshay. *Som* —1G 13
All Saints South Elmham. *Suff* —2F 67

Allscott. *Shrp* —1B 60
Allscott. *Telf* —4A 72
All Stretton. *Shrp* —1G 59
Allt. *Carm* —5F 45
Alltami. *Flin* —4E 83
Alltgobhlach. *N Ayr* —5G 125
Alltmawr. *Powy* —1D 46
Alltnacaillich. *High* —4E 167
Allt na h-Airbhe. *High* —4F 163
Alltour. *High* —5E 148
Alltsigh. *High* —2G 149
Alltwalis. *Carm* —2E 45
Alltwen. *Neat* —5H 45
Alltyblacca. *Cdgn* —1F 45
Allt-y-goed. *Pemb* —1B 44
Allweston. *Dors* —1B 14
Almeley. *Here* —5F 59
Almeley Wooton. *Here* —5F 59
Almer. *Dors* —3E 15
Almholme. *S Yor* —4F 93
Almington. *Staf* —2B 72
Alminstone Cross. *Devn* —4D 18
Almodington. *W Sus* —3G 17
Almondbank. *Per* —1C 136
Almondbury. *W Yor* —3B 92
Almondsbury. *S Glo* —3B 34
Alne. *N Yor* —3G 99
Alness. *High* —2A 158
Alnessferry. *High* —2A 158
Alnham. *Nmbd* —3D 121
Alnmouth. *Nmbd* —3G 121
Alnwick. *Nmbd* —3F 121
Alphamstone. *Essx* —2B 54
Alpheton. *Suff* —5A 66
Alphington. *Devn* —3C 12
Alpington. *Norf* —5E 79
Alport. *Derbs* —4G 85
Alport. *Powy* —1E 59
Alpraham. *Ches* —5H 83
Alresford. *Essx* —3D 54
Alrewas. *Staf* —4F 73
Alsager. *Ches* —5B 84
Alsagers Bank. *Staf* —1C 72
Alsop en le Dale. *Derbs* —5F 85
Alston. *Cumb* —5A 114
Alstone. *Glos* —2E 49
Alstone. *Som* —2G 21
Alstonefield. *Staf* —5F 85
Alston Sutton. *Som* —1H 21
Alswear. *Devn* —4H 19
Altandhu. *High* —2D 163
Altanduin. *High* —1F 165
Altarnun. *Corn* —4C 10
Altass. *High* —3B 164
Alterwall. *High* —2E 169
Altgaltraig. *Arg* —2B 126
Altham. *Lanc* —1F 91
Althorne. *Essx* —1D 40
Althorpe. *N Lin* —4B 94
Altnabreac. *High* —4C 168
Altnacealgach. *High* —2G 163
Altnafeadh. *High* —3G 141
Altnaharra. *High* —5F 167
Altofts. *W Yor* —2D 92
Alton. *Derbs* —4A 86
Alton. *Hants* —3F 25
Alton. *Staf* —1E 73
Alton Barnes. *Wilts* —5G 35
Altonhill. *E Ayr* —1D 116
Alton Pancras. *Dors* —2C 14
Alton Priors. *Wilts* —5G 35
Altrincham. *G Man* —2B 84
Altrua. *High* —4E 149
Alva. *Clac* —4A 136
Alvanley. *Ches* —3G 83
Alvaston. *Dby C* —2A 74
Alvechurch. *Worc* —3E 61
Alvecote. *Warw* —5G 73
Alvediston. *Wilts* —4E 23
Alveley. *Shrp* —2B 60
Alverdiscott. *Devn* —4F 19
Alverstoke. *Hants* —3E 16
Alverstone. *IOW* —4D 16

Alverthorpe. W Yor —2D 92
Alverton. Notts —1E 75
Alves. Mor —2F 159
Alvescot. Oxon —5A 50
Alveston. S Glo —3B 34
Alveston. Warw —5G 61
Alvie. High —3C 150
Alvingham. Linc —1C 88
Alvington. Glos —5B 48
Alwalton. Pet —1A 64
Alwinton. Nmbd —4D 120
Alwoodley. W Yor —5E 99
Alyth. Per —4B 144
Amatnatua. High —4B 164
Am Baile. W Isl —7C 170
Ambaston. Derbs —2B 74
Ambergate. Derbs —5H 85
Amber Hill. Linc —1B 76
Amberley. Glos —5D 48
Amberley. W Sus —4B 26
Amble. Nmbd —4G 121
Amblecote. W Mid —2C 60
Ambler Thorn. W Yor —2A 92
Ambleside. Cumb —4E 103
Ambleston. Pemb —2D 43
Ambrosden. Oxon —4E 50
Amcotts. N Lin —3B 94
Amersham. Buck —1A 38
Amerton. Staf —3D 73
Amesbury. Wilts —2G 23
Amisfield Town. Dum —1B 112
Amlwch. IOA —1D 80
Amlwch Port. IOA —1D 80
Ammanford. Carm —4G 45
Amotherby. N Yor —2B 100
Ampfield. Hants —4B 24
Ampleforth. N Yor —2H 99
Ampleforth College. N Yor —2H 99
Ampney Crucis. Glos —5F 49
Ampney St Mary. Glos —5F 49
Ampney St Peter. Glos —5F 49
Amport. Hants —2A 24
Ampthill. Beds —2A 52
Ampton. Suff —3A 66
Amroth. Pemb —4F 43
Amulree. Per —5G 143
Amwell. Herts —4B 52
Anaheilt. High —2C 140
Ancaster. Linc —1G 75
Anchor. Shrp —2D 58
Anchorsholme. Lanc —5C 96
An Cnoc. W Isl —4G 171
An Coroghon. High —3A 146
Ancroft. Nmbd —5G 131
Ancrum. Scot —2A 120
Ancton. W Sus —5A 26
Anderby. Linc —3E 89
Anderby Creek. Linc —3E 89
Anderson. Dors —3D 15
Anderton. Ches —3A 84
Andertons Mill. Lanc —3D 90
Andover. Hants —2B 24
Andover Down. Hants —2B 24
Andoversford. Glos —4F 49
Andreas. IOM —2D 108
Andwell. Hants —1E 25
Anelog. Gwyn —3A 68
Anfield. Mers —1F 83
Angarrack. Corn —3C 4
Angelbank. Shrp —3H 59
Angerton. Cumb —4D 112
Angle. Pemb —4C 42
Angmering. W Sus —5B 26
Angmering-on-Sea. W Sus —5B 26
Angram. N Yor —5B 104
(nr. Keld)
Angram. N Yor —5H 99
(nr. York)
Anick. Nmbd —3C 114
Ankerbold. Derbs —4A 86
Ankerville. High —1C 158
Anlaby. E Yor —2D 94
Anlaby Park. Hull —2D 94

An Leth Meadhanach. W Isl
—7C 170
Anmer. Norf —3G 77
Anmore. Hants —1E 17
Annan. Dum —3C 112
Annaside. Cumb —1A 96
Annat. Arg —1H 133
Annat. High —3A 156
Annathill. N Lan —2A 128
Anna Valley. Hants —2B 24
Annbank. S Ayr —2D 116
Annesley. Notts —5C 86
Annesley Woodhouse. Notts —5C 86
Annfield Plain. Dur —4E 115
Annscroft. Shrp —5G 71
Ansdell. Lanc —2B 90
Ansford. Som —3B 22
Ansley. Warw —1H 61
Anslow. Staf —3G 73
Anslow Gate. Staf —3F 73
Ansteadbrook. Surr —2A 26
Anstey. Herts —2E 53
Anstey. Leics —5C 74
Anston. S Lan —5D 128
Anstruther Easter. Fife —3H 137
Anstruther Wester. Fife —3H 137
Ansty. Warw —2A 62
Ansty. W Sus —3D 27
Ansty. Wilts —4E 23
Anthill Common. Hants —1E 17
Anthorn. Cumb —4C 112
Antingham. Norf —2E 79
An-t-Ob. W Isl —9C 171
Anton's Gowt. Linc —1B 76
Antony. Corn —3A 8
Antrobus. Ches —3A 84
Anvil Corner. Devn —2D 11
Anwick. Linc —5A 88
Anwoth. Dum —4C 110
Apethorpe. Nptn —1H 63
Apeton. Staf —4C 72
Apley. Linc —3A 88
Apperknowle. Derbs —3A 86
Apperley. Glos —3D 48
Apperley Dene. Nmbd —4D 114
Appersett. N Yor —5B 104
Appin. Arg —4D 140
Appleby. N Lin —3C 94
Appleby-in-Westmorland.
Cumb —2H 103
Appleby Magna. Leics —5H 73
Appleby Parva. Leics —5H 73
Applecross. High —4G 155
Appledore. Devn —3E 19
(nr. Bideford)
Appledore. Devn —1D 12
(nr. Tiverton)
Appledore. Kent —3D 28
Appledore Heath. Kent —2D 28
Appleford. Oxon —2D 36
Applegarthtown. Dum —1C 112
Applemore. Hants —2B 16
Appleshaw. Hants —2B 24
Applethwaite. Cumb —2D 102
Appleton. Hal —2H 83
Appleton. Oxon —5C 50
Appleton-le-Moors. N Yor —1B 100
Appleton-le-Street. N Yor —2B 100
Appleton Roebuck. N Yor —5H 99
Appleton Thorn. Warr —2A 84
Appleton Wiske. N Yor —4A 106
Appletree. Nptn —1C 50
Appletreehall. Scot —3H 119
Appletreewick. N Yor —3C 98
Appley. Som —4D 20
Appley Bridge. Lanc —4D 90
Apse Heath. IOW —4D 16
Apsley End. Beds —2B 52
Apuldram. W Sus —2G 17
Arabella. High —1C 158
Arbeadie. Aber —4D 152
Arberth. Pemb —3F 43
Arbirlot. Ang —4F 145

Arborfield. Wok —5F 37
Arborfield Cross. Wok —5F 37
Arborfield Garrison. Wok —5F 37
Arbourthorne. S Yor —2A 86
Arbroath. Ang —4F 145
Arbuthnott. Aber —1H 145
Arcan. High —3H 157
Archargary. High —3H 167
Archdeacon Newton. Darl —3F 105
Archiestown. Mor —4G 159
Arclid. Ches —4B 84
Arclid Green. Ches —4B 84
Ardachu. High —3D 164
Ardalanish. Arg —1A 132
Ardaneaskan. High —5H 155
Ardarroch. High —5H 155
Ardbeg. Arg —3B 126
(nr. Bute)
Ardbeg. Arg —1C 126
(nr. Dunoon)
Ardbeg. Arg —5C 124
(nr. Islay)
Ardcharnich. High —5F 163
Ardchiavaig. Arg —1A 132
Ardchonnell. Arg —2G 133
Ardchrishnish. Arg —1B 132
Ardchronie. High —5D 164
Ardchullarie. Stir —2E 135
Ardchyle. Stir —1E 135
Ard-dhubh. High —4G 155
Arddleen. Powy —4E 71
Arddlin. Powy —4E 71
Ardechive. High —4D 148
Ardeley. Herts —3D 52
Ardelve. High —1A 148
Arden. Arg —1E 127
Ardendrain. High —5H 157
Arden Hall. N Yor —5C 106
Ardens Grafton. Warw —5F 61
Ardentinny. Arg —1C 126
Ardeonaig. Stir —5D 142
Ardersier. High —3B 158
Ardery. High —2B 140
Ardessie. High —5E 163
Ardfern. Arg —3F 133
Ardfernal. High —2D 124
Ardfin. Arg —3C 124
Ardgartan. Arg —3B 134
Ardgay. High —5C 164
Ardgour. High —2E 141
Ardheslaig. High —3G 155
Ardindrean. High —5F 163
Ardingly. W Sus —3E 27
Ardington. Oxon —3C 36
Ardlamont House. Arg —3A 126
Ardleigh. Essx —3D 54
Ardler. Per —4B 144
Ardley. Oxon —3D 50
Ardlui. Arg —2C 134
Ardlussa. Arg —1E 125
Ardlussa. High —1E 125
Ardmair. High —4F 163
Ardmay. Arg —3B 134
Ardminish. Arg —5E 125
Ardmolich. High —1B 140
Ardmore. High —3C 166
(nr. Kinlochbervie)
Ardmore. High —5E 164
(nr. Tain)
Ardnacross. Arg —4G 139
Ardnadam. Arg —1C 126
Ardnagrask. High —4H 157
Ardnamurach. High —4G 147
Ardnarff. High —5A 156
Ardnastang. High —2C 140
Ardoch. Per —5H 143
Ardochy House. High —3E 148
Ardpatrick. Arg —3F 125
Ardrishaig. Arg —1G 125
Ardroag. High —4B 154
Ardross. High —1A 158
Ardrossan. N Ayr —5D 126
Ardshealach. High —2A 140

Ardsley. S Yor —4D 93
Ardslignish. High —2G 139
Ardtalla. Arg —4C 124
Ardtalnaig. Per —5E 142
Ardtoe. High —1A 140
Arduaine. Arg —2E 133
Ardullie. High —2H 157
Ardvasar. High —3E 147
Ardvorlich. Per —1F 135
Ardwell. Dum —5G 109
Ardwell. Mor —5A 160
Arean. High —1A 140
Areley Common. Worc —3C 60
Areley Kings. Worc —3B 60
Arford. Hants —3G 25
Argoed. Cphy —2E 33
Argoed Mill. Powy —4B 58
Aridhglas. Arg —2B 132
Arinacrinachd. High —3G 155
Arinagour. Arg —3D 138
Arisaig. High —5E 147
Ariundle. High —2C 140
Arivegaig. High —2A 140
Arkendale. N Yor —3F 99
Arkesden. Essx —2E 53
Arkholme. Lanc —2E 97
Arkle Town. N Yor —4D 104
Arkley. G Lon —1D 38
Arksey. S Yor —4F 93
Arkwright Town. Derbs —3B 86
Arlecdon. Cumb —3B 102
Arlescote. Warw —1B 50
Arlesey. Beds —2B 52
Arleston. Telf —4A 72
Arley. Ches —2A 84
Arlingham. Glos —4C 48
Arlington. Devn —2G 19
Arlington. E Sus —5G 27
Arlington. Glos —5G 49
Arlington Beccott. Devn —2G 19
Armadale. High —2H 167
Armadale. W Lot —3C 128
Armathwaite. Cumb —5G 113
Arminghall. Norf —5E 79
Armitage. Staf —4E 73
Armitage Bridge. W Yor —3B 92
Armley. W Yor —1C 92
Armscote. Warw —1H 49
Arms, The. Norf —1A 66
Armston. Nptn —2H 63
Armthorpe. S Yor —4G 93
Arncliffe. N Yor —2B 98
Arncliffe Cote. N Yor —2B 98
Arncroach. Fife —3H 137
Arne. Devn —4E 15
Arnesby. Leics —1D 62
Arnicle. Arg —2B 122
Arnisdale. High —2G 147
Arnish. High —4E 155
Arniston. Midl —3G 129
Arnol. W Isl —3F 171
Arnold. E Yor —5F 101
Arnold. Notts —1C 74
Arnprior. Stir —4F 135
Arnside. Cumb —2D 96
Aros Mains. Arg —4G 139
Arpafeelie. High —3A 158
Arrad Foot. Cumb —1C 96
Arram. E Yor —5E 101
Arras. E Yor —5D 100
Arrathorne. N Yor —5F 105
Arreton. IOW —4D 16
Arrington. Cambs —5C 64
Arrochar. Arg —3B 134
Arrow. Warw —5E 61
Arscaig. High —2C 164
Artafallie. High —4A 158
Arthington. W Yor —5E 99
Arthingworth. Nptn —2E 63
Arthog. Gwyn —4F 69
Arthrath. Aber —5G 161
Arthurstone. Per —4B 144
Arundel. W Sus —5B 26

Asby. Cumb —2B 102
Ascog. Arg —3C 126
Ascot. Wind —4A 38
Ascott-under-Wychwood. Oxon
—4B 50
Asenby. N Yor —2F 99
Asfordby. Leics —4E 74
Asfordby Hill. Leics —4E 74
Asgarby. Linc —4C 88
(nr. Horncastle)
Asgarby. Linc —1A 76
(nr. Sleaford)
Ash. Devn —4E 9
Ash. Dors —1D 14
Ash. Kent —5G 41
(nr. Sandwich)
Ash. Kent —4H 39
(nr. Swanley)
Ash. Som —4H 21
Ash. Surr —1G 25
Ashampstead. W Ber —4D 36
Ashbocking. Suff —5D 66
Ashbourne. Derbs —1F 73
Ashbrittle. Som —4D 20
Ashbrook. Shrp —1G 59
Ashburton. Devn —2D 8
Ashbury. Devn —3F 11
Ashbury. Oxon —3A 36
Ashby. N Lin —4B 94
Ashby by Partney. Linc —4D 88
Ashby cum Fenby. NE Lin —4F 95
Ashby de la Launde. Linc —5H 87
Ashby-de-la-Zouch. Leics —4A 74
Ashby Folville. Leics —4E 74
Ashby Magna. Leics —1C 62
Ashby Parva. Leics —2C 62
Ashby Puerorum. Linc —3C 88
Ashby St Ledgars. Nptn —4C 62
Ashby St Mary. Norf —5F 79
Ashcombe. Devn —5C 12
Ashcott. Som —3H 21
Ashcurch. Glos —2E 49
Ashdon. Essx —1F 53
Ashe. Hants —1D 24
Asheldham. Essx —5C 54
Ashen. Essx —1H 53
Ashendon. Buck —4F 51
Ashey. IOW —4D 16
Ashfield. Hants —1B 16
Ashfield. Here —3A 48
Ashfield. Shrp —2H 59
Ashfield. Stir —3G 135
Ashfield. Suff —4E 66
Ashfield Green. Suff —3E 67
Ashfold Crossways. W Sus —3D 26
Ashford. Devn —3F 19
(nr. Barnstaple)
Ashford. Devn —4C 8
(nr. Kingsbridge)
Ashford. Hants —1G 15
Ashford. Kent —1E 28
Ashford. Surr —3B 38
Ashford Bowdler. Shrp —3H 59
Ashford Carbonel. Shrp —3H 59
Ashford Hill. Hants —5D 36
Ashford in the Water. Derbs —4F 85
Ashgill. S Lan —5A 128
Ash Green. W Mid —2H 61
Ashgrove. Mor —2G 159
Ashill. Devn —1D 12
Ashill. Norf —5A 78
Ashill. Som —1G 13
Ashingdon. Essx —1C 40
Ashington. Nmbd —1F 115
Ashington. W Sus —4C 26
Ashkirk. Scot —2G 119
Ashlett. Hants —2C 16
Ashleworth. Glos —3D 48
Ashley. Cambs —4F 65
Ashley. Ches —2B 84
Ashley. Dors —2G 15
Ashley. Glos —2E 35

Bagnor—Barrowford

Bagnor. W Ber —5C 36
Bagshot. Surr —4A 38
Bagshot. Wilts —5B 36
Bagstone. S Glo —3B 34
Bagthorpe. Norf —2G 77
Bagthorpe. Notts —5B 86
Bagworth. Leics —5B 74
Bagwy Llydiart. Here —3H 47
Baildon. W Yor —1B 92
Baildon Green. W Yor —1B 92
Baile. W Isl —1E 170
Baile Ailein. W Isl —5E 171
Baile an Truiseil. W Isl —2F 171
Baile Boidheach. Arg —2F 125
Baile Glas. W Isl —3D 170
Bailemeonach. Arg —4A 140
Baile Mhanaich. W Isl —3C 170
Baile Mhartainn. W Isl —1C 170
Baile Mor. Arg —2A 132
Baile Mor. W Isl —2C 170
Baile nan Cailleach. W Isl —3C 170
Baile Raghaill. W Isl —2C 170
Bailey Green. Hants —4E 25
Baileyhead. Cumb —1G 113
Bailiesward. Aber —5B 160
Bail Iochdrach. W Isl —3D 170
Baillieston. Glas —3H 127
Bailrigg. Lanc —4D 97
Bail Uachdraich. W Isl —2D 170
Bail Ur Tholastaidh. W Isl —3H 171
Bainbridge. N Yor —5C 104
Bainsford. Falk —1B 128
Bainshole. Aber —5D 160
Bainton. E Yor —4D 100
Bainton. Oxon —3D 50
Bainton. Pet —5H 75
Baintown. Fife —3F 137
Baker Street. Thur —2H 39
Bakewell. Derbs —4G 85
Bala. Gwyn —2B 70
Balbeg. High —5G 157
(nr. Glen Urquhart)
Balbeg. High —1G 149
(nr. Loch Ness)
Balbeggie. Per —1D 136
Balblair. High —4C 164
(nr. Bonar Bridge)
Balblair. High —2B 158
(nr. Invergordon)
Balblair. High —4H 157
(nr. Inverness)
Balby. S Yor —4F 93
Balcathie. Ang —5F 145
Balcherry. High —5F 165
Balchladich. High —1E 163
Balchraggan. High —4H 157
Balchrick. High —3B 166
Balcombe. W Sus —2E 27
Balcombe Lane. W Sus —2E 27
Balcurvie. Fife —3F 137
Baldersby. N Yor —2F 99
Baldersby St James. N Yor —2F 99
Balderstone. Lanc —1E 91
Balderton. Ches —4F 83
Balderton. Notts —5F 87
Baldinnie. Fife —2G 137
Baldock. Herts —2C 52
Baldrine. IOM —3D 108
Baldslow. E Sus —4C 28
Baldwin. IOM —3C 108
Baldwinholme. Cumb —4E 113
Baldwins Gate. Staf —1B 72
Bale. Norf —2C 78
Balearn. Aber —3H 161
Balemartine. Arg —4A 138
Balephretrish. Arg —4B 138
Balephuil. Arg —4A 138
Balerno. Edin —3E 129
Balevullin. Arg —4A 138
Balfield. Ang —2E 145
Balfour. Orkn —6D 172
Balfron. Stir —1G 127
Balgaveny. Aber —4D 160
Balgonar. Fife —4C 136
Balgowan. High —4A 150
Balgown. High —2C 154
Balgrochan. E Dun —2H 127
Balgy. High —3H 155
Balhalgardy. Aber —1E 153
Baliasta. Shet —1G 173
Baligill. High —2A 168
Balintore. Ang —3B 144
Balintore. High —1C 158
Balintraid. High —1B 158
Balk. N Yor —1G 99
Balkeerie. Ang —4C 144
Balkholme. E Yor —2A 94
Ball. Shrp —3F 71
Ballabeg. IOM —4B 108
Ballacannell. IOM —3D 108
Ballacarnane Beg. IOM —3C 108
Ballachulish. High —3E 141
Ballagyr. IOM —3B 108
Ballajora. IOM —2D 108
Ballaleigh. IOM —3C 108
Ballamodha. IOM —4B 108
Ballantrae. S Ayr —1F 109
Ballards Gore. Essx —1D 40
Ballasalla. IOM —4B 108
(nr. Castletown)
Ballasalla. IOM —2C 108
(nr. Kirk Michael)
Ballater. Aber —4A 152
Ballaugh. IOM —2C 108
Ballencrieff. E Lot —2A 130
Ballencrieff Toll. W Lot —2C 128
Ballentoul. Per —2F 143
Ball Hill. Hants —5C 36
Ballidon. Derbs —5G 85
Balliemore. Arg —1B 126
(nr. Dunoon)
Balliemore. Arg —1F 133
(nr. Oban)
Ballieward. High —5E 159
Ballig. IOM —3B 108
Ballimore. Stir —2E 135
Ballingdon. Suff —1B 54
Ballingdon Bulmer. Essx —1B 54
Ballinger Common. Buck —5H 51
Ballingham. Here —2A 48
Ballingry. Fife —4D 136
Ballinluig. Per —3G 143
Ballintuim. Per —3A 144
Balliveolan. Arg —4C 140
Balloan. High —3C 164
Balloch. High —4B 158
Balloch. N Lan —2A 128
Balloch. Per —2H 135
Balloch. W Dun —1E 127
Ballochan. Aber —4C 152
Ballochgoy. Arg —3B 126
Ballochmyle. E Ayr —2E 117
Ballochroy. Arg —4F 125
Balls Cross. W Sus —3A 26
Ball's Green. E Sus —2F 27
Ballygown. Arg —4F 139
Ballygrant. Arg —3B 124
Ballymichael. N Ayr —2D 122
Balmacara. High —1G 147
Balmaclellan. Dum —2D 110
Balmacqueen. High —1D 154
Balmaha. Stir —4D 134
Balmalcolm. Fife —3F 137
Balmalloch. N Lan —2A 128
Balmeanach. High —5E 155
Balmedie. Aber —2G 153
Balmerino. Fife —1F 137
Balmerlawn. Hants —2B 16
Balmore. E Dun —2H 127
Balmore. High —4B 154
Balmuir. Ang —5D 144
Balmullo. Fife —1G 137
Balmurrie. Dum —3H 109
Balnaboth. Ang —2C 144
Balnabruaich. High —1B 158
Balnabruich. High —5D 168
Balnacoil. High —2F 165
Balnacra. High —4B 156
Balnacroft. Aber —4G 151
Balnageith. Mor —3E 159
Balnaglaic. High —5G 157
Balnagrantach. High —5G 157
Balnaguard. Per —3G 143
Balnahard. Arg —3B 132
Balnain. High —5G 157
Balnakeil. High —2D 166
Balnamoon. Aber —3G 161
Balnamoon. Ang —2E 145
Balnapaling. High —2B 158
Balornock. Glas —3H 127
Balquhidder. Stir —1E 135
Balsall. W Mid —3G 61
Balsall Common. W Mid —3G 61
Balscote. Oxon —1B 50
Balsham. Cambs —5E 65
Balstonia. Thur —2A 40
Baltasound. Shet —1H 173
Balterley. Staf —5B 84
Baltersan. Dum —3B 110
Balthangie. Aber —3F 161
Baltonsborough. Som —3A 22
Balvaird. High —3H 157
Balvaird. Per —2D 136
Balvenie. Mor —4H 159
Balvicar. Arg —2E 133
Balvraid. High —2G 147
Balvraid Lodge. High —5C 158
Bamber Bridge. Lanc —2D 90
Bamber's Green. Essx —3F 53
Bamburgh. Nmbd —1F 121
Bamford. Derbs —2G 85
Bampton. Cumb —3G 103
Bampton. Devn —4C 20
Bampton. Oxon —5B 50
Bampton Grange. Cumb —3G 103
Banavie. High —1F 141
Banbury. Oxon —1C 50
Bancffosfelen. Carm —4E 45
Banchory. Aber —4D 152
Banchory-Devenick. Aber —3G 153
Bancycapel. Carm —4E 45
Bancyfelin. Carm —3H 43
Banc-y-ffordd. Carm —2E 45
Banff. Aber —2D 160
Bangor. Gwyn —3E 81
Bangor-is-y-coed. Wrex —1F 71
Bangors. Corn —3C 10
Bangor's Green. Lanc —4B 90
Bangrove. Suff —3B 66
Banham. Norf —2C 66
Bank. Hants —2A 16
Bankend. Dum —3B 112
Bankfoot. Per —5H 143
Bankglen. E Ayr —3E 117
Bankhead. Aber C —2F 153
Bankhead. Aber —3D 152
Bankhead. S Lan —5B 128
Bankland. Som —4G 21
Bank Newton. N Yor —4B 98
Banknock. Falk —2A 128
Banks. Cumb —3G 113
Banks. Lanc —2B 90
Bankshill. Dum —1C 112
Bank Street. Worc —4A 60
Bank, The. Ches —5C 84
Bank, The. Shrp —1A 60
Bank Top. Lanc —4D 90
Banners Gate. W Mid —1E 61
Banningham. Norf —3E 78
Banniskirk. High —3D 168
Bannister Green. Essx —3G 53
Bannockburn. Stir —4H 135
Banstead. Surr —5D 38
Bantham. Devn —4C 8
Banton. N Lan —2A 128
Banwell. N Som —1G 21
Banyard's Green. Suff —3F 67
Bapchild. Kent —4D 40
Bapton. Wilts —3E 23
Barabhas. W Isl —2F 171
Barabhas Iarach. W Isl —2F 171
Barabhas Uarach. W Isl —2F 171
Baramore. High —1A 140
Barassie. S Ayr —1C 116
Baravullin. Arg —4D 140
Barbaraville. High —1B 158
Barber Booth. Derbs —2F 85
Barber Green. Cumb —1C 96
Barbieston. E Ayr —3C 116
Barbieston. S Ayr —3D 116
Barbon. Cumb —1F 97
Barbourne. Worc —5C 60
Barbridge. Ches —5A 84
Barbrook. Devn —2H 19
Barby. Nptn —3C 62
Barby Nortoft. Nptn —3C 62
Barcaldine. Arg —4D 140
Barcheston. Warw —1A 50
Barclose. Cumb —3F 113
Barcombe. E Sus —4F 27
Barcombe Cross. E Sus —4F 27
Barden. N Yor —5E 105
Barden Scale. N Yor —4C 98
Bardfield End Green. Essx —2G 53
Bardfield Saling. Essx —3G 53
Bardnabeinne. High —4E 164
Bardney. Linc —4A 88
Bardon. Leics —4B 74
Bardon Mill. Nmbd —3A 114
Bardowie. E Dun —2G 127
Bardrainney. Inv —2E 127
Bardsea. Cumb —2C 96
Bardsey. W Yor —5F 99
Bardsley. G Man —4H 91
Bardwell. Suff —3B 66
Bare. Lanc —3D 96
Barelees. Nmbd —1C 120
Barewood. Here —5F 59
Barford. Hants —3G 25
Barford. Norf —5D 78
Barford. Warw —4G 61
Barford St John. Oxon —2C 50
Barford St Martin. Wilts —3F 23
Barford St Michael. Oxon —2C 50
Barfrestone. Kent —5G 41
Bargeddie. N Lan —3A 128
Bargod. Cphy —2E 33
Bargoed. Cphy —2E 33
Bargrennan. Dum —2A 110
Barham. Cambs —3A 64
Barham. Kent —5G 41
Barham. Suff —5D 66
Barharrow. Dum —4D 110
Bar Hill. Cambs —4C 64
Barholm. Linc —4H 75
Barkby. Leics —4D 74
Barkestone-le-Vale. Leics —2E 75
Barkham. Wok —5F 37
Barking. G Lon —2F 39
Barking. Suff —5C 66
Barkingside. G Lon —2F 39
Barking Tye. Suff —5C 66
Barkisland. W Yor —3A 92
Barkston. Linc —1G 75
Barkston Ash. N Yor —1E 93
Barkway. Herts —2D 53
Barlanark. Glas —3H 127
Barlaston. Staf —2C 72
Barlavington. W Sus —4A 26
Barlborough. Derbs —3B 86
Barlby. N Yor —1G 93
Barlestone. Leics —5B 74
Barley. Herts —2D 53
Barley. Lanc —5H 97
Barley Mow. Tyne —4F 115
Barleythorpe. Rut —5F 75
Barling. Essx —2D 40
Barlings. Linc —3H 87
Barlow. Derbs —3H 85
Barlow. N Yor —2G 93
Barlow. Tyne —3E 115
Barmby Moor. E Yor —5B 100
Barmby on the Marsh. E Yor —2G 93
Barmer. Norf —2H 77
Barming Heath. Kent —5B 40
Barmoor. Nmbd —1E 121
Barmouth. Gwyn —4F 69
Barmpton. Darl —3A 106
Barmston. E Yor —4F 101
Barmulloch. Glas —3H 127
Barnack. Pet —5H 75
Barnacle. Warw —2A 62
Barnard Castle. Dur —3D 104
Barnard Gate. Oxon —4C 50
Barnardiston. Suff —1H 53
Barnbarroch. Dum —4F 111
Barnburgh. S Yor —4E 93
Barnby. Suff —2G 67
Barnby Dun. S Yor —4G 93
Barnby in the Willows. Notts —5F 87
Barnby Moor. Notts —2D 86
Barnes. G Lon —3D 38
Barnes Street. Kent —1H 27
Barnet. G Lon —1D 38
Barnetby le Wold. N Lin —4D 94
Barney. Norf —2B 78
Barnham. Suff —3A 66
Barnham. W Sus —5A 26
Barnham Broom. Norf —5C 78
Barnhead. Ang —3F 145
Barnhill. D'dee —5D 145
Barnhill. Mor —3F 159
Barnhill. Per —1D 136
Barnhills. Dum —2E 109
Barningham. Dur —3D 105
Barningham. Suff —3B 66
Barnoldby le Beck. NE Lin —4F 95
Barnoldswick. Lanc —5A 98
Barns Green. W Sus —3C 26
Barnsley. Glos —5F 49
Barnsley. Shrp —1B 60
Barnsley. S Yor —4D 92
Barnstaple. Devn —3F 19
Barnston. Essx —4G 53
Barnston. Mers —2E 83
Barnstone. Notts —2E 75
Barnt Green. Worc —3E 61
Barnton. Ches —3A 84
Barnwell. Cambs —5D 64
Barnwell All Saints. Nptn —2H 63
Barnwell St Andrew. Nptn —2H 63
Barnwood. Glos —4D 48
Barons Cross. Here —5G 59
Barony, The. Orkn —5B 172
Barr. Dum —4G 117
Barr. S Ayr —5B 116
Barra Airport. W Isl —8C 170
Barrachan. Dum —5A 110
Barraglom. W Isl —4D 171
Barrahormid. Arg —1F 125
Barrapol. Arg —4A 138
Barrasford. Nmbd —2C 114
Barravullin. Arg —3F 133
Barregarrow. IOM —3C 108
Barrhead. E Ren —4G 127
Barrhill. S Ayr —1H 109
Barri. V Glam —5E 32
Barrington. Cambs —1D 53
Barrington. Som —1G 13
Barripper. Corn —3D 4
Barrmill. N Ayr —4E 127
Barrock. High —1E 169
Barrow. Lanc —1F 91
Barrow. Rut —4F 75
Barrow. Shrp —5A 72
Barrow. Som —3C 22
Barrow. Suff —4G 65
Barroway Drove. Norf —5E 77
Barrow Bridge. G Man —3E 91
Barrow Burn. Nmbd —3C 120
Barrowby. Linc —2F 75
Barrowcliff. N Yor —1E 101
Barrow Common. N Som —5A 34
Barrowden. Rut —5G 75
Barrowford. Lanc —1G 91

Barrow Gurney—Bennethead

Barrow Gurney. *N Som* —5A **34**
Barrow Haven. *N Lin* —2D **94**
Barrow Hill. *Derbs* —3B **86**
Barrow-in-Furness. *Cumb* —3B **96**
Barrow Nook. *Lanc* —4C **90**
Barrow's Green. *Ches* —2H **83**
Barrows Green. *Cumb* —1E **97**
Barrow Street. *Wilts* —3D **22**
Barrow upon Humber. *N Lin* —2D **94**
Barrow upon Soar. *Leics* —4C **74**
Barrow upon Trent. *Derbs* —3A **74**
Barry. *Ang* —5E **145**
Barry. *V Glam* —5E **32**
Barry Island. *V Glam* —5E **32**
Barsby. *Leics* —4D **74**
Barsham. *Suff* —2F **67**
Barston. *W Mid* —3G **61**
Bartestree. *Here* —1A **48**
Barthol Chapel. *Aber* —5F **161**
Bartholomew Green. *Essx* —3H **53**
Barthomley. *Ches* —5B **84**
Bartley. *Hants* —1B **16**
Bartley Green. *W Mid* —2E **61**
Bartlow. *Cambs* —1F **53**
Barton. *Cambs* —5D **64**
Barton. *Ches* —5G **83**
Barton. *Cumb* —2F **103**
Barton. *Glos* —3F **49**
Barton. *IOW* —4D **16**
Barton. *Lanc* —4B **90**
(nr. Ormskirk)
Barton. *Lanc* —1D **90**
(nr. Preston)
Barton. *N Som* —1G **21**
Barton. *N Yor* —4F **105**
Barton. *Oxon* —5D **50**
Barton. *Torb* —2F **9**
Barton. *Warw* —5F **61**
Barton Bendish. *Norf* —5G **77**
Barton Gate. *Staf* —4F **73**
Barton Green. *Staf* —4F **73**
Barton Hartshthorn. *Buck* —2E **51**
Barton Hill. *N Yor* —3B **100**
Barton in Fabis. *Notts* —2C **74**
Barton in the Beans. *Leics* —5A **74**
Barton-le-Clay. *Beds* —2A **52**
Barton-le-Street. *N Yor* —2B **100**
Barton-le-Willows. *N Yor* —3B **100**
Barton Mills. *Suff* —3G **65**
Barton on Sea. *Hants* —3H **15**
Barton-on-the-Heath. *Warw* —2A **50**
Barton St David. *Som* —3A **22**
Barton Seagrave. *Nptn* —3F **63**
Barton Stacey. *Hants* —2C **24**
Barton Town. *Devn* —2G **19**
Barton Turf. *Norf* —3F **79**
Barton-under-Needwood. *Staf* —4F **73**
Barton-upon-Humber. *N Lin* —2D **94**
Barton Waterside. *N Lin* —2D **94**
Barugh Green. *S Yor* —4D **92**
Barway. *Cambs* —3E **65**
Barwell. *Leics* —1B **62**
Barwick. *Herts* —4D **53**
Barwick. *Som* —1A **14**
Barwick in Elmet. *W Yor* —1D **93**
Baschurch. *Shrp* —3G **71**
Bascote. *Warw* —4B **62**
Basford Green. *Staf* —5D **85**
Bashall Eaves. *Lanc* —5F **97**
Bashall Town. *Lanc* —5G **97**
Bashley. *Hants* —3H **15**
Basildon. *Essx* —2B **40**
Basingstoke. *Hants* —1E **25**
Baslow. *Derbs* —3G **85**
Bason Bridge. *Som* —2G **21**
Bassaleg. *Newp* —3F **33**
Bassendean. *Scot* —5C **130**
Bassenthwaite. *Cumb* —1D **102**
Bassett. *Sotn* —1C **16**
Bassingbourn. *Cambs* —1D **52**
Bassingfield. *Notts* —2D **74**
Bassingham. *Linc* —4G **87**
Bassingthorpe. *Linc* —3G **75**
Bassus Green. *Herts* —3D **52**
Basta. *Shet* —2G **173**
Baston. *Linc* —4A **76**
Bastonford. *Worc* —5C **60**
Bastwick. *Norf* —4G **79**
Batchley. *Worc* —4E **61**
Batchworth. *Herts* —1B **38**
Batcombe. *Dors* —2B **14**
Batcombe. *Som* —3B **22**
Bate Heath. *Ches* —3A **84**
Bath. *Bath* —5C **34**
Bathampton. *Bath* —5C **34**
Bathealton. *Som* —4D **20**
Batheaston. *Bath* —5C **34**
Bathford. *Bath* —5C **34**
Bathgate. *W Lot* —3C **128**
Bathley. *Notts* —5E **87**
Bathpool. *Corn* —5C **10**
Bathpool. *Som* —4F **21**
Bathville. *W Lot* —3C **128**
Bathway. *Som* —1A **22**
Batley. *W Yor* —2C **92**
Batsford. *Glos* —2G **49**
Batson. *Devn* —5D **8**
Battersby. *N Yor* —4C **106**
Battersea. *G Lon* —3D **39**
Battisborough Cross. *Devn* —4C **8**
Battisford. *Suff* —5C **66**
Battisford Tye. *Suff* —5C **66**
Battle. *E Sus* —4B **28**
Battle. *Powy* —2D **46**
Battleborough. *Som* —1G **21**
Battledown. *Glos* —3E **49**
Battlefield. *Shrp* —4H **71**
Battlesbridge. *Essx* —1B **40**
Battlesden. *Beds* —3H **51**
Battlesea Green. *Suff* —3E **66**
Battleton. *Som* —4C **20**
Battramsley. *Hants* —3B **16**
Batt's Corner. *Surr* —2G **25**
Bauds of Cullen. *Mor* —2B **160**
Baugh. *Arg* —4B **138**
Baughton. *Worc* —1D **49**
Baughurst. *Hants* —5D **36**
Baulking. *Oxon* —2B **36**
Baumber. *Linc* —3B **88**
Baunton. *Glos* —5F **49**
Baverstock. *Wilts* —3F **23**
Bawburgh. *Norf* —5D **78**
Bawdeswell. *Norf* —3C **78**
Bawdrip. *Som* —3G **21**
Bawdsey. *Suff* —1G **55**
Bawdsey Manor. *Suff* —2G **55**
Bawsey. *Norf* —4F **77**
Bawtry. *S Yor* —1D **86**
Baxenden. *Lanc* —2F **91**
Baxterley. *Warw* —1G **61**
Baxter's Green. *Suff* —5G **65**
Baybridge. *Hants* —4D **24**
Baybridge. *Nmbd* —4C **114**
Baycliff. *Cumb* —2B **96**
Baydon. *Wilts* —4A **36**
Bayford. *Herts* —5D **52**
Bayford. *Som* —4C **22**
Bayles. *Cumb* —5A **114**
Baylham. *Suff* —5D **66**
Baynard's Green. *Oxon* —3D **50**
Bayston Hill. *Shrp* —5G **71**
Baythorn End. *Essx* —1H **53**
Baythorpe. *Linc* —1B **76**
Bayton. *Worc* —3A **60**
Bayton Common. *Worc* —3B **60**
Bayworth. *Oxon* —5D **50**
Beach. *S Glo* —4C **34**
Beachampton. *Buck* —2F **51**
Beachamwell. *Norf* —5G **77**
Beachley. *Glos* —2A **34**
Beacon. *Devn* —2E **13**
Beacon End. *Essx* —3C **54**
Beacon Hill. *Surr* —3G **25**
Beacon's Bottom. *Buck* —2F **37**
Beaconsfield. *Buck* —1A **38**
Beacontree. *G Lon* —2F **39**
Beacrabhaicg. *W Isl* —8D **171**
Beadlam. *N Yor* —1A **100**
Beadnell. *Nmbd* —2G **121**
Beaford. *Devn* —1F **11**
Beal. *Nmbd* —5G **131**
Beal. *N Yor* —2F **93**
Bealsmill. *Corn* —5D **10**
Beam Hill. *Staf* —3G **73**
Beamhurst. *Staf* —2E **73**
Beaminster. *Dors* —2H **13**
Beamish. *Dur* —4F **115**
Beamond End. *Buck* —1A **38**
Beamsley. *N Yor* —4C **98**
Bean. *Kent* —3G **39**
Beanacre. *Wilts* —5E **35**
Beanley. *Nmbd* —3E **121**
Beanshanger. *Nptn* —2F **51**
Beardwood. *Bkbn* —2E **91**
Beare Green. *Surr* —1C **26**
Bearley. *Warw* —4F **61**
Bearpark. *Dur* —5F **115**
Bearsbridge. *Nmbd* —4A **114**
Bearsden. *E Dun* —2G **127**
Bearsted. *Kent* —5B **40**
Bearstone. *Shrp* —2B **72**
Bearwardcote. *Derbs* —2G **73**
Bearwood. *Pool* —3F **15**
Bearwood. *W Mid* —2E **61**
Beattock. *Dum* —4C **118**
Beauchamp Roding. *Essx* —4F **53**
Beauchief. *S Yor* —2H **85**
Beaufort. *Blae* —4E **47**
Beaulieu. *Hants* —2B **16**
Beauly. *High* —4H **157**
Beaumaris. *IOA* —3F **81**
Beaumont. *Cumb* —4E **113**
Beaumont. *Essx* —3E **55**
Beaumont Hill. *Darl* —3F **105**
Beaumont Leys. *Leic C* —5C **74**
Beausale. *Warw* —3G **61**
Beauvale. *Notts* —1B **74**
Beauworth. *Hants* —4D **24**
Beaworthy. *Devn* —3E **11**
Beazley End. *Essx* —3H **53**
Bebington. *Mers* —2F **83**
Bebside. *Nmbd* —1F **115**
Beccles. *Suff* —2G **67**
Becconsall. *Lanc* —2C **90**
Beckbury. *Shrp* —5B **72**
Beckenham. *G Lon* —4E **39**
Beckermet. *Cumb* —4B **102**
Beckett End. *Norf* —1G **65**
Beckfoot. *Cumb* —1A **96**
(nr. Broughton in Furness)
Beck Foot. *Cumb* —5H **103**
(nr. Kendal)
Beckfoot. *Cumb* —4C **102**
(nr. Seascale)
Beckfoot. *Cumb* —5B **112**
(nr. Silloth)
Beckford. *Worc* —2E **49**
Beckhampton. *Wilts* —5F **35**
Beck Hole. *N Yor* —4F **107**
Beckingham. *Linc* —5F **87**
Beckingham. *Notts* —1E **87**
Beckington. *Som* —1D **22**
Beckley. *E Sus* —3C **28**
Beckley. *Hants* —3H **15**
Beckley. *Oxon* —4D **50**
Beck Row. *Suff* —3F **65**
Beck Side. *Cumb* —1C **96**
(nr. Cartmel)
Beckside. *Cumb* —1F **97**
(nr. Sedbergh)
Beck Side. *Cumb* —1B **96**
(nr. Ulverston)
Beckton. *G Lon* —2F **39**
Beckwithshaw. *N Yor* —4E **99**
Becontree. *G Lon* —2F **39**
Bedale. *N Yor* —1E **99**
Bedburn. *Dur* —1E **105**
Bedchester. *Dors* —1D **14**
Beddau. *Rhon* —3D **32**
Beddgelert. *Gwyn* —1E **69**
Beddingham. *E Sus* —5F **27**
Beddington. *G Lon* —4D **39**
Bedfield. *Suff* —4E **66**
Bedford. *Beds* —1A **52**
Bedford. *G Man* —4E **91**
Bedham. *W Sus* —3B **26**
Bedhampton. *Hants* —2F **17**
Bedingfield. *Suff* —4D **66**
Bedingham Green. *Norf* —1E **67**
Bedlam. *N Yor* —3E **99**
Bedlar's Green. *Essx* —3F **53**
Bedlington. *Nmbd* —1F **115**
Bedlinog. *Mer T* —5D **46**
Bedminster. *Bris* —4A **34**
Bedmond. *Herts* —5A **52**
Bednall. *Staf* —4D **72**
Bedrule. *Scot* —3A **120**
Bedstone. *Shrp* —3F **59**
Bedwas. *Cphy* —3E **33**
Bedwellty. *Cphy* —5E **47**
Bedworth. *Warw* —2A **62**
Beeby. *Leics* —5D **74**
Beech. *Hants* —3E **25**
Beech. *Staf* —2C **72**
Beechcliffe. *W Yor* —5C **98**
Beech Hill. *W Ber* —5E **37**
Beechingstoke. *Wilts* —1F **23**
Beedon. *W Ber* —4C **36**
Beeford. *E Yor* —4F **101**
Beeley. *Derbs* —4G **85**
Beelsby. *NE Lin* —4F **95**
Beenham. *W Ber* —5D **36**
Beeny. *Corn* —3B **10**
Beer. *Devn* —4F **13**
Beer. *Som* —3H **21**
Beer Crocombe. *Som* —4G **21**
Beer Hackett. *Dors* —1B **14**
Beesands. *Devn* —4E **9**
Beesby. *Linc* —3D **88**
Beeson. *Devn* —4E **9**
Beeston. *Beds* —1B **52**
Beeston. *Ches* —5H **83**
Beeston. *Norf* —4B **78**
Beeston. *Notts* —2C **74**
Beeston. *W Yor* —1C **92**
Beeston Regis. *Norf* —1D **78**
Beeswing. *Dum* —3F **111**
Beetham. *Cumb* —2D **97**
Beetham. *Som* —1F **13**
Beetley. *Norf* —4B **78**
Beffcote. *Staf* —4C **72**
Began. *Card* —3F **33**
Begbroke. *Oxon* —4C **50**
Begdale. *Cambs* —5D **76**
Begelly. *Pemb* —4F **43**
Beggar Hill. *Essx* —5G **53**
Beggar's Bush. *Powy* —4E **59**
Beggearn Huish. *Som* —3D **20**
Beguildy. *Powy* —3D **58**
Beighton. *Norf* —5F **79**
Beighton. *S Yor* —2B **86**
Beighton Hill. *Derbs* —5G **85**
Beith. *N Ayr* —4E **127**
Bekesbourne. *Kent* —5F **41**
Belaugh. *Norf* —4E **79**
Belbroughton. *Worc* —3D **60**
Belchalwell. *Dors* —2C **14**
Belchalwell Street. *Dors* —2C **14**
Belchamp Otten. *Essx* —1B **54**
Belchamp St Paul. *Essx* —1A **54**
Belchamp Walter. *Essx* —1B **54**
Belchford. *Linc* —3B **88**
Belfatton. *Aber* —3H **161**
Belford. *Nmbd* —1F **121**
Belgrano. *Cnwy* —3B **82**
Belhaven. *E Lot* —2C **130**
Belhelvie. *Aber* —2G **153**
Belhinnie. *Aber* —1B **152**
Bellabeg. *Aber* —2A **152**
Bellamore. *S Ayr* —1H **109**
Bellanoch. *Arg* —4E **133**
Bell Busk. *N Yor* —4B **98**
Belleau. *Linc* —3D **88**
Belleheiglash. *Mor* —5F **159**
Bell End. *Worc* —3D **60**
Bellerby. *N Yor* —5E **105**
Bellerby Camp. *N Yor* —5D **105**
Bellever. *Devn* —5G **11**
Belle Vue. *Cumb* —1C **102**
Belle Vue. *Shrp* —4G **71**
Bellfield. *S Lan* —1H **117**
Belliehill. *Ang* —2E **145**
Bellingdon. *Buck* —5H **51**
Bellingham. *Nmbd* —1B **114**
Bellmount. *Norf* —3E **77**
Bellochantuy. *Arg* —2A **122**
Bellsbank. *E Ayr* —4D **117**
Bell's Cross. *Suff* —5D **66**
Bellshill. *N Lan* —4A **128**
Bellshill. *Nmbd* —1F **121**
Bellside. *N Lan* —4B **128**
Bellspool. *Scot* —1D **118**
Bellsquarry. *W Lot* —3D **128**
Bells Yew Green. *E Sus* —2H **27**
Belmaduthy. *High* —3A **158**
Belmesthorpe. *Rut* —4H **75**
Belmont. *Bkbn* —3E **91**
Belmont. *Shet* —1G **173**
Belmont. *S Ayr* —3C **116**
Belmore. *Arg* —1D **126**
Belnacraig. *Aber* —2A **152**
Belnie. *Linc* —2B **76**
Belowda. *Corn* —2D **6**
Belper. *Derbs* —1A **74**
Belper Lane End. *Derbs* —1H **73**
Belph. *Derbs* —3C **86**
Belsay. *Nmbd* —2E **115**
Belsford. *Devn* —3D **8**
Belsize. *Herts* —5A **52**
Belstead. *Suff* —1E **55**
Belston. *S Ayr* —2C **116**
Belstone. *Devn* —3G **11**
Belstone Corner. *Devn* —3G **11**
Belthorn. *Lanc* —2F **91**
Beltinge. *Kent* —4F **41**
Beltoft. *N Lin* —4B **94**
Belton. *Leics* —3B **74**
Belton. *Linc* —2G **75**
Belton. *Norf* —5G **79**
Belton. *N Lin* —4A **94**
Belton. *Rut* —5F **75**
Beltring. *Kent* —1A **28**
Belts of Collonach. *Aber* —4D **152**
Belvedere. *G Lon* —3G **39**
Belvoir. *Leics* —2F **75**
Bembridge. *IOW* —4E **17**
Bemersyde. *Scot* —1H **119**
Bemerton. *Wilts* —3G **23**
Bempton. *E Yor* —2F **101**
Benacre. *Suff* —2H **67**
Ben Alder Lodge. *High* —1C **142**
Ben Armine Lodge. *High* —2E **164**
Benbecula Airport. *W Isl* —3C **170**
Benbuie. *Dum* —5G **117**
Benchill. *G Man* —2C **84**
Benderloch. *Arg* —5D **140**
Bendish. *Herts* —3B **52**
Bendronaig Lodge. *High* —5C **156**
Benenden. *Kent* —2C **28**
Benera. *High* —1G **147**
Benfieldside. *Dur* —4D **115**
Bengate. *Norf* —3F **79**
Bengeworth. *Worc* —1F **49**
Bengrove. *Glos* —2E **49**
Benhall Green. *Suff* —4F **67**
Benholm. *Aber* —2H **145**
Benington. *Herts* —3D **52**
Benington. *Linc* —1C **76**
Benington Sea End. *Linc* —1D **76**
Benllech. *IOA* —2E **81**
Benmore Lodge. *High* —2H **163**
Bennacott. *Corn* —3C **10**
Bennah. *Devn* —4B **12**
Bennecarngan. *N Ayr* —3D **122**
Bennethead. *Cumb* —2F **103**

Benningbrough—Bishopton

Benningbrough. N Yor—4H 99
Benniworth. Linc—2B 88
Benover. Kent—1B 28
Benson. Oxon—2E 36
Bent. Aber—1F 145
Benthall. Nmbd—2G 121
Benthall. Shrp—5A 72
Bentham. Glos—4E 49
Benthoul. Aber C—3F 153
Bentlawn. Shrp—5F 71
Bentley. E Yor—1D 94
Bentley. Hants—2F 25
Bentley. S Yor—4F 93
Bentley. Suff—2E 54
Bentley. Warw—1G 61
Bentley. W Mid—1D 61
Bentley Heath. Herts—1D 38
Bentley Heath. W Mid—3F 61
Bentpath. Dum—5F 119
Bents. W Lot—3C 128
Bentworth. Hants—2E 25
Benvie. D'dee—5C 144
Benville Lane. Dors—2A 14
Benwell. Tyne—3F 115
Benwick. Cambs—1C 64
Beoley. Worc—4E 61
Beoraidbeg. High—4E 147
Bepton. W Sus—1G 17
Berden. Essx—3E 53
Bere Alston. Devn—2A 8
Bere Ferrers. Devn—2A 8
Berepper. Corn—4D 4
Bere Regis. Dors—3D 14
Bergh Apton. Norf—5F 79
Berinsfield. Oxon—2D 36
Berkeley. Glos—2B 34
Berkhamsted. Herts—5H 51
Berkley. Som—2D 22
Berkswell. W Mid—3G 61
Bermondsey. G Lon—3E 39
Bernice. Arg—4A 134
Bernisdale. High—3D 154
Berrick Salome. Oxon—2E 36
Berriedale. High—1H 165
Berrier. Cumb—2F 103
Berriew. Powy—5D 70
Berrington. Nmbd—5G 131
Berrington. Shrp—5H 71
Berrington. Worc—4H 59
Berrington Green. Worc—4H 59
Berrington Law. Nmbd—5F 131
Berrow. Som—1G 21
Berrow Green. Worc—5B 60
Berry Cross. Devn—1E 11
Berry Down Cross. Devn—2F 19
Berry Hill. Glos—4A 48
Berry Hill. Pemb—1A 44
Berryhillock. Mor—2C 160
Berrynarbor. Devn—2F 19
Berry Pomeroy. Devn—2E 9
Berryscaur. Dum—5D 118
Berry's Green. G Lon—5F 39
Bersham. Wrex—1F 71
Berthengam. Flin—3D 82
Berwick. E Sus—5G 27
Berwick Bassett. Wilts—4G 35
Berwick Hill. Nmbd—2E 115
Berwick St James. Wilts—3F 23
Berwick St John. Wilts—4E 23
Berwick St Leonard. Wilts—3E 23
Berwick-upon-Tweed. Nmbd—4G 131
Berwyn. Den—1D 70
Bescaby. Leics—3F 75
Bescar. Lanc—3B 90
Besford. Worc—1E 49
Bessacarr. S Yor—4G 93
Bessels Leigh. Oxon—5C 50
Bessingby. E Yor—3F 101
Bessingham. Norf—2D 78
Best Beech Hill. E Sus—2H 27
Besthorpe. Norf—1C 66
Besthorpe. Notts—4F 87
Bestwood Village. Notts—1C 74
Beswick. E Yor—5E 101
Betchworth. Surr—5D 38
Bethania. Cdgn—4E 57
Bethania. Gwyn—1G 69
(nr. Blaenau Ffestiniog)
Bethania. Gwyn—5F 81
(nr. Caernarfon)
Bethel. Gwyn—2B 70
(nr. Bala)
Bethel. Gwyn—4E 81
(nr. Caernarfon)
Bethel. IOA—3C 80
Bethersden. Kent—1D 28
Bethesda. Gwyn—4F 81
Bethesda. Pemb—3E 43
Bethlehem. Carm—3G 45
Bethnal Green. G Lon—2E 39
Betishill. N Lan—3A 128
Betley. Staf—1B 72
Betsham. Kent—3H 39
Betteshanger. Kent—5H 41
Bettiscombe. Dors—3H 13
Bettisfield. Wrex—2G 71
Betton. Shrp—2A 72
Betton Strange. Shrp—5H 71
Bettws. B'End—3B 32
Bettws. Newp—2F 33
Bettws Bledrws. Cdgn—5E 57
Bettws Cedewain. Powy—1D 58
Bettws Gwerfil Goch. Den—1C 70
Bettws Ifan. Cdgn—1D 44
Bettws Newydd. Mon—5G 47
Bettyhill. High—2H 167
Betws. Carm—4G 45
Betws Garmon. Gwyn—5E 81
Betws-y-Coed. Cnwy—5G 81
Betws-yn-Rhos. Cnwy—3B 82
Beulah. Cdgn—1C 44
Beulah. Powy—5B 58
Bevendean. Brig—5E 27
Bevercotes. Notts—3D 86
Beverley. E Yor—1D 94
Beverston. Glos—2D 34
Bevington. Glos—2B 34
Bewaldeth. Cumb—1D 102
Bewcastle. Cumb—2G 113
Bewdley. Worc—3B 60
Bewerley. N Yor—3D 98
Bewholme. E Yor—5F 101
Bexfield. Norf—3C 78
Bexhill. E Sus—5B 28
Bexley. G Lon—3F 39
Bexleyheath. G Lon—3F 39
Bexleyhill. W Sus—3A 26
Bexwell. Norf—5F 77
Beyton. Suff—4B 66
Beyton Green. Suff—4B 66
Bhalton. W Isl—4C 171
Bhatarsaigh. W Isl—9B 170
Bibbington. Derbs—3E 85
Bibury. Glos—5G 49
Bicester. Oxon—3D 50
Bickenhall. Som—1F 13
Bickenhill. W Mid—2F 61
Bicker. Linc—2B 76
Bicker Bar. Linc—2B 76
Bicker Gauntlet. Linc—2B 76
Bickershaw. G Man—4E 91
Bickerstaffe. Lanc—4C 90
Bickerton. Ches—5H 83
Bickerton. Nmbd—4D 121
Bickerton. N Yor—4G 99
Bickford. Staf—4C 72
Bickington. Devn—3F 19
(nr. Barnstaple)
Bickington. Devn—5A 12
(nr. Newton Abbot)
Bickleigh. Devn—2B 8
(nr. Plymouth)
Bickleigh. Devn—2C 12
(nr. Tiverton)
Bickleton. Devn—3F 19
Bickley. N Yor—5G 107
Bickley Moss. Ches—1H 71
Bickmarsh. Warw—5F 61
Bicknacre. Essx—5A 54
Bicknoller. Som—3E 20
Bicknor. Kent—5C 40
Bickton. Hants—1G 15
Bicton. Here—4G 59
Bicton. Shrp—2E 59
(nr. Bishop's Castle)
Bicton. Shrp—4G 71
(nr. Shrewsbury)
Bicton Heath. Shrp—4G 71
Bidborough. Kent—1G 27
Biddenden. Kent—2C 28
Biddenden Green. Kent—1C 28
Biddenham. Beds—1A 52
Biddestone. Wilts—4D 34
Biddisham. Som—1G 21
Biddlesden. Buck—1E 51
Biddlestone. Nmbd—4D 120
Biddulph. Staf—5C 84
Biddulph Moor. Staf—5D 84
Bideford. Devn—4E 19
Bidford-on-Avon. Warw—5E 61
Bidlake. Devn—4F 11
Bidston. Mers—2E 83
Bielby. E Yor—5B 100
Bieldside. Aber C—3F 153
Bierley. IOW—5D 16
Bierley. W Yor—1B 92
Bierton. Buck—4G 51
Bigbury. Devn—4C 8
Bigbury-on-Sea. Devn—4C 8
Bigby. Linc—4D 94
Big Corlae. Dum—5F 117
Biggar. Cumb—3A 96
Biggar. S Lan—1C 118
Biggin. Derbs—5F 85
(nr. Hartington)
Biggin. Derbs—1G 73
(nr. Hulland)
Biggin. N Yor—1F 93
Biggings. Shet—5C 173
Biggin Hill. G Lon—5F 39
Biggin Hill (London) Airport. Kent—4F 39
Biggleswade. Beds—1B 52
Bighouse. High—2A 168
Bighton. Hants—3E 24
Biglands. Cumb—4D 112
Bignor. W Sus—4A 26
Big Sand. High—1G 155
Bigton. Shet—9E 173
Bilberry. Corn—2E 6
Bilborough. Not C—1C 74
Bilbrook. Som—2D 20
Bilbrook. Staf—5C 72
Bilbrough. N Yor—5H 99
Bilbster. High—3E 169
Bilby. Notts—2D 86
Bildershaw. Dur—2F 105
Bildeston. Suff—1C 54
Billericay. Essx—1A 40
Billesdon. Leics—5E 74
Billesley. Warw—5F 61
Billingborough. Linc—2A 76
Billinge. Mers—4D 90
Billingford. Norf—3D 66
(nr. Diss)
Billingford. Norf—3C 78
(nr. East Dereham)
Billingham. Stoc T—2B 106
Billinghay. Linc—5A 88
Billingley. S Yor—4E 93
Billingshurst. W Sus—3B 26
Billingsley. Shrp—2B 60
Billington. Beds—3H 51
Billington. Lanc—1F 91
Billington. Staf—3C 72
Billockby. Norf—4G 79
Billy Row. Dur—1E 105
Bilsborrow. Lanc—5E 97
Bilsby. Linc—3D 88
Bilsham. W Sus—5A 26
Bilsington. Kent—2E 29
Bilson Green. Glos—4B 48
Bilsthorpe. Notts—4D 86
Bilsthorpe Moor. Notts—5D 86
Bilston. Midl—3F 129
Bilston. W Mid—1D 60
Bilstone. Leics—5A 74
Bilting. Kent—1E 29
Bilton. E Yor—1E 95
Bilton. Nmbd—3G 121
Bilton. N Yor—4E 99
(nr. Harrogate)
Bilton. N Yor—5G 99
(nr. York)
Bilton. Warw—3B 62
Bilton Banks. Nmbd—3G 121
Binbrook. Linc—1B 88
Binchester Blocks. Dur—1F 105
Bincombe. Dors—4B 14
Bindal. High—5G 165
Binegar. Som—2B 22
Bines Green. W Sus—4C 26
Binfield. Brac—4G 37
Binfield Heath. Oxon—4F 37
Bingfield. Nmbd—2C 114
Bingham. Notts—1E 74
Bingham's Melcombe. Dors—2C 14
Bingley. W Yor—1B 92
Bings Heath. Shrp—4H 71
Binham. Norf—2B 78
Binley. Hants—1C 24
Binley. W Mid—3A 62
Binnegar. Dors—4D 15
Binniehill. Falk—2B 128
Binsoe. N Yor—2E 99
Binstead. IOW—3D 16
Binstead. W Sus—5A 26
Binsted. Hants—2F 25
Binton. Warw—5F 61
Bintree. Norf—3C 78
Binweston. Shrp—5F 71
Birch. Essx—4C 54
Birchall. Staf—5D 85
Bircham Newton. Norf—2G 77
Bircham Tofts. Norf—2G 77
Birchanger. Essx—3F 53
Birchburn. N Ayr—3D 122
Birch Cross. Staf—2F 73
Bircher. Here—4G 59
Birch Green. Essx—4C 54
Birchgrove. Card—4E 33
Birchgrove. Swan—3G 31
Birch Heath. Ches—4H 83
Birch Hill. Ches—3H 83
Birchington. Kent—4G 41
Birch Langley. G Man—4G 91
Birchley Heath. Warw—1G 61
Birchmoor. Warw—5G 73
Birchmoor Green. Beds—2H 51
Birchover. Derbs—4G 85
Birch Vale. Derbs—2E 85
Birchview. Mor—5F 159
Birchwood. Linc—4G 87
Birchwood. Som—1F 13
Birchwood. Warr—1A 84
Bircotes. Notts—1D 86
Birdbrook. Essx—1H 53
Birdham. W Sus—2G 17
Birdingbury. Warw—4B 62
Birdlip. Glos—4E 49
Birdsall. N Yor—3C 100
Birds Edge. W Yor—4C 92
Birds Green. Essx—5F 53
Birdsgreen. Shrp—2B 60
Birdsmoor Gate. Dors—2G 13
Birdston. E Dun—2H 127
Birdwell. S Yor—4D 92
Birdwood. Glos—4C 48
Birgham. Scot—1B 120
Birichen. High—4E 165
Birkby. Cumb—1B 102
Birkby. N Yor—4A 106
Birkdale. Mers—3B 90
Birkenhead. Mers—2F 83
Birkenhills. Aber—4E 161
Birkenshaw. N Lan—3H 127
Birkenshaw. W Yor—2C 92
Birkhall. Aber—4H 151
Birkhill. Ang—5C 144
Birkholme. Linc—3G 75
Birkin. N Yor—2F 93
Birley. Here—5G 59
Birling. Kent—4A 40
Birling. Nmbd—4G 121
Birling Gap. E Sus—5G 27
Birlingham. Worc—1E 49
Birmingham. W Mid—2E 61
Birmingham Airport. W Mid—2F 61
Birnam. Per—4H 143
Birsay. Orkn—5B 172
Birse. Aber—4C 152
Birsemore. Aber—4C 152
Birstall. Leics—5C 74
Birstall Smithies. W Yor—2C 92
Birstwith. N Yor—4E 99
Birthorpe. Linc—2A 76
Birtle. Lanc—3G 91
Birtley. Here—4F 59
Birtley. Nmbd—2B 114
Birtley. Tyne—4F 115
Birtsmorton. Worc—2D 48
Birts Street. Worc—2C 48
Bisbrooke. Rut—1F 63
Bisham. Wind—3G 37
Bishampton. Worc—5D 61
Bish Mill. Devn—4H 19
Bishop Auckland. Dur—2F 105
Bishopbridge. Linc—1H 87
Bishopbriggs. E Dun—2H 127
Bishop Burton. E Yor—5D 101
Bishopdown. Wilts—3G 23
Bishop Middleham. Dur—1A 106
Bishopmill. Mor—2G 159
Bishop Monkton. N Yor—3F 99
Bishop Norton. Linc—1G 87
Bishopsbourne. Kent—5F 41
Bishops Cannings. Wilts—5F 35
Bishop's Castle. Shrp—2F 59
Bishop's Caundle. Dors—1B 14
Bishop's Cleeve. Glos—3E 49
Bishop's Down. Dors—1B 14
Bishop's Frome. Here—1B 48
Bishop's Green. Essx—4G 53
Bishop's Green. Hants—5D 36
Bishop's Hull. Som—4F 21
Bishop's Itchington. Warw—5A 62
Bishop's Lydeard. Som—4E 21
Bishop's Norton. Glos—3D 48
Bishop's Nympton. Devn—4A 20
Bishop's Offley. Staf—3B 72
Bishop's Stortford. Herts—3E 53
Bishops Sutton. Hants—3E 24
Bishop's Tachbrook. Warw—4H 61
Bishop's Tawton. Devn—3F 19
Bishopsteignton. Devn—5C 12
Bishopstoke. Hants—1C 16
Bishopston. Swan—4E 31
Bishopstone. Buck—4G 51
Bishopstone. E Sus—5F 27
Bishopstone. Here—1H 47
Bishopstone. Swin—3H 35
Bishopstone. Wilts—4F 23
Bishopstrow. Wilts—2D 23
Bishop Sutton. Bath—1A 22
Bishop's Waltham. Hants—1D 16
Bishopswood. Som—1F 13
Bishop's Wood. Staf—5C 72
Bishopsworth. Bris—5A 34
Bishop Thornton. N Yor—3E 99
Bishopthorpe. York—5H 99
Bishopton. Darl—2A 106
Bishopton. Dum—5B 110
Bishopton. N Yor—2F 99
Bishopton. Ren—2F 127
Bishopton. Warw—5F 61

Bont —Bramley

Bont. Mon —4G 47
Bontddu. Gwyn —4F 69
Bont Dolgadfan. Powy —5A 70
Bontgoch. Cdgn —2F 57
Bonthorpe. Linc —3D 89
Bontnewydd. Cdgn —4F 57
Bont-newydd. Cnwy —3C 82
Bontnewydd. Gwyn —4D 81
(nr. Caernarfon)
Bont Newydd. Gwyn —1G 69
(nr. Ffestiniog)
Bontuchel. Den —5C 82
Bonvilston. V Glam —4D 32
Bon-y-maen. Swan —3F 31
Booker. Buck —2G 37
Booley. Shrp —3H 71
Boorley Green. Hants —1D 16
Boosbeck. Red C —3D 106
Boot. Cumb —4C 102
Booth. W Yor —2A 92
Boothby Graffoe. Linc —5G 87
Boothby Pagnell. Linc —2G 75
Booth Green. Ches —2D 84
Booth of Toft. Shet —4F 173
Boothstown. G Man —4F 91
Boothville. Nptn —4E 63
Booth Wood. W Yor —3A 92
Bootle. Cumb —1A 96
Bootle. Mers —1F 83
Booton. Norf —3D 78
Booze. N Yor —4D 104
Boquhan. Stir —1G 127
Boraston. Shrp —3A 60
Borden. Kent —4C 40
Borden. W Sus —4G 25
Bordlands. Scot —5E 129
Bordley. N Yor —3B 98
Bordon. Hants —3G 25
Boreham. Essx —5A 54
Boreham. Wilts —2D 23
Boreham Street. E Sus —4A 28
Borehamwood. Herts —1C 38
Boreland. Dum —5D 118
Boreston. Devn —3D 8
Borestone Brae. Stir —4H 135
Boreton. Shrp —5H 71
Borgh. W Isl —8B 170
(on Barra)
Borgh. W Isl —3C 170
(on Benbecula)
Borgh. W Isl —1E 170
(on Berneray)
Borgh. W Isl —2G 171
(on Lewis)
Borghastan. W Isl —3D 171
Borgie. High —3G 167
Borgue. Dum —5D 110
Borgue. High —1H 165
Borley. Essx —1B 54
Borley Green. Essx —1B 54
Borley Green. Suff —4B 66
Borlum. High —1H 149
Bornais. W Isl —6C 170
Bornesketaig. High —1C 154
Boroughbridge. N Yor —3F 99
Borough Green. Kent —5H 39
Borras Head. Wrex —5F 83
Borreraig. High —3A 154
Borrobol Lodge. High —1F 165
Borrodale. High —4A 154
Borrowash. Derbs —2A 74
Borrowby. N Yor —1G 99
(nr. Northallerton)
Borrowby. N Yor —3E 107
(nr. Whitby)
Borrowdale. Cumb —3D 102
Borrowston. High —4F 169
Borrowstoun. Falk —1C 128
Borstal. Medw —4B 40
Borth. Cdgn —2F 57
Borthwick. Midl —4G 129
Borth-y-Gest. Gwyn —2E 69
Borve. High —4D 154
Borwick. Lanc —2E 97
Bosbury. Here —1B 48
Boscastle. Corn —3B 10
Boscombe. Bour —3G 15
Boscombe. Wilts —3H 23
Boscoppa. Corn —3E 7
Bosham. W Sus —2G 17
Bosherston. Pemb —5D 42
Bosley. Ches —4D 84
Bossall. N Yor —3B 100
Bossiney. Corn —4A 10
Bossingham. Kent —1F 29
Bossington. Som —2B 20
Bostadh. W Isl —3D 171
Bostock Green. Ches —4A 84
Boston. Linc —1C 76
Boston Spa. W Yor —5G 99
Boswarthen. Corn —3B 4
Boswinger. Corn —4D 6
Botallack. Corn —3A 4
Botany Bay. G Lon —1D 39
Botcheston. Leics —5B 74
Botesdale. Suff —3C 66
Bothal. Nmbd —1F 115
Bothampstead. W Ber —4D 36
Bothamsall. Notts —3D 86
Bothel. Cumb —1C 102
Bothenhampton. Dors —3H 13
Bothwell. S Lan —4H 127
Botley. Buck —5H 51
Botley. Hants —1D 16
Botley. Oxon —5C 50
Botloe's Green. Glos —3C 48
Botolph Claydon. Buck —3F 51
Botolphs. W Sus —5C 26
Bottacks. High —2G 157
Bottesford. Leics —2F 75
Bottesford. N Lin —4B 94
Bottisham. Cambs —4E 65
Bottlesford. Wilts —1G 23
Bottomcraig. Fife —1F 137
Bottom o' th' Moor. G Man —3E 91
Botton Head. Lanc —3F 97
Botusfleming. Corn —2A 8
Botwnnog. Gwyn —2B 68
Bough Beech. Kent —1F 27
Boughrood. Powy —2E 47
Boughspring. Glos —2A 34
Boughton. Norf —5F 77
Boughton. Nptn —4E 63
Boughton. Notts —4D 86
Boughton Aluph. Kent —1E 29
Boughton Green. Kent —5B 40
Boughton Lees. Kent —1E 28
Boughton Malherbe. Kent —1C 28
Boughton Monchelsea. Kent —5B 40
Boughton under Blean. Kent —5E 41
Boulby. Red C —3E 107
Bouldnor. IOW —4B 16
Bouldon. Shrp —2H 59
Boulmer. Nmbd —3G 121
Boulston. Pemb —3D 42
Boultham. Linc —4G 87
Boulton. Dby C —2A 74
Boundary. Staf —1D 73
Bounds. Here —2B 48
Bourn. Cambs —5C 64
Bournbrook. W Mid —2E 61
Bourne. Linc —3H 75
Bourne End. Beds —1H 51
(nr. Cranfield)
Bourne End. Beds —4H 63
(nr. Sharnbrook)
Bourne End. Buck —3G 37
Bourne End. Herts —5A 52
Bournemouth. Bour —3F 15
Bournemouth Airport. Dors —3G 15
Bournes Green. Glos —5E 49
Bournes Green. S'end —2D 40
Bourne, The. Surr —2G 25
Bournheath. Worc —3D 60
Bournmoor. Dur —4G 115
Bournville. W Mid —2E 61
Bourton. Dors —3C 22
Bourton. N Som —5G 33
Bourton. Oxon —3H 35
Bourton. Shrp —1H 59
Bourton. Wilts —5F 35
Bourton on Dunsmore. Warw —3B 62
Bourton-on-the-Hill. Glos —2G 49
Bourton-on-the-Water. Glos —3G 49
Bousd. Arg —2D 138
Boustead Hill. Cumb —4D 112
Bouth. Cumb —1C 96
Bouthwaite. N Yor —2D 98
Boveney. Buck —3A 38
Boveridge. Dors —1F 15
Boverton. V Glam —5C 32
Bovey Tracey. Devn —5B 12
Bovingdon. Herts —5A 52
Bovingdon Green. Buck —3G 37
Bovinger. Essx —5F 53
Bovington Camp. Dors —4D 14
Bow. Devn —2H 11
Bowbank. Dur —2C 104
Bow Brickhill. Mil —2H 51
Bowbridge. Glos —5D 48
Bowburn. Dur —1A 106
Bowcombe. IOW —4C 16
Bowd. Devn —4E 12
Bowden. Devn —4E 9
Bowden. Scot —1H 119
Bowden Hill. Wilts —5E 35
Bowdon. G Man —2B 84
Bower. Nmbd —1A 114
Bowerchalke. Wilts —4F 23
Bowerhill. Wilts —5E 35
Bower Hinton. Som —1H 13
Bowermadden. High —2E 169
Bowers. Staf —2C 72
Bowers Gifford. Essx —2B 40
Bowershall. Fife —4C 136
Bowertower. High —2E 169
Bowes. Dur —3C 104
Bowgreave. Lanc —5D 97
Bowhousebog. N Lan —4B 128
Bowithick. Corn —4B 10
Bowland Bridge. Cumb —1D 96
Bowlees. Dur —2C 104
Bowley. Here —5H 59
Bowlhead Green. Surr —2A 26
Bowling. W Dun —2F 127
Bowling. W Yor —1B 92
Bowling Bank. Wrex —1G 71
Bowling Green. Worc —5C 60
Bowlish. Som —2B 22
Bowmanstead. Cumb —5E 102
Bowmore. Arg —4B 124
Bowness-on-Solway. Cumb —3D 112
Bowness-on-Windermere. Cumb —5F 103
Bow of Fife. Fife —2F 137
Bowood. Dors —3H 13
Bowriefauld. Ang —4E 145
Bowscale. Cumb —1E 103
Bowsden. Nmbd —5F 131
Bowside Lodge. High —2A 168
Bowston. Cumb —5F 103
Bow Street. Cdgn —2F 57
Bowthorpe. Norf —5D 78
Box. Glos —5D 48
Box. Wilts —5D 34
Boxbush. Glos —3B 48
Box End. Beds —1A 52
Boxford. Suff —1C 54
Boxford. W Ber —4C 36
Boxgrove. W Sus —5A 26
Boxley. Kent —5B 40
Box's Shop. Corn —2C 10
Boxted. Essx —2C 54
Boxted. Suff —5H 65
Boxted Cross. Essx —2D 54
Boxworth. Cambs —4C 64
Boxworth End. Cambs —4C 64
Boyden End. Suff —5G 65
Boyden Gate. Kent —4G 41
Boylestone. Derbs —2F 73
Boylestonfield. Derbs —2F 73
Boyndie. Aber —2D 160
Boyndlie. Aber —2G 161
Boynton. E Yor —3F 101
Boys Hill. Dors —1B 14
Boythorpe. Derbs —4A 86
Boyton. Corn —3D 10
Boyton. Suff —1G 55
Boyton. Wilts —3E 23
Boyton Cross. Essx —5G 53
Boyton End. Essx —2G 53
Boyton End. Suff —1H 53
Bozeat. Nptn —5G 63
Braaid. IOM —4C 108
Braal Castle. High —3D 168
Brabling Green. Suff —4E 67
Brabourne. Kent —1F 29
Brabourne Lees. Kent —1E 29
Brabster. High —2F 169
Bracadale. High —5C 154
Braceborough. Linc —4H 75
Bracebridge. Linc —4G 87
Bracebridge Heath. Linc —4G 87
Bracebridge Low Fields. Linc —4G 87
Braceby. Linc —2H 75
Bracewell. Lanc —5A 98
Brackenfield. Derbs —5A 86
Brackenlands. Cumb —5D 112
Brackenthwaite. Cumb —5D 112
Brackenthwaite. N Yor —4E 99
Brackla. B'End —4C 32
Brackla. High —3C 158
Bracklesham. W Sus —3G 17
Brackletter. High —5D 148
Brackley. Nptn —2D 50
Brackley Hatch. Nptn —1E 51
Bracknell. Brac —5G 37
Braco. Per —3H 135
Bracobrae. Mor —3C 160
Bracon. N Lin —4A 94
Bracon Ash. Norf —1D 66
Bracora. High —4F 147
Bradbourne. Derbs —5G 85
Bradbury. Dur —2A 106
Bradda. IOM —4A 108
Bradden. Nptn —1E 51
Bradenham. Buck —2G 37
Bradenham. Norf —5B 78
Bradenstoke. Wilts —4F 35
Bradfield. Essx —2E 55
Bradfield. Norf —2E 79
Bradfield. W Ber —4E 36
Bradfield Combust. Suff —5A 66
Bradfield Green. Ches —5A 84
Bradfield Heath. Essx —3E 55
Bradfield St Clare. Suff —5B 66
Bradfield St George. Suff —4B 66
Bradford. Derbs —4G 85
Bradford. Devn —2E 11
Bradford. Nmbd —1F 121
Bradford. W Yor —1B 92
Bradford Abbas. Dors —1A 14
Bradford Barton. Devn —1B 12
Bradford Leigh. Wilts —5D 34
Bradford-on-Avon. Wilts —5D 34
Bradford-on-Tone. Som —4E 21
Bradford Peverell. Dors —3B 14
Bradiford. Devn —3F 19
Brading. IOW —4E 16
Bradley. Ches —3H 83
Bradley. Cumb —1H 103
Bradley. Derbs —1G 73
Bradley. Glos —2C 34
Bradley. Hants —2E 25
Bradley. NE Lin —4F 95
Bradley. N Yor —1C 98
Bradley. Staf —4C 72
Bradley. W Mid —1D 60
Bradley. W Yor —2B 92
Bradley. Wrex —5F 83
Bradley Cross. Som —1H 21
Bradley Green. Ches —1H 71
Bradley Green. Som —3F 21
Bradley Green. Warw —5G 73
Bradley Green. Worc —4D 61
Bradley in the Moors. Staf —1E 73
Bradley Mount. Ches —3D 84
Bradley Stoke. S Glo —3B 34
Bradlow. Here —2C 48
Bradmore. Notts —2C 74
Bradmore. W Mid —1C 60
Bradninch. Devn —2D 12
Bradnop. Staf —5E 85
Bradpole. Dors —3H 13
Bradshaw. G Man —3F 91
Bradstone. Devn —4D 11
Bradwall Green. Ches —4B 84
Bradway. S Yor —3H 85
Bradwell. Derbs —2F 85
Bradwell. Essx —3B 54
Bradwell. Mil —2G 51
Bradwell. Norf —5H 79
Bradwell-on-Sea. Essx —5D 54
Bradwell Waterside. Essx —5C 54
Bradworthy. Devn —1D 10
Brae. High —5C 162
Brae. Shet —5E 173
Braeantra. High —1H 157
Braefield. High —5G 157
Braefindon. High —3A 158
Braegrum. Per —1C 136
Braehead. Ang —3F 145
Braehead. Dum —4B 110
Braehead. S Lan —1H 117
(nr. Coalburn)
Braehead. S Lan —4C 128
(nr. Forth)
Braehoulland. Shet —4D 173
Braemar. Aber —4F 151
Braemore. High —5C 168
(nr. Dunbeath)
Braemore. High —1D 156
(nr. Ullapool)
Brae of Achnahaird. High —2E 163
Brae Roy Lodge. High —4F 149
Braeside. Aber —5G 161
Braeside. Inv —2D 126
Braes of Coul. Ang —3B 144
Braetongue. High —3F 167
Braeval. Stir —3E 135
Braevallich. Arg —3G 133
Brafferton. Darl —2F 105
Brafferton. N Yor —2G 99
Brafield-on-the-Green. Nptn —5F 63
Bragar. W Isl —3E 171
Bragbury End. Herts —3C 52
Bragleenbeg. Arg —1G 133
Braichmelyn. Gwyn —4F 81
Braides. Lanc —4D 96
Braidwood. S Lan —5B 128
Braigo. Arg —3A 124
Brailsford. Derbs —1G 73
Braintree. Essx —3A 54
Braiseworth. Suff —3D 66
Braishfield. Hants —4B 24
Braithwaite. Cumb —2D 102
Braithwaite. S Yor —3G 93
Braithwaite. W Yor —5C 98
Braithwell. S Yor —1C 86
Brakefield Green. Norf —5C 78
Bramber. W Sus —4C 26
Brambledown. Kent —3D 40
Brambridge. Hants —4C 24
Bramcote. Notts —2C 74
Bramcote. Warw —2B 62
Bramdean. Hants —4E 24
Bramerton. Norf —5E 79
Bramfield. Herts —4C 52
Bramfield. Suff —3F 67
Bramford. Suff —1E 54
Bramhall. G Man —2C 84
Bramham. W Yor —5G 99
Bramhope. W Yor —5E 99
Bramley. Hants —1E 25
Bramley. S Yor —1B 86

Broad, The—Budle

Broad, The. Here —4G 59
Broad Town. Wilts —4F 35
Broadwas. Worc —5B 60
Broadwath. Cumb —4F 113
Broadway. Carm —5D 45
(nr. Kidwelly)
Broadway. Carm —3G 43
(nr. Laugharne)
Broadway. Pemb —3C 42
Broadway. Som —1G 13
Broadway. Suff —3F 67
Broadway. Worc —2G 49
Broadwell. Glos —4A 48
(nr. Cinderford)
Broadwell. Glos —3H 49
(nr. Stow-on-the-Wold)
Broadwell. Oxon —5A 50
Broadwell. Warw —4B 62
Broadwell House. Nmbd —4C 114
Broadwey. Dors —4B 14
Broadwindsor. Dors —2H 13
Broadwoodkelly. Devn —2G 11
Broadwoodwidger. Devn —4E 11
Broallan. High —4G 157
Brobury. Here —1G 47
Brochel. High —4E 155
Brockamin. Worc —5B 60
Brockbridge. Hants —1E 16
Brockdish. Norf —3E 66
Brockencote. Worc —3C 60
Brock End. Worc —1D 48
Brockenhurst. Hants —2A 16
Brocketsbrae. S Lan —1H 117
Brockford Street. Suff —4D 66
Brockhall. Nptn —4D 62
Brockham. Surr —1C 26
Brockhampton. Glos —3E 49
(nr. Bishop's Cleeve)
Brockhampton. Glos —3F 49
(nr. Sevenhampton)
Brockhampton. Here —2A 48
Brockhill. Scot —2F 119
Brockholes. W Yor —3B 92
Brockhouse. S Yor —2C 86
Brockhurst. Hants —2E 16
Brocklesby. Linc —3E 95
Brockley. N Som —5H 33
Brockley. Suff —3H 65
Brockley Green. Suff —1H 53
(nr. Bury St Edmunds)
Brockley Green. Suff —5H 65
(nr. Haverhill)
Brockleymoor. Cumb —1F 103
Brockmoor. W Mid —2C 60
Brockton. Shrp —2F 59
(nr. Bishop's Castle)
Brockton. Shrp —5B 72
(nr. Madeley)
Brockton. Shrp —1H 59
(nr. Much Wenlock)
Brockton. Shrp —5F 71
(nr. Pontesbury)
Brockton. Staf —2C 72
Brockton. Telf —4B 72
Brockweir. Glos —5A 48
Brockworth. Glos —4D 49
Brocton. Staf —4D 72
Brodick. N Ayr —2E 123
Brodie. Mor —3D 159
Brodsworth. S Yor —4F 93
Brogaig. High —2D 154
Brogborough. Beds —2H 51
Brokenborough. Wilts —3E 35
Broken Cross. Ches —3C 84
Bromborough. Mers —2F 83
Bromdon. Shrp —2A 60
Brome. Suff —3D 66
Brome Street. Suff —3D 66
Bromeswell. Suff —5F 67
Bromfield. Cumb —5C 112
Bromfield. Shrp —3G 59
Bromford. W Mid —1F 61
Bromham. Beds —5H 63
Bromham. Wilts —5E 35
Bromley. G Lon —4F 39
Bromley. Herts —3E 53
Bromley. Shrp —1B 60
Bromley Cross. G Man —3F 91
Bromley Green. Kent —2D 28
Bromley Wood. Staf —3F 73
Brompton. Medw —4B 40
Brompton. N Yor —5A 106
(nr. Northallerton)
Brompton. N Yor —1D 100
(nr. Scarborough)
Brompton. Shrp —5H 71
Brompton-on-Swale. N Yor —5F 105
Brompton Ralph. Som —3D 20
Brompton Regis. Som —3C 20
Bromsash. Here —3B 48
Bromsberrow. Glos —2C 48
Bromsberrow Heath. Glos —2C 48
Bromsgrove. Worc —3D 60
Bromstead Heath. Staf —4B 72
Bromyard. Here —5A 60
Bromyard Downs. Here —5A 60
Bronaber. Gwyn —2G 69
Broncroft. Shrp —2H 59
Brongest. Cdgn —1D 44
Brongwyn. Cdgn —1C 44
Bronington. Wrex —2G 71
Bronllys. Powy —2E 47
Bronnant. Cdgn —4F 57
Bronwydd Arms. Carm —3E 45
Bronydd. Powy —1F 47
Bronygarth. Shrp —2E 71
Brook. Carm —4G 43
Brook. Devn —5E 11
Brook. Hants —1A 16
(nr. Cadnam)
Brook. Hants —4B 24
(nr. Romsey)
Brook. IOW —4B 16
Brook. Kent —1E 29
Brook. Surr —1B 26
(nr. Guildford)
Brook. Surr —2A 26
(nr. Haslemere)
Brooke. Norf —1E 67
Brooke. Rut —5F 75
Brookend. Glos —5B 48
Brook End. Worc —1D 48
Brookfield. Lanc —1D 90
Brookfield. Ren —3F 127
Brookhouse. Lanc —3E 97
Brookhouse Green. Ches —4C 84
Brookhouses. Staf —1D 73
Brookhurst. Mers —2F 83
Brookland. Kent —3D 28
Brooklands. G Man —1B 84
Brooklands. Shrp —1H 71
Brookmans Park. Herts —5C 52
Brooks. Powy —1D 58
Brooksby. Leics —4D 74
Brooks Green. W Sus —3C 26
Brook Street. Essx —1G 39
Brook Street. Kent —2D 28
Brook Street. W Sus —3E 27
Brookthorpe. Glos —4D 48
Brookville. Norf —1G 65
Brookwood. Surr —5A 38
Broom. Beds —1B 52
Broom. Fife —3F 137
Broom. Warw —5E 61
Broome. Norf —1F 67
Broome. Shrp —1H 59
(nr. Cardington)
Broome. Shrp —2G 59
(nr. Craven Arms)
Broome. Worc —3D 60
Broomedge. Warr —2B 84
Broomend. Aber —2E 153
Broome Park. Nmbd —3F 121
Broomer's Corner. W Sus —3C 26
Broomfield. Aber —5G 161
Broomfield. Essx —4H 53
Broomfield. Kent —4F 41
(nr. Herne Bay)
Broomfield. Kent —5C 40
(nr. Maidstone)
Broomfield. Som —3F 21
Broomfleet. E Yor —2B 94
Broom Green. Norf —3B 78
Broomhall. Surr —4A 38
Broomhaugh. Nmbd —3D 114
Broomhill. Bris —4B 34
Broom Hill. Dors —2F 15
Broomhill. High —1D 151
(nr. Grantown-on-Spey)
Broomhill. High —1B 158
(nr. Invergordon)
Broomhill. Norf —5F 77
Broomhill. Nmbd —4G 121
Broom Hill. S Yor —4E 93
Broom Hill. Worc —3D 60
Broomholm. Norf —2F 79
Broomlands. Dum —4C 118
Broomley. Nmbd —3D 114
Broom of Moy. Mor —3E 159
Broompark. Dur —5F 115
Broom's Green. Glos —2C 48
Brora. High —3G 165
Broseley. Shrp —5A 72
Brotherhouse Bar. Linc —4B 76
Brotheridge Green. Worc —1D 48
Brotherlee. Dur —1C 104
Brothertoft. Linc —1B 76
Brotherton. N Yor —2E 93
Brotton. Red C —2D 107
Broubster. High —2C 168
Brough. Cumb —3A 104
Brough. Derbs —2F 85
Brough. E Yor —2C 94
Brough. High —1E 169
Brough. Notts —5F 87
Brough. Shet —4F 173
(nr. Boath of Toft)
Brough. Shet —5G 173
(on Whalsay)
Broughall. Shrp —1H 71
Brougham. Cumb —2G 103
Brough Sowerby. Cumb —3A 104
Broughton. Cambs —3B 64
Broughton. Flin —4F 83
Broughton. Hants —3B 24
Broughton. Lanc —1D 90
Broughton. Mil —2G 51
Broughton. Nptn —3F 63
Broughton. N Lin —4C 94
Broughton. N Yor —2B 100
(nr. Malton)
Broughton. N Yor —4B 98
(nr. Skipton)
Broughton. Oxon —2C 50
Broughton. Scot —1D 118
Broughton. Staf —2B 72
Broughton. V Glam —4C 32
Broughton Astley. Leics —1C 62
Broughton Beck. Cumb —1B 96
Broughton Cross. Cumb —1B 102
Broughton Gifford. Wilts —5D 35
Broughton Green. Worc —4D 60
Broughton Hackett. Worc —5D 60
Broughton in Furness. Cumb —1B 96
Broughton Mills. Cumb —5D 102
Broughton Moor. Cumb —1B 102
Broughton Park. G Man —4G 91
Broughton Poggs. Oxon —5H 49
Broughtown. Orkn —3F 172
Broughty Ferry. D'dee —5D 144
Brownber. Cumb —4A 104
Brownbread Street. E Sus —4A 28
Brown Candover. Hants —3D 24
Brown Edge. Lanc —3B 90
Brown Edge. Staf —5D 84
Brownhill. Bkbn —1E 91
Brownhill. Shrp —3G 71
Brownhills. Shrp —2A 72
Brownhills. W Mid —5E 73
Brown Knowl. Ches —5G 83
Brownlow. Ches —4C 84
Brownlow Heath. Ches —4C 84
Brown's Green. W Mid —1E 61
Brownshill. Glos —5D 49
Brownston. Devn —3C 8
Brownstone. Devn —2A 12
Browston Green. Norf —5G 79
Broxa. N Yor —5G 107
Broxbourne. Herts —5D 52
Broxburn. E Lot —2C 130
Broxburn. W Lot —2D 129
Broxholme. Linc —3G 87
Broxted. Essx —3F 53
Broxton. Ches —5G 83
Broxwood. Here —5F 59
Broyle Side. E Sus —4F 27
Bru. W Isl —3F 171
Bruach Mairi. W Isl —4G 171
Bruairnis. W Isl —8C 170
Bruan. High —5F 169
Bruar Lodge. Per —1F 143
Brucehill. W Dun —2E 127
Brucklay. Aber —3G 161
Bruera. Ches —4G 83
Bruichladdich. Arg —3A 124
Bruisyard. Suff —4F 67
Bruisyard Street. Suff —4F 67
Brumby. N Lin —4B 94
Brund. Staf —4F 85
Brundall. Norf —5F 79
Brundish. Norf —1F 67
Brundish. Suff —4E 67
Brundish Street. Suff —3E 67
Brunery. High —1B 140
Brunswick Village. Tyne —2F 115
Brunthwaite. W Yor —5C 98
Bruntingthorpe. Leics —1D 62
Brunton. Fife —1F 137
Brunton. Nmbd —2G 121
Brunton. Wilts —1H 23
Brushford. Devn —2G 11
Brushford. Som —4C 20
Brusta. W Isl —1E 170
Bruton. Som —3B 22
Bryanston. Dors —2D 14
Bryant's Bottom. Buck —2G 37
Brydekirk. Dum —2C 112
Brymbo. Cnwy —3H 81
Brymbo. Wrex —5E 83
Brympton. Som —1A 14
Bryn. Carm —5F 45
Bryn. G Man —4D 90
Bryn. Neat —2B 32
Bryn. Shrp —2E 59
Brynamman. Carm —4H 45
Brynberian. Pemb —1F 43
Brynbryddan. Neat —2A 32
Bryncae. Rhon —3C 32
Bryncethin. B'End —3C 32
Bryncir. Gwyn —1D 69
Bryn-coch. Neat —3G 31
Bryncroes. Gwyn —2B 68
Bryncrug. Gwyn —5F 69
Bryn Du. IOA —3C 80
Bryn Eden. Gwyn —3G 69
Bryneglwys. Den —1D 70
Bryn Eglwys. Gwyn —4F 81
Brynford. Flin —3D 82
Bryn Gates. G Man —4D 90
Bryn Golau. Rhon —3D 32
Bryngwran. IOA —3C 80
Bryngwyn. Mon —5G 47
Bryngwyn. Powy —1E 47
Bryn-henllan. Pemb —1E 43
Brynhoffnant. Cdgn —5C 56
Bryn-llwyn. Flin —2C 82
Brynllywarch. Powy —2D 58
Bryn-mawr. Blae —4E 47
Bryn-mawr. Gwyn —2B 68
Brynmenyn. B'End —3C 32
Brynmill. Swan —3F 31
Brynna. Rhon —3C 32
Brynrefail. Gwyn —4E 81
Brynrefail. IOA —2D 81
Brynsadler. Rhon —3D 32
Bryn-Saith Marchog. Den —5C 82
Brynsiencyn. IOA —4D 81
Brynteg. IOA —2D 81
Brynteg. Wrex —5F 83
Brynygwenyn. Mon —4G 47
Bryn-y-maen. Cnwy —3H 81
Buaile nam Bodach. W Isl —8C 170
Bualintur. High —1C 146
Bubbenhall. Warw —3A 62
Bubwith. E Yor —1H 93
Buccleuch. Scot —3F 119
Buchanan Smithy. Stir —1F 127
Buchanhaven. Aber —4H 161
Buchanty. Per —1B 136
Buchany. Stir —3G 135
Buchley. E Dun —2G 127
Buchlyvie. Stir —4E 135
Buckabank. Cumb —5E 113
Buckden. Cambs —4A 64
Buckden. N Yor —2B 98
Buckenham. Norf —5F 79
Buckerell. Devn —2E 13
Buckfast. Devn —2D 8
Buckfastleigh. Devn —2D 8
Buckhaven. Fife —4F 137
Buckholm. Scot —1G 119
Buckholt. Here —4A 48
Buckhorn Weston. Dors —4C 22
Buckhurst Hill. Essx —1F 39
Buckie. Mor —2B 160
Buckingham. Buck —2E 51
Buckland. Buck —4G 51
Buckland. Devn —4C 8
Buckland. Glos —2F 49
Buckland. Here —5H 59
Buckland. Herts —2D 52
Buckland. Kent —1H 29
Buckland. Oxon —2B 36
Buckland. Surr —5D 38
Buckland Brewer. Devn —4E 19
Buckland Common. Buck —5H 51
Buckland Dinham. Som —1C 22
Buckland Filleigh. Devn —2E 11
Buckland in the Moor. Devn —5H 11
Buckland Monachorum. Corn —2A 8
Buckland Newton. Dors —2B 14
Buckland Ripers. Dors —4B 14
Buckland St Mary. Som —1F 13
Buckland-tout-Saints. Devn —4D 8
Bucklebury. W Ber —4D 36
Bucklegate. Linc —2C 76
Buckleigh. Devn —4E 19
Bucklers Hard. Hants —3C 16
Bucklesham. Suff —1F 55
Buckley. Flin —4E 83
Buckley Green. Warw —4F 61
Buckley Hill. Mers —1F 83
Bucklow Hill. Ches —2B 84
Buckminster. Leics —3F 75
Bucknall. Linc —4A 88
Bucknall. Stoke —1D 72
Bucknell. Oxon —3D 50
Bucknell. Shrp —3F 59
Buckpool. Mor —2B 160
Bucksburn. Aber C —3F 153
Buck's Cross. Devn —4D 18
Bucks Green. W Sus —2B 26
Bucks Hill. Herts —5A 52
Bucks Horn Oak. Hants —2G 25
Buck's Mills. Devn —4D 18
Buckton. E Yor —2F 101
Buckton. Here —3F 59
Buckton. Nmbd —1E 121
Buckton Vale. G Man —4H 91
Buckworth. Cambs —3A 64
Budby. Notts —4D 86
Bude. Corn —2C 10
Budge's Shop. Corn —3H 7
Budlake. Devn —2C 12
Budle. Nmbd —1F 121

Budleigh Salterton. *Devn* —4D 12
Budock Water. *Corn* —5B 6
Buerton. *Ches* —1A 72
Buffler's Holt. *Buck* —2E 51
Bugbrooke. *Nptn* —5D 62
Buglawton. *Ches* —4C 84
Bugle. *Corn* —3E 6
Bugthorpe. *E Yor* —4B 100
Buildwas. *Shrp* —5A 72
Builth Road. *Powy* —5C 58
Builth Wells. *Powy* —5C 58
Bulbourne. *Herts* —4H 51
Bulby. *Linc* —3H 75
Bulcote. *Notts* —1D 74
Buldoo. *High* —2C 168
Bulford. *Wilts* —2G 23
Bulford Camp. *Wilts* —2G 23
Bulkeley. *Ches* —5H 83
Bulkington. *Warw* —2A 62
Bulkington. *Wilts* —1E 23
Bulkworthy. *Devn* —1D 11
Bullamoor. *N Yor* —5A 106
Bull Bay. *IOA* —1D 80
Bullbridge. *Derbs* —5A 86
Bullgill. *Cumb* —1B 102
Bull Hill. *Hants* —3B 16
Bullinghope. *Here* —2A 48
Bull's Green. *Herts* —4C 52
Bullwood. *Arg* —2C 126
Bulmer. *Essx* —1B 54
Bulmer. *N Yor* —3A 100
Bulmer Tye. *Essx* —2B 54
Bulphan. *Thur* —2H 39
Bulverhythe. *E Sus* —5B 28
Bulwark. *Aber* —4G 161
Bulwell. *Not C* —1C 74
Bulwick. *Nptn* —1G 63
Bumble's Green. *Essx* —5E 53
Bun Abhainn Eadarra. *W Isl* —7D 171
Bunacaimb. *High* —5E 147
Bun a Mhuillinn. *W Isl* —7C 170
Bunarkaig. *High* —5D 148
Bunbury. *Ches* —5H 83
Bunchrew. *High* —4A 158
Bundalloch. *High* —1A 148
Bunessan. *Arg* —1A 132
Bungay. *Suff* —2F 67
Bunkegivie. *High* —2H 149
Bunker's Hill. *Cambs* —5D 76
Bunkers Hill. *Linc* —5B 88
Bunker's Hill. *Suff* —5H 79
Bunloit. *High* —1H 149
Bunnahabhain. *Arg* —2C 124
Bunny. *Notts* —3C 74
Bunoich. *High* —3F 149
Bunree. *High* —2E 141
Bunroy. *High* —5E 149
Buntait. *High* —5F 157
Buntingford. *Herts* —3D 52
Buntings Green. *Essx* —2B 54
Bunwell. *Norf* —1D 66
Burbage. *Derbs* —3E 85
Burbage. *Leics* —1B 62
Burbage. *Wilts* —5H 35
Burcher. *Here* —4F 59
Burchett's Green. *Wind* —3G 37
Burcombe. *Wilts* —3F 23
Burcot. *Oxon* —2D 36
Burcote. *Shrp* —1B 60
Burcott. *Buck* —3G 51
Burcott. *Som* —2A 22
Burdale. *N Yor* —3C 100
Burdrop. *Oxon* —2B 50
Bures. *Suff* —2C 54
Burford. *Oxon* —4A 50
Burford. *Shrp* —4H 59
Burf, The. *Worc* —4C 60
Burg. *Arg* —4E 139
Burgate Great Green. *Suff* —3C 66
Burgate Little Green. *Suff* —3C 66
Burgess Hill. *W Sus* —4E 27
Burgh. *Suff* —5E 67
Burgh by Sands. *Cumb* —4E 113

Burgh Castle. *Norf* —5G 79
Burghclere. *Hants* —5C 36
Burghead. *Mor* —2F 159
Burghfield. *W Ber* —5E 37
Burghfield Common. *W Ber* —5E 37
Burghfield Hill. *W Ber* —5E 37
Burgh Heath. *Surr* —5D 38
Burghill. *Here* —1H 47
Burgh le Marsh. *Linc* —4E 89
Burgh Muir. *Aber* —2E 153
Burgh next Aylsham. *Norf* —3F 78
Burgh on Bain. *Linc* —2B 88
Burgh St Margaret. *Norf* —4G 79
Burgh St Peter. *Norf* —1G 67
Burghwallis. *S Yor* —3F 93
Burgie. *Mor* —3E 159
Burham. *Kent* —4B 40
Buriton. *Hants* —4F 25
Burland. *Ches* —5A 84
Burland. *Shet* —8E 173
Burlawn. *Corn* —2D 6
Burleigh. *Brac* —3A 38
Burleigh. *Glos* —5D 48
Burlescombe. *Devn* —1D 12
Burleston. *Dors* —3C 14
Burlestone. *Devn* —4E 9
Burley. *Hants* —2H 15
Burley. *Rut* —4F 75
Burley. *W Yor* —1C 92
Burley Gate. *Here* —1A 48
Burley in Wharfedale. *W Yor* —5D 98
Burley Street. *Hants* —2H 15
Burley Woodhead. *W Yor* —5D 98
Burlingjobb. *Powy* —5E 59
Burlton. *Shrp* —3G 71
Burmantofts. *W Yor* —1D 92
Burmarsh. *Kent* —2F 29
Burmington. *Warw* —2A 50
Burn. *N Yor* —2F 93
Burnage. *G Man* —1C 84
Burnaston. *Derbs* —2G 73
Burnbanks. *Cumb* —3G 103
Burnby. *E Yor* —5C 100
Burncross. *S Yor* —1H 85
Burneside. *Cumb* —5G 103
Burness. *Orkn* —3F 172
Burneston. *N Yor* —1F 99
Burnett. *Bath* —5B 34
Burnfoot. *Per* —3B 136
Burnfoot. *Scot* —3H 119
(nr. Hawick)
Burnfoot. *Scot* —3G 119
(nr. Roberton)
Burngreave. *S Yor* —2A 86
Burnham. *Buck* —2A 38
Burnham. *N Lin* —3D 94
Burnham Deepdale. *Norf* —1H 77
Burnham Green. *Herts* —4C 52
Burnham Market. *Norf* —1H 77
Burnham Norton. *Norf* —1H 77
Burnham-on-Crouch. *Essx* —1D 40
Burnham-on-Sea. *Som* —2G 21
Burnham Overy Staithe. *Norf* —1H 77
Burnham Overy Town. *Norf* —1H 77
Burnham Thorpe. *Norf* —1A 78
Burnhaven. *Aber* —4H 161
Burnhead. *Dum* —5A 118
Burnhervie. *Aber* —2E 153
Burnhill Green. *Staf* —5B 72
Burnhope. *Dur* —5E 115
Burnhouse. *N Ayr* —4E 127
Burniston. *N Yor* —5H 107
Burnlee. *W Yor* —4B 92
Burnley. *Lanc* —1G 91
Burnleydam. *Wrex* —1A 72
Burnmouth. *Scot* —3F 131
Burn Naze. *Lanc* —5C 96
Burnopfield. *Dur* —4E 115
Burnsall. *N Yor* —3C 98
Burnside. *Ang* —3E 145
Burnside. *E Ayr* —3E 117
Burnside. *Per* —3D 136

Burnside. *Shet* —4D 173
Burnside. *S Lan* —4H 127
Burnside. *W Lot* —2D 129
(nr. Broxburn)
Burnside. *W Lot* —2D 128
(nr. Winchburgh)
Burntcommon. *Surr* —5B 38
Burntheath. *Derbs* —2G 73
Burnt Heath. *Essx* —3D 54
Burnt Hill. *W Ber* —4D 36
Burnt Houses. *Dur* —2E 105
Burntisland. *Fife* —1F 129
Burnt Oak. *G Lon* —1D 38
Burnton. *E Ayr* —4D 117
Burntstalk. *Norf* —2G 77
Burntwood. *Staf* —5E 73
Burntwood Green. *Staf* —5E 73
Burnt Yates. *N Yor* —3E 99
Burnwynd. *Edin* —3E 129
Burpham. *Surr* —5B 38
Burpham. *W Sus* —5B 26
Burradon. *Nmbd* —4D 121
Burradon. *Tyne* —2F 115
Burrafirth. *Shet* —1H 173
Burras. *Corn* —5A 6
Burraton. *Corn* —3A 8
Burray Village. *Orkn* —8D 172
Burrells. *Cumb* —3H 103
Burrelton. *Per* —5A 144
Burridge. *Devn* —2G 13
Burridge. *Hants* —1D 16
Burrigill. *High* —5E 169
Burrill. *N Yor* —1E 99
Burringham. *N Lin* —4B 94
Burrington. *Devn* —1G 11
Burrington. *Here* —3G 59
Burrington. *N Som* —1H 21
Burrough End. *Cambs* —5F 65
Burrough Green. *Cambs* —5F 65
Burrough on the Hill. *Leics* —4E 75
Burrow. *Devn* —4D 12
Burrow. *Som* —2C 20
Burrowbridge. *Som* —4G 21
Burrowhill. *Surr* —4A 38
Burry. *Swan* —3D 30
Burry Green. *Swan* —3D 30
Burry Port. *Carm* —5E 45
Burscough. *Lanc* —3C 90
Burscough Bridge. *Lanc* —3C 90
Bursea. *E Yor* —1B 94
Burshill. *E Yor* —5E 101
Bursledon. *Hants* —2C 16
Burslem. *Stoke* —1C 72
Burstall. *Suff* —1D 54
Burstock. *Dors* —2H 13
Burston. *Devn* —2H 11
Burston. *Norf* —2D 66
Burston. *Staf* —2D 72
Burstow. *Surr* —1E 27
Burstwick. *E Yor* —2F 95
Burtersett. *N Yor* —1A 98
Burtholme. *Cumb* —3G 113
Burthorpe. *Suff* —4G 65
Burthwaite. *Cumb* —5F 113
Burtle. *Som* —2H 21
Burtoft. *Linc* —2B 76
Burton. *Ches* —4H 83
(nr. Kelsall)
Burton. *Ches* —3F 83
(nr. Neston)
Burton. *Dors* —3G 15
(nr. Christchurch)
Burton. *Dors* —3B 14
(nr. Dorchester)
Burton. *Linc* —3G 87
Burton. *Nmbd* —1F 121
Burton. *Pemb* —4D 43
Burton. *Som* —2E 21
Burton. *Wilts* —4D 34
(nr. Chippenham)
Burton. *Wilts* —3D 22
(nr. Warminster)

Burton. *Wrex* —5F 83
Burton Agnes. *E Yor* —3F 101
Burton Bradstock. *Dors* —4H 13
Burton Coggles. *Linc* —3G 75
Burton Constable. *E Yor* —1E 95
Burton Corner. *Linc* —1C 76
Burton End. *Cambs* —1G 53
Burton End. *Essx* —3F 53
Burton Fleming. *E Yor* —2E 101
Burton Green. *W Mid* —3G 61
Burton Green. *Wrex* —5F 83
Burton Hastings. *Warw* —2B 62
Burton-in-Kendal. *Cumb* —2E 97
Burton in Lonsdale. *N Yor* —2F 97
Burton Joyce. *Notts* —1D 74
Burton Latimer. *Nptn* —3G 63
Burton Lazars. *Leics* —4E 75
Burton Leonard. *N Yor* —3F 99
Burton on the Wolds. *Leics* —3C 74
Burton Overy. *Leics* —1D 62
Burton Pedwardine. *Linc* —1A 76
Burton Pidsea. *E Yor* —1F 95
Burton Salmon. *N Yor* —2E 93
Burton's Green. *Essx* —3B 54
Burton Stather. *N Lin* —3B 94
Burton upon Stather. *N Lin* —3B 94
Burton upon Trent. *Staf* —3G 73
Burton Wolds. *Leics* —3D 74
Burtonwood. *Warr* —1H 83
Burwardsley. *Ches* —5H 83
Burwarton. *Shrp* —2A 60
Burwash. *E Sus* —3A 28
Burwash Common. *E Sus* —3H 27
Burwash Weald. *E Sus* —3A 28
Burwell. *Cambs* —4E 65
Burwell. *Linc* —3C 88
Burwen. *IOA* —1D 80
Burwick. *Orkn* —9D 172
Bury. *Cambs* —2B 64
Bury. *G Man* —3G 91
Bury. *Som* —4C 20
Bury. *W Sus* —4B 26
Bury End. *Worc* —2F 49
Bury Green. *Herts* —3E 53
Bury Hill. *S Glo* —3C 34
Bury St Edmunds. *Suff* —4A 66
Burythorpe. *N Yor* —3B 100
Busbridge. *Surr* —1A 26
Busby. *E Ren* —4G 127
Busby. *Per* —1C 136
Buscot. *Oxon* —2H 35
Bush. *Corn* —2C 10
Bush Bank. *Here* —5G 59
Bushbury. *W Mid* —5D 72
Bushby. *Leics* —5D 74
Bushey. *Dors* —4E 15
Bushey. *Herts* —1C 38
Bushey Heath. *Herts* —1C 38
Bush Green. *Norf* —1C 66
(nr. Attleborough)
Bush Green. *Norf* —2E 66
(nr. Harleston)
Bush Green. *Suff* —5B 66
Bushley. *Worc* —2D 48
Bushley Green. *Worc* —2D 48
Bushmead. *Beds* —4A 64
Bushmoor. *Shrp* —2G 59
Bushton. *Wilts* —4F 35
Bushy Common. *Norf* —4B 78
Busk. *Cumb* —5H 113
Buslingthorpe. *Linc* —2H 87
Bussage. *Glos* —5D 49
Bussex. *Som* —3G 21
Busta. *Shet* —5E 173
Bustard Green. *Essx* —3G 53
Butcher's Cross. *E Sus* —3G 27
Butcombe. *N Som* —5A 34
Bute Town. *Cphy* —5E 46
Butleigh. *Som* —3A 22
Butleigh Wootton. *Som* —3A 22
Butlers Marston. *Warw* —5H 61
Butley. *Suff* —5F 67
Butley High Corner. *Suff* —1G 55

Butterburn. *Cumb* —2H 113
Buttercrambe. *N Yor* —4B 100
Butterknowle. *Dur* —2E 105
Butterleigh. *Devn* —2C 12
Buttermere. *Cumb* —3C 102
Buttermere. *Wilts* —5B 36
Buttershaw. *W Yor* —2B 92
Butterstone. *Per* —4H 143
Butterton. *Staf* —5E 85
(nr. Leek)
Butterton. *Staf* —1C 72
(nr. Stoke-on-Trent)
Butterwick. *Dur* —2A 106
Butterwick. *Linc* —1C 76
Butterwick. *N Yor* —2B 100
(nr. Malton)
Butterwick. *N Yor* —2D 101
(nr. Weaverthorpe)
Butteryhaugh. *Nmbd* —5A 120
Butt Green. *Ches* —5A 84
Buttington. *Powy* —5E 71
Buttonbridge. *Shrp* —3B 60
Buttonoak. *Shrp* —3B 60
Buttsash. *Hants* —2C 16
Butt's Green. *Essx* —5A 54
Butt Yeats. *Lanc* —3E 97
Buxhall. *Suff* —5C 66
Buxted. *E Sus* —3F 27
Buxton. *Derbs* —3E 85
Buxton. *Norf* —3E 79
Buxworth. *Derbs* —2E 85
Bwcle. *Flin* —4E 83
Bwlch. *Powy* —3E 47
Bwlchderwin. *Gwyn* —1D 68
Bwlchgwyn. *Wrex* —5E 83
Bwlch-Llan. *Cdgn* —5E 57
Bwlchnewydd. *Carm* —3D 44
Bwlchtocyn. *Gwyn* —3C 68
Bwlch-y-cibau. *Powy* —4D 70
Bwlchyddar. *Powy* —3D 70
Bwlch-y-fadfa. *Cdgn* —1E 45
Bwlch-y-ffridd. *Powy* —1C 58
Bwlch y Garreg. *Powy* —1C 58
Bwlch-y-groes. *Pemb* —1G 43
Bwlch-yr-haiarn. *Cnwy* —5G 81
Bwlch-y-sarnau. *Powy* —3C 58
Bybrook. *Kent* —1E 28
Byermoor. *Tyne* —4E 115
Byers Garth. *Dur* —5G 115
Byers Green. *Dur* —1F 105
Byfield. *Nptn* —5C 62
Byfleet. *Surr* —4B 38
Byford. *Here* —1G 47
Bygrave. *Herts* —2C 52
Byker. *Tyne* —3F 115
Byland Abbey. *N Yor* —2H 99
Bylchau. *Cnwy* —4B 82
Byley. *Ches* —4B 84
Bynea. *Carm* —3E 31
Byram. *N Yor* —2E 93
Byrness. *Nmbd* —4B 120
Bythorn. *Cambs* —3H 63
Byton. *Here* —4F 59
Bywell. *Nmbd* —3D 114
Byworth. *W Sus* —3A 26

C

Cabourne. *Linc* —4E 95
Cabrach. *Arg* —3C 124
Cabrach. *Mor* —1A 152
Cabus. *Lanc* —5D 97
Cadbury. *Devn* —2C 12
Cadder. *E Dun* —2H 127
Caddington. *Beds* —4A 52
Caddonfoot. *Scot* —1G 119
Cadeby. *Leics* —5B 74
Cadeby. *S Yor* —4F 93
Cadeleigh. *Devn* —2C 12
Cade Street. *E Sus* —3H 27
Cadgwith. *Corn* —5E 5
Cadham. *Fife* —3E 137
Cadishead. *G Man* —1B 84
Cadley. *Lanc* —1D 90

Cadley. *Wilts* —1H 23
(nr. Ludgershall)
Cadley. *Wilts* —5H 35
(nr. Marlborough)
Cadmore End. *Buck* —2F 37
Cadnam. *Hants* —1B 16
Cadney. *N Lin* —4D 94
Cadole. *Flin* —4E 82
Cadoxton-Juxta-Neath. *Neat* —2A 32
Cadwell. *Herts* —2B 52
Cadwst. *Den* —2C 70
Cadzow. *S Lan* —4A 128
Caeathro. *Gwyn* —4E 81
Caehopkin. *Powy* —4B 46
Caenby. *Linc* —2H 87
Caenn-na-Cleithe. *W Isl* —8D 171
Caerau. *B'End* —2B 32
Caerau. *Card* —4E 33
Cae'r-bont. *Powy* —4B 46
Cae'r-bryn. *Carm* —4F 45
Caerdeon. *Gwyn* —4F 69
Caerdydd. *Card* —4E 33
Caerfarchell. *Pemb* —2B 42
Caerffili. *Cphy* —3E 33
Caerfyrddin. *Carm* —4E 45
Caergeiliog. *IOA* —3C 80
Caergwrle. *Flin* —5F 83
Caergybi. *IOA* —2B 80
Caerlaverock. *Per* —2A 136
Caerleon. *Newp* —2G 33
Caerlleon. *Carm* —2G 43
Caerllion. *Newp* —2G 33
Caernarfon. *Gwyn* —4D 81
Caerphilly. *Cphy* —3E 33
Caersws. *Powy* —1C 58
Caerwedros. *Cdgn* —5C 56
Caerwent. *Mon* —2H 33
Caerwys. *Flin* —3D 82
Caigenhouses. *Arg* —3D 124
Caim. *IOA* —2F 81
Caio. *Carm* —2G 45
Cairinis. *W Isl* —2D 170
Cairisiadar. *W Isl* —4C 171
Cairminis. *W Isl* —9C 171
Cairnbaan. *Arg* —4F 133
Cairnbulg. *Aber* —2H 161
Cairncross. *Ang* —1D 145
Cairndow. *Arg* —2A 134
Cairness. *Aber* —2H 161
Cairneyhill. *Fife* —1D 128
Cairngarroch. *Dum* —4F 109
Cairnhill. *Aber* —5D 160
Cairnie. *Aber* —4B 160
Cairnorrie. *Aber* —4F 161
Cairnryan. *Dum* —3F 109
Cairntable. *E Ayr* —3D 116
Caister-on-Sea. *Norf* —4H 79
Caister St Edmund. *Norf* —5E 79
Caistor. *Linc* —4E 95
Caistron. *Nmbd* —4D 121
Cakebole. *Worc* —3C 60
Cake Street. *Suff* —3F 65
Calais Street. *Suff* —1C 54
Calanais. *W Isl* —4E 171
Calbost. *W Isl* —6G 171
Calbourne. *IOW* —4C 16
Calceby. *Linc* —3C 88
Calcot. *Glos* —4F 49
Calcot Row. *W Ber* —4E 37
Calcott. *Kent* —4F 41
Calcott. *Shrp* —4G 71
Caldback. *Shet* —1H 173
Caldbeck. *Cumb* —1E 102
Caldbergh. *N Yor* —1C 98
Caldecote. *Cambs* —5C 64
(nr. Cambridge)
Caldecote. *Cambs* —2A 64
(nr. Peterborough)
Caldecote. *Herts* —2C 52
Caldecote. *Warw* —1A 62
Caldecott. *Nptn* —4G 63
Caldecott. *Oxon* —2C 36
Caldecott. *Rut* —1F 63

Calderbank. *N Lan* —3A 128
Calder Bridge. *Cumb* —4B 102
Calderbrook. *G Man* —3H 91
Caldercruix. *N Lan* —3B 128
Calder Grove. *W Yor* —3D 92
Calder Mains. *High* —3C 168
Caldermill. *S Lan* —5H 127
Calder Vale. *Lanc* —5E 97
Calderwood. *S Lan* —4H 127
Caldescote. *Nptn* —5D 62
Caldicot. *Mon* —3H 33
Caldwell. *N Yor* —3E 105
Caldy. *Mers* —2E 83
Calebrack. *Cumb* —1E 103
Caledfwlch. *Carm* —3G 45
Calford Green. *Suff* —1G 53
Calfsound. *Orkn* —4E 172
Calgary. *Arg* —3E 139
Califer. *Mor* —3E 159
California. *Falk* —2C 128
California. *Norf* —4H 79
California. *Suff* —1E 55
Calke. *Derbs* —3A 74
Callakille. *High* —3F 155
Callaly. *Nmbd* —4E 121
Callander. *Stir* —3F 135
Callaughton. *Shrp* —1A 60
Callendoun. *Arg* —1E 127
Callestick. *Corn* —3B 6
Calligarry. *High* —3E 147
Callington. *Corn* —2H 7
Callingwood. *Staf* —3F 73
Callow. *Here* —2H 47
Callowell. *Glos* —5D 48
Callow End. *Worc* —1D 48
Callow Hill. *Wilts* —3F 35
Callow Hill. *Worc* —3B 60
(nr. Bewdley)
Callow Hill. *Worc* —4E 61
(nr. Redditch)
Calmore. *Hants* —1B 16
Calmsden. *Glos* —5F 49
Calne. *Wilts* —4E 35
Calow. *Derbs* —3B 86
Calshot. *Hants* —2C 16
Calstock. *Corn* —2A 8
Calstone Wellington. *Wilts* —5F 35
Calthorpe. *Norf* —2D 78
Calthorpe Street. *Norf* —3G 79
Calthwaite. *Cumb* —5F 113
Calton. *N Yor* —4B 98
Calveley. *Ches* —5H 83
Calver. *Derbs* —3G 85
Calverhall. *Shrp* —2A 72
Calverleigh. *Devn* —1C 12
Calverley. *W Yor* —1C 92
Calvert. *Buck* —3E 51
Calverton. *Mil* —2F 51
Calverton. *Notts* —1D 74
Calvine. *Per* —2F 143
Calvo. *Cumb* —4C 112
Cam. *Glos* —2C 34
Camaghael. *High* —1F 141
Camas-luinie. *High* —1B 148
Camasnacroise. *High* —3C 140
Camastianavaig. *High* —5E 155
Camasunary. *High* —2D 146
Camault Muir. *High* —4H 157
Camb. *Shet* —2G 173
Camber. *E Sus* —4D 28
Camberley. *Surr* —5G 37
Camberwell. *G Lon* —3E 39
Camblesforth. *N Yor* —2G 93
Cambo. *Nmbd* —1D 114
Cambois. *Nmbd* —1G 115
Camborne. *Corn* —5A 6
Cambourne. *Cambs* —5C 64
Cambridge. *Cambs* —5D 64
Cambridge. *Glos* —5C 48
Cambridge Airport. *Cambs* —5D 65
Cambrose. *Corn* —4A 6
Cambus. *Clac* —4A 136
Cambusbarron. *Stir* —4G 135

Cambuskenneth. *Stir* —4H 135
Cambuslang. *S Lan* —3H 127
Cambusnethan. *N Lan* —4B 128
Cambus o'May. *Aber* —4B 152
Camden Town. *G Lon* —2D 39
Cameley. *Bath* —1B 22
Camelford. *Corn* —4B 10
Camelon. *Falk* —1B 128
Camelsdale. *Surr* —2A 26
Camer's Green. *Worc* —2C 48
Camerton. *Bath* —1B 22
Camerton. *Cumb* —1B 102
Camerton. *E Yor* —2F 95
Camghouran. *Per* —3C 142
Cammachmore. *Aber* —4G 153
Cammeringham. *Linc* —2G 87
Camore. *High* —4E 165
Campbelton. *N Ayr* —4C 126
Campbeltown. *Arg* —3B 122
Campbeltown Airport. *Arg* —3A 122
Cample. *Dum* —5B 118
Campmuir. *Per* —5B 144
Campsall. *S Yor* —3F 93
Campsea Ashe. *Suff* —5F 67
Camps End. *Cambs* —1G 53
Camp, The. *Glos* —5E 49
Campton. *Beds* —2B 52
Camptoun. *E Lot* —2B 130
Camptown. *Scot* —3A 120
Camrose. *Pemb* —3D 42
Camserney. *Per* —4F 143
Camster. *High* —4E 169
Camus Croise. *High* —2E 147
Camusdarach. *High* —4E 147
Camusnagaul. *High* —1E 141
(nr. Fort William)
Camusnagaul. *High* —5E 163
(nr. Loch Broom)
Camusteel. *High* —4G 155
Camusterrach. *High* —4G 155
Camusvrachan. *Per* —4D 142
Canada. *Hants* —1A 16
Canadia. *E Sus* —4B 28
Canaston Bridge. *Pemb* —3E 43
Candlesby. *Linc* —4D 88
Candle Street. *Suff* —3C 66
Candy Mill. *S Lan* —5D 128
Cane End. *Oxon* —4E 37
Canewdon. *Essx* —1C 40
Canford Cliffs. *Pool* —4F 15
Canford Magna. *Pool* —3F 15
Cangate. *Norf* —3F 79
Canham's Green. *Suff* —4C 66
Canholes. *Derbs* —3E 85
Canisbay. *High* —1F 169
Canley. *W Mid* —3H 61
Cann. *Dors* —4D 22
Cann Common. *Dors* —4D 23
Cannich. *High* —5F 157
Cannington. *Som* —3F 21
Cannock. *Staf* —4D 73
Cannock Wood. *Staf* —4E 73
Canonbie. *Dum* —2E 113
Canon Bridge. *Here* —1H 47
Canon Frome. *Here* —1B 48
Canon Pyon. *Here* —1H 47
Canons Ashby. *Nptn* —5C 62
Canonstown. *Corn* —3C 4
Canterbury. *Kent* —5F 41
Cantley. *Norf* —5F 79
Cantley. *S Yor* —4G 93
Cantlop. *Shrp* —5H 71
Canton. *Card* —4E 33
Cantray. *High* —4B 158
Cantraybruich. *High* —4B 158
Cantraywood. *High* —4B 158
Cantsdam. *Fife* —4D 136
Cantsfield. *Lanc* —2F 97
Canvey Island. *Essx* —2B 40
Canwick. *Linc* —4G 87
Canworthy Water. *Corn* —3C 10
Caol. *High* —1F 141
Caolas. *W Isl* —9B 170

Caolas Liubharsaigh. *W Isl* —4D 170
Caolas Stocinis. *W Isl* —8D 171
Caoles. *Arg* —4B 138
Caol Ila. *Arg* —3C 124
Capel. *Kent* —1H 27
Capel. *Surr* —1C 26
Capel Bangor. *Cdgn* —2F 57
Capel Betws Lleucu. *Cdgn* —5F 57
Capel Coch. *IOA* —2D 80
Capel Curig. *Cnwy* —5G 81
Capel Cynon. *Cdgn* —1D 45
Capel Dewi. *Carm* —3E 45
Capel Dewi. *Cdgn* —2F 57
(nr. Aberystwyth)
Capel Dewi. *Cdgn* —1E 45
(nr. Llandysul)
Capel Garmon. *Cnwy* —5H 81
Capel Green. *Suff* —1G 55
Capel Gwyn. *IOA* —3C 80
Capel Gwynfe. *Carm* —3H 45
Capel Hendre. *Carm* —4F 45
Capel Isaac. *Carm* —3G 45
Capel Iwan. *Carm* —1G 43
Capel-le-Ferne. *Kent* —2G 29
Capel Llanilterne. *Card* —4D 32
Capel Mawr. *IOA* —3D 80
Capel Newydd. *Pemb* —1G 43
Capel St Andrew. *Suff* —1G 55
Capel St Mary. *Suff* —2D 54
Capel Seion. *Carm* —4F 45
Capel Seion. *Cdgn* —3F 57
Capel Uchaf. *Gwyn* —1D 68
Capel-y-ffin. *Powy* —2F 47
Capenhurst. *Ches* —3F 83
Capernwray. *Lanc* —2E 97
Capheaton. *Nmbd* —1D 114
Cappercleuch. *Scot* —2E 119
Capplegill. *Dum* —3D 118
Capton. *Devn* —3E 9
Capton. *Som* —3D 20
Caputh. *Per* —5H 143
Caradon Town. *Corn* —5C 10
Carbis Bay. *Corn* —3C 4
Carbost. *High* —5C 154
(nr. Loch Harport)
Carbost. *High* —4D 154
(nr. Portree)
Carbrook. *S Yor* —2A 86
Carbrooke. *Norf* —5B 78
Carburton. *Notts* —3D 86
Carcluie. *S Ayr* —3C 116
Car Colston. *Notts* —1E 74
Carcroft. *S Yor* —4F 93
Cardenden. *Fife* —4E 136
Cardeston. *Shrp* —4F 71
Cardewlees. *Cumb* —4E 113
Cardiff. *Card* —4E 33
Cardiff Airport. *V Glam* —5D 32
Cardigan. *Cdgn* —1B 44
Cardinal's Green. *Cambs* —1G 53
Cardington. *Beds* —1A 52
Cardington. *Shrp* —1H 59
Cardinham. *Corn* —2F 7
Cardno. *Aber* —2G 161
Cardow. *Mor* —4F 159
Cardross. *Arg* —2E 127
Cardurnock. *Cumb* —4C 112
Careby. *Linc* —4H 75
Careston. *Ang* —2E 145
Carew. *Pemb* —4E 43
Carew Cheriton. *Pemb* —4E 43
Carew Newton. *Pemb* —4E 43
Carey. *Here* —2A 48
Carfin. *N Lan* —4A 128
Carfrae. *Scot* —4B 130
Cargate Green. *Norf* —4F 79
Cargenbridge. *Dum* —2G 111
Cargill. *Per* —5A 144
Cargo. *Cumb* —4E 113
Cargreen. *Corn* —2A 8
Carham. *Nmbd* —1B 120
Carhampton. *Som* —2D 20
Carharrack. *Corn* —4B 6

Carie. *Per* —3D 142
(nr. Loch Rannah)
Carie. *Per* —5D 142
(nr. Loch Tay)
Carisbrooke. *IOW* —4C 16
Cark. *Cumb* —2C 96
Carkeel. *Corn* —2A 8
Carlabhagh. *W Isl* —3E 171
Carland Cross. *Corn* —3C 6
Carlbury. *Darl* —3F 105
Carlby. *Linc* —4H 75
Carlecotes. *S Yor* —4B 92
Carleen. *Corn* —4D 4
Carlesmoor. *N Yor* —2D 98
Carleton. *Cumb* —4F 113
(nr. Carlisle)
Carleton. *Cumb* —4B 102
(nr. Egremont)
Carleton. *Cumb* —2G 103
(nr. Penrith)
Carleton. *Lanc* —1B 90
Carleton. *N Yor* —5B 98
Carleton. *W Yor* —2E 93
Carleton Forehoe. *Norf* —5C 78
Carleton Rode. *Norf* —1D 66
Carleton St Peter. *Norf* —5F 79
Carlidnack. *Corn* —4E 5
Carlingcott. *Bath* —1B 22
Carlin How. *Red C* —3E 107
Carlisle. *Cumb* —4E 113
Carloonan. *Arg* —2H 133
Carlops. *Scot* —4E 129
Carlton. *Beds* —5G 63
Carlton. *Cambs* —5F 65
Carlton. *Leics* —5A 74
Carlton. *N Yor* —1A 100
(nr. Helmsley)
Carlton. *N Yor* —1C 98
(nr. Middleham)
Carlton. *N Yor* —2G 93
(nr. Selby)
Carlton. *Notts* —1C 74
Carlton. *S Yor* —3D 92
Carlton. *Stoc T* —2A 106
Carlton. *Suff* —4F 67
Carlton. *W Yor* —2D 92
Carlton Colville. *Suff* —1H 67
Carlton Curlieu. *Leics* —1D 62
Carlton Husthwaite. *N Yor* —2G 99
Carlton in Cleveland. *N Yor* —4C 106
Carlton in Lindrick. *Notts* —2C 86
Carlton-le-Moorland. *Linc* —5G 87
Carlton Miniott. *N Yor* —1F 99
Carlton Scroop. *Linc* —1G 75
Carluke. *S Lan* —4B 128
Carlyon Bay. *Corn* —3E 7
Carmarthen. *Carm* —4E 45
Carmel. *Carm* —4F 45
Carmel. *Flin* —3D 82
Carmel. *Gwyn* —5D 81
Carmel. *IOA* —2D 80
Carmichael. *S Lan* —1B 118
Carmunnock. *Glas* —4H 127
Carmyle. *Glas* —3H 127
Carmyllie. *Ang* —4E 145
Carnaby. *E Yor* —3F 101
Carnach. *High* —1C 148
(nr. Lochcarron)
Carnach. *High* —4E 163
(nr. Ullapool)
Carnach. *Mor* —4E 159
Carnach. *W Isl* —8E 171
Carnachy. *High* —3H 167
Carnain. *Arg* —3B 124
Carnais. *W Isl* —4C 171
Carnan. *Arg* —4B 138
Carnan. *W Isl* —4C 170
Carnbee. *Fife* —3H 137
Carnbo. *Per* —3C 136
Carn Brea. *Corn* —4A 6
Carndu. *High* —1A 148
Carne. *Corn* —5D 6

Clyne—Cookhill

Clyne. Neat —5B 46
Clynelish. High —3F 165
Clynnog-fawr. Gwyn —1D 68
Clyro. Powy —1F 47
Clyst Honiton. Devn —3C 12
Clyst Hydon. Devn —2D 12
Clyst St George. Devn —4C 12
Clyst St Lawrence. Devn —2D 12
Clyst St Mary. Devn —3C 12
Clyth. High —5E 169
Cnip. W Isl —4C 171
Cnwcau. Pemb —1C 44
Cnwch Coch. Cdgn —3F 57
Coad's Green. Corn —5C 10
Coal Aston. Derbs —3A 86
Coalbrookdale. Telf —5A 72
Coalbrookvale. Blae —5F 47
Coalburn. S Lan —1H 117
Coalburns. Tyne —3E 115
Coalcleugh. Nmbd —5B 114
Coaley. Glos —5C 48
Coalford. Aber —4F 153
Coalhall. E Ayr —3D 116
Coalhill. Essx —1B 40
Coalpit Heath. S Glo —3B 34
Coal Pool. W Mid —5E 73
Coalport. Telf —5A 72
Coalsnaughton. Clac —4B 136
Coaltown of Balgonie. Fife —4F 137
Coaltown of Wemyss. Fife —4F 137
Coalville. Leics —4B 74
Coalway. Glos —4A 48
Coanwood. Nmbd —4H 113
Coat. Som —4H 21
Coatbridge. N Lan —3A 128
Coatdyke. N Lan —3A 128
Coate. Swin —3G 35
Coate. Wilts —5F 35
Coates. Cambs —1C 64
Coates. Glos —5E 49
Coates. Linc —2G 87
Coates. W Sus —4A 26
Coatham. Red C —2C 106
Coatham Mundeville. Darl —2F 105
Cobbaton. Devn —4G 19
Coberley. Glos —4E 49
Cobhall Common. Here —2H 47
Cobham. Kent —4A 40
Cobham. Surr —4C 38
Cobnash. Here —4G 59
Coburg. Devn —5B 12
Cockayne. N Yor —5D 106
Cockayne Hatley. Beds —1C 52
Cock Bank. Wrex —1F 71
Cock Bridge. Aber —3G 151
Cockburnspath. Scot —2D 130
Cock Clarks. Essx —5B 54
Cockenzie & Port Seton. E Lot —2H 129
Cockerham. Lanc —4D 96
Cockermouth. Cumb —1C 102
Cockernhoe. Herts —3B 52
Cockfield. Dur —2E 105
Cockfield. Suff —5B 66
Cockfosters. G Lon —1D 39
Cock Gate. Here —4G 59
Cock Green. Essx —4G 53
Cocking. W Sus —1G 17
Cocking Causeway. W Sus —1G 17
Cockington. Torb —2F 9
Cocklake. Som —2H 21
Cocklaw. Aber —4H 161
Cocklaw. Nmbd —2C 114
Cockley Beck. Cumb —4D 102
Cockley Cley. Norf —5G 77
Cockmuir. Aber —3G 161
Cockpole Green. Wind —3G 37
Cockshutford. Shrp —2H 59
Cockshutt. Shrp —3G 71
Cockthorpe. Norf —1B 78
Cockwood. Devn —4C 12
Cockyard. Derbs —3E 85
Cockyard. Here —2H 47
Codda. Corn —5B 10
Coddenham. Suff —5D 66
Coddenham Green. Suff —5D 66
Coddington. Ches —5G 83
Coddington. Here —1C 48
Coddington. Notts —5F 87
Codford St Mary. Wilts —3E 23
Codford St Peter. Wilts —3E 23
Codicote. Herts —4C 52
Codmore Hill. W Sus —3B 26
Codnor. Derbs —1B 74
Codrington. S Glo —4C 34
Codsall. Staf —5C 72
Codsall Wood. Staf —5C 72
Coed Duon. Cphy —2E 33
Coedely. Rhon —3D 32
Coedglasson. Powy —4C 58
Coedkernew. Newp —3F 33
Coed Morgan. Mon —4G 47
Coedpoeth. Wrex —5E 83
Coedway. Powy —4F 71
Coed-y-bryn. Cdgn —1D 44
Coed-y-paen. Mon —2G 33
Coed-yr-ynys. Powy —3E 47
Coed Ystumgwern. Gwyn —3E 69
Coelbren. Powy —4B 46
Coffinswell. Devn —2E 9
Cofton Hackett. Worc —3E 61
Cogan. V Glam —4E 33
Cogenhoe. Nptn —4F 63
Cogges. Oxon —5B 50
Coggeshall. Essx —3B 54
Coggeshall Hamlet. Essx —3B 54
Coggins Mill. E Sus —3G 27
Coignafearn Lodge. High —2A 150
Coig Peighinnean. W Isl —1H 171
Coig Peighinnean Bhuirgh. W Isl —2G 171
Coille Mhorgil. High —3D 148
Coilliemore. High —1A 158
Coillore. High —5C 154
Coire an Fhuarain. W Isl —4E 171
Coity. B'End —3C 32
Cokhay Green. Derbs —3G 73
Col. W Isl —3G 171
Colaboll. High —2C 164
Colan. Corn —2C 6
Colaton Raleigh. Devn —4D 12
Colbost. High —4B 154
Colburn. N Yor —5E 105
Colby. Cumb —2H 103
Colby. IOM —4B 108
Colby. Norf —2E 78
Colchester. Essx —3D 54
Cold Ash. W Ber —5D 36
Cold Ashby. Nptn —3D 62
Cold Ashton. S Glo —4C 34
Cold Aston. Glos —4G 49
Coldbackie. High —3G 167
Cold Blow. Pemb —3F 43
Cold Brayfield. Mil —5G 63
Cold Cotes. N Yor —2G 97
Coldean. Brig —5E 27
Coldeast. Devn —5B 12
Colden. W Yor —2H 91
Colden Common. Hants —4C 24
Coldfair Green. Suff —4G 67
Coldham. Cambs —5D 76
Coldham. Staf —5C 72
Cold Hanworth. Linc —2H 87
Coldharbour. Corn —4B 6
Cold Harbour. Dors —3E 15
Coldharbour. Glos —5A 48
Coldharbour. Kent —5G 39
Coldharbour. Surr —1C 26
Cold Hatton. Telf —3A 72
Cold Hatton Heath. Telf —3A 72
Cold Hesledon. Dur —5H 115
Cold Hiendley. W Yor —3D 92
Cold Higham. Nptn —5D 62
Coldingham. Scot —3F 131
Cold Kirby. N Yor —1H 99
Coldmeece. Staf —2C 72
Cold Northcott. Corn —4C 10
Cold Norton. Essx —5B 54
Cold Overton. Leics —5F 75
Coldrain. Per —3C 136
Coldred. Kent —1G 29
Coldridge. Devn —2H 11
Cold Row. Lanc —5C 96
Coldstream. Scot —5E 131
Coldwaltham. W Sus —4B 26
Coldwell. Here —2H 47
Coldwells. Aber —5H 161
Coldwells Croft. Aber —1C 152
Cole. Shet —5E 173
Cole. Som —3B 22
Colebatch. Shrp —2F 59
Colebrook. Devn —2D 12
Colebrooke. Devn —2A 12
Coleburn. Mor —3G 159
Coleby. Linc —4G 87
Coleby. N Lin —3B 94
Cole End. Warw —2F 61
Coleford. Devn —2A 12
Coleford. Glos —4A 48
Coleford. Som —2B 22
Colegate End. Norf —2D 66
Cole Green. Herts —4C 52
Cole Henley. Hants —1C 24
Colehill. Dors —2F 15
Coleman Green. Herts —4B 52
Coleman's Hatch. E Sus —2F 27
Colemere. Shrp —2G 71
Colemore. Hants —3F 25
Colemore Green. Shrp —1B 60
Colenden. Per —1D 136
Coleorton. Leics —4B 74
Colerne. Wilts —4D 34
Colesbourne. Glos —4E 49
Colesden. Beds —5A 64
Coles Green. Worc —5B 60
Coleshill. Buck —1A 38
Coleshill. Oxon —2H 35
Coleshill. Warw —2G 61
Colestocks. Devn —2D 12
Colethrop. Glos —4D 48
Coley. Bath —1A 22
Colgate. W Sus —2D 26
Colinsburgh. Fife —3G 137
Colinton. Edin —3F 129
Colintraive. Arg —2B 126
Colkirk. Norf —3B 78
Collace. Per —5B 144
Collam. W Isl —8D 171
Collaton. Devn —5D 8
Collaton St Mary. Torb —3E 9
College of Roseisle. Mor —2F 159
Collessie. Fife —2E 137
Collier Row. G Lon —1F 39
Colliers End. Herts —3D 52
Collier Street. Kent —1B 28
Colliery Row. Tyne —5G 115
Collieston. Aber —1H 153
Collin. Dum —2B 112
Collingbourne Ducis. Wilts —1H 23
Collingbourne Kingston. Wilts —1H 23
Collingham. Notts —4F 87
Collingham. W Yor —5F 99
Collingtree. Nptn —5E 63
Collins Green. Warr —1H 83
Collins Green. Worc —5B 60
Colliston. Ang —4F 145
Colliton. Devn —2D 12
Collydean. Fife —3E 137
Collyweston. Nptn —5G 75
Colmonell. S Ayr —1G 109
Colmworth. Beds —5A 64
Colnbrook. Buck —3B 38
Colne. Cambs —3C 64
Colne. Lanc —5A 98
Colne Engaine. Essx —2B 54
Colney. Norf —5D 78
Colney Heath. Herts —5C 52
Colney Street. Herts —5B 52
Coln Rogers. Glos —5F 49
Coln St Aldwyns. Glos —5G 49
Coln St Dennis. Glos —4F 49
Colpitts Grange. Nmbd —4C 114
Colpy. Aber —5D 160
Colscott. Devn —1D 10
Colsterdale. N Yor —1D 98
Colsterworth. Linc —3G 75
Colston Bassett. Notts —2D 74
Colstoun House. E Lot —2B 130
Coltfield. Mor —2F 159
Colthouse. Cumb —5E 103
Coltishall. Norf —4E 79
Coltness. N Lan —4A 128
Colton. Cumb —1C 96
Colton. Norf —5D 78
Colton. N Yor —5H 99
Colton. Staf —3E 73
Colton. W Yor —1D 92
Colt's Hill. Kent —1H 27
Col Uarach. W Isl —4G 171
Colvend. Dum —4F 111
Colwall Green. Here —1C 48
Colwall Stone. Here —1C 48
Colwell. Nmbd —2C 114
Colwich. Staf —3E 73
Colwick. Notts —1D 74
Colwinston. V Glam —4C 32
Colworth. W Sus —5A 26
Colwyn Bay. Cnwy —3A 82
Colyford. Devn —3F 13
Colyton. Devn —3F 13
Combe. Devn —2D 8
Combe. Here —4F 59
Combe. Oxon —4C 50
Combe. W Ber —5B 36
Combe Almer. Dors —3E 15
Combebow. Devn —4E 11
Combe Common. Surr —2A 26
Combe Down. Bath —5C 34
Combe Fishacre. Devn —2E 9
Combe Florey. Som —3E 21
Combe Hay. Bath —1C 22
Combeinteignhead. Devn —5C 12
Combe Martin. Devn —2F 19
Combe Moor. Here —4F 59
Combe Raleigh. Devn —2E 13
Comberbach. Ches —3A 84
Comberford. Staf —5F 73
Comberton. Cambs —5C 64
Comberton. Here —4G 59
Combe St Nicholas. Som —1G 13
Combpyne. Devn —3F 13
Combridge. Staf —2E 73
Combrook. Warw —5H 61
Combs. Derbs —3E 85
Combs. Suff —5C 66
Combs Ford. Suff —5C 66
Combwich. Som —2F 21
Comers. Aber —3D 152
Comhampton. Worc —4C 60
Comins Coch. Cdgn —2F 57
Comley. Shrp —1G 59
Commercial End. Cambs —4E 65
Commins. Powy —3D 70
Commins Coch. Powy —5H 69
Commondale. N Yor —3D 106
Common End. Cumb —2B 102
Common Hill. Here —2A 48
Common Moor. Corn —2G 7
Common Platt. Wilts —3G 35
Commonside. Ches —3H 83
Common Side. Derbs —3H 85
(nr. Chesterfield)
Commonside. Derbs —1G 73
(nr. Derby)
Common, The. Wilts —3H 23
(nr. Salisbury)
Common, The. Wilts —3F 35
(nr. Swindon)
Compstall. G Man —1D 84
Compton. Devn —2E 9
Compton. Hants —4C 24
Compton. Plym —3A 8
Compton. Staf —2C 60
Compton. Surr —1A 26
Compton. W Ber —4D 36
Compton. W Sus —1F 17
Compton. Wilts —1G 23
Compton Abbas. Dors —1D 15
Compton Abdale. Glos —4F 49
Compton Bassett. Wilts —4F 35
Compton Beauchamp. Oxon —3A 36
Compton Bishop. Som —1G 21
Compton Chamberlayne. Wilts —4F 23
Compton Dando. Bath —5B 34
Compton Dundon. Som —3H 21
Compton Greenfield. S Glo —3A 34
Compton Martin. Bath —1A 22
Compton Pauncefoot. Som —4B 22
Compton Valence. Dors —3A 14
Comrie. Fife —1D 128
Comrie. Per —1G 135
Conaglen. High —2E 141
Conchra. Arg —1B 126
Conchra. High —1A 148
Conder Green. Lanc —4D 96
Conderton. Worc —2E 49
Condicote. Glos —3G 49
Condorrat. N Lan —2A 128
Condover. Shrp —5G 71
Coneyhurst Common. W Sus —3C 26
Coneysthorpe. N Yor —2B 100
Coneythorpe. N Yor —4F 99
Coney Weston. Suff —3B 66
Conford. Hants —3G 25
Congdon's Shop. Corn —5C 10
Congerstone. Leics —5A 74
Congham. Norf —3G 77
Congleton. Ches —4C 84
Congl-y-wal. Gwyn —1G 69
Congresbury. N Som —5H 33
Congreve. Staf —4D 72
Conham. S Glo —4B 34
Conicaval. Mor —3D 159
Coningsby. Linc —5B 88
Conington. Cambs —4C 64
(nr. Fenstanton)
Conington. Cambs —2A 64
(nr. Sawtry)
Conisbrough. S Yor —1C 86
Conisby. Arg —3A 124
Conisholme. Linc —1D 88
Coniston. Cumb —5E 102
Coniston. E Yor —1E 95
Coniston Cold. N Yor —4B 98
Conistone. N Yor —3B 98
Connah's Quay. Flin —4E 83
Connel. Arg —5D 140
Connel Park. E Ayr —3F 117
Connista. High —1D 154
Connor Downs. Corn —3C 4
Conock. Wilts —1F 23
Conon Bridge. High —3H 157
Cononley. N Yor —5B 98
Cononsyth. Ang —4E 145
Conordan. High —5E 155
Consall. Staf —1D 73
Consett. Dur —4E 115
Constable Burton. N Yor —5E 105
Constantine. Corn —4E 5
Constantine Bay. Corn —1C 6
Contin. High —3G 157
Contullich. High —1A 158
Conwy. Cnwy —3G 81
Conyer. Kent —4D 40
Conyers Green. Suff —4A 66
Cooden. E Sus —5B 28
Cooil. IOM —4C 108
Cookbury. Devn —2E 11
Cookbury Wick. Devn —2D 11
Cookham. Wind —3G 37
Cookham Dean. Wind —3G 37
Cookham Rise. Wind —3G 37
Cookhill. Worc —5E 61

Craiglockhart—Croxden

Craiglockhart. Edin —2F 129
Craig Lodge. Arg —2B 126
Craigmalloch. E Ayr —5D 117
Craigmaud. Aber —3F 161
Craigmill. Stir —4H 135
Craigmillar. Edin —2F 129
Craigmore. Arg —3C 126
Craigmuie. Dum —1E 111
Craignair. Dum —3F 111
Craignant. Shrp —2E 71
Craigneuk. N Lan —3A 128
(nr. Airdrie)
Craigneuk. N Lan —4A 128
(nr. Motherwell)
Craignure. Arg —5B 140
Craigo. Ang —2F 145
Craigrory. High —4A 158
Craigrothie. Fife —2F 137
Craigs. Dum —2D 112
Craigsglen. Aber —3E 161
Craigshill. W Lot —3D 128
Craigside. Dur —1E 105
Craigs, The. High —4B 164
Craigton. Aber C —3F 153
Craigton. Aber —3E 152
Craigton. Ang —5E 145
(nr. Carnoustie)
Craigton. Ang —3C 144
(nr. Kirriemuir)
Craigton. High —4A 158
Craigtown. High —3A 168
Craig-y-Duke. Neat —5H 45
Craigyloch. Ang —3B 144
Craig-y-nos. Powy —4B 46
Craik. Scot —4F 119
Crail. Fife —3H 137
Crailing. Scot —2A 120
Crailinghall. Scot —2B 120
Craiselound. N Lin —1E 87
Crakehill. N Yor —2G 99
Crakemarsh. Staf —2E 73
Crambe. N Yor —3B 100
Crambeck. N Yor —3B 100
Cramlington. Nmbd —2F 115
Cramond. Edin —2E 129
Cramond Bridge. Edin —2E 129
Cranage. Ches —4B 84
Cranberry. Staf —2C 72
Cranborne. Dors —1F 15
Cranbourne. Brac —3A 38
Cranbrook. Kent —2B 28
Cranbrook Common. Kent —2B 28
Crane Moor. S Yor —4D 92
Crane's Corner. Norf —4B 78
Cranfield. Beds —1H 51
Cranford. G Lon —3B 38
Cranford St Andrew. Nptn —3G 63
Cranford St John. Nptn —3G 63
Cranham. Glos —4D 49
Cranham. G Lon —2G 39
Crank. Mers —1H 83
Cranleigh. Surr —2B 26
Cranley. Suff —3D 66
Cranloch. Mor —3G 159
Cranmer Green. Suff —3C 66
Cranmore. IOW —3B 16
Cranmore. Linc —5A 76
Crannich. Arg —4G 139
Crannoch. Mor —3B 160
Cranoe. Leics —1E 63
Cransford. Suff —4F 67
Cranshaws. Scot —3C 130
Cranstal. IOM —1D 108
Crantock. Corn —2B 6
Cranwell. Linc —5H 87
Cranwich. Norf —1G 65
Cranworth. Norf —5B 78
Craobh Haven. Arg —3E 133
Craobhnaclag. High —4G 157
Crapstone. Devn —2B 8
Crarae. Arg —4G 133
Crask. High —2H 167
Crask Inn. High —1C 164
Crask of Aigas. High —4G 157
Craster. Nmbd —3G 121
Cratfield. Suff —3F 67
Crathes. Aber —4E 153
Crathie. Aber —4G 151
Crathie. High —4H 149
Crathorne. N Yor —4B 106
Craven Arms. Shrp —2G 59
Crawcrook. Tyne —3E 115
Crawford. Lanc —4C 90
Crawford. S Lan —2B 118
Crawforddyke. S Lan —4B 128
Crawfordjohn. S Lan —2A 118
Crawick. Dum —3G 117
Crawley. Devn —2F 13
Crawley. Hants —3C 24
Crawley. Oxon —4B 50
Crawley. W Sus —2D 26
Crawley Down. W Sus —2E 27
Crawley Side. Dur —5C 114
Crawshawbooth. Lanc —2G 91
Crawton. Aber —5F 153
Cray. N Yor —2B 98
Cray. Per —2A 144
Crayford. G Lon —3G 39
Crayke. N Yor —2H 99
Craymere Beck. Norf —2C 78
Crays Hill. Essx —1B 40
Cray's Pond. Oxon —3E 37
Crazies Hill. Wok —3F 37
Creacombe. Devn —1B 12
Creagan. Arg —4D 141
Creag Aoil. High —1F 141
Creag Ghoraidh. W Isl —4C 170
Creaguaineach Lodge. High —2H 141
Creamore Bank. Shrp —2H 71
Creaton. Nptn —3E 62
Creca. Dum —2D 112
Credenhill. Here —1H 47
Crediton. Devn —2B 12
Creebridge. Dum —3B 110
Creech. Dors —4E 15
Creech Heathfield. Som —4F 21
Creech St Michael. Som —4F 21
Creed. Corn —4D 6
Creekmoor. Pool —3E 15
Creekmouth. G Lon —2F 39
Creeting St Mary. Suff —5C 66
Creeting St Peter. Suff —5C 66
Creeton. Linc —3H 75
Creetown. Dum —4B 110
Creggans. Arg —3H 133
Cregneash. IOM —5A 108
Cregrina. Powy —5D 58
Creighton. Staf —2E 73
Creigiau. Card —3D 32
Cremyll. Corn —3A 8
Crendell. Dors —1F 15
Crepkill. High —4D 154
Cressage. Shrp —5H 71
Cressbrook. Derbs —3F 85
Cresselly. Pemb —4E 43
Cressing. Essx —3A 54
Cresswell. Nmbd —5G 121
Cresswell. Staf —2D 73
Cresswell Quay. Pemb —4E 43
Creswell. Derbs —3C 86
Creswell Green. Staf —4E 73
Cretingham. Suff —4E 67
Crewe. Ches —5G 83
(nr. Farndon)
Crewe. Ches —5B 84
(nr. Nantwich)
Crewgreen. Powy —4F 71
Crewkerne. Som —2H 13
Crews Hill. G Lon —5D 52
Crewton. Dby C —2A 74
Crianlarich. Stir —1C 134
Cribbs Causeway. S Glo —4A 34
Cribyn. Cdgn —5E 57
Criccieth. Gwyn —2D 69
Crich. Derbs —5A 86
Crichton. Midl —3G 129
Crick. Mon —2H 33
Crick. Nptn —3C 62
Crickadarn. Powy —1D 46
Cricket Hill. Hants —5G 37
Cricket Malherbie. Som —1G 13
Cricket St Thomas. Som —2G 13
Crickham. Som —2H 21
Crickheath. Shrp —3E 71
Crickhowell. Powy —4F 47
Cricklade. Wilts —2G 35
Cricklewood. G Lon —2D 38
Cridling Stubbs. N Yor —2F 93
Criech. Fife —1F 137
Criftins. Shrp —2F 71
Crieff. Per —1A 136
Criggion. Powy —4E 71
Crigglestone. W Yor —3D 92
Crimchard. Som —2G 13
Crimdon Park. Dur —1B 106
Crimond. Aber —3H 161
Crimonmogate. Aber —3H 161
Crimplesham. Norf —5F 77
Crimscote. Warw —1H 49
Crinan. Arg —4E 133
Cringleford. Norf —5D 78
Crinow. Pemb —3F 43
Cripplesease. Corn —3C 4
Cripplestyle. Dors —1F 15
Cripp's Corner. E Sus —3B 28
Croanford. Corn —5A 10
Crockenhill. Kent —4G 39
Crocker End. Oxon —3F 37
Crockerhill. Hants —2D 16
Crockernwell. Devn —3A 12
Crocker's Ash. Here —4A 48
Crockerton. Wilts —2D 22
Crocketford. Dum —2F 111
Crockey Hill. York —5A 100
Crockham Hill. Kent —5F 39
Crockhurst Street. Kent —1H 27
Crockleford Heath. Essx —3D 54
Croeserw. Neat —2B 32
Croes-Goch. Pemb —1C 42
Croes Hywel. Mon —4G 47
Croes-lan. Cdgn —1D 45
Croesor. Gwyn —1F 69
Croesowallt. Shrp —3E 71
Croesyceiliog. Carm —4E 45
Croesyceiliog. Torf —2G 33
Croes-y-mwyalch. Newp —2G 33
Croesywaun. Gwyn —5E 81
Croford. Som —4E 20
Croft. Leics —1C 62
Croft. Linc —4E 89
Croft. Warr —1A 84
Croftamie. Stir —1F 127
Croftfoot. Glas —3H 127
Croftmill. Per —5F 143
Crofton. Cumb —4E 112
Crofton. W Yor —3D 93
Crofton. Wilts —5A 36
Croft-on-Tees. N Yor —4F 105
Crofts. Dum —2E 111
Crofts of Benachielt. High —5D 169
Crofts of Dipple. Mor —3H 159
Crofty. Swan —3E 31
Croggan. Arg —1E 132
Croglin. Cumb —5G 113
Croich. High —4B 164
Croick. High —3A 168
Croig. Arg —3E 139
Croir. W Isl —4D 171
Cromarty. High —2B 158
Crombie. Fife —1D 128
Cromdale. High —1E 151
Cromer. Herts —3C 52
Cromer. Norf —1E 78
Cromford. Derbs —5G 85
Cromhall. S Glo —2B 34
Cromhall Common. S Glo —3B 34
Cromor. W Isl —5G 171
Cromra. High —5H 149
Cromwell. Notts —4E 87
Cronberry. E Ayr —2F 117
Crondall. Hants —2F 25
Cronk, The. IOM —2C 108
Cronk-y-Voddy. IOM —3C 108
Cronton. Mers —2G 83
Crook. Cumb —5F 103
Crook. Dur —1E 105
Crookdake. Cumb —5C 112
Crooke. G Man —4D 90
Crookedholm. E Ayr —1D 116
Crooked Soley. Wilts —4B 36
Crookes. S Yor —2H 85
Crookgate Bank. Dur —4E 115
Crookhall. Dur —4E 115
Crookham. Nmbd —1D 120
Crookham. W Ber —5D 36
Crookham Village. Hants —1F 25
Crooklands. Cumb —1E 97
Crook of Devon. Per —3C 136
Crookston. Ren —3G 127
Cropredy. Oxon —1C 50
Cropston. Leics —4C 74
Cropthorne. Worc —1E 49
Cropton. N Yor —1B 100
Cropwell Bishop. Notts —2D 74
Cropwell Butler. Notts —2D 74
Cros. W Isl —1H 171
Crosbie. N Ayr —4D 126
Crosbost. W Isl —5F 171
Crosby. Cumb —1B 102
Crosby. IOM —4C 108
Crosby. Mers —1F 83
Crosby. N Lin —3B 94
Crosby Court. N Yor —5A 106
Crosby Garrett. Cumb —4A 104
Crosby Ravensworth. Cumb —3H 103
Crosby Villa. Cumb —1B 102
Croscombe. Som —2A 22
Crosland Moor. W Yor —3B 92
Cross. Som —1H 21
Crossaig. Arg —4G 125
Crossapol. Arg —4A 138
Cross Ash. Mon —4H 47
Cross-at-Hand. Kent —1B 28
Crossbush. W Sus —5B 26
Crosscanonby. Cumb —1B 102
Crossdale Street. Norf —2E 79
Cross End. Essx —2B 54
Crossens. Mers —3B 90
Crossford. Fife —1D 128
Crossford. S Lan —5B 128
Cross Foxes. Gwyn —4G 69
Crossgate. Orkn —6D 172
Crossgate. Staf —2D 72
Crossgatehall. E Lot —3G 129
Crossgates. Fife —1E 129
Crossgates. N Yor —1E 101
Crossgates. Powy —4C 58
Cross Gates. W Yor —1D 92
Crossgill. Lanc —3E 97
Cross Green. Devn —4D 11
Cross Green. Staf —5D 72
Cross Green. Suff —5A 66
(nr. Cockfield)
Cross Green. Suff —5B 66
(nr. Hitcham)
Cross Hands. Carm —4F 45
(nr. Ammanford)
Crosshands. Carm —2F 43
(nr. Whitland)
Crosshands. E Ayr —1D 117
Crosshill. E Ayr —2D 117
Crosshill. Fife —4D 136
Cross Hill. Glos —2A 34
Crosshill. S Ayr —4C 116
Crosshills. High —2A 158
Cross Hills. N Yor —5C 98
Cross Holme. N Yor —5C 106
Crosshouse. E Ayr —1C 116
Cross Houses. Shrp —5H 71
Crossings. Cumb —2G 113
Cross in Hand. E Sus —3G 27
Cross Inn. Cdgn —4E 57
(nr. Aberaeron)
Cross Inn. Cdgn —5C 56
(nr. New Quay)
Cross Inn. Rhon —3D 32
Crosskeys. Cphy —2F 33
Crosskirk. High —2C 168
Crosslands. Cumb —1C 96
Cross Lane Head. Shrp —1B 60
Cross Lanes. Corn —4D 5
Cross Lanes. Dur —3D 104
Cross Lanes. N Yor —3H 99
Crosslanes. Shrp —4F 71
Cross Lanes. Wrex —1F 71
Crosslee. Ren —3F 127
Crossmichael. Dum —3E 111
Crossmoor. Lanc —1C 90
Cross Oak. Powy —3E 46
Cross of Jackston. Aber —5E 161
Cross o' th' Hands. Derbs —1G 73
Crossroads. Aber —3G 153
(nr. Aberdeen)
Crossroads. Aber —4E 153
(nr. Banchory)
Crossroads. E Ayr —1D 116
Cross Side. Devn —4B 20
Cross Street. Suff —3D 66
Crosston. Ang —3E 145
Cross Town. Ches —3B 84
Crossway. Mon —4H 47
Crossway. Powy —5C 58
Crossway Green. Mon —2A 34
Crossway Green. Worc —4C 60
Crossways. Dors —4C 14
Crosswell. Pemb —1F 43
Crosswood. Cdgn —3F 57
Crosthwaite. Cumb —5F 103
Croston. Lanc —3C 90
Crostwick. Norf —4E 79
Crostwight. Norf —3F 79
Crothair. W Isl —4D 171
Crouch. Kent —5H 39
Croucheston. Wilts —4F 23
Crouch Hill. Dors —1C 14
Croughton. Nptn —2D 50
Crovie. Aber —2F 161
Crow. Hants —2G 15
Crowan. Corn —3D 4
Crowborough. E Sus —2G 27
Crowcombe. Som —3E 21
Crowcroft. Worc —5B 60
Crowdecote. Derbs —4F 85
Crowden. Derbs —1E 85
Crowden. Devn —3E 11
Crowdhill. Hants —1C 16
Crowdon. N Yor —5G 107
Crow Edge. S Yor —4B 92
Crow End. Cambs —5C 64
Crowfield. Nptn —1E 50
Crowfield. Suff —5D 66
Crow Green. Essx —1G 39
Crow Hill. Here —3B 48
Crowhurst. E Sus —4B 28
Crowhurst. Surr —1E 27
Crowhurst Lane End. Surr —1E 27
Crowland. Linc —4B 76
Crowland. Suff —3C 66
Crowlas. Corn —3C 4
Crowle. N Lin —3A 94
Crowle. Worc —5D 60
Crowle Green. Worc —5D 60
Crowmarsh Gifford. Oxon —3E 36
Crown Corner. Suff —3E 67
Crownthorpe. Norf —5C 78
Crowntown. Corn —3D 4
Crows-an-wra. Corn —4A 4
Crowshill. Norf —5B 78
Crowthorne. Brac —5G 37
Crowton. Ches —3H 83
Croxall. Staf —4F 73
Croxby. Linc —1A 88
Croxdale. Dur —1F 105
Croxden. Staf —2E 73

Dartmeet. *Devn* —5G 11
Dartmouth. *Devn* —3E 9
Darton. *S Yor* —3D 92
Darvel. *E Ayr* —1E 117
Darwen. *Bkbn* —2E 91
Dassels. *Herts* —3D 53
Datchet. *Wind* —3A 38
Datchworth. *Herts* —4C 52
Datchworth Green. *Herts* —4C 52
Daubhill. *G Man* —4F 91
Dauntsey. *Wilts* —3E 35
Dauntsey Green. *Wilts* —3E 35
Dauntsey Lock. *Wilts* —3E 35
Dava. *Mor* —5E 159
Davenham. *Ches* —3A 84
Daventry. *Nptn* —4C 62
Davidson's Mains. *Edin* —2F 129
Davidston. *High* —2B 158
Davidstow. *Corn* —4B 10
David's Well. *Powy* —3C 58
Davington. *Dum* —4E 119
Daviot. *Aber* —1E 153
Daviot. *High* —5B 158
Davyhulme. *G Man* —1B 84
Daw Cross. *N Yor* —4F 99
Dawdon. *Dur* —5H 115
Dawesgreen. *Surr* —1D 26
Dawley. *Telf* —5A 72
Dawlish. *Devn* —5C 12
Dawlish Warren. *Devn* —5C 12
Dawn. *Cnwy* —3A 82
Daws Heath. *Essx* —2C 40
Dawshill. *Worc* —5C 60
Daw's House. *Corn* —4D 10
Dawsmere. *Linc* —2D 76
Dayhills. *Staf* —2D 72
Dayhouse Bank. *Worc* —3D 60
Daylesford. *Glos* —3H 49
Daywall. *Shrp* —2E 71
Ddol. *Flin* —3D 82
Ddol Cownwy. *Powy* —4C 70
Deadwater. *Nmbd* —5A 120
Deaf Hill. *Dur* —1A 106
Deal. *Kent* —5H 41
Dean. *Cumb* —2B 102
Dean. *Devn* —2G 19
 (nr. Combe Martin)
Dean. *Devn* —2F 19
 (nr. Ilfracombe)
Dean. *Devn* —2H 19
 (nr. Lynton)
Dean. *Dors* —1E 15
Dean. *Hants* —1D 16
 (nr. Bishop's Waltham)
Dean. *Hants* —3C 24
 (nr. Winchester)
Dean. *Som* —2B 22
Dean Bank. *Dur* —1F 105
Deanburnhaugh. *Scot* —3F 119
Deane. *Hants* —1D 24
Deanich Lodge. *High* —5A 164
Deanland. *Dors* —1E 15
Deanlane End. *W Sus* —1F 17
Dean Park. *Shrp* —4H 59
Dean Prior. *Devn* —2D 8
Dean Row. *Ches* —2C 84
Deans. *W Lot* —3D 128
Deanscales. *Cumb* —2B 102
Deanshanger. *Nptn* —2F 51
Deanston. *Stir* —3G 135
Dearham. *Cumb* —1B 102
Dearne. *S Yor* —4E 93
Dearne Valley. *S Yor* —4E 93
Debach. *Suff* —5E 67
Debden. *Essx* —2F 53
Debden Green. *Essx* —1F 39
 (nr. Loughton)
Debden Green. *Essx* —2F 53
 (nr. Saffron Walden)
Debenham. *Suff* —4D 66
Dechmont. *W Lot* —2D 128
Deddington. *Oxon* —2C 50
Dedham. *Essx* —2D 54

Dedham Heath. *Essx* —2D 54
Deebank. *Aber* —4D 152
Deene. *Nptn* —1G 63
Deenethorpe. *Nptn* —1G 63
Deepcar. *S Yor* —1G 85
Deepcut. *Surr* —5A 38
Deepdale. *Cumb* —1G 97
Deepdale. *N Lin* —3D 94
Deepdale. *N Yor* —2A 98
Deeping Gate. *Pet* —5A 76
Deeping St James. *Linc* —5A 76
Deeping St Nicholas. *Linc* —4B 76
Deerhill. *Mor* —3B 160
Deerhurst. *Glos* —3D 48
Deerhurst Walton. *Glos* —3D 49
Deerness. *Orkn* —7E 172
Defford. *Worc* —1E 49
Defynnog. *Powy* —3C 46
Deganwy. *Cnwy* —3G 81
Deighton. *N Yor* —4A 106
Deighton. *W Yor* —3B 92
Deighton. *York* —5A 100
Deiniolen. *Gwyn* —4E 81
Delabole. *Corn* —4A 10
Delamere. *Ches* —4H 83
Delfour. *High* —3C 150
Dellieture. *High* —5E 159
Dell, The. *Suff* —1G 67
Delly End. *Oxon* —4B 50
Delny. *High* —1B 158
Delph. *G Man* —4H 91
Delves. *Dur* —5E 115
Delves, The. *W Mid* —1E 61
Delvin End. *Essx* —2A 54
Dembleby. *Linc* —2H 75
Demelza. *Corn* —2D 6
Denaby Main. *S Yor* —1B 86
Denbeath. *Fife* —4F 137
Denbigh. *Den* —4C 82
Denbury. *Devn* —2E 9
Denby. *Derbs* —1A 74
Denby Common. *Derbs* —1B 74
Denby Dale. *W Yor* —4C 92
Denchworth. *Oxon* —2B 36
Dendron. *Cumb* —2B 96
Deneside. *Dur* —5H 115
Denford. *Nptn* —3G 63
Dengie. *Essx* —5C 54
Denham. *Buck* —2B 38
Denham. *Suff* —4G 65
 (nr. Bury St Edmunds)
Denham. *Suff* —3D 66
 (nr. Eye)
Denham Green. *Buck* —2B 38
Denham Street. *Suff* —3D 66
Denhead. *Aber* —5G 161
 (nr. Ellon)
Denhead. *Aber* —3G 161
 (nr. Strichen)
Denhead. *Fife* —2G 137
Denholm. *Scot* —3H 119
Denholme. *W Yor* —1A 92
Denholme Clough. *W Yor* —1A 92
Denholme Gate. *W Yor* —1A 92
Denio. *Gwyn* —2C 68
Denmead. *Hants* —1E 17
Dennington. *Suff* —4E 67
Denny. *Falk* —1B 128
Denny End. *Cambs* —4D 65
Dennyloanhead. *Falk* —1B 128
Den of Lindores. *Fife* —2E 137
Denshaw. *G Man* —3H 91
Denside. *Aber* —4F 153
Densole. *Kent* —1G 29
Denston. *Suff* —5G 65
Denstone. *Staf* —1F 73
Denstroude. *Kent* —4F 41
Dent. *Cumb* —1G 97
Den, The. *N Ayr* —4E 127
Denton. *Cambs* —2A 64
Denton. *Darl* —3F 105
Denton. *E Sus* —5F 27
Denton. *G Man* —1D 84

Denton. *Kent* —1G 29
Denton. *Linc* —2F 75
Denton. *Norf* —2E 67
Denton. *Nptn* —5F 63
Denton. *N Yor* —5D 98
Denton. *Oxon* —5D 50
Denver. *Norf* —5F 77
Denwick. *Nmbd* —3G 121
Deopham. *Norf* —5C 78
Deopham Green. *Norf* —1C 66
Depden. *Suff* —5G 65
Depden Green. *Suff* —5G 65
Deptford. *G Lon* —3E 39
Deptford. *Wilts* —3F 23
Derby. *Dby C* —2A 74
Derbyhaven. *IOM* —5B 108
Derculich. *Per* —3F 143
Dereham. *Norf* —4B 78
Deri. *Cphy* —5E 47
Derril. *Devn* —2D 10
Derringstone. *Kent* —1G 29
Derrington. *Shrp* —1A 60
Derrington. *Staf* —3C 72
Derriton. *Devn* —2D 10
Derryguaig. *Arg* —5F 139
Derry Hill. *Wilts* —4E 35
Derrythorpe. *N Lin* —4B 94
Dersingham. *Norf* —2F 77
Dervaig. *Arg* —3F 139
Derwen. *Den* —5C 82
Derwen Gam. *Cdgn* —5D 56
Derwenlas. *Powy* —1G 57
Desborough. *Nptn* —2F 63
Desford. *Leics* —5B 74
Detchant. *Nmbd* —1E 121
Dethick. *Derbs* —5H 85
Detling. *Kent* —5B 40
Deuchar. *Ang* —2D 144
Deuddwr. *Powy* —4E 71
Devauden. *Mon* —2H 33
Devil's Bridge. *Cdgn* —3G 57
Devitts Green. *Warw* —1G 61
Devizes. *Wilts* —5F 35
Devonport. *Plym* —3A 8
Devonside. *Clac* —4B 136
Devoran. *Corn* —5B 6
Dewartown. *Midl* —3G 129
Dewlish. *Dors* —3C 14
Dewsbury. *W Yor* —2C 92
Dewshall Court. *Here* —2H 47
Dexbeer. *Devn* —2C 10
Dhoon. *IOM* —3D 108
Dhoor. *IOM* —2D 108
Dhowin. *IOM* —1D 108
Dial Green. *W Sus* —3A 26
Dial Post. *W Sus* —4C 26
Dibberford. *Dors* —2H 13
Dibden. *Hants* —2C 16
Dibden Purlieu. *Hants* —2C 16
Dickleburgh. *Norf* —2D 66
Didbrook. *Glos* —2F 49
Didcot. *Oxon* —2D 36
Diddington. *Cambs* —4A 64
Diddlebury. *Shrp* —2H 59
Didley. *Here* —2H 47
Didling. *W Sus* —1G 17
Didmarton. *Glos* —3D 34
Didsbury. *G Man* —1C 84
Didworthy. *Devn* —2C 8
Digby. *Linc* —5H 87
Digg. *High* —2D 154
Diggle. *G Man* —4A 92
Digmoor. *Lanc* —4C 90
Digswell. *Herts* —4C 52
Dihewyd. *Cdgn* —5D 57
Dilham. *Norf* —3F 79
Dilhorne. *Staf* —1D 73
Dillarburn. *S Lan* —5B 128
Dillington. *Cambs* —4A 64
Dilston. *Nmbd* —3C 114
Dilton Marsh. *Wilts* —2D 22
Dilwyn. *Here* —5G 59
Dimmer. *Som* —3B 22

Dimple. *G Man* —3F 91
Dinas. *Carm* —1G 43
Dinas. *Gwyn* —5D 81
Dinas. *Gwyn* —2B 68
Dinas. *Pemb* —1E 43
Dinas Dinlle. *Gwyn* —5D 80
Dinas Mawddwy. *Gwyn* —4A 70
Dinas Powys. *V Glam* —4E 33
Dinbych. *Den* —4C 82
Dinbych-y-Pysgod. *Pemb* —4F 43
Dinckley. *Lanc* —1E 91
Dinder. *Som* —2A 22
Dinedor. *Here* —2A 48
Dinedor Cross. *Here* —2A 48
Dingestow. *Mon* —4H 47
Dingle. *Mers* —2F 83
Dingleden. *Kent* —2C 28
Dingleton. *Scot* —1H 119
Dingley. *Nptn* —2E 63
Dingwall. *High* —3H 157
Dinmael. *Cnwy* —1C 70
Dinnet. *Aber* —4B 152
Dinnington. *Som* —1H 13
Dinnington. *S Yor* —2C 86
Dinnington. *Tyne* —2F 115
Dinorwic. *Gwyn* —4E 81
Dinton. *Buck* —4F 51
Dinton. *Wilts* —3F 23
Dinworthy. *Devn* —1D 10
Dipley. *Hants* —1F 25
Dippen. *Arg* —2B 122
Dippenhall. *Surr* —2G 25
Dippertown. *Devn* —4E 11
Dippin. *N Ayr* —3E 123
Dipple. *S Ayr* —4B 116
Diptford. *Devn* —3D 8
Dipton. *Dur* —4E 115
Dirleton. *E Lot* —1B 130
Dirt Pot. *Nmbd* —5B 114
Discoed. *Powy* —4E 59
Diseworth. *Leics* —3B 74
Dishforth. *N Yor* —2F 99
Disley. *Ches* —2D 85
Diss. *Norf* —3D 66
Disserth. *Powy* —5C 58
Distington. *Cumb* —2B 102
Ditchampton. *Wilts* —3F 23
Ditcheat. *Som* —3B 22
Ditchingham. *Norf* —1F 67
Ditchling. *E Sus* —4E 27
Ditteridge. *Wilts* —5D 34
Dittisham. *Devn* —3E 9
Ditton. *Hal* —2G 83
Ditton. *Kent* —5B 40
Ditton Green. *Cambs* —5F 65
Ditton Priors. *Shrp* —2A 60
Divach. *High* —1G 149
Dixonfield. *High* —2D 168
Dixton. *Glos* —2F 49
Dixton. *Mon* —4A 48
Dizzard. *Corn* —3B 10
Dobcross. *G Man* —4H 91
Dobs Hill. *Flin* —4F 83
Dobson's Bridge. *Shrp* —2G 71
Dobwalls. *Corn* —2G 7
Doccombe. *Devn* —4A 12
Dochgarroch. *High* —4A 158
Docking. *Norf* —2G 77
Docklow. *Here* —5H 59
Dockray. *Cumb* —2E 103
Doc Penfro. *Pemb* —4D 42
Dodbrooke. *Devn* —4D 8
Doddenham. *Worc* —5B 60
Doddinghurst. *Essx* —1G 39
Doddington. *Cambs* —1C 64
Doddington. *Kent* —5D 40
Doddington. *Linc* —4F 87
Doddington. *Nmbd* —1D 121
Doddington. *Shrp* —3A 60
Doddiscombsleigh. *Devn* —4B 12
Doddshill. *Norf* —2G 77
Dodford. *Nptn* —4D 62
Dodford. *Worc* —3D 60

Dodington. *Som* —2E 21
Dodington. *S Glo* —4C 34
Dodleston. *Ches* —4F 83
Dods Leigh. *Staf* —2E 73
Dodworth. *S Yor* —4D 92
Doe Lea. *Derbs* —4B 86
Dogdyke. *Linc* —5B 88
Dogmersfield. *Hants* —1F 25
Dogsthorpe. *Pet* —5B 76
Dog Village. *Devn* —3C 12
Dolanog. *Powy* —4C 70
Dolau. *Powy* —4D 58
Dolau. *Rhon* —3D 32
Dolbenmaen. *Gwyn* —1E 69
Doley. *Shrp* —3B 72
Dol-fach. *Powy* —5B 70
 (nr. Llanbrynmair)
Dolfach. *Powy* —3B 58
 (nr. Llanidloes)
Dolfor. *Powy* —2D 58
Dolgarrog. *Cnwy* —4G 81
Dolgellau. *Gwyn* —4G 69
Dolgoch. *Gwyn* —5F 69
Dol-gran. *Carm* —2E 45
Dolhelfa. *Powy* —3B 58
Doll. *High* —3F 165
Dollar. *Clac* —4B 136
Dolley Green. *Powy* —4E 59
Dollwen. *Cdgn* —2F 57
Dolphin. *Flin* —3D 82
Dolphingstone. *E Lot* —2G 129
Dolphinholme. *Lanc* —4E 97
Dolphinton. *S Lan* —5E 129
Dolton. *Devn* —1F 11
Dolwen. *Cnwy* —3A 82
Dolwyddelan. *Cnwy* —5G 81
Dol-y-Bont. *Cdgn* —2F 57
Dolyhir. *Powy* —5E 59
Domgay. *Powy* —4E 71
Doncaster. *S Yor* —4F 93
Donhead St Andrew. *Wilts* —4E 23
Donhead St Mary. *Wilts* —4E 23
Doniford. *Som* —2D 20
Donington. *Linc* —2B 76
Donington. *Shrp* —5C 72
Donington Eaudike. *Linc* —2B 76
Donington on Bain. *Linc* —2B 88
Donington South Ing. *Linc* —2B 76
Donisthorpe. *Leics* —4H 73
Donkey Town. *Surr* —4A 38
Donna Nook. *Linc* —1D 88
Donnington. *Glos* —3G 49
Donnington. *Here* —2C 48
Donnington. *Shrp* —5H 71
Donnington. *Telf* —4B 72
Donnington. *W Ber* —5C 36
Donnington. *W Sus* —2G 17
Donnington le Heath. *Leics* —4B 74
Donyatt. *Som* —1G 13
Doomsday Green. *W Sus* —2C 26
Doonbank. *E Ayr* —4D 116
Doonfoot. *S Ayr* —3C 116
Doonholm. *S Ayr* —3C 116
Dorback Lodge. *High* —2E 151
Dorchester. *Dors* —3B 14
Dorchester. *Oxon* —2D 36
Dordon. *Warw* —5G 73
Dore. *S Yor* —2H 85
Dores. *High* —5H 157
Dorking. *Surr* —1C 26
Dorking Tye. *Suff* —2C 54
Dormansland. *Surr* —1F 27
Dormans Park. *Surr* —1E 27
Dormanstown. *Red C* —2C 106
Dormington. *Here* —1A 48
Dormston. *Worc* —5D 60
Dorn. *Glos* —2H 49
Dorney. *Buck* —3A 38
Dornie. *High* —1A 148
Dornoch. *High* —5E 165
Dornock. *Dum* —3D 112
Dorridge. *W Mid* —3F 61
Dorrington. *Linc* —5H 87

Dunton—East Molesey

Dunton. *Norf* —2A **78**
Dunton Bassett. *Leics* —1C **62**
Dunton Green. *Kent* —5G **39**
Dunton Patch. *Norf* —2A **78**
Duntulm. *High* —1D **154**
Dunure. *S Ayr* —3B **116**
Dunvant. *Swan* —3E **31**
Dunvegan. *High* —4B **154**
Dunwich. *Suff* —3G **67**
Dunwood. *Staf* —5D **84**
Durdar. *Cumb* —4F **113**
Durgates. *E Sus* —2H **27**
Durham. *Dur* —5F **115**
Durisdeer. *Dum* —4A **118**
Durisdeermill. *Dum* —4A **118**
Durkar. *W Yor* —3D **92**
Durleigh. *Som* —3F **21**
Durley. *Hants* —1D **16**
Durley. *Wilts* —5H **35**
Durley Street. *Hants* —1D **16**
Durlow Common. *Here* —2B **48**
Durnamuck. *High* —4E **163**
Durness. *High* —2E **166**
Durno. *Aber* —1E **152**
Durns Town. *Hants* —3A **16**
Duror. *High* —3D **141**
Durran. *Arg* —3G **133**
Durran. *High* —2D **169**
Durrant Green. *Kent* —2C **28**
Durrants. *Hants* —1F **17**
Durrington. *W Sus* —5C **26**
Durrington. *Wilts* —2G **23**
Dursley. *Glos* —2C **34**
Dursley Cross. *Glos* —4B **48**
Durston. *Som* —4F **21**
Durweston. *Dors* —2D **14**
Duston. *Nptn* —4E **62**
Duthil. *High* —1D **150**
Dutlas. *Powy* —3E **58**
Duton Hill. *Essx* —3G **53**
Dutson. *Corn* —4D **10**
Dutton. *Ches* —3H **83**
Duxford. *Cambs* —1E **53**
Duxford. *Oxon* —2B **36**
Dwygyfylchi. *Cnwy* —3G **81**
Dwyran. *IOA* —4D **80**
Dyce. *Aber C* —2F **153**
Dye House. *Nmbd* —4C **114**
Dyffryn. *B'End* —2B **32**
Dyffryn. *Carm* —2H **43**
Dyffryn. *IOA* —3B **80**
Dyffryn. *Pemb* —1D **42**
Dyffryn. *V Glam* —4D **32**
Dyffryn Ardudwy. *Gwyn* —3E **69**
Dyffryn Castell. *Cdgn* —2G **57**
Dyffryn Ceidrych. *Carm* —3H **45**
Dyffryn Cellwen. *Neat* —5B **46**
Dyke. *Linc* —3A **76**
Dyke. *Mor* —3D **159**
Dykehead. *Ang* —2C **144**
Dykehead. *N Lan* —3B **128**
Dykehead. *Stir* —4E **135**
Dykends. *Ang* —3B **144**
Dykesfield. *Cumb* —4E **112**
Dylife. *Powy* —1A **58**
Dymchurch. *Kent* —3F **29**
Dymock. *Glos* —2C **48**
Dyrham. *S Glo* —4C **34**
Dysart. *Fife* —4F **137**
Dyserth. *Den* —3C **82**

E

Eachwick. *Nmbd* —2E **115**
Eadar Dha Fhadhail. *W Isl* —4C **171**
Eagland Hill. *Lanc* —5D **96**
Eagle. *Linc* —4F **87**
Eagle Barnsdale. *Linc* —4F **87**
Eagle Moor. *Linc* —4F **87**
Eaglescliffe. *Stoc T* —3B **106**
Eaglesfield. *Cumb* —2B **102**
Eaglesfield. *Dum* —2D **112**
Eaglesham. *E Ren* —4G **127**
Eaglethorpe. *Nptn* —1H **63**
Eagley. *G Man* —3F **91**
Eairy. *IOM* —4C **108**
Eakley Lanes. *Mil* —5F **63**
Eakring. *Notts* —4D **86**
Ealand. *N Lin* —3A **94**
Ealing. *G Lon* —2C **38**
Eallabus. *Arg* —3B **124**
Eals. *Nmbd* —4H **113**
Eamont Bridge. *Cumb* —2G **103**
Earby. *Lanc* —5B **98**
Earcroft. *Bkbn* —2E **91**
Eardington. *Shrp* —1B **60**
Eardisland. *Here* —5G **59**
Eardisley. *Here* —1G **47**
Eardiston. *Shrp* —3F **71**
Eardiston. *Worc* —4A **60**
Earith. *Cambs* —3C **64**
Earle. *Nmbd* —2D **121**
Earlesfield. *Linc* —2G **75**
Earlestown. *Mers* —1H **83**
Earley. *Wok* —4F **37**
Earlham. *Norf* —5D **78**
Earlish. *High* —2C **154**
Earls Barton. *Nptn* —4F **63**
Earls Colne. *Essx* —3B **54**
Earls Common. *Worc* —5D **60**
Earl's Croome. *Worc* —1D **48**
Earlsdon. *W Mid* —3H **61**
Earlsferry. *Fife* —3G **137**
Earlsford. *Aber* —5F **161**
Earl's Green. *Suff* —4C **66**
Earlsheaton. *W Yor* —2C **92**
Earl Shilton. *Leics* —1B **62**
Earl Soham. *Suff* —4E **67**
Earl Sterndale. *Derbs* —4E **85**
Earlston. *E Ayr* —1D **116**
Earlston. *Scot* —1H **119**
Earl Stonham. *Suff* —5D **66**
Earlstoun. *Dum* —1D **110**
Earlswood. *Mon* —2H **33**
Earlswood. *Warw* —3F **61**
Earlyvale. *Scot* —4F **129**
Earnley. *W Sus* —3G **17**
Earsairidh. *W Isl* —9C **170**
Earsdon. *Tyne* —2G **115**
Earsham. *Norf* —2F **67**
Earsham Street. *Suff* —3E **67**
Earswick. *York* —4A **100**
Eartham. *W Sus* —5A **26**
Earthcott Green. *S Glo* —3B **34**
Easby. *N Yor* —4C **106**
(nr. Great Ayton)
Easby. *N Yor* —4E **105**
(nr. Richmond)
Easdale. *Arg* —2E **133**
Easebourne. *W Sus* —4G **25**
Easenhall. *Warw* —3B **62**
Eashing. *Surr* —1A **26**
Easington. *Buck* —4E **51**
Easington. *Dur* —5H **115**
Easington. *E Yor* —3G **95**
Easington. *Nmbd* —1F **121**
Easington. *Oxon* —2C **50**
(nr. Banbury)
Easington. *Oxon* —2E **37**
(nr. Watlington)
Easington. *Red C* —3E **107**
Easington Colliery. *Dur* —5H **115**
Easington Lane. *Tyne* —5G **115**
Easingwold. *N Yor* —3H **99**
Easole Street. *Kent* —5G **41**
Eassie. *Ang* —4C **144**
Eassie & Nevay. *Ang* —4C **144**
East Aberthaw. *V Glam* —5D **32**
Eastacombe. *Devn* —4F **19**
Eastacott. *Devn* —4G **19**
East Allington. *Devn* —4D **8**
East Anstey. *Devn* —4B **20**
East Anton. *Hants* —2B **24**
East Appleton. *N Yor* —5F **105**
East Ardsley. *W Yor* —2D **92**
East Ashley. *Devn* —1G **11**
East Ashling. *W Sus* —2G **17**
East Aston. *Hants* —2C **24**
East Ayton. *N Yor* —1D **101**
East Bagborough. *Som* —3E **21**
East Barkwith. *Linc* —2A **88**
East Barming. *Kent* —5B **40**
East Barnby. *N Yor* —3F **107**
East Barnet. *G Lon* —1D **39**
East Barns. *E Lot* —2D **130**
East Barsham. *Norf* —2B **78**
East Beach. *W Sus* —3G **17**
East Beckham. *Norf* —1D **78**
East Bedfont. *G Lon* —3B **38**
East Bennan. *N Ayr* —3D **123**
East Bergholt. *Suff* —2D **54**
East Bierley. *W Yor* —2B **92**
East Blatchington. *E Sus* —5F **27**
East Bliney. *Norf* —4B **78**
East Bloxworth. *Dors* —3D **15**
East Boldre. *Hants* —2B **16**
East Bolton. *Nmbd* —3F **121**
Eastbourne. *Darl* —3F **105**
Eastbourne. *E Sus* —5H **27**
East Brent. *Som* —1G **21**
Eastbridge. *Devn* —1E **11**
East Bridge. *Suff* —4G **67**
East Bridgford. *Notts* —1D **74**
East Briscoe. *Dur* —3C **104**
East Brunton. *Tyne* —2F **115**
East Buckland. *Devn* —3G **19**
East Budleigh. *Devn* —4D **12**
Eastburn. *W Yor* —5C **98**
East Burnham. *Buck* —2A **38**
East Burrafirth. *Shet* —6E **173**
East Burton. *Dors* —4D **14**
Eastbury. *Herts* —1B **38**
Eastbury. *W Ber* —4B **36**
East Butsfield. *Dur* —5E **115**
East Butterleigh. *Devn* —2C **12**
East Butterwick. *N Lin* —4B **94**
Eastby. *N Yor* —4C **98**
East Calder. *W Lot* —3D **129**
East Carleton. *Norf* —5D **78**
East Carlton. *Nptn* —2F **63**
East Carlton. *W Yor* —5E **98**
East Chaldon. *Dors* —4C **14**
East Challow. *Oxon* —3B **36**
East Charlton. *Devn* —4D **8**
East Chelborough. *Dors* —2A **14**
East Chiltington. *E Sus* —4E **27**
East Chinnock. *Som* —1H **13**
East Chisenbury. *Wilts* —1G **23**
Eastchurch. *Kent* —3D **40**
East Clandon. *Surr* —5B **38**
East Claydon. *Buck* —3F **51**
East Clevedon. *N Som* —4H **33**
East Clyne. *High* —3F **165**
East Clyth. *High* —5E **169**
East Coker. *Som* —1A **14**
Eastcombe. *Glos* —5D **49**
East Combe. *Som* —3E **21**
East Common. *N Yor* —1G **93**
East Compton. *Som* —2B **22**
East Cornworthy. *Devn* —3E **9**
Eastcote. *G Lon* —2C **38**
Eastcote. *Nptn* —5D **62**
Eastcote. *W Mid* —3F **61**
Eastcott. *Corn* —1C **10**
Eastcott. *Wilts* —1F **23**
East Cottingwith. *E Yor* —5B **100**
East Coulston. *Wilts* —1E **23**
Eastcourt. *Wilts* —5H **35**
(nr. Pewsey)
Eastcourt. *Wilts* —2E **35**
(nr. Tetbury)
East Cowes. *IOW* —3D **16**
East Cowick. *E Yor* —2G **93**
East Cowton. *N Yor* —4A **106**
East Cramlington. *Nmbd* —2F **115**
East Cranmore. *Som* —2B **22**
East Creech. *Dors* —4E **15**
East Croachy. *High* —1A **150**
East Dean. *E Sus* —5G **27**
East Dean. *Glos* —3B **48**
East Dean. *Hants* —4A **24**
East Dean. *W Sus* —4A **26**
East Down. *Devn* —2G **19**
East Drayton. *Notts* —3E **87**
East Dundry. *N Som* —5A **34**
East Ella. *Hull* —2D **94**
East End. *Cambs* —3C **64**
East End. *Dors* —3E **15**
East End. *E Yor* —4F **101**
(nr. Ulrome)
East End. *E Yor* —2F **95**
(nr. Withernsea)
East End. *Hants* —3B **16**
(nr. Lymington)
East End. *Hants* —5C **36**
(nr. Newbury)
East End. *Herts* —3E **53**
East End. *Kent* —3D **40**
(nr. Minster)
East End. *Kent* —2C **28**
(nr. Tenterden)
East End. *N Som* —5H **33**
East End. *Oxon* —4B **50**
East End. *Som* —1A **22**
East End. *Suff* —2E **54**
Easter Ardross. *High* —1A **158**
Easter Balgedie. *Per* —3D **136**
Easter Balmoral. *Aber* —4G **151**
Easter Brae. *High* —2A **158**
Easter Buckieburn. *Stir* —1A **128**
Easter Bush. *Midl* —3F **129**
Easter Compton. *S Glo* —3A **34**
Easter Fearn. *High* —5D **164**
Easter Galcantray. *High* —4C **158**
Eastergate. *W Sus* —5A **26**
Easterhouse. *Glas* —3H **127**
Easter Howgate. *Midl* —3F **129**
Easter Kinkell. *High* —3H **157**
Easter Lednathie. *Ang* —2C **144**
Easter Ogil. *Ang* —2D **144**
Easter Ord. *Aber* —3F **153**
Easter Quarff. *Shet* —8F **173**
Easter Skeld. *Shet* —7E **173**
Easter Suddie. *High* —3A **158**
Easterton. *Wilts* —1F **23**
Eastertown. *Som* —1G **21**
Eastertown of Auchleuchries. *Aber* —5H **161**
Easter Tulloch. *Aber* —1G **145**
East Everleigh. *Wilts* —1H **23**
East Farleigh. *Kent* —5B **40**
East Farndon. *Nptn* —2E **62**
East Ferry. *Linc* —1F **87**
Eastfield. *N Lan* —3B **128**
(nr. Caldercruix)
Eastfield. *N Lan* —3B **128**
(nr. Harthill)
Eastfield. *N Yor* —1E **101**
Eastfield. *S Lan* —3H **127**
Eastfield Hall. *Nmbd* —4G **121**
East Fortune. *E Lot* —2B **130**
East Garforth. *W Yor* —1E **93**
East Garston. *W Ber* —4B **36**
Eastgate. *Dur* —1C **104**
Eastgate. *Norf* —3D **78**
East Ginge. *Oxon* —3C **36**
East Gores. *Essx* —3B **54**
East Goscote. *Leics* —4D **74**
East Grafton. *Wilts* —5A **36**
East Grimstead. *Wilts* —4H **23**
East Grinstead. *W Sus* —2E **27**
East Guldeford. *E Sus* —3D **28**
East Haddon. *Nptn* —4D **62**
East Hagbourne. *Oxon* —3D **36**
East Halton. *N Lin* —2E **95**
East Ham. *G Lon* —2F **39**
Eastham. *Mers* —2F **83**
Eastham. *Worc* —4A **60**
Eastham Ferry. *Mers* —2F **83**
Easthampstead. *Brac* —5G **37**
Easthampton. *Here* —4G **59**
East Hanney. *Oxon* —2C **36**
East Hanningfield. *Essx* —5A **54**
East Hardwick. *W Yor* —3E **93**
East Harling. *Norf* —2B **66**
East Harlsey. *N Yor* —5B **106**
East Harnham. *Wilts* —4G **23**
East Harptree. *Bath* —1A **22**
East Hartford. *Nmbd* —2F **115**
East Harting. *W Sus* —1G **17**
East Hatch. *Wilts* —4E **23**
East Hatley. *Cambs* —5B **64**
Easthaugh. *Norf* —4C **78**
East Hauxwell. *N Yor* —5E **105**
East Haven. *Ang* —5E **145**
Eastheath. *Wok* —5G **37**
East Heckington. *Linc* —1A **76**
East Hedleyhope. *Dur* —5E **115**
East Hendred. *Oxon* —3C **36**
East Heslerton. *N Yor* —2D **100**
East Hoathly. *E Sus* —4G **27**
Easthope. *Shrp* —1H **59**
Easthorpe. *Essx* —3C **54**
Easthorpe. *Leics* —2F **75**
East Horrington. *Som* —2A **22**
East Horsley. *Surr* —5B **38**
East Horton. *Nmbd* —1E **121**
Easthouses. *Midl* —3G **129**
East Howe. *Bour* —3F **15**
East Huntspill. *Som* —2G **21**
East Hyde. *Beds* —4B **52**
East Ilsley. *W Ber* —3C **36**
Eastington. *Devn* —2H **11**
Eastington. *Glos* —4G **49**
(nr. Northleach)
Eastington. *Glos* —5C **48**
(nr. Stonehouse)
East Keal. *Linc* —4C **88**
East Kennett. *Wilts* —5G **35**
East Keswick. *W Yor* —5F **99**
East Kilbride. *S Lan* —4H **127**
East Kirkby. *Linc* —4C **88**
East Knapton. *N Yor* —2C **100**
East Knighton. *Dors* —4D **14**
East Knowstone. *Devn* —4B **20**
East Knoyle. *Wilts* —3D **23**
East Kyloe. *Nmbd* —1E **121**
East Lambrook. *Som* —1H **13**
East Langdon. *Kent* —1H **29**
East Langton. *Leics* —1E **63**
East Langwell. *High* —3E **164**
East Lavant. *W Sus* —2G **17**
East Lavington. *W Sus* —4A **26**
East Layton. *N Yor* —4E **105**
Eastleach Martin. *Glos* —5H **49**
Eastleach Turville. *Glos* —5G **49**
East Leake. *Notts* —3C **74**
East Learmouth. *Nmbd* —1C **120**
Eastleigh. *Devn* —4E **19**
(nr. Bideford)
East Leigh. *Devn* —2H **11**
(nr. Crediton)
East Leigh. *Devn* —3C **8**
(nr. Modbury)
Eastleigh. *Hants* —1C **16**
East Lexham. *Norf* —4A **78**
East Lilburn. *Nmbd* —2E **121**
Eastling. *Kent* —5D **40**
East Linton. *E Lot* —2B **130**
East Liss. *Hants* —4F **25**
East Lockinge. *Oxon* —3C **36**
East Looe. *Corn* —3G **7**
East Lound. *N Lin* —1E **87**
East Lulworth. *Dors* —4D **14**
East Lutton. *N Yor* —3D **100**
East Lydford. *Som* —3A **22**
East Mains. *Aber* —4D **152**
East Malling. *Kent* —5B **40**
East Marden. *W Sus* —1G **17**
East Markham. *Notts* —3E **87**
East Marton. *N Yor* —4B **98**
East Meon. *Hants* —4E **25**
East Mersea. *Essx* —4D **54**
East Mey. *High* —1F **169**
East Midlands Airport. *Leics* —3B **74**
East Molesey. *Surr* —4C **38**

Eastmoor. Norf —5G 77
East Morden. Dors —3E 15
East Morton. W Yor —5C 98
East Ness. N Yor —2A 100
East Newton. E Yor —1F 95
East Newton. N Yor —2A 100
Eastney. Port —3E 17
Eastnor. Here —2C 48
East Norton. Leics —5E 75
East Oakley. Hants —1D 24
Eastoft. N Lin —3B 94
East Ogwell. Devn —5B 12
Easton. Cambs —3A 64
Easton. Cumb —4D 112
(nr. Burgh by Sands)
Easton. Cumb —2F 113
(nr. Longtown)
Easton. Devn —4H 11
Easton. Dors —5B 14
Easton. Hants —3D 24
Easton. Linc —3G 75
Easton. Norf —4D 78
Easton. Som —2A 22
Easton. Suff —5E 67
Easton. Wilts —4D 35
Easton Grey. Wilts —3D 35
Easton-in-Gordano. N Som —4A 34
Easton Maudit. Nptn —5F 63
Easton on the Hill. Nptn —5H 75
Easton Royal. Wilts —5H 35
East Orchard. Dors —1D 14
East Ord. Nmbd —4F 131
East Panson. Devn —3D 10
East Peckham. Kent —1A 28
East Pennard. Som —3A 22
East Perry. Cambs —4A 64
East Pitcorthie. Fife —3H 137
East Portlemouth. Devn —5D 8
East Prawle. Devn —5D 9
East Preston. W Sus —5B 26
East Putford. Devn —1D 10
East Quantoxhead. Som —2E 21
East Rainton. Tyne —5G 115
East Ravendale. NE Lin —1B 88
East Raynham. Norf —3A 78
Eastrea. Cambs —1B 64
East Rhidorroch Lodge. High
—4G 163
Eastriggs. Dum —3D 112
East Rigton. W Yor —5F 99
Eastrington. E Yor —1A 94
East Rounton. N Yor —4B 106
East Row. N Yor —3F 107
East Rudham. Norf —3H 77
East Runton. Norf —1D 78
East Ruston. Norf —3F 79
Eastry. Kent —5H 41
East Saltoun. E Lot —3A 130
East Shaws. Dur —3D 105
East Shefford. W Ber —4B 36
Eastshore. Shet —10F 173
East Sleekburn. Nmbd —1F 115
East Somerton. Norf —4G 79
East Stockwith. Linc —1E 87
East Stoke. Dors —4D 14
East Stoke. Notts —1E 75
East Stoke. Som —1H 13
East Stour. Dors —4D 22
East Stourmouth. Kent —4G 41
East Stowford. Devn —4G 19
East Stratton. Hants —2D 24
East Studdal. Kent —1H 29
East Taphouse. Corn —2F 7
East-the-Water. Devn —4E 19
East Thirston. Nmbd —5F 121
East Tilbury. Thur —3A 40
East Tisted. Hants —3F 25
East Torrington. Linc —2A 88
East Tuddenham. Norf —4C 78
East Tytherley. Hants —4A 24
East Tytherton. Wilts —4E 35
East Village. Devn —2B 12
Eastville. Linc —5D 88

East Wall. Shrp —1H 59
East Walton. Norf —4G 77
East Week. Devn —3G 11
East Wellow. Hants —4B 24
East Wemyss. Fife —4F 137
East Whitburn. W Lot —3C 128
Eastwick. Herts —4E 53
Eastwick. Shet —4E 173
East Williamston. Pemb —4E 43
East Winch. Norf —4F 77
East Winterslow. Wilts —3H 23
East Wittering. W Sus —3F 17
East Witton. N Yor —1D 98
Eastwood. Notts —1B 74
Eastwood. S'end —2C 40
East Woodburn. Nmbd —1C 114
Eastwood End. Cambs —1D 64
East Woodhay. Hants —5C 36
East Woodlands. Som —2C 22
East Worldham. Hants —3F 25
East Worlington. Devn —1A 12
East Youlstone. Devn —1C 10
Eathorpe. Warw —4A 62
Eaton. Ches —4C 84
(nr. Congleton)
Eaton. Ches —4H 83
(nr. Kelsall)
Eaton. Leics —3E 75
Eaton. Norf —2F 77
(nr. Heacham)
Eaton. Norf —5E 78
(nr. Norwich)
Eaton. Notts —3E 86
Eaton. Oxon —5C 50
Eaton. Shrp —2F 59
(nr. Bishop's Castle)
Eaton. Shrp —1H 59
(nr. Church Stretton)
Eaton Bishop. Here —2H 47
Eaton Bray. Beds —3H 51
Eaton Constantine. Shrp —5H 71
Eaton Green. Beds —3H 51
Eaton Hastings. Oxon —2A 36
Eaton Socon. Cambs —5A 64
Eaton upon Tern. Shrp —3A 72
Eau Brink. Norf —4E 77
Eaves Green. W Mid —2G 61
Ebberston. N Yor —1C 100
Ebbesbourne Wake. Wilts —4E 23
Ebblake. Dors —2G 15
Ebbw Vale. Blae —5E 47
Ebchester. Dur —4E 115
Ebford. Devn —4C 12
Ebley. Glos —5D 48
Ebnal. Ches —1G 71
Ebrington. Glos —1G 49
Ebsworthy Town. Devn —3F 11
Ecchinswell. Hants —1D 24
Ecclefechan. Dum —2C 112
Eccles. G Man —1B 84
Eccles. Kent —4B 40
Eccles. Scot —5D 130
Ecclesall. S Yor —2H 85
Ecclesfield. S Yor —1A 86
Eccles Green. Here —1G 47
Eccleshall. Staf —3C 72
Eccleshill. W Yor —1B 92
Ecclesmachan. W Lot —2D 128
Eccles on Sea. Norf —3G 79
Eccles Road. Norf —1C 66
Eccleston. Ches —4G 83
Eccleston. Lanc —3D 90
Eccleston. Mers —1G 83
Eccup. W Yor —5E 99
Echt. Aber —3E 153
Eckford. Scot —2B 120
Eckington. Derbs —3B 86
Eckington. Worc —1E 49
Ecton. Nptn —4F 63
Edale. Derbs —2F 85
Eday Airport. Orkn —4E 172
Edburton. W Sus —4D 26

Edderside. Cumb —5C 112
Edderton. High —5E 164
Eddington. W Ber —5B 36
Eddleston. Scot —5F 129
Eddlewood. S Lan —4A 128
Edenbridge. Kent —1F 27
Edendonich. Arg —1A 134
Edenfield. Lanc —3G 91
Edenhall. Cumb —1G 103
Edenham. Linc —3H 75
Edensor. Derbs —4G 85
Edentaggart. Arg —4C 134
Edenthorpe. S Yor —4G 93
Eden Vale. Dur —1B 106
Edern. Gwyn —2B 68
Edgarley. Som —3A 22
Edgbaston. W Mid —2E 61
Edgcott. Buck —3E 51
Edgcott. Som —3B 20
Edge. Glos —5D 48
Edge. Shrp —5F 71
Edgebolton. Shrp —3H 71
Edge End. Glos —4A 48
Edgefield. Norf —2C 78
Edgefield Street. Norf —2C 78
Edge Green. Ches —5G 83
Edgehead. Midl —3G 129
Edgeley. Shrp —1H 71
Edgeside. Lanc —2G 91
Edgeworth. Glos —5E 49
Edgiock. Worc —4E 61
Edgmond. Telf —4B 72
Edgmond Marsh. Telf —3B 72
Edgton. Shrp —2F 59
Edgware. G Lon —1C 38
Edgworth. Bkbn —3F 91
Edinbane. High —3C 154
Edinburgh. Edin —2F 129
Edinburgh Airport. Edin —2E 129
Edingale. Staf —4G 73
Edingley. Notts —5D 86
Edingthorpe. Norf —2F 79
Edington. Som —3G 21
Edington. Wilts —1E 23
Edingworth. Som —1G 21
Edistone. Devn —4C 18
Edithmead. Som —2G 21
Edith Weston. Rut —5G 75
Edlaston. Derbs —1F 73
Edlesborough. Buck —4H 51
Edlingham. Nmbd —4F 121
Edlington. Linc —3B 88
Edmondsham. Dors —1F 15
Edmondsley. Dur —5F 115
Edmondthorpe. Leics —4F 75
Edmonstone. Orkn —5E 172
Edmonton. Corn —1D 6
Edmonton. G Lon —1E 39
Edmundbyers. Dur —4D 114
Ednam. Scot —1B 120
Ednaston. Derbs —1G 73
Edney Common. Essx —5G 53
Edrom. Scot —4E 131
Edstaston. Shrp —2H 71
Edstone. Warw —4F 61
Edwalton. Notts —2D 74
Edwardstone. Suff —1C 54
Edwardsville. Mer T —2D 32
Edwinsford. Carm —2G 45
Edwinstowe. Notts —4D 86
Edworth. Beds —1C 52
Edwyn Ralph. Here —5A 60
Edzell. Ang —2F 145
Efail-fach. Neat —2A 32
Efail Isaf. Rhon —3D 32
Efailnewydd. Gwyn —2C 68
Efail-rhyd. Powy —3D 70
Efailwen. Carm —2F 43
Efenechtyd. Den —5D 82
Effingham. Surr —5C 38
Effingham Common. Surr —5C 38
Effirth. Shet —6E 173
Efflinch. Staf —4F 73

Efford. Devn —2B 12
Egbury. Hants —1C 24
Egdon. Worc —5D 60
Egerton. G Man —3F 91
Egerton. Kent —1D 28
Egerton Forstal. Kent —1C 28
Eggborough. N Yor —2F 93
Eggbuckland. Plym —3A 8
Eggesford. Devn —1G 11
Eggington. Beds —3H 51
Eggington. Derbs —3G 73
Egglescliffe. Stoc T —3B 106
Eggleston. Dur —2C 104
Egham. Surr —3B 38
Egham Hythe. Surr —3B 38
Egleton. Rut —5F 75
Eglingham. Nmbd —3F 121
Egloshayle. Corn —5A 10
Egloskerry. Corn —4C 10
Eglwysbach. Cnwy —3H 81
Eglwys Brewis. V Glam —5D 32
Eglwys Fach. Cdgn —1F 57
Eglwyswrw. Pemb —1F 43
Egmanton. Notts —4E 87
Egremont. Cumb —3B 102
Egremont. Mers —1F 83
Egton. N Yor —4F 107
Egton Bridge. N Yor —4F 107
Egypt. Buck —2A 38
Egypt. Hants —2C 24
Eight Ash Green. Essx —3C 54
Eight Mile Burn. Midl —4E 129
Eignaig. High —4B 140
Eilanreach. High —2G 147
Eildon. Scot —1H 119
Eileanach Lodge. High —2H 157
Eilean Iarmain. High —2F 147
Eisgean. W Isl —6F 171
Eishken. W Isl —6F 171
Eisingrug. Gwyn —2F 69
Elan Village. Powy —4B 58
Elberton. S Glo —3B 34
Elbridge. W Sus —5A 26
Elburton. Plym —3B 8
Elcho. Per —1D 136
Elcombe. Swin —3G 35
Elcot. W Ber —5B 36
Eldernell. Cambs —1C 64
Eldersfield. Worc —2D 48
Elderslie. Ren —3F 127
Elder Street. Essx —2F 53
Eldon. Dur —2F 105
Eldroth. N Yor —3G 97
Eldwick. W Yor —5D 98
Elfhowe. Cumb —5F 103
Elford. Nmbd —1F 121
Elford. Staf —4F 73
Elford Closes. Cambs —3D 65
Elgin. Mor —2G 159
Elgol. High —2D 146
Elham. Kent —1F 29
Elie. Fife —3G 137
Eling. Hants —1B 16
Eling. W Ber —4D 36
Elishaw. Nmbd —5C 120
Elizafield. Dum —2B 112
Elkesley. Notts —3D 86
Elkington. Nptn —3D 62
Elkins Green. Essx —5G 53
Elkstone. Glos —4E 49
Ellan. High —1C 150
Ellanbeich. Arg —2E 133
Elland. W Yor —2B 92
Ellary. Arg —2F 125
Ellastone. Staf —1F 73
Ellbridge. Corn —2A 8
Ellel. Lanc —4D 97
Ellemford. Scot —3D 130
Ellenborough. Cumb —1B 102
Ellenbrook. Herts —5C 52
Ellenhall. Staf —3C 72
Ellen's Green. Surr —2B 26

Ellerbec. N Yor —5B 106
Ellerburn. N Yor —1C 100
Ellerby. N Yor —3E 107
Ellerdine. Telf —3A 72
Ellerdine Heath. Telf —3A 72
Ellerhayes. Devn —2C 12
Elleric. Arg —4E 141
Ellerker. E Yor —2C 94
Ellerton. E Yor —1H 93
Ellerton. N Yor —5F 105
Ellerton. Shrp —3B 72
Ellesborough. Buck —5G 51
Ellesmere. Shrp —2G 71
Ellesmere Port. Ches —3G 83
Ellingham. Hants —2G 15
Ellingham. Norf —1F 67
Ellingham. Nmbd —2F 121
Ellingstring. N Yor —1D 98
Ellington. Cambs —3A 64
Ellington. Nmbd —5G 121
Ellington Thorpe. Cambs —3A 64
Ellisfield. Hants —2E 25
Elishadder. High —2E 155
Ellistown. Leics —4B 74
Ellon. Aber —5G 161
Ellonby. Cumb —1F 103
Ellough. Suff —2G 67
Elloughton. E Yor —2C 94
Ellwood. Glos —5A 48
Elm. Cambs —5D 76
Elmbridge. Glos —4D 48
Elmbridge. Worc —4D 60
Elmdon. Essx —2E 53
Elmdon. W Mid —2F 61
Elmdon Heath. W Mid —2F 61
Elmesthorpe. Leics —1B 62
Elmfield. IOW —3D 16
Elm Hill. Dors —4D 22
Elmhurst. Staf —4F 73
Elmley Castle. Worc —1E 49
Elmley Lovett. Worc —4C 60
Elmore. Glos —4C 48
Elmore Back. Glos —4C 48
Elm Park. G Lon —2G 39
Elmscott. Devn —4C 18
Elmsett. Suff —1D 54
Elmstead. Essx —3D 54
Elmstead Heath. Essx —3D 54
Elmstead Market. Essx —3D 54
Elmsted. Kent —1F 29
Elmstone. Kent —4G 41
Elmstone Hardwicke. Glos —3E 49
Elmswell. E Yor —4D 101
Elmswell. Suff —4B 66
Elmton. Derbs —3C 86
Elphin. High —2G 163
Elphinstone. E Lot —2G 129
Elrick. Aber —3F 153
Elrick. Mor —1B 152
Elrig. Dum —5A 110
Elsdon. Nmbd —5D 120
Elsecar. S Yor —1A 86
Elsenham. Essx —3F 53
Elsfield. Oxon —4D 50
Elsham. N Lin —3D 94
Elsing. Norf —4C 78
Elslack. N Yor —5B 98
Elsrickle. S Lan —5D 128
Elstead. Surr —1A 26
Elsted. W Sus —1G 17
Elsted Marsh. W Sus —4G 25
Elsthorpe. Linc —3H 75
Elstob. Dur —2A 106
Elston. Devn —2A 12
Elston. Lanc —1E 90
Elston. Notts —1E 75
Elston. Wilts —2F 23
Elstone. Devn —1G 11
Elstow. Beds —1A 52
Elstree. Herts —1C 38
Elstronwick. E Yor —1F 95
Elswick. Lanc —1C 90
Elswick. Tyne —3F 115

Furzebrook—Glaspwll

Furzebrook. Dors —4E 15
Furzehill. Devn —2H 19
Furzeley Corner. Hants —1E 17
Furzey Lodge. Hants —2B 16
Furzley. Hants —1A 16
Fyfield. Essx —5F 53
Fyfield. Glos —5H 49
Fyfield. Hants —2A 24
Fyfield. Oxon —2C 36
Fyfield. Wilts —5G 35
Fylingthorpe. N Yor —4G 107
Fyning. W Sus —4G 25
Fyvie. Aber —5E 161

Gabhsann bho Dheas. W Isl —2G 171
Gabhsann bho Thuath. W Isl —2G 171
Gabroc Hill. E Ayr —4F 127
Gadbrook. Surr —1D 26
Gaddesby. Leics —4D 74
Gadgirth. S Ayr —2D 116
Gaer. Powy —3E 47
Gaerwen. IOA —3D 81
Gagingwell. Oxon —3C 50
Gaick Lodge. High —5B 150
Gailey. Staf —4D 72
Gainford. Dur —3E 105
Gainsborough. Linc —1F 87
Gainsborough. Suff —1E 55
Gainsford End. Essx —2H 53
Gairletter. Arg —1C 126
Gairloch. Aber —3E 153
Gairloch. High —1H 155
Gairlochy. High —5D 148
Gairney Bank. Per —4D 136
Gairnshiel Lodge. Aber —3G 151
Gaisgill. Cumb —4H 103
Gaitsgill. Cumb —5E 113
Galashiels. Scot —1G 119
Galgate. Lanc —4D 97
Galhampton. Som —4B 22
Gallatown. Fife —4E 137
Galley Common. Warw —1H 61
Galleyend. Essx —5H 53
Galleywood. Essx —5H 53
Gallin. Per —4C 142
Gallowfauld. Ang —4D 144
Gallowhill. E Dun —2H 127
Gallowhill. Per —5A 144
Gallowhill. Ren —3F 127
Gallowhills. Aber —3H 161
Gallows Green. Staf —1E 73
Gallows Green. Worc —4D 60
Gallowstree Common. Oxon —3E 37
Galltair. High —1G 147
Gallt Melyd. Den —2C 82
Galmington. Som —4F 21
Galmisdale. High —5C 146
Galmpton. Devn —4C 8
Galmpton. Torb —3E 9
Galmpton Warborough. Torb —3E 9
Galphay. N Yor —2E 99
Galston. E Ayr —1D 117
Galton. Dors —4C 14
Galtrigill. High —3A 154
Gamblesby. Cumb —1H 103
Gamelsby. Cumb —4D 112
Gamesley. Derbs —1E 85
Gamlingay. Cambs —5B 64
Gamlingay Cinques. Cambs —5B 64
Gamlingay Great Heath. Cambs —5B 64
Gammersgill. N Yor —1C 98
Gamrie. Aber —2E 161
Gamston. Notts —3E 86
(nr. East Retford)
Gamston. Notts —2D 74
(nr. Nottingham)
Ganarew. Here —4A 48
Ganavan. Arg —5C 140
Ganborough. Glos —3G 49
Gang. Corn —2H 7
Ganllwyd. Gwyn —3G 69
Gannochy. Ang —1E 145
Gannochy. Per —1D 136
Gansclet. High —4F 169
Ganstead. E Yor —1E 95
Ganthorpe. N Yor —2A 100
Ganton. N Yor —2D 101
Gappah. Devn —5B 12
Garboldisham. Norf —2C 66
Garden City. Flin —4F 83
Gardeners Green. Wok —5G 37
Gardenstown. Aber —2F 161
Garden Village. S Yor —1G 85
Garden Village. Swan —3E 31
Garden Village. W Yor —1E 93
Garderhouse. Shet —7E 173
Gardham. E Yor —5D 100
Gare Hill. Som —2C 22
Garelochhead. Arg —4B 134
Garford. Oxon —2C 36
Garforth. W Yor —1E 93
Gargrave. N Yor —4B 98
Gargunnock. Stir —4G 135
Garlieston. Dum —5B 110
Garlinge Green. Kent —5F 41
Garlogie. Aber —3E 153
Garmelow. Staf —3B 72
Garmond. Aber —3F 161
Garmondsway. Dur —1A 106
Garmony. Arg —4A 140
Garmouth. Mor —2H 159
Garmston. Shrp —5A 72
Garnant. Carm —4G 45
Garndiffaith. Torf —5F 47
Garndolbenmaen. Gwyn —1D 69
Garnett Bridge. Cumb —5G 103
Garnfadryn. Gwyn —2B 68
Garnkirk. N Lan —3H 127
Garnlydan. Blae —4E 47
Garnsgate. Linc —3D 76
Garnswllt. Swan —5G 45
Garn-yr-erw. Torf —4F 47
Garrabost. W Isl —4H 171
Garrafad. High —2D 155
Garrallan. E Ayr —3E 117
Garras. Corn —4E 5
Garreg. Gwyn —1F 69
Garrigill. Cumb —5A 114
Garriston. N Yor —5E 105
Garrogie Lodge. High —2H 149
Garros. High —2D 155
Garrow. Per —5F 143
Garsdale. Cumb —1G 97
Garsdale Head. Cumb —5A 104
Garsdon. Wilts —3E 35
Garshall Green. Staf —2D 72
Garsington. Oxon —5D 50
Garstang. Lanc —5D 97
Garston. Mers —2G 83
Garswood. Mers —1H 83
Gartcosh. N Lan —3H 127
Garth. B'End —2B 32
Garth. Cdgn —2F 57
Garth. Den —1E 71
Garth. Gwyn —2E 69
Garth. IOM —4C 108
Garth. Powy —1C 46
(nr. Builth Wells)
Garth. Powy —3E 59
(nr. Knighton)
Garthamlock. Glas —3H 127
Garthbrengy. Powy —2D 46
Gartheli. Cdgn —5E 57
Garthmyl. Powy —1D 58
Garthorpe. Leics —3F 75
Garthorpe. N Lin —3B 94
Garth Owen. Powy —1D 58
Garth Row. Cumb —5G 103
Gartly. Aber —5C 160
Gartmore. Stir —4E 135
Gartness. N Lan —3A 128
Gartness. Stir —1G 127
Gartocharn. W Dun —1F 127
Garton. E Yor —1F 95
Garton-on-the-Wolds. E Yor —4D 101
Gartsherrie. N Lan —3A 128
Gartymore. High —2H 165
Garvald. E Lot —2B 130
Garvamore. High —4H 149
Garvard. Arg —4A 132
Garvault. High —5H 167
Garve. High —2F 157
Garvestone. Norf —5C 78
Garvie. Arg —4H 133
Garvock. Aber —1G 145
Garvock. Inv —2D 126
Garway. Here —3H 47
Garway Common. Here —3H 47
Garway Hill. Here —3H 47
Garwick. Linc —1A 76
Gaskan. High —1B 140
Gasper. Wilts —3C 22
Gastard. Wilts —5D 35
Gasthorpe. Norf —2B 66
Gatcombe. IOW —4C 16
Gateacre. Mers —2G 83
Gatebeck. Cumb —1E 97
Gate Burton. Linc —2F 87
Gateforth. N Yor —2F 93
Gatehead. E Ayr —1C 116
Gate Helmsley. N Yor —4A 100
Gatehouse. Nmbd —1A 114
Gatehouse of Fleet. Dum —4C 110
Gatelawbridge. Dum —5B 118
Gateley. Norf —3B 78
Gatenby. N Yor —1F 99
Gatesgarth. Cumb —3C 102
Gateshead. Tyne —3F 115
Gatesheath. Ches —4G 83
Gateside. Ang —4D 144
(nr. Forfar)
Gateside. Ang —4C 144
(nr. Kirriemuir)
Gateside. Fife —3D 136
Gateside. N Ayr —4E 127
Gathurst. G Man —4D 90
Gatley. G Man —2C 84
Gatton. Surr —5D 39
Gattonside. Scot —1H 119
Gatwick (London) Airport. G Lon —1D 27
Gaufron. Powy —4B 58
Gaulby. Leics —5D 74
Gauldry. Fife —1F 137
Gaultree. Norf —5D 77
Gaunt's Common. Dors —2F 15
Gaunt's Earthcott. S Glo —3B 34
Gautby. Linc —3A 88
Gavinton. Scot —4D 130
Gawber. S Yor —4D 92
Gawcott. Buck —2E 51
Gawsworth. Ches —4C 84
Gawthorpe. W Yor —2C 92
Gawthrop. Cumb —1F 97
Gawthwaite. Cumb —1B 96
Gay Bowers. Essx —5A 54
Gaydon. Warw —5A 62
Gayhurst. Mil —1G 51
Gayle. N Yor —1A 98
Gayles. N Yor —4E 105
Gay Street. W Sus —3B 26
Gayton. Mers —2E 83
Gayton. Norf —4G 77
Gayton. Nptn —5E 62
Gayton. Staf —3D 73
Gayton le Marsh. Linc —2D 88
Gayton le Wold. Linc —2B 88
Gayton Thorpe. Norf —4G 77
Gaywood. Norf —3F 77
Gazeley. Suff —4G 65
Geanies. High —1C 158
Gearraidh Bhailteas. W Isl —6C 170
Gearraidh Bhaird. W Isl —6F 171
Gearraidh ma Monadh. W Isl —7C 170
Geary. High —2B 154
Geddes. High —3C 158
Gedding. Suff —5B 66
Geddington. Nptn —2F 63
Gedintailor. High —5E 155
Gedling. Notts —1D 74
Gedney. Linc —3D 76
Gedney Broadgate. Linc —3D 76
Gedney Drove End. Linc —3D 76
Gedney Dyke. Linc —3D 76
Gedney Hill. Linc —4C 76
Gee Cross. G Man —1D 84
Geeston. Rut —5G 75
Geilston. Arg —2E 127
Geirinis. W Isl —4C 170
Geise. High —2D 168
Geisiadar. W Isl —4D 171
Gelder Shiel. Aber —5G 151
Geldeston. Norf —1F 67
Gell. Cnwy —4A 82
Gelli. Pemb —3E 43
Gelli. Rhon —2C 32
Gellifor. Den —4D 82
Gelligaer. Cphy —2E 32
Gellilydan. Gwyn —2F 69
Gellinudd. Neat —5H 45
Gellyburn. Per —5H 143
Gellywen. Carm —2G 43
Gelston. Dum —4E 111
Gelston. Linc —1G 75
Gembling. E Yor —4F 101
Geneva. Cdgn —5D 56
Gentleshaw. Staf —4E 73
Geocrab. W Isl —8D 171
George Green. Buck —2A 38
Georgeham. Devn —3E 19
George Nympton. Devn —4H 19
Georgetown. Blae —5E 47
Georgetown. Ren —3F 127
Georth. Orkn —5C 172
Gerlan. Gwyn —4F 81
Germansweek. Devn —3E 11
Germoe. Corn —4C 4
Gerrard's Bromley. Staf —2B 72
Gerrards Cross. Buck —2A 38
Gerston. High —3D 168
Gervans. Corn —5C 6
Gestingthorpe. Essx —2B 54
Gethsemane. Pemb —1A 44
Geuffordd. Powy —4E 70
Gibraltar. Linc —5E 89
Gibraltar. Suff —5D 66
Gibralter. Buck —4F 51
Gibsmere. Notts —1E 74
Giddeahall. Wilts —4D 34
Gidea Park. G Lon —2G 39
Gidleigh. Devn —4G 11
Giffnock. E Ren —4G 127
Gifford. E Lot —3B 130
Giffordtown. Fife —2E 137
Giggetty. Staf —1C 60
Giggleswick. N Yor —3H 97
Gignog. Pemb —2C 42
Gilberdyke. E Yor —2B 94
Gilbert's End. Worc —1D 48
Gilbert's Green. Warw —3F 61
Gilchriston. E Lot —3A 130
Gilcrux. Cumb —1C 102
Gildersome. W Yor —2C 92
Gildingwells. S Yor —2C 86
Gilesgate Moor. Dur —5F 115
Gileston. V Glam —5D 32
Gilfach. Cphy —2E 33
Gilfach Goch. Rhon —2C 32
Gilfachreda. Cdgn —5D 56
Gill. Cumb —2F 103
Gillamoor. N Yor —1A 100
Gillar's Green. Mers —1G 83
Gillen. High —3B 154
Gilling East. N Yor —2A 100
Gillingham. Dors —4D 22
Gillingham. Medw —4B 40
Gillingham. Norf —1G 67
Gilling West. N Yor —4E 105
Gillock. High —3E 169
Gillow Heath. Staf —5C 84
Gills. High —1F 169
Gill's Green. Kent —2B 28
Gilmanscleuch. Scot —2F 119
Gilmerton. Edin —3F 129
Gilmerton. Per —1A 136
Gilmonby. Dur —3C 104
Gilmorton. Leics —2C 62
Gilsland. Nmbd —3H 113
Gilsland Spa. Cumb —3H 113
Gilston. Midl —4H 129
Giltbrook. Notts —1B 74
Gilwern. Mon —4F 47
Gimingham. Norf —2E 79
Giosla. W Isl —5D 171
Gipping. Suff —4C 66
Gipsey Bridge. Linc —1B 76
Gipton. W Yor —1D 92
Girdle Toll. N Ayr —5E 127
Girlsta. Shet —6F 173
Girsby. N Yor —4A 106
Girthon. Dum —4D 110
Girton. Cambs —4D 64
Girton. Notts —4F 87
Girvan. S Ayr —5A 116
Gisburn. Lanc —5H 97
Gisleham. Suff —2H 67
Gislingham. Suff —3C 66
Gissing. Norf —2D 66
Gittisham. Devn —3E 13
Gladestry. Powy —5E 59
Gladsmuir. E Lot —2A 130
Glaichbea. High —5H 157
Glais. Swan —5H 45
Glaisdale. N Yor —4E 107
Glame. High —4E 155
Glamis. Ang —4C 144
Glamisdale. High —5C 146
Glanaman. Carm —4G 45
Glan-Conwy. Cnwy —5H 81
Glandford. Norf —1C 78
Glan Duar. Carm —1F 45
Glandwr. Blae —5F 47
Glandwr. Pemb —2F 43
Glan-Dwyfach. Gwyn —1D 69
Glandy Cross. Carm —2F 43
Glandyfi. Cdgn —1F 57
Glangrwyney. Powy —4F 47
Glanmule. Powy —1D 58
Glanrhyd. Gwyn —2B 68
Glan-rhyd. Neat —5A 46
Glanrhyd. Pemb —1B 44
(nr. Cardigan)
Glan-rhyd. Pemb —1F 43
(nr. Crymmych)
Glanton. Nmbd —3E 121
Glanton Pike. Nmbd —3E 121
Glanvilles Wootton. Dors —2B 14
Glan-y-don. Flin —3D 82
Glan-y-nant. Powy —2B 58
Glan-yr-afon. Gwyn —1C 70
Glan-yr-afon. IOA —2F 81
Glan-yr-afon. Powy —5C 70
Glan-y-wern. Gwyn —2F 69
Glapthorn. Nptn —1H 63
Glapwell. Derbs —4B 86
Glas Aird. Arg —4A 132
Glas-allt Shiel. Aber —5G 151
Glasbury. Powy —2E 47
Glascoed. Den —3B 82
Glascoed. Mon —5G 47
Glascote. Staf —5G 73
Glascwm. Powy —5D 58
Glasfryn. Cnwy —5B 82
Glasgow. Glas —3G 127
Glasgow Airport. Ren —3F 127
Glashvin. High —2D 154
Glasinfryn. Gwyn —4E 81
Glasnakille. High —2D 146
Glasnarcardoch. High —4E 147
Glaspwll. Powy —1G 57

Glassburn. *High* —5F 157
Glassenbury. *Kent* —2B 28
Glasserton. *Dum* —5B 110
Glassford. *S Lan* —5A 128
Glasshouse. *Glos* —3C 48
Glasshouses. *N Yor* —3D 98
Glasson. *Cumb* —3D 112
Glasson. *Lanc* —4D 96
Glassonby. *Cumb* —1G 103
Glasterlaw. *Ang* —3E 145
Glaston. *Rut* —5F 75
Glastonbury. *Som* —3H 21
Glatton. *Cambs* —2A 64
Glazebrook. *Warr* —1A 84
Glazebury. *Warr* —1A 84
Glazeley. *Shrp* —2B 60
Gleadless. *S Yor* —2A 86
Gleadsmoss. *Ches* —4C 84
Gleann Dail bho Dheas. *W Isl*
　　　　—7C 170
Gleann Tholastaidh. *W Isl* —3H 171
Gleaston. *Cumb* —2B 96
Glecknabae. *Arg* —3B 126
Gledrid. *Shrp* —2E 71
Gleiniant. *Powy* —1B 58
Glemsford. *Suff* —1B 54
Glen. *Dum* —4C 110
Glenancross. *High* —4E 147
Glen Audlyn. *IOM* —2D 108
Glenbarr. *Arg* —2A 122
Glenbeg. *High* —2G 139
Glen Bernisdale. *High* —4D 154
Glenbervie. *Aber* —5E 153
Glenboig. *N Lan* —3A 128
Glenborrodale. *High* —2A 140
Glenbranter. *Arg* —4A 134
Glenbreck. *Scot* —2C 118
Glenbrein Lodge. *High* —2G 149
Glenbrittle. *High* —1C 146
Glenbuchat Lodge. *Aber* —2H 151
Glenbuck. *E Ayr* —2G 117
Glenburn. *Ren* —3F 127
Glencalvie Lodge. *High* —5B 164
Glencaple. *Dum* —3A 112
Glencarron Lodge. *High* —3C 156
Glencarse. *Per* —1D 136
Glencassley Castle. *High* —3B 164
Glencat. *Aber* —4C 152
Glencoe. *High* —3F 141
Glen Cottage. *High* —5E 147
Glencraig. *Fife* —4D 136
Glendale. *High* —4A 154
Glendevon. *Per* —3B 136
Glendoebeg. *High* —3G 149
Glendoick. *Per* —1E 136
Glendoune. *S Ayr* —5A 116
Glenduckie. *Fife* —2E 137
Gleneagles. *Per* —3B 136
Glenegedale. *Arg* —4B 124
Glenegedale Lots. *Arg* —4B 124
Glenelg. *High* —2G 147
Glenernie. *Mor* —4E 159
Glenesslin. *Dum* —1F 111
Glenfarg. *Per* —2D 136
Glenfarquhar Lodge. *Aber* —5E 152
Glenferness Mains. *High* —4D 158
Glenfeshie Lodge. *High* —4C 150
Glenfiddich Lodge. *Mor* —5H 159
Glenfield. *Leics* —5C 74
Glenfinnan. *High* —5B 148
Glenfintaig Lodge. *High* —5E 149
Glenfoot. *Per* —2D 136
Glenfyne Lodge. *Arg* —2B 134
Glengap. *Dum* —4D 110
Glengarnock. *N Ayr* —4E 126
Glengolly. *High* —2C 168
Glengorm Castle. *Arg* —3F 139
Glengrasco. *High* —4D 154
Glenhead Farm. *Ang* —2B 144
Glenholm. *Scot* —1D 118
Glen House. *Scot* —1E 119
Glenhurich. *High* —2C 140
Glenkerry. *Scot* —3E 119

Glenkiln. *Dum* —2F 111
Glenkindie. *Aber* —2B 152
Glenkinglass Lodge. *Arg* —5F 141
Glenkirk. *Scot* —1C 118
Glenlean. *Arg* —1B 126
Glenlee. *Dum* —1D 110
Glenleraig. *High* —5B 166
Glenlichorn. *Per* —2G 135
Glenlivet. *Mor* —1F 151
Glenlochar. *Dum* —3E 111
Glenlochsie Lodge. *Per* —1H 143
Glenluce. *Dum* —4G 109
Glenmarskie. *High* —3F 157
Glenmassan. *Arg* —1C 126
Glenmavis. *N Lan* —3A 128
Glenmaye. *IOM* —3B 108
Glenmazeran Lodge. *High* —1B 150
Glenmidge. *Dum* —1F 111
Glen Mona. *IOM* —3D 108
Glenmore. *High* —2G 139
　(nr. Glenborrodale)
Glenmore. *High* —3D 151
　(nr. Kingussie)
Glenmore. *High* —5D 154
　(on Skye)
Glenmoy. *Ang* —2D 144
Glennoe. *Arg* —5E 141
Glen of Coachford. *Aber* —4B 160
Glenogil. *Ang* —2D 144
Glen Parva. *Leics* —1C 62
Glenprosen Village. *Ang* —2C 144
Glenree. *N Ayr* —3D 122
Glenridding. *Cumb* —3E 103
Glenrisdell. *Arg* —4G 125
Glenrosa. *N Ayr* —2E 123
Glenrothes. *Fife* —3E 137
Glensanda. *High* —4C 140
Glensaugh. *Aber* —1F 145
Glenshero Lodge. *High* —4H 149
Glensluain. *Arg* —4H 133
Glenstockadale. *Dum* —3F 109
Glenstriven. *Arg* —2B 126
Glen Tanar House. *Aber* —4B 152
Glentham. *Linc* —1H 87
Glenton. *Aber* —1D 152
Glentress. *Scot* —1E 119
Glentromie Lodge. *High* —4B 150
Glentrool Lodge. *Dum* —1B 110
Glentrool Village. *Dum* —2A 110
Glentruim House. *High* —4A 150
Glentworth. *Linc* —2G 87
Glenuig. *High* —1A 140
Glen Village. *Falk* —2B 128
Glen Vine. *IOM* —4C 108
Glenwhilly. *Dum* —2G 109
Glenzierfoot. *Dum* —2E 113
Glespin. *S Lan* —2H 117
Gletness. *Shet* —6F 173
Glewstone. *Here* —3A 48
Glib Cheois. *W Isl* —5F 171
Glinton. *Pet* —5A 76
Glooston. *Leics* —1E 63
Glossop. *Derbs* —1E 85
Gloster Hill. *Nmbd* —4G 121
Gloucester. *Glos* —4D 48
Gloup. *Shet* —1G 173
Glusburn. *N Yor* —5C 98
Glutt Lodge. *High* —5B 168
Glutton Bridge. *Derbs* —4E 85
Gluvian. *Corn* —2D 6
Glympton. *Oxon* —3C 50
Glyn. *Cnwy* —3A 82
Glynarthen. *Cdgn* —1D 44
Glynbrochan. *Powy* —2B 58
Glyn Ceiriog. *Wrex* —2E 70
Glyncoch. *Rhon* —2D 32
Glyncorrwg. *Neat* —2B 32
Glynde. *E Sus* —5F 27
Glyndebourne. *E Sus* —4F 27
Glyndyfrdwy. *Den* —1D 70
Glyn Ebwy. *Blae* —5E 47
Glynllan. *B'End* —3C 32
Glyn-neath. *Neat* —5B 46

Glynogwr. *B'End* —3C 32
Glyntaff. *Rhon* —3D 32
Glyntawe. *Powy* —4B 46
Glynteg. *Carm* —2D 44
Gnosall. *Staf* —3C 72
Gnosall Heath. *Staf* —3C 72
Goadby. *Leics* —1E 63
Goadby Marwood. *Leics* —3E 75
Goatacre. *Wilts* —4F 35
Goathill. *Dors* —1B 14
Goathland. *N Yor* —4F 107
Goathurst. *Som* —3F 21
Goathurst Common. *Kent* —5F 39
Goat Lees. *Kent* —1E 28
Gobernuisgach Lodge. *High* —4E 167
Gobernuisgeach. *High* —5B 168
Gobhaig. *W Isl* —7C 171
Gobowen. *Shrp* —2F 71
Godalming. *Surr* —1A 26
Goddard's Corner. *Suff* —4E 67
Goddard's Green. *Kent* —2C 28
　(nr. Benenden)
Goddard's Green. *Kent* —2B 28
　(nr. Cranbrook)
Goddards Green. *W Sus* —3D 27
Godford Cross. *Devn* —2E 13
Godleybrook. *Staf* —1D 73
Godmanchester. *Cambs* —3B 64
Godmanstone. *Dors* —3B 14
Godmersham. *Kent* —5E 41
Godolphin Cross. *Corn* —3D 4
Godre'r-graig. *Neat* —5A 46
Godshill. *Hants* —1G 15
Godshill. *IOW* —4D 16
Godstone. *Staf* —2E 73
Godstone. *Surr* —5E 39
Godwell. *Devn* —3C 8
Goetre. *Mon* —5G 47
Goff's Oak. *Herts* —5D 52
Gogar. *Edin* —2E 129
Goginan. *Cdgn* —2F 57
Golan. *Gwyn* —1E 69
Golant. *Corn* —3F 7
Golberdon. *Corn* —5D 10
Golborne. *G Man* —1A 84
Golcar. *W Yor* —3A 92
Goldcliff. *Newp* —3G 33
Golden Cross. *E Sus* —4G 27
Golden Green. *Kent* —1H 27
Golden Grove. *Carm* —4F 45
Golden Grove. *N Yor* —4F 107
Golden Hill. *Pemb* —2D 43
Goldenhill. *Stoke* —5C 84
Golden Pot. *Hants* —2F 25
Golden Valley. *Glos* —3E 49
Golders Green. *G Lon* —2D 38
Goldhanger. *Essx* —5C 54
Gold Hill. *Norf* —1E 65
Golding. *Shrp* —5H 71
Goldington. *Beds* —5H 63
Goldsborough. *N Yor* —4F 99
　(nr. Harrogate)
Goldsborough. *N Yor* —3F 107
　(nr. Whitby)
Goldsithney. *Corn* —3C 4
Goldstone. *Kent* —4G 41
Goldstone. *Shrp* —3B 72
Goldthorpe. *S Yor* —4E 93
Goldworthy. *Devn* —4D 19
Golfa. *Powy* —3D 70
Gollanfield. *High* —3D 158
Gollinglith Foot. *N Yor* —1D 98
Golsoncott. *Som* —3D 20
Golspie. *High* —4F 165
Gomeldon. *Wilts* —3G 23
Gomersal. *W Yor* —2C 92
Gometra House. *Arg* —4E 139
Gomshall. *Surr* —1B 26
Gonalston. *Notts* —1D 74
Gonerby Hill Foot. *Linc* —2G 75
Gonnabarn. *Corn* —3D 6
Good Easter. *Essx* —4G 53
Gooderstone. *Norf* —5G 77

Goodleigh. *Devn* —3G 19
Goodmanham. *E Yor* —5C 100
Goodmayes. *G Lon* —2F 39
Goodnestone. *Kent* —5G 41
　(nr. Aylesham)
Goodnestone. *Kent* —4E 41
　(nr. Faversham)
Goodrich. *Here* —4A 48
Goodrington. *Torb* —3E 9
Goodshaw. *Lanc* —2G 91
Goodshaw Fold. *Lanc* —2G 91
Goodstone. *Devn* —5A 12
Goodwick. *Pemb* —1D 42
Goodworth Clatford. *Hants* —2B 24
Goole. *E Yor* —2H 93
Goom's Hill. *Worc* —5E 61
Goonbell. *Corn* —4B 6
Goonhavern. *Corn* —3B 6
Goonvrea. *Corn* —4B 6
Goose Green. *Cumb* —1E 97
Goose Green. *S Glo* —3C 34
Gooseham. *Corn* —1C 10
Goosewell. *Plym* —3B 8
Goosey. *Oxon* —2B 36
Goosnargh. *Lanc* —1D 90
Goostrey. *Ches* —4B 84
Gorcott Hill. *Warw* —4E 61
Gordon. *Scot* —5C 130
Gordonbush. *High* —3F 165
Gordonstown. *Aber* —3C 160
　(nr. Cornhill)
Gordonstown. *Aber* —5E 160
　(nr. Fyvie)
Gorebridge. *Midl* —3G 129
Gorefield. *Cambs* —4D 76
Gores. *Wilts* —1G 23
Gorgie. *Edin* —2F 129
Goring. *Oxon* —3E 36
Goring-by-Sea. *W Sus* —5C 26
Goring Heath. *Oxon* —4E 37
Gorleston-on-Sea. *Norf* —5H 79
Gornalwood. *W Mid* —1D 60
Gorran Churchtown. *Corn* —4D 6
Gorran Haven. *Corn* —4E 6
Gorran High Lanes. *Corn* —4D 6
Gors. *Cdgn* —3F 57
Gorsedd. *Flin* —3D 82
Gorseinon. *Swan* —3E 31
Gorseness. *Orkn* —6D 172
Gorseybank. *Derbs* —5G 85
Gorsgoch. *Cdgn* —5D 57
Gorslas. *Carm* —4F 45
Gorsley. *Glos* —3B 48
Gorsley Common. *Here* —3B 48
Gorstan. *High* —2F 157
Gorstella. *Ches* —4F 83
Gorsty Common. *Here* —2H 47
Gorsty Hill. *Staf* —3E 73
Gortantaoid. *Arg* —2B 124
Gortenfern. *High* —2A 140
Gorton. *G Man* —1C 84
Gosbeck. *Suff* —5D 66
Gosberton. *Linc* —2B 76
Gosberton Clough. *Linc* —3A 76
Goseley Dale. *Derbs* —3H 73
Gosfield. *Essx* —3A 54
Gosford. *Oxon* —4D 50
Gosforth. *Cumb* —4B 102
Gosforth. *Tyne* —3F 115
Gosmore. *Herts* —3B 52
Gospel End Village. *Staf* —1C 60
Gosport. *Hants* —2D 16
Gossabrough. *Shet* —3G 173
Gossington. *Glos* —5C 48
Gossops Green. *W Sus* —2D 26
Goswick. *Nmbd* —5G 131
Gotham. *Notts* —2C 74
Gotherington. *Glos* —3E 49
Gott. *Arg* —4B 138
Goudhurst. *Kent* —2B 28
Goulceby. *Linc* —3B 88
Gourdon. *Aber* —1H 145

Gourock. *Inv* —2D 126
Govan. *Glas* —3G 127
Govanhill. *Glas* —3G 127
Goverton. *Notts* —5E 86
Goveton. *Devn* —4D 8
Govilon. *Mon* —4F 47
Gowanhill. *Aber* —2H 161
Gowdall. *E Yor* —2G 93
Gowerton. *Swan* —3E 31
Gowkhall. *Fife* —1D 128
Gowthorpe. *E Yor* —4B 100
Goxhill. *E Yor* —5F 101
Goxhill. *N Lin* —2E 94
Goxhill Haven. *N Lin* —2E 94
Goytre. *Neat* —3A 32
Grabhair. *W Isl* —6F 171
Graby. *Linc* —3H 75
Graffham. *W Sus* —4A 26
Grafham. *Cambs* —4A 64
Grafham. *Surr* —1B 26
Grafton. *Here* —2H 47
Grafton. *N Yor* —3G 99
Grafton. *Oxon* —5A 50
Grafton. *Shrp* —4G 71
Grafton. *Worc* —2E 49
　(nr. Evesham)
Grafton. *Worc* —4H 59
　(nr. Leominster)
Grafton Flyford. *Worc* —5D 60
Grafton Regis. *Nptn* —1F 51
Grafton Underwood. *Nptn* —2G 63
Grafty Green. *Kent* —1C 28
Graianrhyd. *Den* —5E 82
Graig. *Carm* —5E 45
Graig. *Cnwy* —3H 81
Graig. *Den* —3D 82
Graig-fechan. *Den* —5D 82
Graig Penllyn. *V Glam* —4C 32
Grain. *Medw* —3C 40
Grainsby. *Linc* —1B 88
Grainthorpe. *Linc* —1C 88
Grainthorpe Fen. *Linc* —1C 88
Gramasdail. *W Isl* —3D 170
Grampound. *Corn* —4D 6
Grampound Road. *Corn* —3D 6
Granborough. *Buck* —3F 51
Granby. *Notts* —2E 75
Grandborough. *Warw* —4B 62
Grandpont. *Oxon* —5D 50
Grandtully. *Per* —3G 143
Grange. *Cumb* —3D 102
Grange. *E Ayr* —1D 116
Grange. *Here* —3G 59
Grange. *Mers* —2E 83
Grange. *Per* —1E 137
Grange Crossroads. *Mor* —3B 160
Grange Hill. *G Lon* —1F 39
Grangemill. *Derbs* —5G 85
Grange Moor. *W Yor* —3C 92
Grangemouth. *Falk* —1C 128
Grange of Lindores. *Fife* —2E 137
Grange-over-Sands. *Cumb* —2D 96
Grangepans. *Falk* —1D 128
Grange, The. *N Yor* —5C 106
Grangetown. *Card* —4E 33
Grangetown. *Red C* —2C 106
Grange Villa. *Dur* —4F 115
Granish. *High* —2C 150
Gransmoor. *E Yor* —4F 101
Granston. *Pemb* —1C 42
Grantchester. *Cambs* —5D 64
Grantham. *Linc* —2G 75
Grantley. *N Yor* —3E 99
Grantlodge. *Aber* —2E 152
Granton. *Edin* —2F 129
Grantown-on-Spey. *High* —1E 151
Grantshouse. *Scot* —3E 130
Grappenhall. *Warr* —2A 84
Grasby. *Linc* —4D 94
Grasmere. *Cumb* —4E 103
Grasscroft. *G Man* —4H 91
Grassendale. *Mers* —2F 83
Grassgarth. *Cumb* —5E 113

Grassholme. *Dur* —2C 104
Grassington. *N Yor* —3C 98
Grassmoor. *Derbs* —4B 86
Grassthorpe. *Notts* —4E 87
Grateley. *Hants* —2A 24
Gratton. *Devn* —1D 11
Gratton. *Staf* —5D 84
Gratwich. *Staf* —2E 73
Graveley. *Cambs* —4B 64
Graveley. *Herts* —3C 52
Gravelhill. *Shrp* —4G 71
Gravel Hole. *G Man* —4H 91
Gravelly Hill. *W Mid* —1F 61
Graven. *Shet* —4F 173
Graveney. *Kent* —4E 41
Gravesend. *Kent* —3H 39
Grayingham. *Linc* —1G 87
Grayrigg. *Cumb* —5G 103
Grays. *Thur* —3H 39
Grayshott. *Hants* —3G 25
Grayson Green. *Cumb* —2A 102
Grayswood. *Surr* —2A 26
Graythorp. *Hart* —2C 106
Grazeley. *Wok* —5E 37
Grealin. *High* —2E 155
Greasby. *Mers* —2E 83
Greasebrough. *S Yor* —1B 86
Great Abington. *Cambs* —1F 53
Great Addington. *Nptn* —3G 63
Great Alne. *Warw* —5F 61
Great Altcar. *Lanc* —4B 90
Great Amwell. *Herts* —4D 52
Great Asby. *Cumb* —3H 103
Great Ashfield. *Suff* —4B 66
Great Ayton. *N Yor* —3C 106
Great Baddow. *Essx* —5H 53
Great Bardfield. *Essx* —2G 53
Great Barford. *Beds* —5A 64
Great Barr. *W Mid* —1E 61
Great Barrington. *Glos* —4H 49
Great Barrow. *Ches* —4G 83
Great Barton. *Suff* —4A 66
Great Barugh. *N Yor* —2B 100
Great Bavington. *Nmbd* —1C 114
Great Bealings. *Suff* —1F 55
Great Bedwyn. *Wilts* —5A 36
Great Bentley. *Essx* —3E 54
Great Billing. *Nptn* —4F 63
Great Bircham. *Norf* —2G 77
Great Blakenham. *Suff* —5D 66
Great Blencow. *Cumb* —1F 103
Great Bolas. *Telf* —3A 72
Great Bookham. *Surr* —5C 38
Great Bosullow. *Corn* —3B 4
Great Bourton. *Oxon* —1C 50
Great Bowden. *Leics* —2E 63
Great Bradley. *Suff* —5F 65
Great Braxted. *Essx* —4B 54
Great Bricett. *Suff* —5C 66
Great Brickhill. *Buck* —2H 51
Great Bridgeford. *Staf* —3C 72
Great Brington. *Nptn* —4D 62
Great Bromley. *Essx* —3D 54
Great Broughton. *Cumb* —1B 102
Great Broughton. *N Yor* —4C 106
Great Budworth. *Ches* —3A 84
Great Burdon. *Darl* —3A 106
Great Burstead. *Essx* —1A 40
Great Busby. *N Yor* —4C 106
Great Canfield. *Essx* —4F 53
Great Carlton. *Linc* —2D 88
Great Casterton. *Rut* —5H 75
Great Chalfield. *Wilts* —5D 34
Great Chart. *Kent* —1D 28
Great Chatwell. *Staf* —4B 72
Great Chesterford. *Essx* —1F 53
Great Cheverell. *Wilts* —1E 23
Great Chilton. *Dur* —1F 105
Great Chishill. *Cambs* —2E 53
Great Clacton. *Essx* —4E 55
Great Cliff. *W Yor* —3D 92
Great Clifton. *Cumb* —2B 102
Great Coates. *NE Lin* —3F 95

Great Comberton. *Worc* —1E 49
Great Corby. *Cumb* —4F 113
Great Cornard. *Suff* —1B 54
Great Cowden. *E Yor* —5G 101
Great Coxwell. *Oxon* —2A 36
Great Crakehall. *N Yor* —1E 99
Great Cransley. *Nptn* —3F 63
Great Cressingham. *Norf* —5H 77
Great Crosby. *Mers* —1F 83
Great Cubley. *Derbs* —2F 73
Great Dalby. *Leics* —4E 75
Great Doddington. *Nptn* —4F 63
Great Doward. *Here* —4A 48
Great Dunham. *Norf* —4A 78
Great Dunmow. *Essx* —3G 53
Great Durnford. *Wilts* —3G 23
Great Easton. *Essx* —3G 53
Great Easton. *Leics* —1F 63
Great Eccleston. *Lanc* —5D 96
Great Edstone. *N Yor* —1B 100
Great Ellingham. *Norf* —1C 66
Great Elm. *Som* —2C 22
Great Eppleton. *Tyne* —5G 115
Great Eversden. *Cambs* —5C 64
Great Fencote. *N Yor* —5F 105
Great Finborough. *Suff* —5C 66
Greatford. *Linc* —4H 75
Great Fransham. *Norf* —4A 78
Great Gaddesden. *Herts* —4A 52
Greatgate. *Staf* —1E 73
Great Gidding. *Cambs* —2A 64
Great Givendale. *E Yor* —4C 100
Great Glemham. *Suff* —4F 67
Great Glen. *Leics* —1D 62
Great Gonerby. *Linc* —2G 75
Great Gransden. *Cambs* —5B 64
Great Green. *Norf* —2E 67
Great Green. *Suff* —5B 66
(nr. Lavenham)
Great Green. *Suff* —3D 66
(nr. Palgrave)
Great Habton. *N Yor* —2B 100
Great Hale. *Linc* —1A 76
Great Hallingbury. *Essx* —4F 53
Greatham. *Hants* —3F 25
Greatham. *Hart* —2B 106
Greatham. *W Sus* —4B 26
Great Hampden. *Buck* —5G 51
Great Harrowden. *Nptn* —3F 63
Great Harwood. *Lanc* —1F 91
Great Haseley. *Oxon* —5E 51
Great Hatfield. *E Yor* —5F 101
Great Haywood. *Staf* —3D 73
Great Heath. *W Mid* —2H 61
Great Heck. *N Yor* —2F 93
Great Henny. *Essx* —2B 54
Great Hinton. *Wilts* —1E 23
Great Hockham. *Norf* —1B 66
Great Holland. *Essx* —4F 55
Great Horkesley. *Essx* —2C 54
Great Hormead. *Herts* —2E 53
Great Horton. *W Yor* —1B 92
Great Horwood. *Buck* —2F 51
Great Houghton. *Nptn* —5E 63
Great Houghton. *S Yor* —4E 93
Great Hucklow. *Derbs* —3F 85
Great Kelk. *E Yor* —4F 101
Great Kendale. *E Yor* —4E 101
Great Kimble. *Buck* —5G 51
Great Kingshill. *Buck* —2G 37
Great Langdale. *Cumb* —4D 102
Great Langton. *N Yor* —5F 105
Great Leighs. *Essx* —4H 53
Great Limber. *Linc* —4E 95
Great Linford. *Mil* —1G 51
Great Livermere. *Suff* —3A 66
Great Longstone. *Derbs* —3G 85
Great Lumley. *Dur* —5F 115
Great Lyth. *Shrp* —5G 71
Great Malvern. *Worc* —1C 48
Great Maplestead. *Essx* —2B 54
Great Marton. *Bkpl* —1B 90
Great Massingham. *Norf* —3G 77

Great Melton. *Norf* —5D 78
Great Milton. *Oxon* —5E 51
Great Missenden. *Buck* —5G 51
Great Mitton. *Lanc* —1F 91
Great Mongeham. *Kent* —5H 41
Great Moulton. *Norf* —1D 66
Great Munden. *Herts* —3D 52
Great Musgrave. *Cumb* —3A 104
Great Ness. *Shrp* —4G 71
Great Notley. *Essx* —3H 53
Great Oak. *Mon* —5G 47
Great Oakley. *Essx* —3E 55
Great Oakley. *Nptn* —2F 63
Great Offley. *Herts* —3B 52
Great Ormside. *Cumb* —3A 104
Great Orton. *Cumb* —4E 113
Great Ouseburn. *N Yor* —3G 99
Great Oxendon. *Nptn* —2E 63
Great Oxney Green. *Essx* —5G 53
Great Parndon. *Essx* —5E 53
Great Paxton. *Cambs* —4B 64
Great Plumpton. *Lanc* —1B 90
Great Plumstead. *Norf* —4F 79
Great Ponton. *Linc* —2G 75
Great Potheridge. *Devn* 1F 11
Great Preston. *W Yor* —2E 93
Great Raveley. *Cambs* —2B 64
Great Rissington. *Glos* —4G 49
Great Rollright. *Oxon* —2B 50
Great Ryburgh. *Norf* —3B 78
Great Ryle. *Nmbd* —3E 121
Great Ryton. *Shrp* —5G 71
Great Saling. *Essx* —3G 53
Great Salkeld. *Cumb* —1G 103
Great Sampford. *Essx* —2G 53
Great Sankey. *Warr* —2H 83
Great Saredon. *Staf* —5D 72
Great Saxham. *Suff* —4G 65
Great Shefford. *W Ber* —4B 36
Great Shelford. *Cambs* —5D 64
Great Shoddesden. *Hants* —2A 24
Great Smeaton. *N Yor* —4A 106
Great Snoring. *Norf* —2B 78
Great Somerford. *Wilts* —3E 35
Great Stainton. *Darl* —2A 106
Great Stambridge. *Essx* —1C 40
Great Staughton. *Cambs* —4A 64
Great Steeping. *Linc* —4D 88
Great Stonar. *Kent* —5H 41
Greatstone-on-Sea. *Kent* —3E 29
Great Strickland. *Cumb* —2G 103
Great Stukeley. *Cambs* —3B 64
Great Sturton. *Linc* —3B 88
Great Sutton. *Ches* —3F 83
Great Sutton. *Shrp* —2H 59
Great Swinburne. *Nmbd* —2C 114
Great Tew. *Oxon* —3B 50
Great Tey. *Essx* —3B 54
Great Thirkleby. *N Yor* —2G 99
Great Thorness. *IOW* —3C 16
Great Thurlow. *Suff* —5F 65
Great Torr. *Devn* —4C 8
Great Torrington. *Devn* —1E 11
Great Tosson. *Nmbd* —4E 121
Great Totham North. *Essx* —4B 54
Great Totham South. *Essx* —4B 54
Great Tows. *Linc* —1B 88
Great Urswick. *Cumb* —2B 96
Great Wakering. *Essx* —2D 40
Great Waldingfield. *Suff* —1C 54
Great Walsingham. *Norf* —2B 78
Great Waltham. *Essx* —4G 53
Great Warley. *Essx* —1G 39
Great Washbourne. *Glos* —2E 49
Great Welnetham. *Suff* —5A 66
Great Wenham. *Suff* —2D 54
Great Whittington. *Nmbd* —2D 114
Great Wigborough. *Essx* —4C 54
Great Wilbraham. *Cambs* —5E 65
Great Wilne. *Derbs* —2B 74
Great Wishford. *Wilts* —3F 23
Great Witchingham. *Norf* —4D 78
Great Witcombe. *Glos* —4E 49

Great Witley. *Worc* —4B 60
Great Wolford. *Warw* —2H 49
Greatworth. *Nptn* —1D 50
Great Wratting. *Suff* —1G 53
Great Wymondley. *Herts* —3C 52
Great Wyrley. *Staf* —5D 73
Great Wytheford. *Shrp* —4H 71
Great Yarmouth. *Norf* —5H 79
Great Yeldham. *Essx* —2A 54
Grebby. *Linc* —4D 88
Creeba Castle. *IOM* —3C 108
Greenbank. *Shet* —1G 173
Green Bottom. *Corn* —4B 6
Greenburn. *W Lot* —3C 128
Greencroft. *Dur* —4E 115
Greencroft Hall. *Dur* —5E 115
Greendikes. *Nmbd* —2E 121
Greendown. *Som* —1A 22
Green End. *Beds* —1A 52
Green End. *Herts* —2D 52
(nr. Buntingford)
Green End. *Herts* —3D 52
(nr. Stevenage)
Green End. *Warw* —2G 61
Greenfield. *Arg* —4B 134
Greenfield. *Beds* —2A 52
Greenfield. *Flin* —3D 82
Greenfield. *G Man* —4H 91
Greenfield. *Oxon* —2F 37
Greenfoot. *N Lan* —3A 128
Greenford. *G Lon* —2C 38
Greengairs. *N Lan* —2A 128
Greengate. *Norf* —4C 78
Greengill. *Cumb* —1C 102
Greenhalgh. *Lanc* —1C 90
Greenham. *Dors* —2H 13
Greenham. *Som* —4D 20
Greenham. *W Ber* —5C 36
Green Hammerton. *N Yor* —4G 99
Greenhaugh. *Nmbd* —1A 114
Greenhead. *Nmbd* —3H 113
Green Heath. *Staf* —4D 73
Greenhill. *Dum* —2C 112
Greenhill. *Falk* —2B 128
Greenhill. *Kent* —4F 41
Greenhill. *S Yor* —2H 85
Greenhill. *Worc* —4D 60
Greenhills. *N Ayr* —4E 127
Greenhithe. *Kent* —3G 39
Greenholm. *E Ayr* —1E 117
Greenhow Hill. *N Yor* —3D 98
Greenigo. *Orkn* —7D 172
Greenland. *High* —2E 169
Greenland Mains. *High* —2E 169
Greenlands. *Worc* —4E 61
Green Lane. *Shrp* —3A 72
Green Lane. *Warw* —4E 61
Greenlaw. *Scot* —5D 130
Greenlea. *Dum* —2B 112
Greenloaning. *Per* —3H 135
Greenmount. *G Man* —3F 91
Greenock. *Inv* —2D 126
Greenodd. *Cumb* —1C 96
Green Ore. *Som* —1A 22
Greenrow. *Cumb* —4C 112
Greens. *Aber* —4F 161
Greensgate. *Norf* —4C 78
Greenside. *Tyne* —3E 115
Greensidehill. *Nmbd* —3D 121
Greens Norton. *Nptn* —1E 51
Greenstead Green. *Essx* —3B 54
Greensted Green. *Essx* —5F 53
Green Street. *Herts* —1C 38
Green Street. *Suff* —3D 66
Green Street Green. *G Lon* —4F 39
Green Street Green. *Kent* —3G 39
Greenstreet Green. *Suff* —1D 54
Green, The. *Cumb* —1A 96
Green, The. *Wilts* —3D 22
Green Tye. *Herts* —4E 53
Greenway. *Pemb* —2E 43
Greenway. *V Glam* —4D 32

Greenwell. *Cumb* —4G 113
Greenwich. *G Lon* —3E 39
Greet. *Glos* —2F 49
Greete. *Shrp* —3H 59
Greetham. *Linc* —3C 88
Greetham. *Rut* —4G 75
Greetland. *W Yor* —2A 92
Gregson Lane. *Lanc* —2D 90
Grein. *W Isl* —8B 170
Greinetobht. *W Isl* —1D 170
Greinton. *Som* —3H 21
Grenaby. *IOM* —4B 108
Grendon. *Nptn* —4F 63
Grendon. *Warw* —1G 61
Grendon Common. *Warw* —1G 61
Grendon Green. *Here* —5H 59
Grendon Underwood. *Buck* —3E 51
Grenofen. *Devn* —5E 11
Grenoside. *S Yor* —1H 85
Greosabhagh. *W Isl* —8D 171
Gresford. *Wrex* —5F 83
Gresham. *Norf* —2D 78
Greshornish. *High* —3C 154
Gressenhall. *Norf* —4B 78
Gressingham. *Lanc* —2E 97
Greta Bridge. *Dur* —3D 105
Gretna. *Dum* —3E 112
Gretna Green. *Dum* —3E 112
Gretton. *Glos* —2F 49
Gretton. *Nptn* —1G 63
Gretton. *Shrp* —1H 59
Grewelthorpe. *N Yor* —2E 99
Greygarth. *N Yor* —2D 98
Grey Green. *N Lin* —4A 94
Greylake. *Som* —3G 21
Greysouthern. *Cumb* —2B 102
Greystoke. *Cumb* —1F 103
Greystone. *Ang* —4E 145
Greystones. *S Yor* —2H 85
Greywell. *Hants* —1F 25
Griais. *W Isl* —3G 171
Grianan. *W Isl* —4G 171
Gribthorpe. *E Yor* —1A 94
Gribun. *Arg* —5F 139
Griff. *Warw* —2A 62
Griffithstown. *Torf* —2F 33
Griffydam. *Leics* —4B 74
Grigghall. *Cumb* —5F 103
Griggs Green. *Hants* —3G 25
Grimbister. *Orkn* —6C 172
Grimeford Village. *Lanc* —3E 90
Grimethorpe. *S Yor* —4E 93
Griminis. *W Isl* —3C 170
(on Benbecula)
Griminis. *W Isl* —1C 170
(on North Uist)
Grimister. *Shet* —2F 173
Grimley. *Worc* —4C 60
Grimoldby. *Linc* —2C 88
Grimpo. *Shrp* —3F 71
Grimsargh. *Lanc* —1D 90
Grimsby. *NE Lin* —3F 95
Grimscote. *Nptn* —5D 62
Grimscott. *Corn* —2C 10
Grimshaw. *Bkbn* —2F 91
Grimshaw Green. *Lanc* —3C 90
Grimsthorpe. *Linc* —3H 75
Grimston. *E Yor* —1F 95
Grimston. *Leics* —3D 74
Grimston. *Norf* —3G 77
Grimston. *York* —4A 100
Grimstone. *Dors* —3B 14
Grimstone End. *Suff* —4B 66
Grinacombe Moor. *Devn* —3E 11
Grindale. *E Yor* —2F 101
Grindhill. *Devn* —3E 11
Grindiscol. *Shet* —8F 173
Grindle. *Shrp* —5B 72
Grindleford. *Derbs* —3G 85
Grindleton. *Lanc* —5G 97
Grindley. *Staf* —3E 73
Grindley Brook. *Shrp* —1H 71
Grindlow. *Derbs* —3F 85

Grindon. *Nmbd* —5F **131**
Grindon. *Staf* —5E **85**
Gringley on the Hill. *Notts* —1E **87**
Grinsdale. *Cumb* —4E **113**
Grinshill. *Shrp* —3H **71**
Grinton. *N Yor* —5D **104**
Griomsidar. *W Isl* —5G **171**
Grishipoll. *Arg* —3C **138**
Grisling Common. *E Sus* —3F **27**
Gristhorpe. *N Yor* —1E **101**
Griston. *Norf* —1B **66**
Gritley. *Orkn* —7E **172**
Grittenham. *Wilts* —3F **35**
Grizebeck. *Cumb* —1B **96**
Grizedale. *Cumb* —5E **103**
Grobister. *Orkn* —5F **172**
Grobsness. *Shet* —5E **173**
Groby. *Leics* —5C **74**
Groes. *Cnwy* —4C **82**
Groes. *Neat* —3A **32**
Groes-faen. *Rhon* —3D **32**
Groesffordd. *Gwyn* —2B **68**
Groesffordd. *Powy* —3D **46**
Groeslon. *Gwyn* —5D **81**
Groes-lwyd. *Powy* —4E **70**
Groes-wen. *Cphy* —3E **33**
Grogport. *Arg* —5G **125**
Groigearraidh. *W Isl* —4C **170**
Gromford. *Suff* —5F **67**
Gronant. *Flin* —2D **82**
Groombridge. *E Sus* —2G **27**
Grosmont. *Mon* —3H **47**
Grosmont. *N Yor* —4F **107**
Groton. *Suff* —1C **54**
Grove. *Dors* —5B **14**
Grove. *Kent* —4G **41**
Grove. *Notts* —3E **87**
Grove. *Oxon* —2B **36**
Grovehill. *E Yor* —5E **101**
Grove Park. *G Lon* —3E **39**
Grovesend. *Swan* —5F **45**
Grove, The. *Dum* —2A **112**
Grove, The. *Worc* —1D **48**
Grub Street. *Staf* —3B **72**
Grudie. *High* —2F **157**
Gruids. *High* —3C **164**
Gruinard House. *High* —4D **162**
Gruinart. *Arg* —3A **124**
Grulinbeg. *Arg* —3A **124**
Gruline. *Arg* —4G **139**
Grummore. *High* —5G **167**
Grundisburgh. *Suff* —5E **66**
Gruting. *Shet* —7D **173**
Gualachulain. *High* —4F **141**
Guardbridge. *Fife* —2G **137**
Guarlford. *Worc* —1D **48**
Guay. *Per* —4H **143**
Gubblecote. *Herts* —4H **51**
Guestling Green. *E Sus* —4C **28**
Guestling Thorn. *E Sus* —4C **28**
Guestwick. *Norf* —3C **78**
Guestwick Green. *Norf* —3C **78**
Guide. *Bkbn* —2F **91**
Guide Post. *Nmbd* —1F **115**
Guilden Down. *Shrp* —2F **59**
Guilden Morden. *Cambs* —1C **52**
Guilden Sutton. *Ches* —4G **83**
Guildford. *Surr* —1A **26**
Guildtown. *Per* —5A **144**
Guilsborough. *Nptn* —3D **62**
Guilsfield. *Powy* —4E **70**
Guineaford. *Devn* —3F **19**
Guisborough. *Red C* —3D **106**
Guiseley. *W Yor* —5D **98**
Guist. *Norf* —3B **78**
Guiting Power. *Glos* —3F **49**
Gulberwick. *Shet* —8F **173**
Gullane. *E Lot* —1A **130**
Gulling Green. *Suff* —5H **65**
Gulval. *Corn* —3B **4**
Gumfreston. *Pemb* —4F **43**
Gumley. *Leics* —1D **62**

Gunby. *E Yor* —1H **93**
Gunby. *Linc* —3G **75**
Gundleton. *Hants* —3E **24**
Gun Green. *Kent* —2B **28**
Gun Hill. *E Sus* —4G **27**
Gunn. *Devn* —3G **19**
Gunnerside. *N Yor* —5C **104**
Gunnerton. *Nmbd* —2C **114**
Gunness. *N Lin* —3B **94**
Gunnislake. *Corn* —5E **11**
Gunsgreenhill. *Scot* —3F **131**
Gunstone. *Staf* —5C **72**
Gunthorpe. *Norf* —2C **78**
Gunthorpe. *N Lin* —1F **87**
Gunthorpe. *Notts* —1D **74**
Gunthorpe. *Pet* —5A **76**
Gunville. *IOW* —4C **16**
Gupworthy. *Som* —3C **20**
Gurnard. *IOW* —3C **16**
Gurney Slade. *Som* —2B **22**
Gurnos. *Powy* —5A **46**
Gussage All Saints. *Dors* —1F **15**
Gussage St Andrew. *Dors* —1E **15**
Gussage St Michael. *Dors* —1E **15**
Guston. *Kent* —1H **29**
Gutcher. *Shet* —2G **173**
Guthram Gowt. *Linc* —3A **76**
Guthrie. *Ang* —3E **145**
Guyhirn. *Cambs* —5D **76**
Guyhirn Gull. *Cambs* —5C **76**
Guy's Head. *Linc* —3D **77**
Guy's Marsh. *Dors* —4D **22**
Guyzance. *Nmbd* —4G **121**
Gwaelod-y-garth. *Card* —3E **32**
Gwaenynog Bach. *Den* —4C **82**
Gwaenysgor. *Flin* —2C **82**
Gwalchmai. *IOA* —3C **80**
Gwastad. *Pemb* —2E **43**
Gwaun-Cae-Gurwen. *Neat* —4H **45**
Gwaun-y-bara. *Cphy* —3E **33**
Gwbert. *Cdgn* —5A **56**
Gweek. *Corn* —4E **5**
Gwehelog. *Mon* —5G **47**
Gwenddwr. *Powy* —1D **46**
Gwennap. *Corn* —4B **6**
Gwenter. *Corn* —5E **5**
Gwernaffield. *Flin* —4E **82**
Gwernesney. *Mon* —5H **47**
Gwernogle. *Carm* —2F **45**
Gwern-y-go. *Powy* —1E **58**
Gwernymynydd. *Flin* —4E **82**
Gwersylt. *Wrex* —5F **83**
Gwespyr. *Flin* —2D **82**
Gwinear. *Corn* —3D **4**
Gwithian. *Corn* —2C **4**
Gwredog. *IOA* —2D **80**
Gwyddelwern. *Den* —1C **70**
Gwyddgrug. *Carm* —2E **45**
Gwynfryn. *Wrex* —5E **83**
Gwystre. *Powy* —4C **58**
Gwytherin. *Cnwy* —4A **82**
Gyfelia. *Wrex* —1F **71**
Gyffin. *Cnwy* —3G **81**

H

Habberley. *Shrp* —5F **71**
Habergham. *Lanc* —1G **91**
Habin. *W Sus* —4G **25**
Habrough. *NE Lin* —3E **95**
Hacconby. *Linc* —3A **76**
Haceby. *Linc* —2H **75**
Hacheston. *Suff* —5F **67**
Hackenthorpe. *S Yor* —2B **86**
Hackford. *Norf* —5C **78**
Hackforth. *N Yor* —5F **105**
Hackleton. *Nptn* —5F **63**
Hackness. *N Yor* —5G **107**
Hackness. *Orkn* —8C **172**
Hackney. *G Lon* —2E **39**
Hackthorn. *Linc* —2G **87**
Hackthorpe. *Cumb* —2G **103**
Haclait. *W Isl* —4D **170**
Hadden. *Scot* —1B **120**

Haddenham. *Buck* —5F **51**
Haddenham. *Cambs* —3D **64**
Haddenham End. *Cambs* —3D **64**
Haddington. *E Lot* —2B **130**
Haddington. *Linc* —4F **87**
Haddiscoe. *Norf* —1G **67**
Haddo. *Aber* —5F **161**
Haddon. *Cambs* —1A **64**
Hademore. *Staf* —5F **73**
Hadfield. *Derbs* —1E **85**
Hadham Cross. *Herts* —4E **53**
Hadham Ford. *Herts* —3E **53**
Hadleigh. *Essx* —2C **40**
Hadleigh. *Suff* —1D **54**
Hadleigh Heath. *Suff* —1C **54**
Hadley. *Telf* —4A **72**
Hadley. *Worc* —4C **60**
Hadley End. *Staf* —3F **73**
Hadley Wood. *G Lon* —1D **38**
Hadlow. *Kent* —1H **27**
Hadlow Down. *E Sus* —3G **27**
Hadnall. *Shrp* —3H **71**
Hadstock. *Essx* —1F **53**
Hady. *Derbs* —3B **86**
Hadzor. *Worc* —4D **60**
Haffenden Quarter. *Kent* —1C **28**
Haggate. *Lanc* —1G **91**
Haggbeck. *Cumb* —2F **113**
Haggerston. *Nmbd* —5G **131**
Hagget End. *Cumb* —3B **102**
Haggrister. *Shet* —4E **173**
Hagley. *Here* —1A **48**
Hagley. *Worc* —2D **60**
Hagnaby. *Linc* —4C **88**
Hagworthingham. *Linc* —4C **88**
Haigh. *G Man* —4E **90**
Haigh Moor. *W Yor* —2C **92**
Haighton Green. *Lanc* —1D **90**
Haile. *Cumb* —4B **102**
Hailes. *Glos* —2F **49**
Hailey. *Oxon* —4D **52**
Hailsham. *E Sus* —5G **27**
Hail Weston. *Cambs* —4A **64**
Hainault. *G Lon* —1F **39**
Hainford. *Norf* —4E **78**
Hainton. *Linc* —2A **88**
Hainworth. *W Yor* —1A **92**
Haisthorpe. *E Yor* —3F **101**
Hakin. *Pemb* —4C **42**
Halam. *Notts* —5D **86**
Halbeath. *Fife* —1E **129**
Halberton. *Devn* —1D **12**
Halcro. *High* —2E **169**
Hale. *Cumb* —2E **97**
Hale. *G Man* —2B **84**
Hale. *Hal* —2G **83**
Hale. *Hants* —1G **15**
Hale. *Surr* —2G **25**
Hale Bank. *Hal* —2G **83**
Halebarns. *G Man* —2B **84**
Hales. *Norf* —1F **67**
Hales. *Staf* —2B **72**
Halesgate. *Linc* —3C **76**
Hales Green. *Derbs* —1F **73**
Halesowen. *W Mid* —2D **60**
Hale Street. *Kent* —1A **28**
Halesworth. *Suff* —3F **67**
Halewood. *Mers* —2G **83**
Halford. *Devn* —5B **12**
Halford. *Shrp* —2G **59**
Halford. *Warw* —1A **50**
Halfpenny. *Cumb* —1E **97**
Halfpenny Furze. *Carm* —3G **43**
Halfpenny Green. *Staf* —1C **60**
Halfway. *Carm* —2G **45**
Halfway. *Powy* —2B **46**
Halfway. *S Yor* —2B **86**
Halfway House. *Shrp* —4F **71**
Halfway Houses. *Kent* —3D **40**
Halgabron. *Corn* —4A **10**
Halifax. *W Yor* —2A **92**
Halistra. *High* —3B **154**

Halket. *E Ayr* —4F **127**
Halkirk. *High* —3D **168**
Halkyn. *Flin* —3E **82**
Hall. *E Ren* —4F **127**
Hallam Fields. *Derbs* —1B **74**
Halland. *E Sus* —4G **27**
Hallands, The. *N Lin* —2D **94**
Hallaton. *Leics* —1E **63**
Hallatrow. *Bath* —1B **22**
Hallbank. *Cumb* —5H **103**
Hallbankgate. *Cumb* —4G **113**
Hall Dunnerdale. *Cumb* —5D **102**
Hallen. *S Glo* —3A **34**
Hall End. *Beds* —1A **52**
Halley. *Herts* —4D **52**
Hallgarth. *Dur* —5G **115**
Hall Green. *Ches* —5C **84**
Hall Green. *Norf* —2D **66**
Hall Green. *W Mid* —2F **61**
Hall Green. *W Yor* —3D **92**
Halliburton. *Scot* —5C **130**
Hallin. *High* —3B **154**
Halling. *Medw* —4B **40**
Hallington. *Linc* —2C **88**
Hallington. *Nmbd* —2C **114**
Halloughton. *Notts* —5D **86**
Hallow. *Worc* —5C **60**
Hallow Heath. *Worc* —5C **60**
Hallowsgate. *Ches* —4H **83**
Hallsands. *Devn* —5E **9**
Hall's Green. *Herts* —3C **52**
Hallspill. *Devn* —4E **19**
Hallthwaites. *Cumb* —1A **96**
Hall Waberthwaite. *Cumb* —5C **102**
Hallwood Green. *Glos* —2B **48**
Hallworthy. *Corn* —4B **10**
Hallyne. *Scot* —5E **129**
Halmer End. *Staf* —1C **72**
Halmond's Frome. *Here* —1B **48**
Halmore. *Glos* —5B **48**
Halnaker. *W Sus* —5A **26**
Halsall. *Lanc* —3B **90**
Halse. *Nptn* —1D **50**
Halse. *Som* —4E **21**
Halsetown. *Corn* —3C **4**
Halsham. *E Yor* —2F **95**
Halsinger. *Devn* —3F **19**
Halstead. *Essx* —2B **54**
Halstead. *Kent* —4F **39**
Halstead. *Leics* —5E **75**
Halstock. *Dors* —2A **14**
Halstow. *Devn* —3B **12**
Halsway. *Som* —3E **21**
Haltcliff Bridge. *Cumb* —1E **103**
Haltham. *Linc* —4B **88**
Haltoft End. *Linc* —1C **76**
Halton. *Buck* —5G **51**
Halton. *Hal* —2H **83**
Halton. *Lanc* —3E **97**
Halton. *Nmbd* —3C **114**
Halton. *W Yor* —1D **92**
Halton. *Wrex* —2F **71**
Halton East. *N Yor* —4C **98**
Halton Fenside. *Linc* —4D **88**
Halton Gill. *N Yor* —2A **98**
Halton Holegate. *Linc* —4D **88**
Halton Lea Gate. *Nmbd* —4H **113**
Halton Moor. *W Yor* —1D **92**
Halton Shields. *Nmbd* —3D **114**
Halton West. *N Yor* —4H **97**
Haltwhistle. *Nmbd* —3A **114**
Halvergate. *Norf* —5G **79**
Halwell. *Devn* —3D **9**
Halwill. *Devn* —3E **11**
Halwill Junction. *Devn* —3E **11**
Ham. *Devn* —2F **13**
Ham. *Glos* —2B **34**
Ham. *G Lon* —3C **38**
Ham. *High* —1E **169**
Ham. *Kent* —5H **41**
Ham. *Plym* —3A **8**
Ham. *Shet* —8A **173**

Ham. *Som* —1F **13**
(nr. Ilminster)
Ham. *Som* —4F **21**
(nr. Taunton)
Ham. *Wilts* —5B **36**
Hambleden. *Buck* —3F **37**
Hambledon. *Hants* —1E **17**
Hambledon. *Surr* —2A **26**
Hamble-le-Rice. *Hants* —2C **16**
Hambleton. *Lanc* —5C **96**
Hambleton. *N Yor* —1F **93**
Hambridge. *Som* —4G **21**
Hambrook. *S Glo* —4B **34**
Hambrook. *W Sus* —2F **17**
Ham Common. *Dors* —4D **22**
Hameringham. *Linc* —4C **88**
Hamerton. *Cambs* —3A **64**
Ham Green. *Here* —1C **48**
Ham Green. *Kent* —4C **40**
Ham Green. *N Som* —4A **34**
Ham Green. *Worc* —4E **61**
Ham Hill. *Kent* —4A **40**
Hamilton. *Leics* —5D **74**
Hamilton. *S Lan* —4A **128**
Hammer. *W Sus* —3G **25**
Hammersmith. *G Lon* —3D **38**
Hammerwich. *Staf* —5E **73**
Hammerwood. *E Sus* —2F **27**
Hammill. *Kent* —5G **41**
Hammond Street. *Herts* —5D **52**
Hammoon. *Dors* —1D **14**
Hamnavoe. *Shet* —8E **173**
(nr. Burland)
Hamnavoe. *Shet* —3F **173**
(on Yell)
Hamp. *Som* —3G **21**
Hampden Park. *E Sus* —5H **27**
Hampen. *Glos* —3F **49**
Hamperden End. *Essx* —2F **53**
Hamperley. *Shrp* —2G **59**
Hampnett. *Glos* —4F **49**
Hampole. *S Yor* —3F **93**
Hampreston. *Dors* —3F **15**
Hampstead. *G Lon* —2D **38**
Hampstead Norreys. *W Ber* —4D **36**
Hampsthwaite. *N Yor* —4E **99**
Hampton. *Devn* —3F **13**
Hampton. *G Lon* —3C **38**
Hampton. *Kent* —4F **41**
Hampton. *Shrp* —2B **60**
Hampton. *Swin* —2G **35**
Hampton. *Worc* —1F **49**
Hampton Bishop. *Here* —2A **48**
Hampton Fields. *Glos* —2D **35**
Hampton Heath. *Ches* —1H **71**
Hampton in Arden. *W Mid* —2G **61**
Hampton Loade. *Shrp* —2B **60**
Hampton Lovett. *Worc* —4C **60**
Hampton Lucy. *Warw* —5G **61**
Hampton Magna. *Warw* —4G **61**
Hampton on the Hill. *Warw* —4G **61**
Hampton Poyle. *Oxon* —4D **50**
Hampton Wick. *G Lon* —4C **38**
Hamptworth. *Wilts* —1H **15**
Hamrow. *Norf* —3B **78**
Hamsey. *E Sus* —4F **27**
Hamsey Green. *Surr* —5E **39**
Hamstall Ridware. *Staf* —4F **73**
Hamstead. *IOW* —3B **16**
Hamstead. *W Mid* —1E **61**
Hamstead Marshall. *W Ber* —5C **36**
Hamsterley. *Dur* —4E **115**
(nr. Consett)
Hamsterley. *Dur* —1E **105**
(nr. Wolsingham)
Hamsterley Mill. *Dur* —4E **115**
Hamstreet. *Kent* —2E **28**
Ham Street. *Som* —3A **22**
Hamworthy. *Pool* —3E **15**
Hanbury. *Staf* —3F **73**
Hanbury. *Worc* —4D **60**
Hanbury Woodend. *Staf* —3F **73**
Hanby. *Linc* —2H **75**

Hanchurch. *Staf* —1C 72
Hand and Pen. *Devn* —3D 12
Handbridge. *Ches* —4G 83
Handcross. *W Sus* —3D 26
Handforth. *Ches* —2C 84
Handley. *Ches* —5G 83
Handley. *Derbs* —4A 86
Handsacre. *Staf* —4E 73
Handsworth. *S Yor* —2B 86
Handsworth. *W Mid* —1E 61
Handy Cross. *Buck* —2G 37
Hanford. *Stoke* —1C 72
Hangersley Hill. *Hants* —2G 15
Hanging Haughton. *Nptn* —3E 63
Hanging Langford. *Wilts* —3F 23
Hangleton. *Brig* —5D 26
Hangleton. *W Sus* —5B 26
Hanham. *S Glo* —4B 34
Hanham Green. *S Glo* —4B 34
Hankelow. *Ches* —1A 72
Hankerton. *Wilts* —2E 35
Hankham. *E Sus* —5H 27
Hanley. *Stoke* —1C 72
Hanley Castle. *Worc* —1D 48
Hanley Childe. *Worc* —4A 60
Hanley Swan. *Worc* —1D 48
Hanley William. *Worc* —4A 60
Hanlith. *N Yor* —3B 98
Hanmer. *Wrex* —2G 71
Hannaborough. *Devn* —2F 11
Hannaford. *Devn* —4G 19
Hannah. *Linc* —3E 89
Hannington. *Hants* —1D 24
Hannington. *Nptn* —3F 63
Hannington. *Swin* —2G 35
Hannington Wick. *Swin* —2G 35
Hanscombe End. *Beds* —2B 52
Hanslope. *Mil* —1G 51
Hanthorpe. *Linc* —3H 75
Hanwell. *G Lon* —2C 38
Hanwell. *Oxon* —1C 50
Hanwood. *Shrp* —5G 71
Hanworth. *G Lon* —3C 38
Hanworth. *Norf* —2D 78
Happas. *Ang* —4D 144
Happendon. *S Lan* —1A 118
Happisburgh. *Norf* —2F 79
Happisburgh Common. *Norf*
—3F 79
Hapsford. *Ches* —3G 83
Hapton. *Lanc* —1F 91
Hapton. *Norf* —1D 66
Harberton. *Devn* —3D 9
Harbertonford. *Devn* —3D 9
Harbledown. *Kent* —5F 41
Harborne. *W Mid* —2E 61
Harborough Magna. *Warw* —3B 62
Harbottle. *Nmbd* —4D 120
Harbourneford. *Devn* —2D 8
Harbours Hill. *Worc* —4D 60
Harbridge. *Hants* —1G 15
Harbury. *Warw* —5A 62
Harby. *Leics* —2E 75
Harby. *Notts* —3F 87
Harcombe. *Devn* —3E 13
Harcombe Bottom. *Devn* —3G 13
Harcourt. *Corn* —5E 5
Harden. *W Yor* —1A 92
Hardenhuish. *Wilts* —4E 35
Hardgate. *Aber* —3E 153
Hardgate. *Dum* —3F 111
Hardham. *W Sus* —4B 26
Hardingham. *Norf* —5C 78
Hardingstone. *Nptn* —5E 63
Hardings Wood. *Ches* —5C 84
Hardington. *Som* —1C 22
Hardington Mandeville. *Som* —1A 14
Hardington Marsh. *Som* —2A 14
Hardington Moor. *Som* —1A 14
Hardley. *Hants* —2C 16
Hardley Street. *Norf* —5F 79
Hardmead. *Mil* —1H 51
Hardraw. *N Yor* —5B 104

Hardstott. *Derbs* —4B 86
Hardway. *Hants* —2E 16
Hardway. *Som* —3C 22
Hardwick. *Buck* —4G 51
Hardwick. *Cambs* —5C 64
Hardwick. *Norf* —2E 66
Hardwick. *Nptn* —4F 63
Hardwick. *Oxon* —3D 50
(nr. Bicester)
Hardwick. *Oxon* —5B 50
(nr. Witney)
Hardwick. *Shrp* —1F 59
Hardwick. *S Yor* —2B 86
Hardwick. *Stoc T* —2B 106
Hardwick. *W Mid* —1E 61
Hardwicke. *Glos* —3E 49
(nr. Cheltenham)
Hardwicke. *Glos* —4C 48
(nr. Gloucester)
Hardwicke. *Here* —1F 47
Hardwick Village. *Notts* —3D 86
Hardy's Green. *Essx* —3C 54
Hareby. *Linc* —4C 88
Hareden. *Lanc* —4F 97
Harefield. *G Lon* —1B 38
Hare Green. *Essx* —3D 54
Hare Hatch. *Wok* —4G 37
Harehill. *Derbs* —2F 73
Harehills. *W Yor* —1C 92
Harehope. *Nmbd* —2E 121
Harelaw. *Dum* —2F 113
Harelaw. *Dur* —4E 115
Hareplain. *Kent* —2C 28
Haresceugh. *Cumb* —5H 113
Harescombe. *Glos* —4D 48
Haresfield. *Glos* —4D 48
Haresfinch. *Mers* —1H 83
Hareshaw. *N Lan* —3B 128
Hare Street. *Essx* —5E 53
Hare Street. *Herts* —3D 53
Harewood. *W Yor* —5F 99
Harewood End. *Here* —3A 48
Harford. *Devn* —3D 8
Hargate. *Norf* —1D 66
Hargatewall. *Derbs* —3F 85
Hargrave. *Ches* —4G 83
Hargrave. *Nptn* —3H 63
Hargrave. *Suff* —5G 65
Harker. *Cumb* —3E 113
Harkstead. *Suff* —2E 55
Harlaston. *Staf* —4G 73
Harlaxton. *Linc* —2F 75
Harlech. *Gwyn* —2E 69
Harlequin. *Notts* —2D 74
Harlescott. *Shrp* —4H 71
Harleston. *Devn* —4D 9
Harleston. *Norf* —2E 67
Harleston. *Suff* —4C 66
Harlestone. *Nptn* —4E 62
Harley. *Shrp* —5H 71
Harley. *S Yor* —1A 86
Harling Road. *Norf* —2B 66
Harlington. *Beds* —2A 52
Harlington. *G Lon* —3B 38
Harlington. *S Yor* —4E 93
Harlosh. *High* —4B 154
Harlow. *Essx* —5E 53
Harlow Hill. *Nmbd* —3D 115
Harlsey Castle. *N Yor* —5B 106
Harlthorpe. *E Yor* —1H 93
Harlton. *Cambs* —5C 64
Harlyn. *Corn* —1C 6
Harman's Cross. *Dors* —4E 15
Harmby. *N Yor* —1D 98
Harmer Green. *Herts* —4C 52
Harmer Hill. *Shrp* —3G 71
Harmondsworth. *G Lon* —3B 38
Harmston. *Linc* —4G 87
Harnage. *Shrp* —5H 71
Harnham. *Nmbd* —1D 115
Harnhill. *Glos* —5F 49
Harold Hill. *G Lon* —1G 39
Haroldston West. *Pemb* —3C 42

Haroldswick. *Shet* —1H 173
Harold Wood. *G Lon* —1G 39
Harome. *N Yor* —1A 100
Harpenden. *Herts* —4B 52
Harpford. *Devn* —3D 12
Harpham. *E Yor* —3E 101
Harpley. *Norf* —3G 77
Harpley. *Worc* —4A 60
Harpole. *Nptn* —4D 62
Harpsdale. *High* —3D 168
Harpsden. *Oxon* —3F 37
Harpswell. *Linc* —2G 87
Harpurhey. *G Man* —4G 91
Harpur Hill. *Derbs* —3E 85
Harraby. *Cumb* —4F 113
Harracott. *Devn* —4F 19
Harrapool. *High* —1E 147
Harrietfield. *Per* —1B 136
Harrietsham. *Kent* —5C 40
Harrington. *Cumb* —2A 102
Harrington. *Linc* —3C 88
Harrington. *Nptn* —2E 63
Harringworth. *Nptn* —1G 63
Harriseahead. *Staf* —5C 84
Harriston. *Cumb* —5C 112
Harrogate. *N Yor* —4F 99
Harrold. *Beds* —5G 63
Harrop Dale. *G Man* —4A 92
Harrow. *G Lon* —2C 38
Harrowbarrow. *Corn* —2H 7
Harrowden. *Beds* —1A 52
Harrowgate Hill. *Darl* —3F 105
Harrow on the Hill. *G Lon* —2C 38
Harrow Weald. *G Lon* —1C 38
Harry Stoke. *S Glo* —4B 34
Harston. *Cambs* —5D 64
Harston. *Leics* —2F 75
Harswell. *E Yor* —5C 100
Hart. *Hart* —1B 106
Hartburn. *Nmbd* —1D 115
Hartburn. *Stoc T* —3B 106
Hartest. *Suff* —5H 65
Hartfield. *E Sus* —2F 27
Hartford. *Cambs* —3B 64
Hartford. *Ches* —3A 84
Hartford End. *Essx* —4G 53
Harthill. *Ches* —5H 83
Harthill. *N Lan* —3C 128
Harthill. *S Yor* —2B 86
Hartington. *Derbs* —4F 85
Hartland. *Devn* —4C 18
Hartland Quay. *Devn* —4C 18
Hartle. *Worc* —3D 60
Hartlebury. *Worc* —3C 60
Hartlepool. *Hart* —1C 106
Hartley. *Cumb* —4A 104
Hartley. *Kent* —2B 28
(nr. Cranbrook)
Hartley. *Kent* —4H 39
(nr. Dartford)
Hartley. *Nmbd* —2G 115
Hartley Green. *Staf* —2D 73
Hartley Mauditt. *Hants* —3F 25
Hartley Wespall. *Hants* —1E 25
Hartley Wintney. *Hants* —1F 25
Hartlip. *Kent* —4C 40
Hartmount. *High* —1B 158
Hartoft End. *N Yor* —5E 107
Harton. *N Yor* —3B 100
Harton. *Shrp* —2G 59
Harton. *Tyne* —3G 115
Hartpury. *Glos* —3C 48
Hartshead. *W Yor* —2B 92
Hartshill. *Warw* —1H 61
Hartshorne. *Derbs* —3H 73
Hartsop. *Cumb* —3F 103
Hart Station. *Hart* —1B 106
Hartswell. *Som* —4D 20
Hartwell. *Nptn* —5E 63
Hartwood. *Lanc* —3D 90
Hartwood. *N Lan* —4B 128
Harvel. *Kent* —4A 40

Harvington. *Worc* —1F 49
(nr. Evesham)
Harvington. *Worc* —3C 60
(nr. Kidderminster)
Harwell. *Oxon* —3C 36
Harwich. *Essx* —2F 55
Harwood. *Dur* —1B 104
Harwood. *G Man* —3F 91
Harwood Dale. *N Yor* —5G 107
Harworth. *Notts* —1D 86
Hascombe. *Surr* —1A 26
Haselbech. *Nptn* —3E 62
Haselbury Plucknett. *Som* —1H 13
Haseley. *Warw* —4G 61
Haselor. *Warw* —5F 61
Hasfield. *Glos* —3D 48
Hasguard. *Pemb* —4C 42
Haskayne. *Lanc* —4B 90
Hasketon. *Suff* —5E 67
Hasland. *Derbs* —4A 86
Haslemere. *Surr* —2A 26
Haslingden. *Lanc* —2F 91
Haslingden Grane. *Lanc* —2F 91
Haslingfield. *Cambs* —5D 64
Haslington. *Ches* —5B 84
Hassall. *Ches* —5B 84
Hassall Green. *Ches* —5B 84
Hassell Street. *Kent* —1E 29
Hassendean. *Scot* —2H 119
Hassingham. *Norf* —5F 79
Hassness. *Cumb* —3C 102
Hassocks. *W Sus* —4E 27
Hassop. *Derbs* —3G 85
Haste Hill. *Surr* —2A 26
Haster. *High* —3F 169
Hasthorpe. *Linc* —4D 89
Hastigrow. *High* —2E 169
Hastingleigh. *Kent* —1E 29
Hastings. *E Sus* —5C 28
Hastingwood. *Essx* —5E 53
Hastoe. *Herts* —5H 51
Haston. *Shrp* —3H 71
Haswell. *Dur* —5G 115
Haswell Plough. *Dur* —5G 115
Hatch. *Beds* —1B 52
Hatch Beauchamp. *Som* —4G 21
Hatch End. *G Lon* —1C 38
Hatch Green. *Som* —1G 13
Hatching Green. *Herts* —4B 52
Hatchmere. *Ches* —3H 83
Hatch Warren. *Hants* —2E 24
Hatcliffe. *NE Lin* —4F 95
Hatfield. *Here* —5H 59
Hatfield. *Herts* —5C 52
Hatfield. *S Yor* —4G 93
Hatfield. *Worc* —5C 60
Hatfield Broad Oak. *Essx* —4F 53
Hatfield Heath. *Essx* —4F 53
Hatfield Hyde. *Herts* —4C 52
Hatfield Peverel. *Essx* —4A 54
Hatfield Woodhouse. *S Yor* —4G 93
Hatford. *Oxon* —2B 36
Hatherden. *Hants* —1B 24
Hatherleigh. *Devn* —2F 11
Hathern. *Leics* —3C 74
Hatherop. *Glos* —5G 49
Hathersage. *Derbs* —2G 85
Hathersage Booths. *Derbs* —2G 85
Hatherton. *Ches* —1A 72
Hatherton. *Staf* —4D 72
Hatley St George. *Cambs* —5B 64
Hatt. *Corn* —2H 7
Hattersley. *G Man* —1D 85
Hattingley. *Hants* —3E 25
Hatton. *Aber* —5H 161
Hatton. *Derbs* —2G 73
Hatton. *G Lon* —3B 38
Hatton. *Linc* —3A 88
Hatton. *Shrp* —1G 59
Hatton. *Warr* —2H 83
Hatton. *Warw* —4G 61
Hattoncrook. *Aber* —1F 153
Hatton Heath. *Ches* —4G 83

Hatton of Fintray. *Aber* —2F 153
Haugh. *E Ayr* —2D 117
Haugh. *Linc* —3D 88
Haugham. *Linc* —2C 88
Haugh Head. *Nmbd* —2E 121
Haughley. *Suff* —4C 66
Haughley Green. *Suff* —4C 66
Haugh of Ballechin. *Per* —3G 143
Haugh of Glass. *Mor* —5B 160
Haugh of Urr. *Dum* —3F 111
Haughton. *Notts* —3D 86
Haughton. *Shrp* —1A 60
(nr. Bridgnorth)
Haughton. *Shrp* —3F 71
(nr. Oswestry)
Haughton. *Shrp* —5B 72
(nr. Shifnal)
Haughton. *Shrp* —4H 71
(nr. Shrewsbury)
Haughton. *Staf* —3C 72
Haughton Green. *G Man* —1D 84
Haughton le Skerne. *Darl* —3A 106
Haughton Moss. *Ches* —5H 83
Haultwick. *Herts* —3D 52
Haunn. *Arg* —4E 139
Haunn. *W Isl* —7C 170
Haunton. *Staf* —4G 73
Hauxley. *Nmbd* —4G 121
Hauxton. *Cambs* —5D 64
Havannah. *Ches* —4C 84
Havant. *Hants* —2F 17
Haven. *Here* —5G 59
Haven Bank. *Linc* —5B 88
Havenside. *E Yor* —2E 95
Havenstreet. *IOW* —3D 16
Haven, The. *W Sus* —2B 26
Havercroft. *W Yor* —3D 93
Haverfordwest. *Pemb* —3D 42
Haverhill. *Suff* —1G 53
Haverigg. *Cumb* —2A 96
Havering-atte-Bower. *G Lon* —1G 39
Havering's Grove. *Essx* —1A 40
Haversham. *Mil* —1G 51
Haverthwaite. *Cumb* —1C 96
Havyatt. *Som* —3A 22
Hawarden. *Flin* —4F 83
Hawcoat. *Cumb* —2B 96
Hawcross. *Glos* —2C 48
Hawen. *Cdgn* —1D 44
Hawes. *N Yor* —1A 98
Hawes Green. *Norf* —1E 67
Hawick. *Scot* —3H 119
Hawkchurch. *Devn* —2G 13
Hawkedon. *Suff* —5G 65
Hawkenbury. *Kent* —1C 28
Hawkeridge. *Wilts* —1D 22
Hawkerland. *Devn* —4D 12
Hawkesbury. *S Glo* —3C 34
Hawkesbury Upton. *S Glo* —3C 34
Hawkes End. *W Mid* —2G 61
Hawk Green. *G Man* —2D 84
Hawkhill. *Nmbd* —3G 121
Hawkhurst. *Kent* —2B 28
Hawkhurst Common. *E Sus* —4G 27
Hawkinge. *Kent* —2G 29
Hawkley. *Hants* —4F 25
Hawkridge. *Som* —3B 20
Hawksdale. *Cumb* —5E 113
Hawkshaw. *G Man* —3F 91
Hawkshead. *Cumb* —5E 103
Hawkshead Hill. *Cumb* —5E 103
Hawkswick. *N Yor* —2B 98
Hawksworth. *Notts* —1E 75
Hawksworth. *W Yor* —5D 98
Hawkwell. *Essx* —1C 40
Hawley. *Hants* —1G 25
Hawley. *Kent* —3G 39
Hawling. *Glos* —3F 49
Hawnby. *N Yor* —1H 99
Haworth. *W Yor* —1A 92
Hawstead. *Suff* —5A 66
Hawthorn. *Dur* —5H 115

Heythrop—Hoggard's Green

Heythrop. Oxon —3B 50
Heywood. G Man —3G 91
Heywood. Wilts —1D 22
Hibaldstow. N Lin —4C 94
Hickleton. S Yor —4E 93
Hickling. Norf —3G 79
Hickling. Notts —3D 74
Hickling Green. Norf —3G 79
Hickling Heath. Norf —3G 79
Hickstead. W Sus —3D 26
Hidcote Bartrim. Glos —1G 49
Hidcote Boyce. Glos —1G 49
Higford. Shrp —5B 72
High Ackworth. W Yor —3E 93
Higham. Derbs —5A 86
Higham. Kent —3B 40
Higham. Lanc —1G 91
Higham. S Yor —4D 92
Higham. Suff —2D 54
(nr. Ipswich)
Higham. Suff —4G 65
(nr. Newmarket)
Higham Dykes. Nmbd —2E 115
Higham Ferrers. Nptn —4G 63
Higham Gobion. Beds —2B 52
Higham on the Hill. Leics —1A 62
Highampton. Devn —2E 11
Higham Wood. Kent —1G 27
High Angerton. Nmbd —1D 115
High Auldgirth. Dum —1G 111
High Bankhill. Cumb —5G 113
High Banton. N Lan —1A 128
High Barnet. G Lon —1D 38
High Beech. Essx —1F 39
High Bentham. N Yor —3F 97
High Bickington. Devn —4G 19
High Biggins. Cumb —2F 97
High Birkwith. N Yor —2G 97
High Blantyre. S Lan —4H 127
High Bonnybridge. Falk —2B 128
High Borrans. Cumb —4F 103
High Bradfield. S Yor —1G 85
High Bray. Devn —3G 19
Highbridge. Cumb —5E 113
Highbridge. High —5D 148
Highbridge. Som —2G 21
Highbrook. W Sus —2E 27
High Brooms. Kent —1G 27
High Bullen. Devn —4F 19
Highburton. W Yor —3B 92
Highbury. Som —2B 22
High Buston. Nmbd —4G 121
High Callerton. Nmbd —2E 115
High Carlingill. Cumb —4H 103
High Catton. E Yor —4B 100
High Church. Nmbd —1E 115
Highclere. Hants —5C 36
Highcliffe. Dors —3H 15
High Cogges. Oxon —5B 50
High Common. Norf —5B 78
High Coniscliffe. Darl —3F 105
High Crosby. Cumb —4F 113
High Cross. Hants —4F 25
High Cross. Herts —4D 52
High Dougarie. N Ayr —2C 122
High Easter. Essx —4G 53
High Eggborough. N Yor —2F 93
High Ellington. N Yor —1D 98
Higher Alham. Som —2B 22
Higher Ansty. Dors —2C 14
Higher Ashton. Devn —4B 12
Higher Ballam. Lanc —1B 90
Higher Bartle. Lanc —1D 90
Higher Bockhampton. Dors —3C 14
High Ercall. Telf —4H 71
Higher Clovelly. Devn —4D 18
Higher Dinting. Derbs —1E 85
Higher End. G Man —4D 90
Higher Gabwell. Devn —2F 9
Higher Heysham. Lanc —3D 96
Higher Hurdsfield. Ches —3D 84
Higher Kingcombe. Dors —3A 14
Higher Kinnerton. Flin —4F 83
Higher Penwortham. Lanc —2D 90
Higher Porthpean. Corn —3E 7
Higher Poynton. Ches —2D 84
Higher Shotton. Flin —4F 83
Higher Shurlach. Ches —3A 84
Higher Tale. Devn —2D 12
Highertown. Corn —4C 6
Higher Town. IOS —1B 4
Higher Town. Som —2C 20
Higher Walton. Lanc —2D 90
Higher Walton. Warr —2A 84
Higher Whatcombe. Dors —2D 14
Higher Wheelton. Lanc —2E 90
Higher Whiteleigh. Corn —3C 10
Higher Whitley. Ches —3A 84
Higher Wincham. Ches —3A 84
Higher Wych. Ches —1G 71
High Etherley. Dur —2E 105
High Ferry. Linc —1C 76
Highfield. E Yor —1H 93
Highfield. N Ayr —4E 126
Highfield. Tyne —4E 115
Highfields. Cambs —5C 64
Highfields. Nmbd —4F 131
High Garrett. Essx —3A 54
Highgate. G Lon —2D 39
Highgate. N Ayr —4E 127
Highgate. Powy —1D 58
High Grange. Dur —1E 105
High Green. Cumb —4F 103
High Green. Norf —5D 78
High Green. Shrp —2B 60
High Green. S Yor —1H 85
High Green. W Yor —3B 92
High Green. Worc —1D 49
Highgreen Manor. Nmbd —5C 120
High Halden. Kent —2C 28
High Halstow. Medw —3B 40
High Ham. Som —3H 21
High Harrington. Cumb —2B 102
High Haswell. Dur —5G 115
High Hatton. Shrp —3A 72
High Hawkser. N Yor —4G 107
High Hesket. Cumb —5F 113
High Hesleden. Dur —1B 106
High Hoyland. S Yor —4C 92
High Hunsley. E Yor —1C 94
High Hurstwood. E Sus —3F 27
High Hutton. N Yor —3B 100
High Ireby. Cumb —1D 102
High Keil. Arg —5A 122
High Kelling. Norf —1D 78
High Kilburn. N Yor —2H 99
High Killerby. N Yor —1E 101
High Knipe. Cumb —3G 103
High Lands. Dur —2E 105
Highlands, The. Shrp —2A 60
Highlane. Ches —4C 84
Highlane. Derbs —2B 86
High Lane. G Man —2D 84
High Lane. Here —4A 60
High Laver. Essx —5F 53
Highlaws. Cumb —5C 112
Highleadon. Glos —3C 48
High Legh. Ches —2A 84
Highleigh. W Sus —3G 17
High Leven. Stoc T —3B 106
Highley. Shrp —2B 60
High Littleton. Bath —1B 22
High Longthwaite. Cumb —5D 112
High Lorton. Cumb —2C 102
High Marishes. N Yor —2C 100
High Marnham. Notts —3F 87
High Melton. S Yor —4F 93
High Mickley. Nmbd —3D 115
Highmoor. Cumb —5D 112
High Moor. Lanc —3D 90
Highmoor. Oxon —3F 37
Highmoor Hill. Mon —3H 33
High Mowthorpe. N Yor —3C 100
Highnam. Glos —4C 48
High Newport. Tyne —4G 115
High Newton. Cumb —1D 96
High Newton-by-the-Sea. Nmbd —2G 121
High Nibthwaite. Cumb —1B 96
High Offley. Staf —3B 72
High Ongar. Essx —5F 53
High Onn. Staf —4C 72
High Orchard. Glos —4D 48
High Park. Mers —3B 90
High Pennyvenie. E Ayr —4E 117
High Roding. Essx —4G 53
High Row. Cumb —1E 103
High Salvington. W Sus —5C 26
High Scales. Cumb —5C 112
High Seaton. Cumb —1B 102
High Shaw. N Yor —5B 104
High Side. Cumb —1D 102
High Spen. Tyne —3E 115
Highsted. Kent —4D 40
High Stoop. Dur —5E 115
High Street. Corn —3D 6
High Street. Suff —5G 67
(nr. Aldeburgh)
High Street. Suff —2F 67
(nr. Bungay)
High Street. Suff —3G 67
(nr. Yoxford)
Highstreet Green. Essx —2A 54
High Street Green. Suff —5C 66
Highstreet Green. Surr —2A 26
Hightae. Dum —2B 112
High Throston. Hart —1B 106
Hightown. Ches —4C 84
Hightown. Mers —4A 90
High Town. Staf —4D 73
Hightown Green. Suff —5B 66
High Toynton. Linc —4B 88
High Trewhitt. Nmbd —4E 121
High Valleyfield. Fife —1D 128
Highway. Here —1H 47
Highweek. Devn —5B 12
High Westwood. Dur —4E 115
Highwood. Staf —2E 73
Highwood. Worc —4A 60
High Worsall. N Yor —4A 106
Highworth. Swin —2H 35
High Wray. Cumb —5E 103
High Wych. Herts —4E 53
High Wycombe. Buck —2G 37
Hilborough. Norf —5H 77
Hilcott. Wilts —1G 23
Hildenborough. Kent —1G 27
Hildersham. Cambs —1F 53
Hilderstone. Staf —2D 72
Hilderthorpe. E Yor —3F 101
Hilfield. Dors —2B 14
Hilgay. Norf —1F 65
Hill. S Glo —2B 34
Hill. Warw —4B 62
Hill. Worc —1E 49
Hillam. N Yor —2F 93
Hillbeck. Cumb —3A 104
Hillberry. IOM —4C 108
Hillborough. Kent —4G 41
Hillbourne. Pool —3F 15
Hillbrae. Aber —4D 160
(nr. Aberchirder)
Hillbrae. Aber —1E 153
(nr. Inverurie)
Hillbrae. Aber —5F 161
(nr. Methlick)
Hill Brow. Hants —4F 25
Hillbutts. Dors —2E 15
Hillclifflane. Derbs —1G 73
Hill Deverill. Wilts —2D 22
Hilldyke. Linc —1C 76
Hill End. Dur —1D 104
Hillend. Fife —1E 129
(nr. Inverkeithing)
Hill End. Fife —4C 136
(nr. Saline)
Hillend. N Lan —3B 128
Hill End. N Yor —4C 98
Hillend. Shrp —1C 60
Hillend. Swan —3D 30
Hillersland. Glos —4A 48
Hillerton. Devn —3H 11
Hillesden. Buck —3E 51
Hillesley. Glos —3C 34
Hillfarrance. Som —4E 21
Hill Furze. Worc —1E 49
Hill Gate. Here —3H 47
Hill Green. Essx —2E 53
Hillgreen. W Ber —4C 36
Hillhead. E Ayr —3D 116
Hill Head. Hants —2D 16
Hillhead. Torb —3F 9
Hilliard's Cross. Staf —4F 73
Hilliclay. High —2D 168
Hillingdon. G Lon —2B 38
Hillington. Norf —3G 77
Hillington. Ren —3G 127
Hillmorton. Warw —3C 62
Hill of Beath. Fife —4D 136
Hill of Fearn. High —1C 158
Hill of Fiddes. Aber —1G 153
Hill of Keillor. Ang —4B 144
Hill of Overbrae. Aber —2F 161
Hill Ridware. Staf —4E 73
Hillsborough. S Yor —1H 85
Hillside. Aber —4G 153
Hillside. Ang —2G 145
Hillside. Devn —2D 8
Hillside. Hants —1F 25
Hillside. Mers —3B 90
Hillside. Orkn —5C 172
Hillside. Shet —5F 173
Hillside. Shrp —2A 60
Hill Side. W Yor —3B 92
Hillside. Worc —4B 60
Hillside of Prieston. Ang —5C 144
Hill Somersal. Derbs —2F 73
Hillstown. Derbs —4B 86
Hillstreet. Hants —1B 16
Hillswick. Shet —4D 173
Hill, The. Cumb —1A 96
Hill Top. Dur —2C 104
(nr. Barnard Castle)
Hill Top. Dur —5F 115
(nr. Durham)
Hill Top. Dur —4E 115
(nr. Stanley)
Hill Top. Hants —2C 16
Hill View. Dors —3E 15
Hill Wootton. Warw —4H 61
Hillyland. Per —1C 136
Hilmarton. Wilts —4F 35
Hilperton. Wilts —1D 22
Hilperton Marsh. Wilts —5D 34
Hilsea. Port —2E 17
Hilston. E Yor —1F 95
Hiltingbury. Hants —4C 24
Hilton. Cambs —4B 64
Hilton. Cumb —2A 104
Hilton. Derbs —2G 73
Hilton. Dors —2C 14
Hilton. Dur —2E 105
Hilton. High —5E 165
Hilton. Shrp —1B 60
Hilton. Staf —5E 73
Hilton. Stoc T —3B 106
Hilton of Cadboll. High —1C 158
Himbleton. Worc —5D 60
Himley. Staf —1C 60
Hincaster. Cumb —1E 97
Hinchcliffe Mill. W Yor —4B 92
Hinchwick. Glos —2G 49
Hinckley. Leics —1B 62
Hinderclay. Suff —3C 66
Hinderwell. N Yor —3E 107
Hindford. Shrp —2F 71
Hindhead. Surr —3G 25
Hindley. G Man —4E 91
Hindley. Nmbd —4D 114
Hindley Green. G Man —4E 91
Hindlip. Worc —5C 60
Hindolveston. Norf —3C 78
Hindon. Wilts —3E 23
Hindringham. Norf —2B 78
Hingham. Norf —5C 78
Hinksford. Staf —2C 60
Hinstock. Shrp —3A 72
Hintlesham. Suff —1D 54
Hinton. Hants —3H 15
Hinton. Here —2G 47
Hinton. Nptn —5C 62
Hinton. Shrp —5G 71
Hinton. S Glo —4C 34
Hinton Ampner. Hants —4D 24
Hinton Blewett. Bath —1A 22
Hinton Charterhouse. Bath —1C 22
Hinton-in-the-Hedges. Nptn —2D 50
Hinton Martell. Dors —2F 15
Hinton on the Green. Worc —1F 49
Hinton Parva. Swin —3H 35
Hinton St George. Som —1H 13
Hinton St Mary. Dors —1C 14
Hinton Waldrist. Oxon —2B 36
Hints. Shrp —3A 60
Hints. Staf —5F 73
Hinwick. Beds —4G 63
Hinxhill. Kent —1E 29
Hinxton. Cambs —1E 53
Hinxworth. Herts —1C 52
Hipley. Hants —1E 16
Hipperholme. W Yor —2B 92
Hipsburn. Nmbd —3G 121
Hipswell. N Yor —5E 105
Hiraeth. Carm —2F 43
Hirn. Aber —3E 153
Hirnant. Powy —3C 70
Hirst. Nmbd —1F 115
Hirst Courtney. N Yor —2G 93
Hirwaen. Den —4D 82
Hirwaun. Rhon —5C 46
Hiscott. Devn —4F 19
Histon. Cambs —4D 64
Hitcham. Suff —5B 66
Hitchin. Herts —3B 52
Hittisleigh. Devn —3H 11
Hittisleigh Barton. Devn —3H 11
Hive. E Yor —1B 94
Hixon. Staf —3E 73
Hoaden. Kent —5G 41
Hoar Cross. Staf —3F 73
Hoarwithy. Here —3A 48
Hoath. Kent —4G 41
Hobarris. Shrp —3F 59
Hobbles Green. Suff —5G 65
Hobbs Cross. Essx —1F 39
Hobkirk. Scot —3H 119
Hobson. Dur —4E 115
Hoby. Leics —4D 74
Hockering. Norf —4C 78
Hockering Heath. Norf —4C 78
Hockerton. Notts —5E 86
Hockley. Essx —1C 40
Hockley. Staf —5G 73
Hockley. W Mid —2G 61
Hockley Heath. W Mid —3F 61
Hockliffe. Beds —3H 51
Hockwold cum Wilton. Norf —2G 65
Hockworthy. Devn —1D 12
Hoddesdon. Herts —5D 52
Hoddlesden. Bkbn —2F 91
Hoddomcross. Dum —2C 112
Hodgeston. Pemb —5E 43
Hodley. Powy —1D 58
Hodnet. Shrp —3A 72
Hodsoll Street. Kent —4H 39
Hodson. Swin —3G 35
Hodthorpe. Derbs —3C 86
Hoe. Norf —4B 78
Hoe Gate. Hants —1E 17
Hoe, The. Plym —3A 8
Hoff. Cumb —3H 103
Hoffleet Stow. Linc —2B 76
Hogaland. Shet —4E 173
Hogben's Hill. Kent —5E 41
Hoggard's Green. Suff —5A 66

Hoggeston—Houghton on the Hill

Hoggeston. Buck—3G 51
Hoggrill's End. Warw—1G 61
Hogha Gearraidh. W Isl—1C 170
Hoghton. Lanc—2E 90
Hoghton Bottoms. Lanc—2E 91
Hognaston. Derbs—5G 85
Hogsthorpe. Linc—3E 89
Hogstock. Dors—2E 15
Holbeach. Linc—3C 76
Holbeach Bank. Linc—3C 76
Holbeach Clough. Linc—3C 76
Holbeach Drove. Linc—4C 76
Holbeach Hurn. Linc—3C 76
Holbeach St Johns. Linc—4C 76
Holbeach St Marks. Linc—2C 76
Holbeach St Matthew. Linc—2D 76
Holbeck. Notts—3C 86
Holbeck. W Yor—1C 92
Holberrow Green. Worc—5E 61
Holbeton. Devn—4C 8
Holborn. G Lon—2E 39
Holbrook. Derbs—1A 74
Holbrook. S Yor—2B 86
Holbrook. Suff—2E 55
Holburn. Nmbd—1E 121
Holbury. Hants—2C 16
Holcombe. Devn—5C 12
Holcombe. G Man—3F 91
Holcombe. Som—2B 22
Holcombe Brook. G Man—3F 91
Holcombe Rogus. Devn—1D 12
Holcot. Nptn—4E 63
Holden. Lanc—5G 97
Holdenby. Nptn—4D 62
Holder's Green. Essx—3G 53
Holdgate. Shrp—2H 59
Holdingham. Linc—1H 75
Holditch. Dors—2G 13
Holemoor. Devn—2E 11
Hole Street. W Sus—4C 26
Holford. Som—2E 21
Holker. Cumb—2C 96
Holkham. Norf—1A 78
Hollacombe. Devn—2D 11
Holland. Orkn—2D 172
Holland Fen. Linc—1B 76
Holland Lees. Lanc—4D 90
Holland-on-Sea. Essx—4E 55
Holland Park. W Mid—5E 73
Hollandstoun. Orkn—2G 172
Hollesley. Suff—1G 55
Hollinfare. Warr—1A 84
Hollingbourne. Kent—5C 40
Hollingbury. Brig—5E 27
Hollingdon. Buck—3G 51
Hollingrove. E Sus—3A 28
Hollington. Derbs—1G 73
Hollington. E Sus—4B 28
Hollington. Staf—2E 73
Hollington Grove. Derbs—2G 73
Hollingworth. G Man—1E 85
Hollins. Derbs—3H 85
Hollins. G Man—4G 91
Hollinsclough. Staf—4E 85
Hollinswood. Telf—5A 72
Hollinthorpe. W Yor—1D 93
Hollinwood. G Man—4H 91
Hollinwood. Shrp—2H 71
Hollocombe. Devn—1G 11
Holloway. Derbs—5H 85
Hollow Court. Worc—5D 61
Hollowell. Nptn—3D 62
Hollow Meadows. S Yor—2G 85
Hollows. Dum—2E 113
Hollybush. Cphy—5E 47
Hollybush. E Ayr—3C 116
Hollybush. Worc—2C 48
Holly End. Norf—5D 77
Holly Hill. N Yor—4E 105
Hollyhurst. Ches—1H 71
Hollym. E Yor—2G 95
Hollywood. Staf—2D 72
Hollywood. Worc—3E 61
Holmacott. Devn—4F 19
Holmbridge. W Yor—4B 92
Holmbury St Mary. Surr—1C 26
Holmbush. Corn—3E 7
Holmcroft. Staf—3D 72
Holme. Cambs—2A 64
Holme. Cumb—2E 97
Holme. N Lin—4C 94
Holme. N Yor—1F 99
Holme. Notts—5F 87
Holme. W Yor—4B 92
Holmebridge. Dors—4D 15
Holme Chapel. Lanc—2G 91
Holme Hale. Norf—5A 78
Holme Lacy. Here—2A 48
Holme Lane. Notts—2D 74
Holme Marsh. Here—5F 59
Holmend. Dum—4C 118
Holme next the Sea. Norf—1G 77
Holme-on-Spalding-Moor. E Yor—1B 94
Holme on the Wolds. E Yor—5D 100
Holme Pierrepont. Notts—2D 74
Holmer. Here—1A 48
Holmer Green. Buck—2G 37
Holmes. Lanc—3C 90
Holme St Cuthbert. Cumb—5C 112
Holmes Chapel. Ches—4B 84
Holmesfield. Derbs—3H 85
Holmeswood. Lanc—3C 90
Holmewood. Derbs—4B 86
Holmfirth. W Yor—4B 92
Holmhead. E Ayr—2E 117
Holmisdale. High—4A 154
Holm of Drumlanrig. Dum—5H 117
Holmpton. E Yor—2G 95
Holmrook. Cumb—5B 102
Holmsey Green. Suff—3F 65
Holmside. Dur—5F 115
Holmwrangle. Cumb—5G 113
Holne. Devn—2D 8
Holsworthy. Devn—2D 10
Holsworthy Beacon. Devn—2D 10
Holt. Dors—2F 15
Holt. Norf—2C 78
Holt. Wilts—5D 34
Holt. Worc—4C 60
Holt. Wrex—5G 83
Holtby. York—4A 100
Holt End. Hants—3E 25
Holt End. Worc—4E 61
Holt Fleet. Worc—4C 60
Holt Green. Lanc—4B 90
Holt Heath. Dors—2F 15
Holt Heath. Worc—4C 60
Holton. Oxon—5E 50
Holton. Som—4B 22
Holton. Suff—3F 67
Holton cum Beckering. Linc—2A 88
Holton Heath. Dors—3E 15
Holton le Clay. Linc—4F 95
Holton le Moor. Linc—1H 87
Holton St Mary. Suff—2D 54
Holt Pound. Hants—2G 25
Holtsmere End. Herts—4A 52
Holtye. E Sus—2F 27
Holwell. Dors—1C 14
Holwell. Herts—2B 52
Holwell. Leics—3E 75
Holwell. Oxon—5H 49
Holwell. Som—2C 22
Holwick. Dur—2C 104
Holworth. Dors—4C 14
Holybourne. Hants—2F 25
Holy Cross. Worc—3D 60
Holyfield. Essx—5D 53
Holyhead. IOA—2B 80
Holy Island. Nmbd—5H 131
Holymoorside. Derbs—4H 85
Holyport. Wind—4G 37
Holystone. Nmbd—4D 120
Holytown. N Lan—3A 128
Holywell. Cambs—3C 64
Holywell. Corn—3B 6
Holywell. Dors—2A 14
Holywell. Flin—3D 82
Holywell. Glos—2C 34
Holywell. Nmbd—2G 115
Holywell. Warw—4F 61
Holywell Green. W Yor—3A 92
Holywell Lake. Som—4E 20
Holywell Row. Suff—3G 65
Holywood. Dum—1G 111
Homer. Shrp—5A 72
Homer Green. Mers—4B 90
Homersfield. Suff—2E 67
Hom Green. Here—3A 48
Homington. Wilts—4G 23
Honeyborough. Pemb—4D 42
Honeybourne. Worc—1G 49
Honeychurch. Devn—2G 11
Honey Hill. Kent—4F 41
Honey Street. Wilts—5G 35
Honey Tye. Suff—2C 54
Honiley. Warw—3G 61
Honing. Norf—3F 79
Honingham. Norf—4D 78
Honington. Linc—1G 75
Honington. Suff—3B 66
Honington. Warw—1A 50
Honiton. Devn—2E 13
Honley. W Yor—3B 92
Honnington. Telf—4B 72
Hoo. Suff—5E 67
Hoobrook. Worc—3C 60
Hood Green. S Yor—4D 92
Hooe. E Sus—5A 28
Hooe. Plym—3A 8
Hooe Common. E Sus—4A 28
Hoohill. Bkpl—1B 90
Hook. Cambs—1D 64
Hook. G Lon—4C 38
Hook. Hants—1F 25
(nr. Basingstoke)
Hook. Hants—2D 16
(nr. Fareham)
Hook. N Lin—2A 94
Hook. Pemb—3D 43
Hook. Wilts—3F 35
Hook-a-Gate. Shrp—5G 71
Hook Bank. Worc—1D 48
Hooke. Dors—2A 14
Hooker Gate. Tyne—4E 115
Hookgate. Staf—2B 72
Hook Green. Kent—2A 28
(nr. Lamberhurst)
Hook Green. Kent—3H 39
(nr. Longfield)
Hook Green. Kent—4H 39
(nr. Meopham)
Hook Norton. Oxon—2B 50
Hook's Cross. Herts—3C 52
Hook Street. Glos—2B 34
Hookway. Devn—3B 12
Hookwood. Surr—1D 26
Hoole. Ches—4G 83
Hooley. Surr—5D 39
Hooley Bridge. G Man—3G 91
Hooley Brow. G Man—3G 91
Hoo St Werburgh. Medw—3B 40
Hooton. Ches—3F 83
Hooton Levitt. S Yor—1C 86
Hooton Pagnell. S Yor—4E 93
Hooton Roberts. S Yor—1B 86
Hope. Derbs—2F 85
Hope. Flin—5F 83
Hope. High—3E 167
Hope. Powy—5E 71
Hope. Shrp—5F 71
Hope. Staf—5F 85
Hope Bagot. Shrp—3H 59
Hope Bowdler. Shrp—1G 59
Hopedale. Staf—5F 85
Hope Green. Ches—2D 84
Hopeman. Mor—2F 159
Hope Mansell. Here—4B 48
Hopesay. Shrp—2F 59
Hope's Green. Essx—2B 40
Hopetown. W Yor—2D 93
Hope under Dinmore. Here—5H 59
Hopley's Green. Here—5F 59
Hopperton. N Yor—4G 99
Hop Pole. Linc—4A 76
Hopstone. Shrp—1B 60
Hopton. Derbs—5G 85
Hopton. Powy—1E 59
Hopton. Shrp—3F 71
(nr. Oswestry)
Hopton. Shrp—3H 71
(nr. Wem)
Hopton. Staf—3D 72
Hopton. Suff—3B 66
Hopton Cangeford. Shrp—2H 59
Hopton Castle. Shrp—3F 59
Hoptonheath. Shrp—3F 59
Hopton Heath. Staf—3D 72
Hopton on Sea. Norf—5H 79
Hopton Waters. Shrp—3A 60
Hopwas. Staf—5F 73
Hopwood. Worc—3E 61
Horam. E Sus—4G 27
Horbling. Linc—2A 76
Horbury. W Yor—3C 92
Horcott. Glos—5G 49
Horden. Dur—5H 115
Horderley. Shrp—2G 59
Hordle. Hants—3A 16
Hordley. Shrp—2F 71
Horeb. Carm—3F 45
(nr. Brechfa)
Horeb. Carm—5E 45
(nr. Llanelli)
Horeb. Cdgn—1D 45
Horfield. Bris—4B 34
Horgabost. W Isl—8C 171
Horham. Suff—3E 66
Horkesley Heath. Essx—3C 54
Horkstow. N Lin—3C 94
Horley. Oxon—1C 50
Horley. Surr—1D 27
Hornblotton Green. Som—3A 22
Hornby. Lanc—3E 97
Hornby. N Yor—4A 106
(nr. Appleton Wiske)
Hornby. N Yor—5F 105
(nr. Catterick Garrison)
Horncastle. Linc—4B 88
Hornchurch. G Lon—2G 39
Horncliffe. Nmbd—5F 131
Horndean. Hants—1E 17
Horndean. Scot—5E 131
Horndon. Devn—4F 11
Horndon on the Hill. Thur—2A 40
Horne. Surr—1E 27
Horner. Som—2C 20
Horning. Norf—4F 79
Horninghold. Leics—1F 63
Horninglow. Staf—3G 73
Horningsea. Cambs—4D 65
Horningsham. Wilts—2D 22
Horningtoft. Norf—3B 78
Hornsby. Cumb—4G 113
Hornsbygate. Cumb—4G 113
Horns Corner. Kent—3B 28
Horns Cross. Devn—4D 19
Hornsea. E Yor—5G 101
Hornsea Burton. E Yor—5G 101
Hornsey. G Lon—2E 39
Hornton. Oxon—1B 50
Horpit. Swin—3H 35
Horrabridge. Devn—2B 8
Horringer. Suff—4H 65
Horringford. IOW—4D 16
Horrocks Fold. G Man—3F 91
Horrocksford. Lanc—5G 97
Horsburgh Ford. Scot—1F 119
Horsebridge. Devn—5E 11
Horsebridge. Hants—3B 24
Horse Bridge. Staf—5D 84
Horsebrook. Staf—4C 72
Horsecastle. N Som—5H 33
Horsehay. Telf—5A 72
Horseheath. Cambs—1G 53
Horsehouse. N Yor—1C 98
Horsell. Surr—5A 38
Horseman's Green. Wrex—1G 71
Horsenden. Buck—5F 51
Horseway. Cambs—2D 64
Horsey. Norf—3G 79
Horsey. Som—3G 21
Horsford. Norf—4D 78
Horsforth. W Yor—1C 92
Horsham. W Sus—2C 26
Horsham. Worc—5B 60
Horsham St Faith. Norf—4E 78
Horsington. Linc—4A 88
Horsington. Som—4C 22
Horsley. Derbs—1A 74
Horsley. Glos—2D 34
Horsley. Nmbd—3D 115
(nr. Prudhoe)
Horsley. Nmbd—5C 120
(nr. Rochester)
Horsley Cross. Essx—3E 54
Horsleycross Street. Essx—3E 54
Horsleyhill. Scot—3H 119
Horsleyhope. Dur—5D 114
Horsley Woodhouse. Derbs—1A 74
Horsmonden. Kent—1A 28
Horspath. Oxon—5D 50
Horstead. Norf—4E 79
Horsted Keynes. W Sus—3E 27
Horton. Buck—4H 51
Horton. Dors—2F 15
Horton. Lanc—4A 98
Horton. Nptn—5F 63
Horton. Shrp—2G 71
Horton. Som—1G 13
Horton. S Glo—3C 34
Horton. Staf—5D 84
Horton. Swan—4D 30
Horton. Wilts—5F 35
Horton. Wind—3B 38
Horton Cross. Som—1G 13
Horton-cum-Studley. Oxon—4D 50
Horton Green. Ches—1G 71
Horton Heath. Hants—1C 16
Horton in Ribblesdale. N Yor—2H 97
Horton Kirby. Kent—4G 39
Hortonwood. Telf—4A 72
Horwich. G Man—3E 91
Horwich End. Derbs—2E 85
Horwood. Devn—4F 19
Hoscar. Lanc—3C 90
Hose. Leics—3E 75
Hosh. Per—1A 136
Hosta. W Isl—1C 170
Hoswick. Shet—9F 173
Hotham. E Yor—1B 94
Hothfield. Kent—1D 28
Hoton. Leics—3C 74
Houbie. Shet—2H 173
Hough. Arg—4A 138
Hough. Ches—5B 84
(nr. Crewe)
Hough. Ches—3C 84
(nr. Wilmslow)
Hougham. Linc—1F 75
Hough Green. Hal—2G 83
Hough-on-the-Hill. Linc—1G 75
Houghton. Cambs—3B 64
Houghton. Cumb—4F 113
Houghton. Hants—3B 24
Houghton. Nmbd—3E 115
Houghton. Pemb—4D 43
Houghton. W Sus—4B 26
Houghton Bank. Darl—2F 105
Houghton Conquest. Beds—1A 52
Houghton Green. E Sus—3D 28
Houghton-le-Side. Darl—2F 105
Houghton-le-Spring. Tyne—5G 115
Houghton on the Hill. Leics—5D 74

Houghton Regis. *Beds* —3A **52**
Houghton St Giles. *Norf* —2B **78**
Houlsyke. *N Yor* —4E **107**
Hound. *Hants* —2C **16**
Hound Green. *Hants* —1F **25**
Houndslow. *Scot* —5C **130**
Houndsmoor. *Som* —4E **21**
Houndwood. *Scot* —3E **131**
Hounsdown. *Hants* —1B **16**
Hounslow. *G Lon* —3C **38**
Housay. *Shet* —4H **173**
Househill. *High* —3C **158**
Housetter. *Shet* —3E **173**
Houss. *Shet* —8E **173**
Houston. *Ren* —3F **127**
Housty. *High* —5D **168**
Houton. *Orkn* —7C **172**
Hove. *Brig* —5D **27**
Hoveringham. *Notts* —1E **74**
Hoveton. *Norf* —4F **79**
Hovingham. *N Yor* —2A **100**
How. *Cumb* —4G **113**
How Caple. *Here* —2B **48**
Howden. *E Yor* —2H **93**
Howden-le-Wear. *Dur* —1F **105**
Howe. *Cumb* —1D **96**
Howe. *High* —2F **169**
Howe. *Norf* —5E **79**
Howe. *N Yor* —1F **99**
Howe Green. *Essx* —5H **53**
(nr. Chelmsford)
Howegreen. *Essx* —5B **54**
(nr. Maldon)
Howell. *Linc* —1A **76**
How End. *Beds* —1A **52**
Howe of Teuchar. *Aber* —4E **161**
Howes. *Dum* —3C **112**
Howe Street. *Essx* —4G **53**
(nr. Chelmsford)
Howe Street. *Essx* —2G **53**
(nr. Finchingfield)
Howe, The. *IOM* —5A **108**
Howey. *Powy* —5C **58**
Howgate. *Midl* —4F **129**
Howgill. *Lanc* —5H **97**
Howgill. *N Yor* —4C **98**
How Green. *Kent* —1F **27**
How Green. *Warw* —2H **61**
How Hill. *Norf* —4F **79**
Howick. *Nmbd* —3G **121**
Howle. *Telf* —3A **72**
Howle Hill. *Here* —3B **48**
Howleigh. *Som* —1F **13**
Howlett End. *Essx* —2F **53**
Howley. *Som* —2F **13**
Howley. *Warr* —2A **84**
Hownam. *Scot* —3B **120**
Howsham. *N Lin* —4D **94**
Howsham. *N Yor* —3B **100**
Howtel. *Nmbd* —1C **120**
Howt Green. *Kent* —4C **40**
Howton. *Here* —3H **47**
Howwood. *Ren* —3F **127**
Hoxne. *Suff* —3D **66**
Hoylake. *Mers* —2E **82**
Hoyland. *S Yor* —4D **92**
Hoylandswaine. *S Yor* —4C **92**
Hoyle. *W Sus* —4A **26**
Hubberholme. *N Yor* —2B **98**
Hubberston. *Pemb* —4C **42**
Hubbert's Bridge. *Linc* —1B **76**
Huby. *N Yor* —5E **99**
(nr. Harrogate)
Huby. *N Yor* —3H **99**
(nr. York)
Huccaby. *Devn* —5G **11**
Hucclecote. *Glos* —4D **48**
Hucking. *Kent* —5C **40**
Hucknall. *Notts* —1C **74**
Huddersfield. *W Yor* —3B **92**
Huddington. *Worc* —5D **60**
Huddlesford. *Staf* —5F **73**
Hudswell. *N Yor* —4E **105**

Huggate. *E Yor* —4C **100**
Hugglescote. *Leics* —4B **74**
Hughenden Valley. *Buck* —2G **37**
Hughley. *Shrp* —1H **59**
Hughton. *High* —4G **157**
Hugh Town. *IOS* —1B **4**
Hugus. *Corn* —4B **6**
Huish. *Wilts* —5G **35**
Huish Champflower. *Som* —4D **20**
Huish Episcopi. *Som* —4H **21**
Huisinis. *W Isl* —6B **171**
Hulcote. *Nptn* —1F **51**
Hulcott. *Buck* —4G **51**
Hulham. *Devn* —4D **12**
Hulland. *Derbs* —1G **73**
Hulland Moss. *Derbs* —1G **73**
Hulland Ward. *Derbs* —1G **73**
Hullavington. *Wilts* —3D **35**
Hullbridge. *Essx* —1C **40**
Hulme. *G Man* —1C **84**
Hulme. *Staf* —1D **72**
Hulme End. *Staf* —5F **85**
Hulme Walfield. *Ches* —4C **84**
Hulverstone. *IOW* —4B **16**
Hulver Street. *Suff* —2G **67**
Humber. *Devn* —5C **12**
Humber Court. *Here* —5H **59**
Humberside Airport. *N Lin* —3D **94**
Humberston. *NE Lin* —4G **95**
Humberstone. *Leic C* —5D **74**
Humbie. *E Lot* —3A **130**
Humbleton. *E Yor* —1F **95**
Humbleton. *Nmbd* —2D **121**
Humby. *Linc* —2H **75**
Hume. *Scot* —5D **130**
Humshaugh. *Nmbd* —2C **114**
Huna. *High* —1F **169**
Huncoat. *Lanc* —1F **91**
Huncote. *Leics* —1C **62**
Hundall. *Derbs* —3A **86**
Hunderthwaite. *Dur* —2C **104**
Hundleby. *Linc* —4C **88**
Hundle Houses. *Linc* —5B **88**
Hundleton. *Pemb* —4D **42**
Hundon. *Suff* —1H **53**
Hundred Acres. *Hants* —1D **16**
Hundred House. *Powy* —5D **58**
Hundred, The. *Here* —4H **59**
Hungarton. *Leics* —5D **74**
Hungerford. *Hants* —1G **15**
Hungerford. *Shrp* —2H **59**
Hungerford. *Som* —2D **20**
Hungerford. *W Ber* —5B **36**
Hungerford Newtown. *W Ber*
　　　　　　　　　　　—4B **36**
Hunger Hill. *G Man* —4E **91**
Hungerton. *Linc* —2F **75**
Hungladder. *High* —1C **154**
Hungryhatton. *Shrp* —3A **72**
Hunmanby. *N Yor* —2E **101**
Hunmanby Sands. *N Yor* —2F **101**
Hunningham. *Warw* —4A **62**
Hunnington. *W Mid* —2D **60**
Hunny Hill. *IOW* —4C **16**
Hunsdon. *Herts* —4E **53**
Hunsingore. *N Yor* —4G **99**
Hunslet. *W Yor* —1D **92**
Hunslet Carr. *W Yor* —2D **92**
Hunsonby. *Cumb* —1G **103**
Hunspow. *High* —1E **169**
Hunstanton. *Norf* —1F **77**
Hunstanworth. *Dur* —5C **114**
Hunston. *Suff* —4B **66**
Hunston. *W Sus* —2G **17**
Hunstrete. *Bath* —5B **34**
Hunt End. *Worc* —4E **61**
Hunterfield. *Midl* —3G **129**
Hunter's Quay. *Arg* —2C **126**
Huntham. *Som* —4G **21**
Hunthill Lodge. *Ang* —1D **144**
Huntingdon. *Cambs* —3B **64**
Huntingfield. *Suff* —3F **67**
Huntingford. *Wilts* —3D **22**

Huntington. *Ches* —4G **83**
Huntington. *E Lot* —2A **130**
Huntington. *Here* —5E **59**
Huntington. *Staf* —4D **72**
Huntington. *Telf* —5A **72**
Huntington. *York* —4A **100**
Huntingtower. *Per* —1C **136**
Huntley. *Glos* —4C **48**
Huntley. *Staf* —1E **73**
Huntly. *Aber* —4C **160**
Huntlywood. *Scot* —5C **130**
Hunton. *Hants* —3C **24**
Hunton. *Kent* —1B **28**
Hunton. *N Yor* —5E **105**
Hunton Bridge. *Herts* —5A **52**
Hunt's Corner. *Norf* —2C **66**
Huntscott. *Som* —2C **20**
Hunt's Cross. *Mers* —2G **83**
Hunts Green. *Warw* —1F **61**
Huntsham. *Devn* —4D **20**
Huntshaw. *Devn* —4F **19**
Huntspill. *Som* —2G **21**
Huntstile. *Som* —3F **21**
Huntstrete. *Bath* —5B **34**
Huntworth. *Som* —3G **21**
Hunwick. *Dur* —1E **105**
Hunworth. *Norf* —2C **78**
Hurcott. *Som* —1G **13**
(nr. Ilminster)
Hurcott. *Som* —4A **22**
(nr. Somerton)
Hurdcott. *Wilts* —3G **23**
Hurdley. *Powy* —1E **59**
Hurdsfield. *Ches* —3D **84**
Hurlet. *Glas* —3G **127**
Hurley. *Warw* —1G **61**
Hurley. *Wind* —3G **37**
Hurlford. *E Ayr* —1D **116**
Hurliston Green. *Lanc* —3B **90**
Hurn. *Dors* —3G **15**
Hursey. *Dors* —2H **13**
Hursley. *Hants* —4C **24**
Hurst. *G Man* —4H **91**
Hurst. *N Yor* —4D **104**
Hurst. *Wok* —4F **37**
Hurstbourne Priors. *Hants* —2C **24**
Hurstbourne Tarrant. *Hants* —1B **24**
Hurst Green. *Ches* —1H **71**
Hurst Green. *E Sus* —3B **28**
Hurst Green. *Essx* —4D **54**
Hurst Green. *Lanc* —1E **91**
Hurst Green. *Surr* —5E **39**
Hurstley. *Here* —1G **47**
Hurstpierpoint. *W Sus* —4D **27**
Hurstway Common. *Here* —1F **47**
Hurst Wickham. *W Sus* —4D **27**
Hurstwood. *Lanc* —1G **91**
Hurtmore. *Surr* —1A **26**
Hurworth-on-Tees. *Darl* —3A **106**
Hurworth Place. *Darl* —3F **105**
Hury. *Dur* —3C **104**
Husbands Bosworth. *Leics* —2D **62**
Husborne Crawley. *Beds* —2H **51**
Husthwaite. *N Yor* —2H **99**
Hutcherleigh. *Devn* —3D **9**
Hut Green. *N Yor* —2F **93**
Huthwaite. *Notts* —5B **86**
Huttoft. *Linc* —3E **89**
Hutton. *Cumb* —2F **103**
Hutton. *Essx* —1H **39**
Hutton. *Lanc* —2C **90**
Hutton. *N Som* —1G **21**
Hutton. *Scot* —4F **131**
Hutton Bonville. *N Yor* —4A **106**
Hutton Buscel. *N Yor* —1D **100**
Hutton Conyers. *N Yor* —2F **99**
Hutton Cranswick. *E Yor* —4E **101**
Hutton End. *Cumb* —1F **103**
Hutton Gate. *Red C* —3C **106**
Hutton Henry. *Dur* —1B **106**
Hutton-le-Hole. *N Yor* —1B **100**
Hutton Magna. *Dur* —3E **105**
Hutton Mulgrave. *N Yor* —3F **107**

Hutton Roof. *Cumb* —2E **97**
(nr. Kirkby Lonsdale)
Hutton Roof. *Cumb* —1E **103**
(nr. Penrith)
Hutton Rudby. *N Yor* —4B **106**
Huttons Ambro. *N Yor* —3B **100**
Hutton Sessay. *N Yor* —2G **99**
Hutton Village. *Red C* —3D **106**
Hutton Wandesley. *N Yor* —4H **99**
Huxham. *Devn* —3C **12**
Huxham Green. *Som* —3A **22**
Huxley. *Ches* —4H **83**
Huyton. *Mers* —1G **83**
Hwlffordd. *Pemb* —3D **42**
Hycemoor. *Cumb* —1A **96**
Hyde. *Glos* —5D **49**
(nr. Stroud)
Hyde. *Glos* —3F **49**
(nr. Winchcombe)
Hyde. *G Man* —1D **84**
Hyde Lea. *Staf* —4D **72**
Hyde Park. *S Yor* —4F **93**
Hydestile. *Surr* —1A **26**
Hykeham Moor. *Linc* —4G **87**
Hyndford Bridge. *S Lan* —5C **128**
Hynish. *Arg* —5A **138**
Hyssington. *Powy* —1F **59**
Hythe. *Hants* —2C **16**
Hythe. *Kent* —2F **29**
Hythe End. *Wind* —3B **38**
Hythie. *Aber* —3H **161**
Hyton. *Cumb* —1A **96**

I anstown. *Mor* —2B **160**
Iarsiadar. *W Isl* —4D **171**
Ibberton. *Dors* —2C **14**
Ible. *Derbs* —5G **85**
Ibrox. *Glas* —3G **127**
Ibsley. *Hants* —2G **15**
Ibstock. *Leics* —4B **74**
Ibstone. *Buck* —2F **37**
Ibthorpe. *Hants* —1B **24**
Iburndale. *N Yor* —4F **107**
Ibworth. *Hants* —1D **24**
Icelton. *N Som* —5G **33**
Ichrachan. *Arg* —5E **141**
Ickburgh. *Norf* —1H **65**
Ickenham. *G Lon* —2B **38**
Ickford. *Buck* —5E **51**
Ickham. *Kent* —5G **41**
Ickleford. *Herts* —2B **52**
Icklesham. *E Sus* —4C **28**
Ickleton. *Cambs* —1E **53**
Icklingham. *Suff* —3G **65**
Ickwell. *Beds* —1B **52**
Icomb. *Glos* —3H **49**
Idbury. *Oxon* —4H **49**
Iddesleigh. *Devn* —2F **11**
Ide. *Devn* —3C **12**
Ideford. *Devn* —5B **12**
Ide Hill. *Kent* —5F **39**
Iden. *E Sus* —3D **28**
Iden Green. *Kent* —2C **28**
(nr. Benenden)
Iden Green. *Kent* —2B **28**
(nr. Goudhurst)
Idle. *W Yor* —1B **92**
Idless. *Corn* —4C **6**
Idlicote. *Warw* —1A **50**
Idmiston. *Wilts* —3G **23**
Idole. *Carm* —4E **45**
Idridgehay. *Derbs* —1G **73**
Idrigill. *High* —2C **154**
Idstone. *Oxon* —3A **36**
Iffley. *Oxon* —5D **50**
Ifield. *W Sus* —2D **26**
Ifieldwood. *W Sus* —2D **26**
Ifold. *W Sus* —2B **26**
Iford. *E Sus* —5F **27**
Ifton Heath. *Shrp* —2F **71**
Ightfield. *Shrp* —2H **71**

Ightham. *Kent* —5G **39**
Iken. *Suff* —5G **67**
Ilam. *Staf* —5F **85**
Ilchester. *Som* —4A **22**
Ilderton. *Nmbd* —2E **121**
Ilford. *G Lon* —2F **39**
Ilford. *Som* —1G **13**
Ilfracombe. *Devn* —2F **19**
Ilkeston. *Derbs* —1B **74**
Ilketshall St Andrew. *Suff* —2F **67**
Ilketshall St Lawrence. *Suff* —2F **67**
Ilketshall St Margaret. *Suff* —2F **67**
Ilkley. *W Yor* —5D **98**
Illand. *Corn* —5C **10**
Illey. *W Mid* —2D **61**
Illidge Green. *Ches* —4B **84**
Illington. *Norf* —2B **66**
Illingworth. *W Yor* —2A **92**
Illogan. *Corn* —4A **6**
Illogan Highway. *Corn* —4A **6**
Illston on the Hill. *Leics* —1E **62**
Ilmer. *Buck* —5F **51**
Ilmington. *Warw* —1H **49**
Ilminster. *Som* —1G **13**
Ilsington. *Devn* —5A **12**
Ilsington. *Dors* —3C **14**
Ilston. *Swan* —3E **31**
Ilton. *N Yor* —2D **98**
Ilton. *Som* —1G **13**
Imachar. *N Ayr* —5G **125**
Imber. *Wilts* —2E **23**
Immingham. *NE Lin* —3E **95**
Immingham Dock. *NE Lin* —3E **95**
Impington. *Cambs* —4D **64**
Ince. *Ches* —3G **83**
Ince Blundell. *Mers* —4B **90**
Ince-in-Makerfield. *G Man* —4D **90**
Inchbae Lodge. *High* —2G **157**
Inchbare. *Ang* —2F **145**
Inchberry. *Mor* —3H **159**
Inchbraoch. *Ang* —3G **145**
Inchbrook. *Glos* —5D **48**
Incheril. *High* —2C **156**
Inchinnan. *Ren* —3F **127**
Inchlaggan. *High* —3D **148**
Inchmichael. *Per* —1E **137**
Inchnadamph. *High* —1G **163**
Inchree. *High* —2E **141**
Inchture. *Per* —1E **137**
Inchyra. *Per* —1D **136**
Indian Queens. *Corn* —3D **6**
Ingatestone. *Essx* —1H **39**
Ingbirchworth. *S Yor* —4C **92**
Ingestre. *Staf* —3D **73**
Ingham. *Linc* —2G **87**
Ingham. *Norf* —3F **79**
Ingham. *Suff* —3A **66**
Ingham Corner. *Norf* —3F **79**
Ingleborough. *Norf* —4D **76**
Ingleby. *Derbs* —3H **73**
Ingleby Arncliffe. *N Yor* —4B **106**
Ingleby Barwick. *Stoc T* —3B **106**
Ingleby Greenhow. *N Yor* —4C **106**
Ingleigh Green. *Devn* —2G **11**
Inglemire. *Hull* —1D **94**
Inglesbatch. *Bath* —5C **34**
Ingleton. *Dur* —2E **105**
Ingleton. *N Yor* —2F **97**
Inglewhite. *Lanc* —5E **97**
Ingoe. *Nmbd* —2D **114**
Ingol. *Lanc* —1D **90**
Ingoldisthorpe. *Norf* —2F **77**
Ingoldmells. *Linc* —4E **89**
Ingoldsby. *Linc* —2H **75**
Ingon. *Warw* —5G **61**
Ingram. *Nmbd* —3E **121**
Ingrave. *Essx* —1H **39**
Ingrow. *W Yor* —1A **92**
Ings. *Cumb* —5F **103**
Ingst. *S Glo* —3A **34**
Ingthorpe. *Rut* —5G **75**
Ingworth. *Norf* —3D **78**
Inkberrow. *Worc* —5E **61**

Kestle Mill—Kinrossie

Kestle Mill. Corn —3C 6
Keston. G Lon —4F 39
Keswick. Cumb —2D 102
Keswick. Norf —2F 79
(nr. North Walsham)
Keswick. Norf —5E 78
(nr. Norwich)
Ketsby. Linc —3C 88
Kettering. Nptn —3F 63
Ketteringham. Norf —5D 78
Kettins. Per —5B 144
Kettlebaston. Suff —5B 66
Kettlebridge. Fife —3F 137
Kettlebrook. Staf —5G 73
Kettleburgh. Suff —4E 67
Kettleholm. Dum —2C 112
Kettleness. N Yor —3F 107
Kettleshulme. Ches —3D 85
Kettlesing. N Yor —4E 99
Kettlesing Bottom. N Yor —4E 99
Kettlestone. Norf —2B 78
Kettlethorpe. Linc —3F 87
Kettletoft. Orkn —4F 172
Kettlewell. N Yor —2B 98
Ketton. Rut —5G 75
Kew. G Lon —3C 38
Kewaigue. IOM —4C 108
Kewstoke. N Som —5G 33
Kexbrough. S Yor —4D 92
Kexby. Linc —2F 87
Kexby. York —4B 100
Keyford. Som —2C 22
Key Green. Ches —4C 84
Key Green. N Yor —4F 107
Keyham. Leics —5D 74
Keyhaven. Hants —3B 16
Keyhead. Aber —3H 161
Keyingham. E Yor —2F 95
Keymer. W Sus —4E 27
Keynsham. Bath —5B 34
Keysoe. Beds —4H 63
Keysoe Row. Beds —4H 63
Key's Toft. Linc —5D 89
Keyston. Cambs —3H 63
Key Street. Kent —4C 40
Keyworth. Notts —2D 74
Kibblesworth. Tyne —4F 115
Kibworth Beauchamp. Leics —1D 62
Kibworth Harcourt. Leics —1D 62
Kidbrooke. G Lon —3F 39
Kidburngill. Cumb —2B 102
Kiddemore Green. Staf —5C 72
Kidderminster. Worc —3C 60
Kiddington. Oxon —3C 50
Kidd's Moor. Norf —5D 78
Kidlington. Oxon —4C 50
Kidmore End. Oxon —4E 37
Kidnal. Ches —1G 71
Kidsgrove. Staf —5C 84
Kidstones. N Yor —1B 98
Kidwelly. Carm —5E 45
Kiel Crofts. Arg —5D 140
Kielder. Nmbd —5A 120
Kiells. Arg —3C 124
Kilbagie. Fife —4B 136
Kilbarchan. Ren —3F 127
Kilbeg. High —3E 147
Kilberry. Arg —3F 125
Kilbirnie. N Ayr —4E 126
Kilbride. Arg —1F 133
Kilbride. High —1D 147
Kilbucho Place. Scot —1C 118
Kilburn. Derbs —1A 74
Kilburn. G Lon —2D 38
Kilburn. N Yor —2H 99
Kilby. Leics —1D 62
Kilchattan. Arg —4C 126
(on Bute)
Kilchattan. Arg —4A 132
(on Colonsay)
Kilchattan Bay. Arg —4B 126
Kilchenzie. Arg —3A 122
Kilcheran. Arg —5C 140
Kilchiaran. Arg —4A 124
Kilchoan. High —4F 147
(nr. Inverie)
Kilchoan. High —2F 139
(nr. Tobermory)
Kilchoman. Arg —3A 124
Kilchrenan. Arg —1H 133
Kilconquhar. Fife —3G 137
Kilcot. Glos —3B 48
Kilcoy. High —3H 157
Kilcreggan. Arg —1D 126
Kildale. N Yor —4D 106
Kildary. High —1B 158
Kildermorie Lodge. High —1H 157
Kildonan. Dum —4F 109
Kildonan. High —1G 165
Kildonan. N Ayr —3E 123
Kildrummy. Aber —2B 152
Kildwick. W Yor —5C 98
Kilfillan. Dum —4H 109
Kilfinan. Arg —2H 125
Kilfinnan. High —4E 149
Kilgetty. Pemb —4F 43
Kilgour. Fife —3E 136
Kilgrammie. S Ayr —4B 116
Kilham. E Yor —3E 101
Kilham. Nmbd —1C 120
Kilkenneth. Arg —4A 138
Kilkhampton. Corn —1C 10
Killamarsh. Derbs —2B 86
Killandrist. Arg —4C 140
Killay. Swan —3F 31
Killean. Arg —5E 125
Killearn. Stir —1G 127
Killellan. Arg —4A 122
Killen. High —3A 158
Killerby. Darl —3E 105
Killichonan. Per —3C 142
Killiechronan. Arg —4G 139
Killiecrankie. Per —2G 143
Killilan. High —5B 156
Killimster. High —3F 169
Killin. Stir —5C 142
Killinghall. N Yor —4E 99
Killinghurst. Surr —2A 26
Killington. Cumb —1F 97
Killingworth. Tyne —2F 115
Killin Lodge. High —3H 149
Killinochonoch. Arg —4F 133
Killochyett. Scot —5A 130
Killundine. High —3G 139
Kilmacolm. Inv —3E 127
Kilmahog. Stir —3F 135
Kilmahumaig. Arg —4E 133
Kilmalieu. High —3C 140
Kilmaluag. High —1D 154
Kilmany. Fife —1F 137
Kilmarie. High —2D 146
Kilmarnock. E Ayr —1D 116
Kilmaron. Fife —2F 137
Kilmartin. Arg —4F 133
Kilmaurs. E Ayr —5F 127
Kilmelford. Arg —2F 133
Kilmeny. Arg —3B 124
Kilmersdon. Som —1B 22
Kilmeston. Hants —4D 24
Kilmichael Glassary. Arg —4F 133
Kilmichael of Inverlussa. Arg —1F 125
Kilmington. Devn —3F 13
Kilmington. Wilts —3C 22
Kilmoluag. Arg —4A 138
Kilmorack. High —4G 157
Kilmore. Arg —1F 133
Kilmore. High —3E 147
Kilmory. Arg —2F 125
Kilmory. High —1G 139
(nr. Kilchoan)
Kilmory. High —3B 146
(on Rhum)
Kilmory. N Ayr —3D 122
Kilmory Lodge. Arg —3E 132
Kilmote. High —2G 165
Kilmuir. High —4B 154
(nr. Dunvegan)
Kilmuir. High —1B 158
(nr. Invergordon)
Kilmuir. High —4A 158
(nr. Inverness)
Kilmuir. High —1C 154
(nr. Uig)
Kilmun. Arg —1C 126
Kilnave. Arg —2A 124
Kilncadzow. S Lan —5B 128
Kilndown. Kent —2B 28
Kiln Green. Here —4A 48
Kiln Green. Wind —4G 37
Kilnhill. Cumb —1D 102
Kilnhurst. S Yor —1B 86
Kilninian. Arg —4E 139
Kilninver. Arg —1F 133
Kiln Pit Hill. Nmbd —4D 114
Kilnsea. E Yor —3H 95
Kilnsey. N Yor —3B 98
Kilnwick. E Yor —5D 101
Kiloran. Arg —3A 132
Kilpatrick. N Ayr —3D 122
Kilpeck. Here —2H 47
Kilpin. E Yor —2A 94
Kilpin Pike. E Yor —2A 94
Kilrenny. Fife —3H 137
Kilsby. Nptn —3C 62
Kilspindie. Per —1E 136
Kilsyth. N Lan —2A 128
Kiltarlity. High —4H 157
Kilton. Som —2E 21
Kilton Thorpe. Red C —3D 107
Kilvaxter. High —2C 154
Kilve. Som —2E 21
Kilvington. Notts —1F 75
Kilwinning. N Ayr —5D 126
Kimberley. Norf —5C 78
Kimberley. Notts —1B 74
Kimblesworth. Dur —5F 115
Kimble Wick. Buck —5G 51
Kimbolton. Cambs —4H 63
Kimbolton. Here —4H 59
Kimcote. Leics —2C 62
Kimmeridge. Dors —5E 15
Kimmerston. Nmbd —1D 120
Kimpton. Hants —2A 24
Kimpton. Herts —4B 52
Kinbeachie. High —2A 158
Kinbrace. High —5A 168
Kinbuck. Stir —3G 135
Kincaple. Fife —2G 137
Kincardine. Fife —1C 128
Kincardine. High —5D 164
Kincardine O'Neil. Aber —4C 152
Kinchrackine. Arg —1A 134
Kincorth. Aber C —3G 153
Kincraig. High —3C 150
Kincraigie. Per —4G 143
Kindallachan. Per —3G 143
Kineton. Glos —3F 49
Kineton. Warw —5H 61
Kinfauns. Per —1D 136
Kingairloch. High —3C 140
Kingarth. Arg —4B 126
Kingcoed. Mon —5H 47
Kingerby. Linc —1H 87
Kingham. Oxon —3A 50
Kingholm Quay. Dum —2A 112
Kinghorn. Fife —1F 129
Kinglassie. Fife —4E 137
Kingledores. Scot —2D 118
Kingodie. Per —1F 137
King o' Muirs. Clac —4A 136
King's Acre. Here —1H 47
Kingsand. Corn —3A 8
Kingsash. Buck —5G 51
Kingsbarns. Fife —2H 137
Kingsbridge. Devn —4D 8
Kingsbridge. Som —3C 20
King's Bromley. Staf —4F 73
Kingsburgh. High —3C 154
Kingsbury. G Lon —2C 38
Kingsbury. Warw —1G 61
Kingsbury Episcopi. Som —4H 21
Kings Caple. Here —3A 48
Kingscavil. W Lot —2D 128
Kingsclere. Hants —1D 24
King's Cliffe. Nptn —1H 63
Kingscote. Glos —2D 34
Kingscott. Devn —1F 11
Kings Coughton. Warw —5E 61
Kingscross. N Ayr —3E 123
Kingsdon. Som —4A 22
Kingsdown. Kent —1H 29
Kingsdown. Swin —3G 35
Kingsdown. Wilts —5D 34
Kingseat. Fife —4D 136
Kingsey. Buck —5F 51
Kingsfold. Lanc —2G 95
Kingsfold. W Sus —2C 26
Kingsford. E Ayr —5F 127
Kingsford. Worc —2C 60
Kingsforth. N Lin —3D 94
Kingsgate. Kent —3H 41
King's Green. Glos —2C 48
Kingshall Street. Suff —4B 66
King's Heath. W Mid —2E 61
Kings Hill. Kent —5A 40
Kingsholm. Glos —4D 48
Kingshouse. High —3G 141
Kingshouse. Stir —1E 135
Kingshurst. W Mid —2F 61
Kingskerswell. Devn —2E 9
Kingskettle. Fife —3F 137
Kingsland. Here —4G 59
Kingsland. IOA —2B 80
Kings Langley. Herts —5A 52
Kingsley. Ches —3H 83
Kingsley. Hants —3F 25
Kingsley. Staf —1E 73
Kingsley Green. W Sus —3G 25
Kingsley Holt. Staf —1E 73
King's Lynn. Norf —3F 77
King's Meaburn. Cumb —2H 103
Kings Moss. Mers —4D 90
Kingsmuir. Ang —4D 145
Kingsmuir. Fife —3H 137
Kings Muir. Scot —1E 119
King's Newnham. Warw —3B 62
Kings Newton. Derbs —3A 74
Kingsnorth. Kent —2E 28
Kingsnorth. Medw —3C 40
King's Norton. Leics —5D 74
King's Norton. W Mid —3E 61
King's Nympton. Devn —1G 11
King's Pyon. Here —5G 59
Kings Ripton. Cambs —3B 64
King's Somborne. Hants —3B 24
King's Stag. Dors —1C 14
King's Stanley. Glos —5D 48
King's Sutton. Nptn —2C 50
Kingstanding. W Mid —1E 61
Kingsteignton. Devn —5B 12
Kingsteps. High —3D 158
King Sterndale. Derbs —3E 85
King's Thorn. Here —2A 48
Kingsthorpe. Nptn —4E 63
Kingston. Cambs —5C 64
Kingston. Devn —4C 8
Kingston. Dors —2C 14
(nr. Sturminster Newton)
Kingston. Dors —5E 15
(nr. Swanage)
Kingston. E Lot —1B 130
Kingston. Hants —2G 15
Kingston. IOW —4C 16
Kingston. Kent —5F 41
Kingston. Mor —2H 159
Kingston. W Sus —5B 26
Kingston Bagpuize. Oxon —2C 36
Kingston Blount. Oxon —2F 37
Kingston by Sea. W Sus —5D 26
Kingston Deverill. Wilts —3D 22
Kingstone. Here —2H 47
Kingstone. Som —1G 13
Kingstone. Staf —3E 73
Kingston Lisle. Oxon —3B 36
Kingston near Lewes. E Sus —5E 27
Kingston on Soar. Notts —3C 74
Kingston Russell. Dors —3A 14
Kingston St Mary. Som —4F 21
Kingston Seymour. N Som —5H 33
Kingston Stert. Oxon —5F 51
Kingston upon Hull. Hull —2D 94
Kingston upon Thames. G Lon —4C 38
King's Walden. Herts —3B 52
Kingswear. Devn —3E 9
Kingswells. Aber C —3F 153
Kingswinford. W Mid —2C 60
Kingswood. Buck —4E 51
Kingswood. Glos —2C 34
Kingswood. Here —5E 59
Kingswood. Kent —5C 40
Kingswood. Per —5H 143
Kingswood. Powy —5E 71
Kingswood. Som —3E 20
Kingswood. S Glo —4B 34
Kingswood. Surr —5D 38
Kingswood. Warw —3F 61
Kingswood Common. Staf —5C 72
Kings Worthy. Hants —3C 24
Kingthorpe. Linc —3A 88
Kington. Here —5F 59
Kington. S Glo —2B 34
Kington. Worc —5D 61
Kington Langley. Wilts —4E 35
Kington Magna. Dors —4C 22
Kington St Michael. Wilts —4E 35
Kingussie. High —3B 150
Kingweston. Som —3A 22
Kinharrachie. Aber —5G 161
Kinhrive. High —1B 158
Kinkell Bridge. Per —2B 136
Kinknockie. Aber —4H 161
Kinkry Hill. Cumb —2G 113
Kinlet. Shrp —2B 60
Kinloch. High —5D 166
(nr. Loch More)
Kinloch. High —3A 140
(nr. Lochaline)
Kinloch. High —4C 146
(on Rhum)
Kinloch. Per —4A 144
Kinlochard. Stir —3D 134
Kinlochbervie. High —3C 166
Kinlocheil. High —1D 141
Kinlochewe. High —2C 156
Kinloch Hourn. High —3B 148
Kinloch Laggan. High —5H 149
Kinlochleven. High —2F 141
Kinloch Lodge. High —3F 167
Kinlochmoidart. High —1B 140
Kinlochmore. High —2F 141
Kinloch Rannoch. Per —3D 142
Kinlochspelve. Arg —1D 132
Kinloid. High —5E 147
Kinloss. Mor —2E 159
Kinmel Bay. Cnwy —2B 82
Kinmuck. Aber —2F 153
Kinnadie. Aber —4G 161
Kinnaird. Per —1E 137
Kinneff. Aber —1H 145
Kinnelhead. Dum —4C 118
Kinnell. Ang —3F 145
Kinnerley. Shrp —3F 71
Kinnernie. Aber —2E 152
Kinnersley. Here —1G 47
Kinnersley. Worc —1D 48
Kinnerton. Powy —4E 59
Kinnerton. Shrp —1F 59
Kinnesswood. Per —3D 136
Kinninvie. Dur —2D 104
Kinnordy. Ang —3C 144
Kinoulton. Notts —2D 74
Kinross. Per —3D 136
Kinrossie. Per —5A 144

Kinsbourne Green. *Herts* —4B 52
Kinsey Heath. *Ches* —1A 72
Kinsham. *Here* —4F 59
Kinsham. *Worc* —2E 49
Kinsley. *W Yor* —3E 93
Kinson. *Bour* —3F 15
Kintbury. *W Ber* —5B 36
Kintessack. *Mor* —2E 159
Kintillo. *Per* —2D 136
Kinton. *Here* —3G 59
Kinton. *Shrp* —4F 71
Kintore. *Aber* —2E 153
Kintour. *Arg* —4C 124
Kintra. *Arg* —2B 132
Kintraw. *Arg* —3F 133
Kinveachy. *High* —2D 150
Kinver. *Staf* —2C 60
Kinwarton. *Warw* —5F 61
Kiplingcotes. *E Yor* —5D 100
Kippax. *W Yor* —1E 93
Kippen. *Stir* —4F 135
Kippford. *Dum* —4F 111
Kipping's Cross. *Kent* —1H 27
Kirbister. *Orkn* —7C 172
Kirby Bedon. *Norf* —5E 79
Kirby Bellars. *Leics* —4E 74
Kirby Cane. *Norf* —1F 67
Kirby Cross. *Essx* —3F 55
Kirby Fields. *Leics* —5C 74
Kirby Grindalythe. *N Yor* —3D 100
Kirby Hill. *N Yor* —4E 105
(nr. Richmond)
Kirby Hill. *N Yor* —3F 99
(nr. Ripon)
Kirby Knowle. *N Yor* —1G 99
Kirby-le-Soken. *Essx* —3F 55
Kirby Misperton. *N Yor* —2B 100
Kirby Muxloe. *Leics* —5C 74
Kirby Row. *Norf* —1F 67
Kirby Sigston. *N Yor* —5B 106
Kirby Underdale. *E Yor* —4C 100
Kirby Wiske. *N Yor* —1F 99
Kirdford. *W Sus* —3B 26
Kirk. *High* —3E 169
Kirkabister. *Shet* —6F 173
Kirkandrews. *Dum* —5D 110
Kirkandrews-on-Eden. *Cumb*
—4E 113
Kirkapol. *Arg* —4B 138
Kirkbampton. *Cumb* —4E 112
Kirkbean. *Dum* —4A 112
Kirk Bramwith. *S Yor* —3G 93
Kirkbride. *Cumb* —4D 112
Kirkbuddo. *Ang* —4E 145
Kirkburn. *E Yor* —4D 101
Kirkburton. *W Yor* —3C 92
Kirkby. *Linc* —1H 87
Kirkby. *Mers* —1G 83
Kirkby. *N Yor* —4C 106
Kirkby Fenside. *Linc* —4C 88
Kirkby Fleetham. *N Yor* —5F 105
Kirkby Green. *Linc* —5H 87
Kirkby in Ashfield. *Notts* —5C 86
Kirkby Industrial Estate. *Mers* —1G 83
Kirkby la Thorpe. *Linc* —1A 76
Kirkby Lonsdale. *Cumb* —2F 97
Kirkby Malham. *N Yor* —3A 98
Kirkby Mallory. *Leics* —5B 74
Kirkby Malzeard. *N Yor* —2E 99
Kirkby Mills. *N Yor* —1B 100
Kirkbymoorside. *N Yor* —1A 100
Kirkby on Bain. *Linc* —4B 88
Kirkby Overblow. *N Yor* —5F 99
Kirkby Stephen. *Cumb* —4A 104
Kirkby Thore. *Cumb* —2H 103
Kirkby Underwood. *Linc* —3H 75
Kirkby Wharfe. *N Yor* —5H 99
Kirkcaldy. *Fife* —4E 137
Kirkcambeck. *Cumb* —3G 113
Kirkcolm. *Dum* —3F 109
Kirkconnel. *Dum* —3G 117

Kirkconnell. *Dum* —3A 112
Kirkcowan. *Dum* —3A 110
Kirkcudbright. *Dum* —4D 111
Kirkdale. *Mers* —1F 83
Kirk Deighton. *N Yor* —4G 99
Kirk Ella. *E Yor* —2D 94
Kirkfield. *S Lan* —4H 127
Kirkfieldbank. *S Lan* —5B 128
Kirkforthar Feus. *Fife* —3E 137
Kirkgunzeon. *Dum* —3F 111
Kirk Hallam. *Derbs* —1B 74
Kirkham. *Lanc* —1C 90
Kirkham. *N Yor* —3B 100
Kirkhamgate. *W Yor* —2C 92
Kirk Hammerton. *N Yor* —4G 99
Kirkharle. *Nmbd* —1D 114
Kirkheaton. *Nmbd* —2D 114
Kirkheaton. *W Yor* —3B 92
Kirkhill. *Ang* —2F 145
Kirkhill. *High* —4H 157
Kirkhope. *S Lan* —4B 118
Kirkhouse. *Scot* —1F 119
Kirkibost. *High* —2D 146
Kirkinch. *Ang* —4C 144
Kirkinner. *Dum* —4B 110
Kirkintilloch. *E Dun* —2H 127
Kirk Ireton. *Derbs* —5G 85
Kirkland. *Cumb* —3B 102
(nr. Cleator Moor)
Kirkland. *Cumb* —1H 103
(nr. Penrith)
Kirkland. *Cumb* —5D 112
(nr. Wigton)
Kirkland. *Dum* —3G 117
(nr. Kirkconnel)
Kirkland. *Dum* —5H 117
(nr. Moniaive)
Kirkland Guards. *Cumb* —5C 112
Kirk Langley. *Derbs* —2G 73
Kirklauchline. *Dum* —4F 109
Kirkleatham. *Red C* —2C 106
Kirklevington. *Stoc T* —4B 106
Kirkley. *Suff* —1H 67
Kirklington. *N Yor* —1F 99
Kirklington. *Notts* —5D 86
Kirklinton. *Cumb* —3F 113
Kirkliston. *Edin* —2E 129
Kirkmabreck. *Dum* —4B 110
Kirkmaiden. *Dum* —5E 109
Kirk Merrington. *Dur* —1F 105
Kirk Michael. *IOM* —2C 108
Kirkmichael. *Per* —2H 143
Kirkmichael. *S Ayr* —4C 116
Kirkmuirhill. *S Lan* —5A 128
Kirknewton. *Nmbd* —1D 120
Kirknewton. *W Lot* —3E 129
Kirkney. *Aber* —5C 160
Kirk of Shotts. *N Lan* —3B 128
Kirkoswald. *Cumb* —5G 113
Kirkoswald. *S Ayr* —4B 116
Kirkpatrick. *Dum* —5B 118
Kirkpatrick Durham. *Dum* —2E 111
Kirkpatrick-Fleming. *Dum* —2D 112
Kirk Sandall. *S Yor* —4G 93
Kirksanton. *Cumb* —1A 96
Kirk Smeaton. *N Yor* —3F 93
Kirkstall. *W Yor* —1C 92
Kirkstile. *Dum* —5F 119
Kirkstyle. *High* —1F 169
Kirkthorpe. *W Yor* —2D 92
Kirkton. *Aber* —2D 152
(nr. Alford)
Kirkton. *Aber* —1D 152
(nr. Insch)
Kirkton. *Aber* —4F 161
(nr. Turriff)
Kirkton. *Ang* —5D 144
(nr. Balgray)
Kirkton. *Ang* —4D 144
(nr. Forfar)
Kirkton. *Ang* —5B 152
(nr. Tarfside)
Kirkton. *Dum* —1A 112

Kirkton. *Fife* —1F 137
Kirkton. *High* —4E 165
(nr. Golspie)
Kirkton. *High* —1G 147
(nr. Kyle of Lochalsh)
Kirkton. *High* —4B 156
(nr. Lochcarron)
Kirkton. *Scot* —3H 119
Kirkton. *S Lan* —2B 118
Kirktonhill. *W Dun* —2E 127
Kirkton Manor. *Scot* —1E 118
Kirkton of Airlie. *Ang* —3C 144
Kirkton of Auchterhouse. *Ang*
—5C 144
Kirkton of Bourtie. *Aber* —1F 153
Kirkton of Collace. *Per* —5A 144
Kirkton of Craig. *Ang* —3G 145
Kirkton of Culsalmond. *Aber* —5D 160
Kirkton of Durris. *Aber* —4E 153
Kirkton of Glenbuchat. *Aber* —2A 152
Kirkton of Glenisla. *Ang* —2B 144
Kirkton of Kingoldrum. *Ang* —3C 144
Kirkton of Largo. *Fife* —3G 137
Kirkton of Lethendy. *Per* —4A 144
Kirkton of Logie Buchan. *Aber*
—1G 153
Kirkton of Maryculter. *Aber* —4F 153
Kirkton of Menmuir. *Ang* —2E 145
Kirkton of Monikie. *Ang* —5E 145
Kirkton of Oyne. *Aber* —1D 152
Kirkton of Rayne. *Aber* —1D 152
Kirkton of Skene. *Aber* —3F 153
Kirktown. *Aber* —2G 161
(nr. Fraserburgh)
Kirktown. *Aber* —3H 161
(nr. Peterhead)
Kirktown of Alvah. *Aber* —3D 160
Kirktown of Auchterless. *Aber*
—4E 160
Kirktown of Deskford. *Mor* —2C 160
Kirktown of Fetteresso. *Aber* —5F 153
Kirktown of Mortlach. *Mor* —5H 159
Kirktown of Slains. *Aber* —1H 153
Kirkurd. *Scot* —5E 129
Kirkwall. *Orkn* —6D 172
Kirkwall Airport. *Orkn* —7D 172
Kirkwhelpington. *Nmbd* —1C 114
Kirk Yetholm. *Scot* —2C 120
Kirmington. *N Lin* —3E 94
Kirmond le Mire. *Linc* —1A 88
Kirn. *Arg* —2C 126
Kirriemuir. *Ang* —3C 144
Kirstead Green. *Norf* —1E 67
Kirtlebridge. *Dum* —2D 112
Kirtleton. *Dum* —2D 112
Kirtling. *Cambs* —5F 65
Kirtling Green. *Cambs* —5F 65
Kirtlington. *Oxon* —4C 50
Kirtomy. *High* —2H 167
Kirton. *Linc* —2C 76
Kirton. *Notts* —4D 86
Kirton. *Suff* —2F 55
Kirton End. *Linc* —1B 76
Kirton Holme. *Linc* —1B 76
Kirton in Lindsey. *N Lin* —1G 87
Kishorn. *High* —4H 155
Kislingbury. *Nptn* —5D 62
Kites Hardwick. *Warw* —4B 62
Kittisford. *Som* —4D 20
Kittle. *Swan* —4E 31
Kittybrewster. *Aber C* —3G 153
Kitwood. *Hants* —3E 25
Kivernoll. *Here* —2H 47
Kiveton Park. *S Yor* —2B 86
Knaith. *Linc* —2F 87
Knaith Park. *Linc* —2F 87
Knap Corner. *Dors* —4D 22
Knaphill. *Surr* —5A 38
Knapp. *Hants* —4C 24
Knapp. *Per* —5B 144
Knapp. *Som* —4G 21
Knapton. *Norf* —2F 79
Knapton. *York* —4H 99

Knapton Green. *Here* —5G 59
Knapwell. *Cambs* —4C 64
Knaresborough. *N Yor* —4F 99
Knarsdale. *Nmbd* —4H 113
Knatts Valley. *Kent* —4G 39
Knaven. *Aber* —4F 161
Knayton. *N Yor* —1G 99
Knebworth. *Herts* —3C 52
Knedlington. *E Yor* —2H 93
Kneesall. *Notts* —4E 86
Kneesworth. *Cambs* —1D 52
Kneeton. *Notts* —1E 74
Knelston. *Swan* —4D 30
Knenhall. *Staf* —2D 72
Knightacott. *Devn* —3G 19
Knightcote. *Warw* —5B 62
Knightcott. *N Som* —1G 21
Knightley. *Staf* —3C 72
Knightley Dale. *Staf* —3C 72
Knightlow Hill. *Warw* —3B 62
Knighton. *Devn* —4B 8
Knighton. *Dors* —1B 14
Knighton. *Leic C* —5D 74
Knighton. *Powy* —3E 59
Knighton. *Som* —2E 21
Knighton. *Staf* —3B 72
Knighton. *Wilts* —4A 36
Knighton. *Worc* —5E 61
Knighton Common. *Worc* —3A 60
Knight's End. *Cambs* —1D 64
Knightswood. *Glas* —3G 127
Knightwick. *Worc* —5B 60
Knill. *Here* —4E 59
Knipton. *Leics* —2F 75
Knitsley. *Dur* —5E 115
Kniveton. *Derbs* —5G 85
Knock. *Arg* —5G 139
Knock. *Cumb* —2H 103
Knock. *Mor* —3C 160
Knockally. *High* —5D 168
Knockan. *Arg* —1B 132
Knockan. *High* —2G 163
Knockandhu. *Mor* —1G 151
Knockando. *Mor* —4F 159
Knockarthur. *High* —3E 165
Knockbain. *High* —3A 158
Knockbreck. *High* —2B 154
Knockdee. *High* —2D 168
Knockdolian. *S Ayr* —1G 109
Knockdon. *S Ayr* —3C 116
Knockdown. *Wilts* —3D 34
Knockenbaird. *Aber* —1D 152
Knockenkelly. *N Ayr* —3E 123
Knockentiber. *E Ayr* —1C 116
Knockfarrel. *High* —3H 157
Knockglass. *High* —2C 168
Knockholt. *Kent* —5F 39
Knockholt Pound. *Kent* —5F 39
Knockie Lodge. *High* —2G 149
Knockin. *Shrp* —3F 71
Knockinlaw. *E Ayr* —1D 116
Knockinnon. *High* —5D 169
Knockrome. *Arg* —2D 124
Knocksharry. *IOM* —3B 108
Knockvennie. *Dum* —2E 111
Knodishall. *Suff* —4G 67
Knole. *Som* —4H 21
Knollbury. *Mon* —3H 33
Knolls Green. *Ches* —3C 84
Knolton. *Wrex* —2F 71
Knook. *Wilts* —2E 23
Knossington. *Leics* —5F 75
Knott. *High* —3C 154
Knott End-on-Sea. *Lanc* —5C 96
Knotting. *Beds* —4H 63
Knotting Green. *Beds* —4H 63
Knottingley. *W Yor* —2E 93
Knotts. *Cumb* —2F 103
Knotty Ash. *Mers* —1G 83
Knotty Green. *Buck* —1A 38
Knowbury. *Shrp* —3H 59
Knowe. *Dum* —2A 110
Knowefield. *Cumb* —4F 113

Knowehead. *Dum* —5F 117
Knowes. *E Lot* —2C 130
Knowesgate. *Nmbd* —1C 114
Knoweside. *S Ayr* —3B 116
Knowle. *Bris* —4B 34
Knowle. *Devn* —3E 19
(nr. Braunton)
Knowle. *Devn* —4D 12
(nr. Budleigh Salterton)
Knowle. *Devn* —2A 12
(nr. Crediton)
Knowle. *Shrp* —3H 59
Knowle. *W Mid* —3F 61
Knowle Green. *Lanc* —1E 91
Knowle St Giles. *Som* —1G 13
Knowl Hill. *Wind* —4G 37
Knowlton. *Kent* —5G 41
Knowsley. *Mers* —1G 83
Knowstone. *Devn* —4B 20
Knucklas. *Powy* —3E 59
Knuston. *Nptn* —4G 63
Knutsford. *Ches* —3B 84
Knypersley. *Staf* —5C 84
Krumlin. *W Yor* —3A 92
Kuggar. *Corn* —5E 5
Kyleakin. *High* —1F 147
Kyle of Lochalsh. *High* —1F 147
Kylerhea. *High* —1F 147
Kylesku. *High* —5C 166
Kyles Lodge. *W Isl* —9B 171
Kylesmorar. *High* —4G 147
Kylestrome. *High* —5C 166
Kymin. *Mon* —4A 48
Kynaston. *Here* —2B 48
Kynaston. *Shrp* —3F 71
Kynnersley. *Telf* —4A 72
Kyre Green. *Worc* —4A 60
Kyre Park. *Worc* —4A 60
Kyrewood. *Worc* —4A 60
Kyrle. *Som* —4D 20

L

Labost. *W Isl* —3E 171
Lacasaigh. *W Isl* —5F 171
Lacasdail. *W Isl* —4G 171
Laceby. *NE Lin* —4F 95
Lacey Green. *Buck* —5G 51
Lach Dennis. *Ches* —3B 84
Lache. *Ches* —4F 83
Lackford. *Suff* —3G 65
Lacock. *Wilts* —5E 35
Ladbroke. *Warw* —5B 62
Laddingford. *Kent* —1A 28
Lade Bank. *Linc* —5C 88
Ladock. *Corn* —3C 6
Ladybank. *Fife* —2F 137
Ladycross. *Corn* —4D 10
Lady Green. *Mers* —4B 90
Lady Hall. *Cumb* —1A 96
Ladykirk. *Scot* —5E 131
Ladysford. *Aber* —2G 161
Ladywood. *W Mid* —2C 61
Ladywood. *Worc* —4C 60
Laga. *High* —2A 140
Lagavulin. *Arg* —5C 124
Lagg. *Arg* —2D 125
Lagg. *N Ayr* —3D 122
Laggan. *Arg* —4A 124
Laggan. *High* —4E 149
(nr. Fort Augustus)
Laggan. *High* —4A 150
(nr. Newtonmore)
Laggan. *Mor* —5H 159
Lagganlia. *High* —3C 150
Laglingarten. *Arg* —3A 134
Lagness. *W Sus* —2G 17
Laid. *High* —3E 166
Laide. *High* —4D 162
Laigh Fenwick. *E Ayr* —5F 127
Laindon. *Essx* —2A 40
Lairg. *High* —3C 164
Lairg Muir. *High* —3C 164
Laithes. *Cumb* —1F 103

Little Down—Llanfaes

Little Down. *Hants* —1B **24**
Little Downham. *Cambs* —2E **65**
Little Drayton. *Shrp* —2A **72**
Little Driffield. *E Yor* —4E **101**
Little Dunham. *Norf* —4A **78**
Little Dunkeld. *Per* —4H **143**
Little Dunmow. *Essx* —3G **53**
Little Easton. *Essx* —3G **53**
Little Eaton. *Derbs* —1A **74**
Little Eccleston. *Lanc* —5D **96**
Little Ellingham. *Norf* —1C **66**
Little Elm. *Som* —2C **22**
Little End. *Essx* —5F **53**
Little Everdon. *Nptn* —5C **62**
Little Eversden. *Cambs* —5C **64**
Little Faringdon. *Oxon* —5H **49**
Little Fencote. *N Yor* —5F **105**
Little Fenton. *N Yor* —1F **93**
Littleferry. *High* —4F **165**
Little Fransham. *Norf* —4B **78**
Little Gaddesden. *Herts* —4H **51**
Little Garway. *Here* —3H **47**
Little Gidding. *Cambs* —2A **64**
Little Glemham. *Suff* —5F **67**
Little Glenshee. *Per* —5G **143**
Little Gransden. *Cambs* —5B **64**
Little Green. *Wrex* —1G **71**
Little Grimsby. *Linc* —1C **88**
Little Habton. *N Yor* —2B **100**
Little Hadham. *Herts* —3E **53**
Little Hale. *Linc* —1A **76**
Little Hallingbury. *Essx* —4E **53**
Littleham. *Devn* —4E **19**
(nr. Bideford)
Littleham. *Devn* —4D **12**
(nr. Exmouth)
Little Hampden. *Buck* —5G **51**
Littlehampton. *W Sus* —5B **26**
Little Haresfield. *Glos* —5D **48**
Little Harrowden. *Nptn* —3F **63**
Little Haseley. *Oxon* —5E **51**
Little Hatfield. *E Yor* —5F **101**
Little Hautbois. *Norf* —3E **79**
Little Haven. *Pemb* —3C **42**
Little Hay. *Staf* —5F **73**
Little Hayfield. *Derbs* —2E **85**
Little Haywood. *Staf* —3E **73**
Little Heath. *W Mid* —2H **61**
Little Heck. *N Yor* —2F **93**
Littlehempston. *Devn* —2E **9**
Little Herbert's. *Glos* —4E **49**
Little Hereford. *Here* —4H **59**
Little Horkesley. *Essx* —2C **54**
Little Hormead. *Herts* —3E **53**
Little Horsted. *E Sus* —4F **27**
Little Horton. *W Yor* —1B **92**
Little Horwood. *Buck* —2F **51**
Little Houghton. *Nptn* —5F **63**
Littlehoughton. *Nmbd* —3G **121**
Little Houghton. *S Yor* —4E **93**
Little Hucklow. *Derbs* —3F **85**
Little Hulton. *G Man* —4F **91**
Little Ingestre. *Staf* —3D **73**
Little Irchester. *Nptn* —4G **63**
Little Kelk. *E Yor* —3E **101**
Little Kimble. *Buck* —5G **51**
Little Kineton. *Warw* —5H **61**
Little Kingshill. *Buck* —2G **37**
Little Langdale. *Cumb* —4E **102**
Little Langford. *Wilts* —3F **23**
Little Laver. *Essx* —5F **53**
Little Lawford. *Warw* —3B **62**
Little Leigh. *Ches* —3A **84**
Little Leighs. *Essx* —4H **53**
Little Leven. *E Yor* —5E **101**
Little Lever. *G Man* —4F **91**
Little Linford. *Mil* —1G **51**
Little London. *Buck* —4E **51**
Little London. *E Sus* —4G **27**
Little London. *Hants* —2B **24**
(nr. Andover)
Little London. *Hants* —1E **24**
(nr. Basingstoke)
Little London. *Linc* —3D **76**
(nr. Long Sutton)
Little London. *Linc* —3B **76**
(nr. Spalding)
Little London. *Norf* —2E **79**
(nr. North Walsham)
Little London. *Norf* —1G **65**
(nr. Northwold)
Little London. *Norf* —2D **78**
(nr. Saxthorpe)
Little London. *Norf* —1F **65**
(nr. Southery)
Little London. *Powy* —2C **58**
Little Longstone. *Derbs* —3F **85**
Little Malvern. *Worc* —1C **48**
Little Maplestead. *Essx* —2B **54**
Little Marcle. *Here* —2B **48**
Little Marlow. *Buck* —3G **37**
Little Massingham. *Norf* —3G **77**
Little Melton. *Norf* —5D **78**
Littlemill. *Aber* —4H **151**
Littlemill. *E Ayr* —3D **116**
Littlemill. *High* —3D **158**
Little Mill. *Mon* —5G **47**
Little Milton. *Oxon* —5E **50**
Little Missenden. *Buck* —1A **38**
Littlemoor. *Derbs* —4A **86**
Littlemoor. *Dors* —4B **14**
Littlemore. *Oxon* —5D **50**
Little Mountain. *Flin* —4E **83**
Little Musgrave. *Cumb* —3A **104**
Little Ness. *Shrp* —4G **71**
Little Neston. *Ches* —3F **83**
Little Newcastle. *Pemb* —2D **43**
Little Newsham. *Dur* —3E **105**
Little Oakley. *Essx* —3F **55**
Little Oakley. *Nptn* —2F **63**
Little Onn. *Staf* —4C **72**
Little Ormside. *Cumb* —3A **104**
Little Orton. *Cumb* —4E **113**
Little Orton. *Leics* —5H **73**
Little Ouse. *Norf* —2F **65**
Little Ouseburn. *N Yor* —3G **99**
Littleover. *Dby C* —2H **73**
Little Packington. *Warw* —2G **61**
Little Paxton. *Cambs* —4A **64**
Little Petherick. *Corn* —1D **6**
Little Plumpton. *Lanc* —1B **90**
Little Plumstead. *Norf* —4F **79**
Little Ponton. *Linc* —2G **75**
Littleport. *Cambs* —2E **65**
Little Posbrook. *Hants* —2D **16**
Little Potheridge. *Devn* —1F **11**
Little Preston. *Nptn* —5C **62**
Little Raveley. *Cambs* —3B **64**
Little Reynoldston. *Swan* —4D **31**
Little Ribston. *N Yor* —4F **99**
Little Rissington. *Glos* —4G **49**
Little Rogart. *High* —3E **165**
Little Rollright. *Oxon* —2A **50**
Little Ryburgh. *Norf* —3B **78**
Little Ryle. *Nmbd* —3E **121**
Little Ryton. *Shrp* —5G **71**
Little Salkeld. *Cumb* —1G **103**
Little Sampford. *Essx* —2G **53**
Little Sandhurst. *Brac* —5G **37**
Little Saredon. *Staf* —5D **72**
Little Saxham. *Suff* —4G **65**
Little Scatwell. *High* —3F **157**
Little Shelford. *Cambs* —5D **64**
Little Shoddesden. *Hants* —2A **24**
Little Singleton. *Lanc* —1B **90**
Little Smeaton. *N Yor* —3F **93**
Little Snoring. *Norf* —2B **78**
Little Sodbury. *S Glo* —3C **34**
Little Somborne. *Hants* —3B **24**
Little Somerford. *Wilts* —3E **35**
Little Soudley. *Shrp* —3B **72**
Little Stainforth. *N Yor* —3H **97**
Little Stainton. *Darl* —2A **106**
Little Stanney. *Ches* —3G **83**
Little Staughton. *Beds* —4A **64**
Little Steeping. *Linc* —4D **88**
Littlester. *Shet* —3G **173**
Little Stoke. *Staf* —2D **72**
Littlestone-on-Sea. *Kent* —3E **29**
Little Stonham. *Suff* —4D **66**
Little Street. *Cambs* —2E **65**
Little Stretton. *Leics* —5D **74**
Little Stretton. *Shrp* —1G **59**
Little Strickland. *Cumb* —3G **103**
Little Stukeley. *Cambs* —3B **64**
Little Sugnall. *Staf* —2C **72**
Little Sutton. *Ches* —3F **83**
Little Sutton. *Linc* —3D **76**
Little Swinburne. *Nmbd* —2C **114**
Little Tew. *Oxon* —3B **50**
Little Tey. *Essx* —3B **54**
Little Thetford. *Cambs* —3E **65**
Little Thirkleby. *N Yor* —2G **99**
Little Thornton. *Lanc* —5C **96**
Littlethorpe. *Leics* —1C **62**
Littlethorpe. *N Yor* —3F **99**
Little Thorpe. *W Yor* —2B **92**
Little Thurlow. *Suff* —5F **65**
Little Thurrock. *Thur* —3H **39**
Littleton. *Ches* —4G **83**
Littleton. *G Lon* —4B **38**
Littleton. *Hants* —3C **24**
Littleton. *Som* —3H **21**
Littleton. *Surr* —1A **26**
Littleton Drew. *Wilts* —3D **34**
Littleton Pannell. *Wilts* —1E **23**
Littleton-upon-Severn. *S Glo* —2A **34**
Little Torboll. *High* —4E **165**
Little Torrington. *Devn* —1E **11**
Little Totham. *Essx* —4B **54**
Little Town. *Cumb* —3D **102**
Littletown. *Dur* —5G **115**
Littletown. *High* —5E **165**
Little Town. *Lanc* —1E **91**
Little Twycross. *Leics* —5H **73**
Little Urswick. *Cumb* —2B **96**
Little Wakering. *Essx* —2D **40**
Little Walden. *Essx* —1F **53**
Little Waldingfield. *Suff* —1C **54**
Little Walsingham. *Norf* —2B **78**
Little Waltham. *Essx* —4H **53**
Little Warley. *Essx* —1H **39**
Little Washbourne. *Glos* —2E **49**
Little Weighton. *E Yor* —1C **94**
Little Welnetham. *Suff* —5A **66**
Little Wenham. *Suff* —2D **54**
Little Wenlock. *Telf* —5A **72**
Little Whittingham Green. *Suff* —3E **67**
Littlewick Green. *Wind* —4G **37**
Little Wilbraham. *Cambs* —5E **65**
Littlewindsor. *Dors* —2H **13**
Little Wisbeach. *Linc* —2A **76**
Little Witcombe. *Glos* —4E **49**
Little Witley. *Worc* —4B **60**
Little Wittenham. *Oxon* —2D **36**
Little Wolford. *Warw* —2A **50**
Littleworth. *Beds* —1A **52**
Littleworth. *Glos* —2G **49**
Littleworth. *Oxon* —2B **36**
Littleworth. *Staf* —4E **73**
(nr. Cannock)
Littleworth. *Staf* —3B **72**
(nr. Eccleshall)
Littleworth. *Staf* —3D **72**
(nr. Stafford)
Littleworth. *W Sus* —3C **26**
Littleworth. *Worc* —4D **61**
(nr. Redditch)
Littleworth. *Worc* —1D **49**
(nr. Worcester)
Little Wratting. *Suff* —1G **53**
Little Wymington. *Nptn* —4G **63**
Little Wymondley. *Herts* —3C **52**
Little Wyrley. *Staf* —5E **73**
Little Yeldham. *Essx* —2A **54**
Littley Green. *Essx* —4G **53**
Litton. *Derbs* —3F **85**
Litton. *N Yor* —2B **98**
Litton. *Som* —1A **22**
Litton Cheney. *Dors* —3A **14**
Liurbost. *W Isl* —5F **171**
Liverpool. *Mers* —1F **83**
Liverpool Airport. *Mers* —2G **83**
Liversedge. *W Yor* —2B **92**
Liverton. *Devn* —5B **12**
Liverton. *Red C* —3E **107**
Liverton Mines. *Red C* —3E **107**
Livingston. *W Lot* —3D **128**
Livingston Village. *W Lot* —3D **128**
Lixwm. *Flin* —3D **82**
Lizard. *Corn* —5E **5**
Llaingoch. *IOA* —2B **80**
Llaithddu. *Powy* —2C **58**
Llampha. *V Glam* —4C **32**
Llan. *Powy* —5A **70**
Llanaber. *Gwyn* —4F **69**
Llanaelhaearn. *Gwyn* —1C **68**
Llanaeron. *Cdgn* —5D **57**
Llanafan. *Cdgn* —3F **57**
Llanafan-fawr. *Powy* —5B **58**
Llanafan-fechan. *Powy* —5B **58**
Llanallgo. *IOA* —2D **81**
Llanandras. *Powy* —4E **59**
Llananno. *Powy* —3C **58**
Llanarmon. *Gwyn* —2D **68**
Llanarmon Dyffryn Ceiriog. *Wrex* —2D **70**
Llanarmon-yn-Ial. *Den* —5D **82**
Llanarth. *Cdgn* —5D **56**
Llanarth. *Mon* —4G **47**
Llanarthney. *Carm* —3F **45**
Llanasa. *Flin* —2D **82**
Llanbabo. *IOA* —2C **80**
Llanbadarn Fawr. *Cdgn* —2F **57**
Llanbadarn Fynydd. *Powy* —3C **58**
Llanbadarn-y-garreg. *Powy* —1E **46**
Llanbadoc. *Mon* —5G **47**
Llanbadrig. *IOA* —1C **80**
Llanbeder. *Newp* —2G **33**
Llanbedr. *Gwyn* —3E **69**
Llanbedr. *Powy* —3F **47**
(nr. Crickhowell)
Llanbedr. *Powy* —1E **47**
(nr. Hay-on-Wye)
Llanbedr-Dyffryn-Clwyd. *Den* —5D **82**
Llanbedrgoch. *IOA* —2E **81**
Llanbedrog. *Gwyn* —2C **68**
Llanbedr Pont Steffan. *Cdgn* —1F **45**
Llanbedr-y-cennin. *Cnwy* —4G **81**
Llanberis. *Gwyn* —4E **81**
Llanbethery. *V Glam* —5D **32**
Llanbister. *Powy* —3D **58**
Llanblethian. *V Glam* —4D **32**
Llanboidy. *Carm* —2G **43**
Llanbradach. *Cphy* —2E **33**
Llanbrynmair. *Powy* —5A **70**
Llanbydderi. *V Glam* —5D **32**
Llancadle. *V Glam* —5D **32**
Llancarfan. *V Glam* —4D **32**
Llancatal. *V Glam* —5D **32**
Llancayo. *Mon* —5G **47**
Llancloudy. *Here* —3H **47**
Llancoch. *Powy* —3E **58**
Llancynfelyn. *Cdgn* —1F **57**
Llandaff. *Card* —4E **33**
Llandanwg. *Gwyn* —3E **69**
Llandarcy. *Neat* —3G **31**
Llandawke. *Carm* —3G **43**
Llanddaniel-Fab. *IOA* —3D **81**
Llanddarog. *Carm* —4F **45**
Llanddeiniol. *Cdgn* —3E **57**
Llanddeiniolen. *Gwyn* —4E **81**
Llandderfel. *Gwyn* —2B **70**
Llanddeusant. *Carm* —3A **46**
Llanddeusant. *IOA* —2C **80**
Llanddew. *Powy* —2D **46**
Llanddewi. *Swan* —4D **30**
Llanddewi Brefi. *Cdgn* —5F **57**
Llanddewi'r Cwm. *Powy* —1D **46**
Llanddewi Rhydderch. *Mon* —4G **47**
Llanddewi Velfrey. *Pemb* —3F **43**
Llanddewi Ystradenni. *Powy* —4D **58**
Llanddoged. *Cnwy* —4H **81**
Llanddona. *IOA* —3E **81**
Llanddowror. *Carm* —3G **43**
Llanddulas. *Cnwy* —3B **82**
Llanddwywe. *Gwyn* —3E **69**
Llanddyfnan. *IOA* —3E **81**
Llandecwyn. *Gwyn* —2F **69**
Llandefaelog Fach. *Powy* —2D **46**
Llandefaelog-tre'r-graig. *Powy* —2E **47**
Llandefalle. *Powy* —2E **46**
Llandegai. *Gwyn* —3E **81**
Llandegfan. *IOA* —3E **81**
Llandegla. *Den* —5D **82**
Llandegley. *Powy* —4D **58**
Llandegveth. *Mon* —2G **33**
Llandeilo. *Carm* —3G **45**
Llandeilo Graban. *Powy* —1D **46**
Llandeilo'r Fan. *Powy* —2B **46**
Llandeloy. *Pemb* —2C **42**
Llandenny. *Mon* —5H **47**
Llandevaud. *Newp* —2H **33**
Llandevenny. *Newp* —3H **33**
Llandilo. *Pemb* —2F **43**
Llandinabo. *Here* —3A **48**
Llandinam. *Powy* —2C **58**
Llandissilio. *Pemb* —2F **43**
Llandogo. *Mon* —5A **48**
Llandough. *V Glam* —4C **32**
(nr. Cowbridge)
Llandough. *V Glam* —4E **33**
(nr. Penarth)
Llandovery. *Carm* —2A **46**
Llandow. *V Glam* —4C **32**
Llandre. *Cdgn* —2F **57**
Llandrillo. *Den* —2C **70**
Llandrillo-yn-Rhos. *Cnwy* —2H **81**
Llandrindod. *Powy* —4C **58**
Llandrindod Wells. *Powy* —4C **58**
Llandrinio. *Powy* —4E **71**
Llandsadwrn. *Carm* —2G **45**
Llandudno. *Cnwy* —2G **81**
Llandudno Junction. *Cnwy* —3G **81**
Llandudoch. *Pemb* —1B **44**
Llandw. *V Glam* —4C **32**
Llandwrog. *Gwyn* —5D **80**
Llandybie. *Carm* —4G **45**
Llandyfaelog. *Carm* —4E **45**
Llandyfan. *Carm* —4G **45**
Llandyfriog. *Cdgn* —1D **44**
Llandyfrydog. *IOA* —2D **80**
Llandygwydd. *Cdgn* —1C **44**
Llandynan. *Den* —1D **70**
Llandyrnog. *Den* —4D **82**
Llandysilio. *Powy* —4E **71**
Llandyssil. *Powy* —1D **58**
Llandysul. *Cdgn* —1E **45**
Llanedeyrn. *Card* —3F **33**
Llaneglwys. *Powy* —2D **46**
Llanegryn. *Gwyn* —5F **69**
Llanegwad. *Carm* —3F **45**
Llaneilian. *IOA* —1D **80**
Llanelian-yn-Rhos. *Cnwy* —3A **82**
Llanelidan. *Den* —5D **82**
Llanelieu. *Powy* —2E **47**
Llanellen. *Mon* —4G **47**
Llanelli. *Carm* —3E **31**
Llanelltyd. *Gwyn* —4G **69**
Llanelly. *Mon* —4F **47**
Llanelly Hill. *Mon* —4F **47**
Llanelwedd. *Powy* —5C **58**
Llanelwy. *Den* —3C **82**
Llanenddwyn. *Gwyn* —3E **69**
Llanengan. *Gwyn* —3B **68**
Llanerch. *Powy* —1F **59**
Llanerchymedd. *IOA* —2D **80**
Llanerfyl. *Powy* —5C **70**
Llaneuddog. *IOA* —2D **80**
Llanfachraeth. *IOA* —2C **80**
Llanfaelog. *IOA* —3C **80**
Llanfaelrhys. *Gwyn* —3B **68**
Llanfaenor. *Mon* —4H **47**
Llanfaes. *IOA* —3F **81**

Londubh—Lowton

Londubh. *High* —5C **162**
Lone. *High* —4D **166**
Lonemore. *High* —5E **165**
(nr. Dornoch)
Lonemore. *High* —1G **155**
(nr. Gairloch)
Long Ashton. *N Som* —4A **34**
Long Bank. *Worc* —3B **60**
Longbar. *N Ayr* —4E **127**
Long Bennington. *Linc* —1F **75**
Longbenton. *Tyne* —3F **115**
Longborough. *Glos* —3G **49**
Long Bredy. *Dors* —3A **14**
Longbridge. *Warw* —4G **61**
Longbridge. *W Mid* —3E **61**
Longbridge Deverill. *Wilts* —2D **22**
Long Buckby. *Nptn* —4D **62**
Long Buckby Wharf. *Nptn* —4D **62**
Longburgh. *Cumb* —4E **112**
Longburton. *Dors* —1B **14**
Long Clawson. *Leics* —3E **74**
Longcliffe. *Derbs* —5G **85**
Long Common. *Hants* —1D **16**
Long Compton. *Staf* —3C **72**
Long Compton. *Warw* —2A **50**
Longcot. *Oxon* —2A **36**
Long Crendon. *Buck* —5E **51**
Long Crichel. *Dors* —1E **15**
Longcroft. *Cumb* —4D **112**
Longcroft. *Falk* —2A **128**
Longcross. *Surr* —4A **38**
Longdale. *Cumb* —4H **103**
Longdales. *Cumb* —5G **113**
Longden. *Shrp* —5G **71**
Longden Common. *Shrp* —5G **71**
Long Ditton. *Surr* —4C **38**
Longdon. *Staf* —4E **73**
Longdon. *Worc* —2D **48**
Longdon Green. *Staf* —4E **73**
Longdon on Tern. *Telf* —4A **72**
Longdown. *Devn* —3B **12**
Longdowns. *Corn* —5B **6**
Long Drax. *N Yor* —2G **93**
Long Duckmanton. *Derbs* —3B **86**
Long Eaton. *Derbs* —2B **74**
Longfield. *Kent* —4H **39**
Longfield Hill. *Kent* —4H **39**
Longford. *Derbs* —2G **73**
Longford. *Glos* —3D **48**
Longford. *G Lon* —3B **38**
Longford. *Shrp* —2A **72**
Longford. *Telf* —4B **72**
Longford. *W Mid* —2H **61**
Longforgan. *Per* —1F **137**
Longformacus. *Scot* —4C **130**
Longframlington. *Nmbd* —4F **121**
Long Gardens. *Essx* —2B **54**
Long Green. *Ches* —3G **83**
Long Green. *Worc* —2D **48**
Longham. *Dors* —3F **15**
Longham. *Norf* —4B **78**
Long Hanborough. *Oxon* —4C **50**
Longhedge. *Wilts* —2D **22**
Long Hermiston. *Edin* —2E **129**
Longhill. *Aber* —3H **161**
Longhirst. *Nmbd* —1F **115**
Longhope. *Glos* —4B **48**
Longhope. *Orkn* —8C **172**
Longhorsley. *Nmbd* —5F **121**
Longhoughton. *Nmbd* —3G **121**
Long Itchington. *Warw* —4B **62**
Longlands. *Cumb* —1D **102**
Longlane. *Derbs* —2G **73**
Long Lane. *Telf* —4A **72**
Longlane. *W Ber* —4C **36**
Long Lawford. *Warw* —3B **62**
Long Lease. *N Yor* —4G **107**
Longley Green. *Worc* —5B **60**
Long Load. *Som* —4H **21**
Longmanhill. *Aber* —2E **161**
Long Marston. *Herts* —4G **51**
Long Marston. *N Yor* —4H **99**
Long Marston. *Warw* —1G **49**
Long Marton. *Cumb* —2H **103**
Long Meadow. *Cambs* —4E **65**
Long Meadowend. *Shrp* —2G **59**
Long Melford. *Suff* —1B **54**
Longmoor Camp. *Hants* —3F **25**
Longmorn. *Mor* —3G **159**
Longmoss. *Ches* —3C **84**
Long Newnton. *Glos* —2E **35**
Longnewton. *Scot* —2H **119**
Long Newton. *Stoc T* —3A **106**
Longney. *Glos* —4C **48**
Longniddry. *E Lot* —2H **129**
Longnor. *Shrp* —5G **71**
Longnor. *Staf* —4E **85**
(nr. Leek)
Longnor. *Staf* —4C **72**
(nr. Stafford)
Longparish. *Hants* —2C **24**
Longpark. *Cumb* —3F **113**
Long Preston. *N Yor* —4H **97**
Longridge. *Lanc* —1E **90**
Longridge. *Staf* —4D **72**
Longridge. *W Lot* —3C **128**
Longriggend. *N Lan* —2B **128**
Long Riston. *E Yor* —5F **101**
Longrock. *Corn* —3C **4**
Longsdon. *Staf* —5D **85**
Longshaw. *G Man* —4D **90**
Longshaw. *Staf* —1E **73**
Longside. *Aber* —4H **161**
Longslow. *Shrp* —2A **72**
Longstanton. *Cambs* —4C **64**
Longstock. *Hants* —3B **24**
Longstowe. *Cambs* —5C **64**
Long Stratton. *Norf* —1D **66**
Long Street. *Mil* —1F **51**
Longstreet. *Wilts* —1G **23**
Long Sutton. *Hants* —2F **25**
Long Sutton. *Linc* —3D **76**
Long Sutton. *Som* —4H **21**
Longthorpe. *Pet* —1A **64**
Long Thurlow. *Suff* —4C **66**
Longthwaite. *Cumb* —2F **103**
Longton. *Lanc* —2C **90**
Longton. *Stoke* —1D **72**
Longtown. *Cumb* —3E **113**
Longtown. *Here* —3G **47**
Longville in the Dale. *Shrp* —1H **59**
Long Whatton. *Leics* —3B **74**
Longwick. *Buck* —5F **51**
Long Wittenham. *Oxon* —2D **36**
Longwitton. *Nmbd* —1D **115**
Longworth. *Oxon* —2B **36**
Longyester. *E Lot* —3B **130**
Lonmore. *High* —4B **154**
Looe. *Corn* —3G **7**
Loose. *Kent* —5B **40**
Loosegate. *Linc* —3C **76**
Loosley Row. *Buck* —5G **51**
Lootcherbrae. *Aber* —3D **160**
Lopcombe Corner. *Wilts* —3A **24**
Lopen. *Som* —1H **13**
Loppington. *Shrp* —3G **71**
Lorbottle. *Nmbd* —4E **121**
Lorbottle Hall. *Nmbd* —4E **121**
Lordington. *W Sus* —2F **17**
Loscoe. *Derbs* —1B **74**
Loscombe. *Dors* —3A **14**
Losgaintir. *W Isl* —8C **171**
Lossiemouth. *Mor* —1G **159**
Lossit. *Arg* —4A **124**
Lostock Gralam. *Ches* —3A **84**
Lostock Green. *Ches* —3A **84**
Lostock Hall. *Lanc* —2D **90**
Lostock Junction. *G Man* —4E **91**
Lostwithiel. *Corn* —3F **7**
Lothbeg. *High* —2G **165**
Lothersdale. *N Yor* —5B **98**
Lothianbridge. *Midl* —3G **129**
Lothianburn. *Edin* —3F **129**
Lothmore. *High* —2G **165**
Lottisham. *Som* —3A **22**
Loudwater. *Buck* —1A **38**
Loughborough. *Leics* —4C **74**
Loughor. *Swan* —3E **31**
Loughton. *Essx* —1F **39**
Loughton. *Mil* —2G **51**
Loughton. *Shrp* —2A **60**
Lound. *Linc* —4H **75**
Lound. *Notts* —2D **86**
Lound. *Suff* —1H **67**
Lound, The. *Cumb* —5G **103**
Lount. *Leics* —4A **74**
Louth. *Linc* —2C **88**
Love Clough. *Lanc* —2G **91**
Lovedean. *Hants* —1E **17**
Lover. *Wilts* —4H **23**
Loversall. *S Yor* —1C **86**
Loves Green. *Essx* —5G **53**
Loveston. *Pemb* —4E **43**
Lovington. *Som* —3A **22**
Low Ackworth. *W Yor* —3E **93**
Low Angerton. *Nmbd* —1D **115**
Low Ardwell. *Dum* —5F **109**
Low Ballochdoan. *S Ayr* —2F **109**
Lowbands. *Glos* —2C **48**
Low Barlings. *Linc* —3H **87**
Low Bell End. *N Yor* —5E **107**
Low Bentham. *N Yor* —3F **97**
Low Bradfield. *S Yor* —1G **85**
Low Bradley. *N Yor* —5C **98**
Low Braithwaite. *Cumb* —5F **113**
Low Brunton. *Nmbd* —2C **114**
Low Burnham. *N Lin* —4A **94**
Lowca. *Cumb* —2A **102**
Low Catton. *E Yor* —4B **100**
Low Coniscliffe. *Dur* —3F **105**
Low Coylton. *S Ayr* —3D **116**
Low Crosby. *Cumb* —4F **113**
Low Dalby. *N Yor* —1C **100**
Lowdham. *Notts* —1D **74**
Low Dinsdale. *Darl* —3A **106**
Lowe. *Shrp* —2H **71**
Low Ellington. *N Yor* —1E **98**
Lower Amble. *Corn* —1D **6**
Lower Ansty. *Dors* —2C **14**
Lower Arboll. *High* —5F **165**
Lower Arncott. *Oxon* —4E **50**
Lower Ashton. *Devn* —4B **12**
Lower Assendon. *Oxon* —3F **37**
Lower Auchenreath. *Mor* —2A **160**
Lower Badcall. *High* —4B **166**
Lower Ballam. *Lanc* —1B **90**
Lower Basildon. *W Ber* —4E **36**
Lower Beeding. *W Sus* —3D **26**
Lower Benefield. *Nptn* —2G **63**
Lower Bentley. *Worc* —4D **61**
Lower Beobridge. *Shrp* —1B **60**
Lower Boddington. *Nptn* —5B **62**
Lower Bordean. *Hants* —4E **25**
Lower Brailes. *Warw* —2B **50**
Lower Breakish. *High* —1E **147**
Lower Broadheath. *Worc* —5C **60**
Lower Brynamman. *Neat* —4H **45**
Lower Bullingham. *Here* —2A **48**
Lower Bullington. *Hants* —2C **24**
Lower Burgate. *Hants* —1G **15**
Lower Cam. *Glos* —5C **48**
Lower Catesby. *Nptn* —5C **62**
Lower Chapel. *Powy* —2D **46**
Lower Chicksgrove. *Wilts* —3E **23**
Lower Chute. *Wilts* —1B **24**
Lower Clopton. *Warw* —5F **61**
Lower Common. *Hants* —2E **25**
Lower Cumberworth. *W Yor* —4C **92**
Lower Darwen. *Bkbn* —2E **91**
Lower Dean. *Beds* —4H **63**
Lower Dean. *Devn* —2D **8**
Lower Diabaig. *High* —2G **155**
Lower Dicker. *E Sus* —4G **27**
Lower Dounreay. *High* —2B **168**
Lower Down. *Shrp* —2F **59**
Lower Dunsforth. *N Yor* —3G **99**
Lower East Carleton. *Norf* —5D **78**
Lower Egleton. *Here* —1B **48**
Lower Ellastone. *Derbs* —1F **73**
Lower End. *Nptn* —4F **63**
Lower Everleigh. *Wilts* —1G **23**
Lower Failand. *N Som* —4A **34**
Lower Faintree. *Shrp* —2A **60**
Lower Farringdon. *Hants* —3F **25**
Lower Foxdale. *IOM* —4B **108**
Lower Frankton. *Shrp* —2F **71**
Lower Froyle. *Hants* —2F **25**
Lower Gabwell. *Devn* —2F **9**
Lower Gledfield. *High* —4C **164**
Lower Godney. *Som* —2H **21**
Lower Gravenhurst. *Beds* —2B **52**
Lower Green. *Essx* —2E **53**
Lower Green. *Norf* —2B **78**
Lower Green. *Staf* —5D **72**
Lower Green. *W Ber* —5B **36**
Lower Halstow. *Kent* —4C **40**
Lower Hardres. *Kent* —5F **41**
Lower Hardwick. *Here* —5G **59**
Lower Hartshay. *Derbs* —5A **86**
Lower Hawthwaite. *Cumb* —1B **96**
Lower Hayton. *Shrp* —2H **59**
Lower Hergest. *Here* —5E **59**
Lower Heyford. *Oxon* —3C **50**
Lower Heysham. *Lanc* —3D **96**
Lower Higham. *Kent* —3B **40**
Lower Holbrook. *Suff* —2E **55**
Lower Hordley. *Shrp* —3F **71**
Lower Horncroft. *W Sus* —4B **26**
Lower Horsebridge. *E Sus* —4G **27**
Lower Kilcott. *Glos* —3C **34**
Lower Killeyan. *Arg* —5A **124**
Lower Kingcombe. *Dors* —3A **14**
Lower Kingswood. *Surr* —5D **38**
Lower Kinnerton. *Ches* —4F **83**
Lower Langford. *N Som* —5H **33**
Lower Largo. *Fife* —3G **137**
Lower Layham. *Suff* —1D **54**
Lower Ledwyche. *Shrp* —3H **59**
Lower Leigh. *Staf* —2E **73**
Lower Lemington. *Glos* —2H **49**
Lower Lenie. *High* —1H **149**
Lower Ley. *Glos* —4C **48**
Lower Llanfadog. *Powy* —4B **58**
Lower Lode. *Glos* —2D **49**
Lower Loxhore. *Devn* —3G **19**
Lower Loxley. *Staf* —2E **73**
Lower Lydbrook. *Glos* —4A **48**
Lower Lye. *Here* —4G **59**
Lower Machen. *Newp* —3F **33**
Lower Maes-coed. *Here* —2G **47**
Lower Meend. *Glos* —5A **48**
Lower Milovaig. *High* —3A **154**
Lower Moor. *Worc* —1E **49**
Lower Morton. *S Glo* —2B **34**
Lower Mountain. *Flin* —5F **83**
Lower Nazeing. *Essx* —5D **53**
Lower Nyland. *Dors* —4C **22**
Lower Oakfield. *Fife* —4D **136**
Lower Oddington. *Glos* —3H **49**
Lower Ollach. *High* —5E **155**
Lower Penarth. *V Glam* —5E **33**
Lower Penn. *Staf* —1C **60**
Lower Pennington. *Hants* —3B **16**
Lower Peover. *Ches* —3B **84**
Lower Pitkerrie. *High* —1C **158**
Lower Place. *G Man* —3H **91**
Lower Quinton. *Warw* —1G **49**
Lower Rainham. *Medw* —4C **40**
Lower Raydon. *Suff* —2D **54**
Lower Seagry. *Wilts* —3E **35**
Lower Shelton. *Beds* —1H **51**
Lower Shiplake. *Oxon* —4F **37**
Lower Shuckburgh. *Warw* —4B **62**
Lower Sketty. *Swan* —3F **31**
Lower Slaughter. *Glos* —3G **49**
Lower Soudley. *Glos* —4B **48**
Lower Stanton St Quintin. *Wilts* —3E **35**
Lower Stoke. *Medw* —3C **40**
Lower Stonnall. *Staf* —5E **73**
Lower Stow Bedon. *Norf* —1B **66**
Lower Street. *Norf* —2E **79**
Lower Strensham. *Worc* —1E **49**
Lower Sundon. *Beds* —3A **52**
Lower Swanwick. *Hants* —2C **16**
Lower Swell. *Glos* —3G **49**
Lower Tale. *Devn* —2D **12**
Lower Tean. *Staf* —2E **73**
Lower Thurlton. *Norf* —1G **67**
Lower Thurnham. *Lanc* —4D **96**
Lower Thurvaston. *Derbs* —2G **73**
Lowertown. *Corn* —4D **4**
Lower Town. *Devn* —5H **11**
Lower Town. *Here* —1B **48**
Lower Town. *IOS* —1B **4**
Lower Town. *Pemb* —1D **42**
Lower Tysoe. *Warw* —1B **50**
Lower Upham. *Hants* —1D **16**
Lower Upnor. *Medw* —3B **40**
Lower Vexford. *Som* —3E **20**
Lower Walton. *Warr* —2A **84**
Lower Wear. *Devn* —4C **12**
Lower Weare. *Som* —1H **21**
Lower Welson. *Here* —5E **59**
Lower Whatcombe. *Dors* —2D **14**
Lower Whitley. *Ches* —3A **84**
Lower Wield. *Hants* —2E **25**
Lower Winchendon. *Buck* —4F **51**
Lower Withington. *Ches* —4C **84**
Lower Woodend. *Buck* —3G **37**
Lower Woodford. *Wilts* —3G **23**
Lower Wych. *Ches* —1G **71**
Lower Wyche. *Worc* —1C **48**
Lowesby. *Leics* —5E **74**
Lowestoft. *Suff* —1H **67**
Loweswater. *Cumb* —2C **102**
Low Etherley. *Dur* —2E **105**
Lowfield Heath. *W Sus* —1D **26**
Lowford. *Hants* —1C **16**
Low Fulney. *Linc* —3B **76**
Low Gate. *Nmbd* —3C **114**
Lowgill. *Cumb* —5H **103**
Lowgill. *Lanc* —3F **97**
Low Grantley. *N Yor* —2E **99**
Low Green. *N Yor* —4E **98**
Low Habberley. *Worc* —3C **60**
Low Ham. *Som* —4H **21**
Low Hameringham. *Linc* —4C **88**
Low Hawkser. *N Yor* —4G **107**
Low Hesket. *Cumb* —5F **113**
Low Hesleyhurst. *Nmbd* —5E **121**
Lowick. *Cumb* —1B **96**
Lowick. *Nptn* —2G **63**
Lowick. *Nmbd* —1E **121**
Lowick Bridge. *Cumb* —1B **96**
Lowick Green. *Cumb* —1B **96**
Low Knipe. *Cumb* —2G **103**
Low Leighton. *Derbs* —2E **85**
Low Lorton. *Cumb* —2C **102**
Low Marishes. *N Yor* —2C **100**
Low Marnham. *Notts* —4F **87**
Low Mill. *N Yor* —5D **106**
Low Moor. *Lanc* —5G **97**
Low Moor. *W Yor* —2B **92**
Low Moorsley. *Tyne* —5G **115**
Low Newton-by-the-Sea. *Nmbd* —2G **121**
Lownie Moor. *Ang* —4D **145**
Lowood. *Scot* —1H **119**
Low Row. *Cumb* —3G **113**
(nr. Brampton)
Low Row. *Cumb* —1E **103**
(nr. Caldbeck)
Low Row. *Cumb* —5C **112**
(nr. Wigton)
Low Row. *N Yor* —5C **104**
Lowsonford. *Warw* —4F **61**
Low Street. *Norf* —5C **78**
Low Team. *Tyne* —3F **115**
Lowther. *Cumb* —2G **103**
Lowthorpe. *E Yor* —3E **101**
Lowton. *Devn* —2G **11**
Lowton. *G Man* —1A **84**
Lowton. *Som* —1E **13**

Meon. *Hants* —2D **15**
Meonstoke. *Hants* —1E **16**
Meopham. *Kent* —4H **39**
Meopham Green. *Kent* —4H **39**
Meopham Station. *Kent* —4H **39**
Mepal. *Cambs* —2D **64**
Meppershall. *Beds* —2B **52**
Merbach. *Here* —1G **47**
Mercaston. *Derbs* —1G **73**
Merchiston. *Edin* —2F **129**
Mere. *Ches* —2B **84**
Mere. *Wilts* —3D **22**
Mere Brow. *Lanc* —3C **90**
Mereclough. *Lanc* —1G **91**
Mere Green. *W Mid* —1F **61**
Mere Green. *Worc* —4D **60**
Mere Heath. *Ches* —3A **84**
Mereside. *Bkpl* —1B **90**
Meretown. *Staf* —3B **72**
Mereworth. *Kent* —5A **40**
Meriden. *W Mid* —2G **61**
Merkadale. *High* —5C **154**
Merkland. *S Ayr* —5B **116**
Merkland Lodge. *High* —1A **164**
Merley. *Pool* —3F **15**
Merlin's Bridge. *Pemb* —3D **42**
Merridge. *Som* —3F **21**
Merrington. *Shrp* —3G **71**
Merrion. *Pemb* —5D **42**
Merriott. *Som* —1H **13**
Merrivale. *Devn* —5F **11**
Merrow. *Surr* —5B **38**
Merrybent. *Darl* —3F **105**
Merry Lees. *Leics* —5B **74**
Merrymeet. *Corn* —2G **7**
Mersham. *Kent* —2E **29**
Merstham. *Surr* —5D **39**
Merston. *W Sus* —2G **17**
Merstone. *IOW* —4D **16**
Merther. *Corn* —4C **6**
Merthyr. *Carm* —3D **44**
Merthyr Cynog. *Powy* —2C **46**
Merthyr Dyfan. *V Glam* —5E **32**
Merthyr Mawr. *B'End* —4B **32**
Merthyr Tudful. *Mer T* —5D **46**
Merthyr Tydfil. *Mer T* —5D **46**
Merthyr Vale. *Mer T* —5D **46**
Merton. *Devn* —1F **11**
Merton. *G Lon* —4D **38**
Merton. *Norf* —1B **66**
Merton. *Oxon* —4D **50**
Meshaw. *Devn* —1A **12**
Messing. *Essx* —4B **54**
Messingham. *N Lin* —4B **94**
Metcombe. *Devn* —3D **12**
Metfield. *Suff* —2E **67**
Metherell. *Corn* —2A **8**
Metheringham. *Linc* —4H **87**
Methil. *Fife* —4F **137**
Methilhill. *Fife* —4F **137**
Methley. *W Yor* —2D **93**
Methley Junction. *W Yor* —2D **93**
Methlick. *Aber* —5F **161**
Methven. *Per* —1C **136**
Methwold. *Norf* —1G **65**
Methwold Hythe. *Norf* —1G **65**
Mettingham. *Suff* —1F **67**
Metton. *Norf* —2D **78**
Mevagissey. *Corn* —4E **6**
Mexborough. *S Yor* —4E **93**
Mey. *High* —1E **169**
Meysey Hampton. *Glos* —2G **35**
Miabhag. *W Isl* —7C **171**
(nr. Cliasmol)
Miabhag. *W Isl* —8D **171**
(nr. Tarbert)
Miabhig. *W Isl* —4C **171**
Mial. *High* —1G **155**
Michael. *IOM* —2C **108**
Michaelchurch. *Here* —3A **48**
Michaelchurch Escley. *Here* —2G **47**
Michaelchurch-on-Arrow. *Powy*
—5E **59**

Michaelcombe. *Devn* —2C **8**
Michaelston-le-Pit. *V Glam* —4E **33**
Michaelston-y-Vedw. *Newp* —3F **33**
Michaelstow. *Corn* —5A **10**
Micheldever. *Hants* —3D **24**
Micheldever Station. *Hants* —2D **24**
Michelmersh. *Hants* —4B **24**
Mickfield. *Suff* —4D **66**
Micklebring. *S Yor* —1C **86**
Mickleby. *N Yor* —3F **107**
Micklefield. *W Yor* —1E **93**
Micklefield Green. *Herts* —1B **38**
Micklenham. *Surr* —5C **38**
Mickleover. *Dby C* —2H **73**
Micklethwaite. *Cumb* —4D **112**
Micklethwaite. *W Yor* —5D **98**
Mickleton. *Dur* —2C **104**
Mickleton. *Glos* —1G **49**
Mickletown. *W Yor* —2D **93**
Mickle Trafford. *Ches* —4G **83**
Mickley. *N Yor* —2E **99**
Mickley Green. *Suff* —5H **65**
Mickley Square. *Nmbd* —3D **115**
Mid Ardlaw. *Aber* —2G **161**
Midbea. *Orkn* —3D **172**
Mid Beltie. *Aber* —3D **152**
Mid Calder. *W Lot* —3D **129**
Mid Clyth. *High* —5E **169**
Middle Assendon. *Oxon* —3F **37**
Middle Aston. *Oxon* —3C **50**
Middle Barton. *Oxon* —3C **50**
Middlebie. *Dum* —2D **112**
Middle Chinnock. *Som* —1H **13**
Middle Claydon. *Buck* —3F **51**
Middlecliff. *S Yor* —4E **93**
Middlecott. *Devn* —4H **11**
Middle Drums. *Ang* —3E **145**
Middle Duntisbourne. *Glos* —5E **49**
Middle Essie. *Aber* —3H **161**
Middleforth Green. *Lanc* —2D **90**
Middleham. *N Yor* —1D **98**
Middle Handley. *Derbs* —3B **86**
Middle Harling. *Norf* —2B **66**
Middlehope. *Shrp* —2G **59**
Middle Littleton. *Worc* —1F **49**
Middle Maes-coed. *Here* —2G **47**
Middlemarsh. *Dors* —2B **14**
Middle Marwood. *Devn* —3F **19**
Middle Mayfield. *Staf* —1F **73**
Middlemuir. *Aber* —4F **161**
(nr. New Deer)
Middlemuir. *Aber* —3G **161**
(nr. Strichen)
Middle Rainton. *Tyne* —5G **115**
Middle Rasen. *Linc* —2H **87**
Middlesbrough. *Midd* —2B **106**
Middlescough. *Cumb* —5E **113**
Middleshaw. *Cumb* —1E **97**
Middlesmoor. *N Yor* —2D **98**
Middles, The. *Dur* —4F **115**
Middlestone. *Dur* —1F **105**
Middlestone Moor. *Dur* —1F **105**
Middle Stoughton. *Som* —2H **21**
Middlestown. *W Yor* —3C **92**
Middle Street. *Glos* —5C **48**
Middle Taphouse. *Corn* —2F **7**
Middleton. *Ang* —4E **145**
Middleton. *Arg* —4A **138**
Middleton. *Cumb* —1E **97**
Middleton. *Derbs* —4F **85**
(nr. Bakewell)
Middleton. *Derbs* —5G **85**
(nr. Wirksworth)
Middleton. *Essx* —2B **54**
Middleton. *G Man* —4G **91**
Middleton. *Hants* —2C **24**
Middleton. *Hart* —1C **106**
Middleton. *Here* —4H **59**
Middleton. *IOW* —4B **16**
Middleton. *Lanc* —4D **96**
Middleton. *Midl* —4G **129**
Middleton. *Norf* —4F **77**
Middleton. *Nptn* —1F **63**

Middleton. *Nmbd* —1F **121**
(nr. Belford)
Middleton. *Nmbd* —1D **114**
(nr. Morpeth)
Middleton. *N Yor* —5D **98**
(nr. Ilkley)
Middleton. *N Yor* —1B **100**
(nr. Pickering)
Middleton. *Per* —3D **136**
Middleton. *Shrp* —3H **59**
(nr. Ludlow)
Middleton. *Shrp* —3F **71**
(nr. Oswestry)
Middleton. *Suff* —4G **67**
Middleton. *Swan* —4D **30**
Middleton. *Warw* —1F **61**
Middleton. *W Yor* —2D **92**
Middleton Cheney. *Nptn* —1D **50**
Middleton Green. *Staf* —2D **73**
Middleton Hall. *Midl* —4G **129**
Middleton Hall. *Nmbd* —2D **121**
Middleton in Teesdale. *Dur* —2C **104**
Middleton One Row. *Darl* —3A **106**
Middleton-on-Leven. *N Yor* —4B **106**
Middleton-on-Sea. *W Sus* —5A **26**
Middleton on the Hill. *Here* —4H **59**
Middleton-on-the-Wolds. *E Yor*
—5D **100**
Middleton Priors. *Shrp* —1A **60**
Middleton Quernhow. *N Yor* —2F **99**
Middleton St George. *Darl* —3A **106**
Middleton Scriven. *Shrp* —2A **60**
Middleton Stoney. *Oxon* —3D **50**
Middleton Tyas. *N Yor* —4F **105**
Middletown. *Cumb* —4A **102**
Middle Town. *IOS* —1B **4**
Middletown. *Powy* —4F **71**
Middle Tysoe. *Warw* —1B **50**
Middle Wallop. *Hants* —3A **24**
Middlewich. *Ches* —4B **84**
Middle Winterslow. *Wilts* —3H **23**
Middlewood. *Corn* —5C **10**
Middlewood. *S Yor* —1H **85**
Middle Woodford. *Wilts* —3G **23**
Middlewood Green. *Suff* —4C **66**
Middleyard. *Glos* —5D **48**
Middlezoy. *Som* —3G **21**
Middridge. *Dur* —2F **105**
Midfield. *High* —2F **167**
Midford. *Bath* —5C **34**
Midge Hall. *Lanc* —2D **90**
Midgeholme. *Cumb* —4H **113**
Midgham. *W Ber* —5D **36**
Midgley. *W Yor* —2A **92**
(nr. Halifax)
Midgley. *W Yor* —3C **92**
(nr. Horbury)
Midhopestones. *S Yor* —1G **85**
Midhurst. *W Sus* —4G **25**
Mid Kirkton. *N Ayr* —4C **126**
Mid Lambrook. *Som* —1H **13**
Midland. *Orkn* —7C **172**
Mid Lavant. *W Sus* —2G **17**
Midlem. *Scot* —2H **119**
Midney. *Som* —4A **22**
Midsomer Norton. *Bath* —1B **22**
Midton. *Inv* —2D **126**
Midtown. *High* —5C **162**
(nr. Poolewe)
Midtown. *High* —2F **167**
(nr. Tongue)
Midville. *Linc* —5C **88**
Midway. *Derbs* —3H **73**
Mid Yell. *Shet* —2G **173**
Migdale. *High* —4D **164**
Migvie. *Aber* —3B **152**
Milborne Port. *Som* —1B **14**
Milborne St Andrew. *Dors* —3D **14**
Milborne Wick. *Som* —4B **22**
Milbourne. *Nmbd* —2E **115**
Milbourne. *Wilts* —3E **35**
Milburn. *Cumb* —2H **103**
Milbury Heath. *S Glo* —2B **34**

Milby. *N Yor* —3G **99**
Milcombe. *Oxon* —2C **50**
Milden. *Suff* —1C **54**
Mildenhall. *Suff* —3G **65**
Mildenhall. *Wilts* —5H **35**
Milebrook. *Powy* —3F **59**
Milebush. *Kent* —1B **28**
Mile End. *Cambs* —2F **65**
Mile End. *Essx* —3C **54**
Mileham. *Norf* —4B **78**
Mile Oak. *Brig* —5D **26**
Miles Green. *Staf* —5C **84**
Miles Hope. *Here* —4H **59**
Milesmark. *Fife* —1D **128**
Mile Town. *Kent* —3D **40**
Milfield. *Nmbd* —1D **120**
Milford. *Derbs* —1A **74**
Milford. *Devn* —4C **18**
Milford. *Powy* —1C **58**
Milford. *Staf* —3D **73**
Milford. *Surr* —1A **26**
Milford Haven. *Pemb* —4D **42**
Milford on Sea. *Hants* —3A **16**
Milkwall. *Glos* —5A **48**
Milkwell. *Wilts* —4E **23**
Milland. *W Sus* —4G **25**
Millbank. *High* —2D **168**
Mill Bank. *W Yor* —2A **92**
Millbeck. *Cumb* —2D **102**
Millbounds. *Orkn* —4E **172**
Millbreck. *Aber* —4H **161**
Millbridge. *Surr* —2G **25**
Millbrook. *Beds* —2A **52**
Millbrook. *Corn* —3A **8**
Millbrook. *G Man* —1D **85**
Millbrook. *Sotn* —1B **16**
Mill Common. *Suff* —2G **67**
Mill Corner. *E Sus* —3C **28**
Milldale. *Staf* —5F **85**
Millden Lodge. *Ang* —1E **145**
Milldens. *Ang* —3E **145**
Millearn. *Per* —2B **136**
Mill End. *Buck* —3F **37**
Mill End. *Cambs* —5F **65**
Millend. *Glos* —2C **34**
(nr. Dursley)
Mill End. *Glos* —4G **49**
(nr. Northleach)
Mill End. *Herts* —2D **52**
Millerhill. *Midl* —3G **129**
Miller's Dale. *Derbs* —3F **85**
Millers Green. *Derbs* —5G **85**
Millerston. *Glas* —3H **127**
Millfield. *Aber* —4B **152**
Millfield. *Pet* —1A **64**
Millgate. *Lanc* —3G **91**
Mill Green. *Norf* —2D **66**
Mill Green. *Shrp* —3A **72**
Mill Green. *Staf* —3E **73**
Mill Green. *Suff* —1C **54**
Mill Greep. *Essx* —5G **53**
Millhalf. *Here* —1F **47**
Millhall. *E Ren* —4G **127**
Millhayes. *Devn* —2F **13**
(nr. Honiton)
Millhayes. *Devn* —1E **13**
(nr. Wellington)
Millhead. *Lanc* —2D **97**
Millheugh. *S Lan* —4A **128**
Mill Hill. *Bkbn* —2E **91**
Mill Hill. *G Lon* —1D **38**
Millholme. *Cumb* —5G **103**
Millhouse. *Arg* —2A **126**
Millhousebridge. *Dum* —1C **112**
Millhouses. *S Yor* —2H **85**
Millikenpark. *Ren* —3F **127**
Millington. *E Yor* —4C **100**
Millington Green. *Derbs* —1G **73**
Mill Knowe. *Arg* —3B **122**
Mill Lane. *Hants* —1F **25**
Millmeece. *Staf* —2C **72**
Mill of Craigievar. *Aber* —2C **152**
Mill of Fintray. *Aber* —2F **153**

Mill of Haldane. *W Dun* —1E **127**
Millom. *Cumb* —1A **96**
Millow. *Beds* —1C **52**
Mill Place. *N Lin* —4C **94**
Millpool. *Corn* —5B **10**
Millport. *N Ayr* —4C **126**
Mill Side. *Cumb* —1D **96**
Mill Street. *Norf* —4C **78**
(nr. Lyng)
Mill Street. *Norf* —4C **78**
(nr. Swanton Morley)
Millthorpe. *Derbs* —3H **85**
Millthorpe. *Linc* —2A **76**
Millthrop. *Cumb* —5H **103**
Milltimber. *Aber C* —3F **153**
Milltown. *Aber* —3G **151**
(nr. Corgarff)
Milltown. *Aber* —2B **152**
(nr. Lumsden)
Milltown. *Corn* —3F **7**
Milltown. *Derbs* —4A **86**
Milltown. *Devn* —3F **19**
Milltown. *Dum* —2E **113**
Milltown. *High* —3E **157**
Milltown. *Mor* —4C **160**
Milltown of Aberdalgie. *Per* —1C **136**
Milltown of Auchindoun. *Mor*
—4A **160**
Milltown of Campfield. *Aber*
—3D **152**
Milltown of Edinville. *Mor* —5G **159**
Milltown of Towie. *Aber* —2B **152**
Milnacraig. *Ang* —3B **144**
Milnathort. *Per* —3D **136**
Milngavie. *E Dun* —2G **127**
Milnholm. *Stir* —1A **128**
Milnrow. *G Man* —3H **91**
Milnthorpe. *Cumb* —1D **97**
Milnthorpe. *W Yor* —3D **92**
Milovaig. *High* —4A **154**
Milson. *Shrp* —3A **60**
Milstead. *Kent* —5D **40**
Milston. *Wilts* —2G **23**
Milthorpe. *Nptn* —1D **50**
Milton. *Ang* —4C **144**
Milton. *Cambs* —4D **65**
Milton. *Cumb* —3G **113**
Milton. *Derbs* —3H **73**
Milton. *Dum* —2F **111**
(nr. Crocketford)
Milton. *Dum* —1F **111**
(nr. Dunscore)
Milton. *Dum* —4H **109**
(nr. Glenluce)
Milton. *E Ayr* —2D **116**
Milton. *Glas* —2H **127**
Milton. *High* —3F **157**
(nr. Achnasheen)
Milton. *High* —4G **155**
(nr. Applecross)
Milton. *High* —5G **157**
(nr. Drumnadrochit)
Milton. *High* —1B **158**
(nr. Invergordon)
Milton. *High* —4H **157**
(nr. Inverness)
Milton. *High* —3F **169**
(nr. Wick)
Milton. *Mor* —2C **160**
(nr. Cullen)
Milton. *Mor* —2F **151**
(nr. Tomintoul)
Milton. *N Som* —5G **33**
Milton. *Notts* —3E **86**
Milton. *Oxon* —2C **50**
(nr. Banbury)
Milton. *Oxon* —2C **36**
(nr. Didcot)
Milton. *Pemb* —4E **43**
Milton. *Per* —3A **144**
Milton. *Port* —3E **17**
Milton. *Som* —4H **21**

Milton—Moulton

Milton. Stir —3E 135
(nr. Aberfoyle)
Milton. Stir —4D 134
(nr. Drymen)
Milton. Stoke —5D 84
Milton. W Dun —2F 127
Milton Abbas. Dors —2D 14
Milton Abbot. Devn —5E 11
Milton Auchlossan. Aber —3C 152
Milton Bridge. Midl —3F 129
Milton Bryan. Beds —2H 51
Milton Clevedon. Som —3B 22
Milton Coldwells. Aber —5G 161
Milton Combe. Devn —2A 8
Milton Damerel. Devn —1D 11
Miltonduff. Mor —2F 159
Milton End. Glos —5G 49
Milton Ernest. Beds —5H 63
Milton Green. Ches —5G 83
Milton Hill. Devn —5C 12
Milton Hill. Oxon —2C 36
Milton Keynes. Mil —2G 51
Milton Keynes Village. Mil —2G 51
Milton Lilbourne. Wilts —5G 35
Milton Malsor. Nptn —5E 63
Milton Morenish. Per —5D 142
Milton of Auchinhove. Aber —3C 152
Milton of Balgonie. Fife —3F 137
Milton of Barras. Aber —1H 145
Milton of Campsie. E Dun —2H 127
Milton of Cultoquhey. Per —1A 136
Milton of Cushnie. Aber —2C 152
Milton of Finavon. Ang —3D 145
Milton of Gollanfield. High —3B 158
Milton of Lesmore. Aber —1B 152
Milton of Tullich. Aber —4A 152
Milton on Stour. Dors —4C 22
Milton Regis. Kent —4C 40
Milton Street. E Sus —5G 27
Milton-under-Wychwood. Oxon —4A 50
Milverton. Som —4E 20
Milverton. Warw —4H 61
Milwich. Staf —2D 72
Mimbridge. Surr —4A 38
Minard. Arg —4G 133
Minchington. Dors —1E 15
Minchinhampton. Glos —5D 49
Mindrum. Nmbd —1C 120
Minehead. Som —2C 20
Minera. Wrex —5E 83
Minety. Wilts —2F 35
Minffordd. Gwyn —2E 69
Mingarrypark. High —2A 140
Mingary. High —2G 139
Miningsby. Linc —4C 88
Minions. Corn —5C 10
Minishant. S Ayr —3C 116
Minllyn. Gwyn —4A 70
Minngearraidh. W Isl —6C 170
Minnigaff. Dum —3B 110
Minorca. IOM —3D 108
Minskip. N Yor —3F 99
Minstead. Hants —1A 16
Minsted. W Sus —4G 25
Minster. Kent —4H 41
(nr. Ramsgate)
Minster. Kent —3D 40
(nr. Sheerness)
Minsteracres. Nmbd —4D 114
Minsterley. Shrp —5F 71
Minster Lovell. Oxon —4B 50
Minsterworth. Glos —4C 48
Minterne Magna. Dors —2B 14
Minterne Parva. Dors —2B 14
Minting. Linc —3A 88
Mintlaw. Aber —4H 161
Minto. Scot —2H 119
Minton. Shrp —1G 59
Minwear. Pemb —3E 43
Minworth. W Mid —1F 61
Miodar. Arg —4B 138
Mirehouse. Cumb —3A 102
Mireland. High —2F 169
Mirfield. W Yor —3C 92
Miserden. Glos —5E 49
Miskin. Rhon —3D 32
Misson. Notts —1D 86
Misterton. Leics —2C 62
Misterton. Notts —1E 87
Misterton. Som —2H 13
Mistley. Essx —2E 54
Mistley Heath. Essx —2E 55
Mitcham. G Lon —4D 39
Mitcheldean. Glos —4B 48
Mitchell. Corn —3C 6
Mitchel Troy. Mon —4H 47
Mitcheltroy Common. Mon —5H 47
Mitford. Nmbd —1E 115
Mithian. Corn —3B 6
Mitton. Staf —4C 72
Mixbury. Oxon —2E 50
Mixenden. W Yor —2A 92
Mixon. Staf —5E 85
Moat. Cumb —2F 113
Moats Tye. Suff —5C 66
Mobberley. Ches —3B 84
Mobberley. Staf —1E 73
Moccas. Here —1G 47
Mochdre. Cnwy —3H 81
Mochdre. Powy —2C 58
Mochrum. Dum —5A 110
Mockbeggar. Hants —2G 15
Mockerkin. Cumb —2B 102
Modbury. Devn —3C 8
Moddershall. Staf —2D 72
Modsarie. High —2G 167
Moelfre. Cnwy —3B 82
Moelfre. IOA —2E 81
Moelfre. Powy —3D 70
Moffat. Dum —4C 118
Mogerhanger. Beds —1B 52
Mogworthy. Devn —1B 12
Moira. Leics —4H 73
Molash. Kent —5E 41
Mol-chlach. High —2C 146
Mold. Flin —4E 83
Molehill Green. Essx —3F 53
Molescroft. E Yor —5E 101
Molesden. Nmbd —1E 115
Molesworth. Cambs —3H 63
Moll. High —5E 155
Molland. Devn —4B 20
Mollington. Ches —3F 83
Mollington. Oxon —1C 50
Mollinsburn. N Lan —2A 128
Monachty. Cdgn —4E 57
Monachylemore. Stir —1D 134
Monar Lodge. High —4E 156
Monaughty. Powy —4E 59
Monewden. Suff —5E 67
Moneydie. Per —1C 136
Moneyrow Green. Wind —4G 37
Moniaive. Dum —5G 117
Monifieth. Ang —5E 145
Monikie. Ang —5E 145
Monimail. Fife —2E 137
Monington. Pemb —1B 44
Monk Bretton. S Yor —4D 92
Monken Hadley. G Lon —1D 38
Monk Fryston. N Yor —2F 93
Monk Hesleden. Dur —1B 106
Monkhide. Here —1B 48
Monkhill. Cumb —4E 113
Monkhopton. Shrp —1A 60
Monkland. Here —5G 59
Monkleigh. Devn —4E 19
Monknash. V Glam —4C 32
Monkokehampton. Devn —2F 11
Monkseaton. Tyne —2G 115
Monks Eleigh. Suff —1C 54
Monk's Gate. W Sus —3D 26
Monk's Heath. Ches —3C 84
Monk Sherborne. Hants —1E 24
Monkshill. Aber —4E 161
Monksilver. Som —3D 20
Monks Kirby. Warw —2B 62
Monk Soham. Suff —4E 66
Monk Soham Green. Suff —4E 66
Monkspath. W Mid —3F 61
Monks Risborough. Buck —5G 51
Monksthorpe. Linc —4D 88
Monk Street. Essx —3G 53
Monkswood. Mon —5G 47
Monkton. Devn —2E 13
Monkton. Kent —4G 41
Monkton. Pemb —4D 42
Monkton. S Ayr —2C 116
Monkton Combe. Bath —5C 34
Monkton Deverill. Wilts —3D 22
Monkton Farleigh. Wilts —5D 34
Monkton Heathfield. Som —4F 21
Monktonhill. S Ayr —2C 116
Monkton Up Wimborne. Dors —1F 15
Monkton Wyld. Dors —3G 13
Monkwearmouth. Tyne —4H 115
Monkwood. Hants —3E 25
Monmarsh. Here —1A 48
Monmouth. Mon —4A 48
Monnington on Wye. Here —1G 47
Monreith. Dum —5A 110
Montacute. Som —1H 13
Montford. Arg —3C 126
Montford. Shrp —4G 71
Montford Bridge. Shrp —4G 71
Montgarrie. Aber —2C 152
Montgarswood. E Ayr —2E 117
Montgomery. Powy —1E 58
Montgreenan. N Ayr —5E 127
Montrave. Fife —3F 137
Montrose. Ang —3G 145
Monxton. Hants —2B 24
Monyash. Derbs —4F 85
Monymusk. Aber —2D 152
Monzie. Per —1A 136
Moodiesburn. N Lan —2H 127
Moon's Green. Kent —3C 28
Moonzie. Fife —2F 137
Moor Allerton. W Yor —1D 92
Moorby. Linc —4B 88
Moorcot. Here —5F 59
Moor Crichel. Dors —2E 15
Moor Cross. Devn —3C 8
Moordown. Bour —3F 15
Moore. Hal —2H 83
Moorend. Dum —2D 112
Moor End. E Yor —1B 94
Moorend. Glos —5C 48
(nr. Dursley)
Moorend. Glos —4D 48
(nr. Gloucester)
Moorends. S Yor —3G 93
Moorgate. S Yor —1B 86
Moorgreen. Hants —1C 16
Moorgreen. Notts —1B 74
Moor Green. Wilts —5D 34
Moorhaigh. Notts —4C 86
Moorhall. Derbs —3H 85
Moorhampton. Here —1G 47
Moorhouse. Cumb —4E 113
(nr. Carlisle)
Moorhouse. Cumb —4D 112
(nr. Wigton)
Moorhouse. Notts —4E 87
Moorhouse. Surr —5F 39
Moorhouses. Linc —5B 88
Moorland. Som —3G 21
Moorlinch. Som —3G 21
Moor Monkton. N Yor —4H 99
Moor of Granary. Mor —3E 159
Moorpath. Dors —3H 13
Moor Row. Cumb —3B 102
(nr. Whitehaven)
Moor Row. Cumb —5D 112
(nr. Wigton)
Moorsholm. Red C —3D 107
Moorside. Dors —1C 14
Moorside. G Man —4H 91
Moor, The. Kent —3B 28
Moortown. Devn —3D 10
Moortown. Hants —2G 15
Moortown. IOW —4C 16
Moortown. Linc —1H 87
Moortown. Telf —4A 72
Moortown. W Yor —1C 92
Morangie. High —5E 165
Morar. High —4E 147
Morborne. Cambs —1A 64
Morchard Bishop. Devn —2A 12
Morcombelake. Dors —3H 13
Morcott. Rut —5G 75
Morda. Shrp —3E 71
Morden. G Lon —4D 38
Mordiford. Here —2A 48
Mordon. Dur —2A 106
More. Shrp —1F 59
Morebath. Devn —4C 20
Morebattle. Scot —2B 120
Morecambe. Lanc —3D 96
Morefield. High —4F 163
Morehouse, The. Shrp —1H 59
Moreleigh. Devn —3D 8
Morely St Botolph. Norf —1C 66
Morenish. Per —5C 142
Moresby. Cumb —2A 102
Moresby Parks. Cumb —3A 102
Morestead. Hants —4D 24
Moreton. Dors —4D 14
Moreton. Essx —5F 53
Moreton. Here —4H 59
Moreton. Mers —1E 83
Moreton. Oxon —5E 51
Moreton. Staf —4B 72
Moreton Corbet. Shrp —3H 71
Moretonhampstead. Devn —4A 12
Moreton-in-Marsh. Glos —2H 49
Moreton Jeffries. Here —1B 48
Moreton Morrell. Warw —5H 61
Moreton on Lugg. Here —1A 48
Moreton Pinkney. Nptn —1D 50
Moreton Say. Shrp —2A 72
Moreton Valence. Glos —5C 48
Morfa. Cdgn —5C 56
Morfa Bach. Carm —4D 44
Morfa Bychan. Gwyn —2E 69
Morfa Glas. Neat —5B 46
Morfa Nefyn. Gwyn —1B 68
Morganstown. Card —3E 33
Morgan's Vale. Wilts —4G 23
Morham. E Lot —2B 130
Moriah. Cdgn —3F 57
Morland. Cumb —2G 103
Morley. Ches —2C 84
Morley. Derbs —1A 74
Morley. Dur —2E 105
Morley. W Yor —2C 92
Morningside. Edin —2F 129
Morningside. N Lan —4B 128
Morningthorpe. Norf —1E 66
Morpeth. Nmbd —1F 115
Morrey. Staf —4F 73
Morridge Side. Staf —5E 85
Morridge Top. Staf —4E 85
Morrington. Dum —1F 111
Morris Green. Essx —2H 53
Morriston. Swan —3F 31
Morston. Norf —1C 78
Mortehoe. Devn —2E 19
Morthen. S Yor —2B 86
Mortimer Common. W Ber —5E 37
Mortimer's Cross. Here —4G 59
Mortimer West End. Hants —5E 37
Mortomley. S Yor —1H 85
Morton. Cumb —1F 103
(nr. Calthwaite)
Morton. Cumb —4E 113
(nr. Carlisle)
Morton. Derbs —4B 86
Morton. Linc —3H 75
(nr. Bourne)
Morton. Linc —1F 87
(nr. Gainsborough)
Morton. Linc —4F 87
(nr. Lincoln)
Morton. Norf —4D 78
Morton. Notts —5E 87
Morton. Shrp —3E 71
Morton. S Glo —2B 34
Morton Bagot. Warw —4F 61
Morton Mill. Shrp —3H 71
Morton-on-Swale. N Yor —5A 106
Morton Tinmouth. Dur —2E 105
Morvah. Corn —3B 4
Morval. Corn —3G 7
Morvich. High —3E 165
(nr. Golspie)
Morvich. High —1B 148
(nr. Shiel Bridge)
Morvil. Pemb —1E 43
Morville. Shrp —1A 60
Morwenstow. Corn —1C 10
Morwick Hall. Nmbd —4G 121
Mosborough. S Yor —2B 86
Moscow. E Ayr —5F 127
Mose. Shrp —1B 60
Mosedale. Cumb —1E 103
Moseley. W Mid —2E 61
(nr. Birmingham)
Moseley. W Mid —5D 72
(nr. Wolverhampton)
Moseley. Worc —5C 60
Moss. Arg —4A 138
Moss. High —2A 140
Moss. S Yor —3F 93
Moss. Wrex —5F 83
Mossatt. Aber —2B 152
Moss Bank. Mers —1H 83
Mossbank. Shet —4F 173
Mossblown. S Ayr —2D 116
Mossbrow. G Man —2B 84
Mossburnford. Scot —3A 120
Mossdale. Dum —2D 110
Mossedge. Cumb —3F 113
Mossend. N Lan —3A 128
Mossgate. Staf —2D 72
Moss Lane. Ches —3D 84
Mossley. Ches —4C 84
Mossley. G Man —4H 91
Mossley Hill. Mers —2F 83
Moss of Barmuckity. Mor —2G 159
Mosspark. Glas —3G 127
Mosspaul. Scot —5G 119
Moss-side. Aber —3G 161
Moss Side. Cumb —4C 112
Moss Side. G Man —1C 84
Moss-side. High —3C 158
Moss Side. Lanc —1B 90
(nr. Blackpool)
Moss Side. Lanc —2D 90
(nr. Preston)
Moss Side. Mers —4B 90
Mosstodloch. Mor —3H 159
Mosswood. Nmbd —4D 114
Mossy Lea. Lanc —3D 90
Mosterton. Dors —2H 13
Moston. Shrp —3H 71
Moston Green. Ches —4B 84
Mostyn. Flin —2D 82
Motcombe. Dors —4D 22
Mothecombe. Devn —4C 8
Motherby. Cumb —2F 103
Motherwell. N Lan —4A 128
Mottingham. G Lon —3F 39
Mottisfont. Hants —4B 24
Mottistone. IOW —4C 16
Mottram in Longdendale. G Man —1D 85
Mottram St Andrew. Ches —3C 84
Mott's Mill. E Sus —2G 27
Mouldsworth. Ches —3H 83
Moulin. Per —3G 143
Moulsecoomb. Brig —5E 27
Moulsford. Oxon —3D 36
Moulsoe. Mil —1H 51
Moulton. Ches —4A 84

Moulton—Netton

Moulton. Linc —3C 76
Moulton. Nptn —4E 63
Moulton. N Yor —4F 105
Moulton. Suff —4F 65
Moulton. V Glam —4D 32
Moulton Chapel. Linc —4B 76
Moulton Eugate. Linc —4B 76
Moulton St Mary. Norf —5F 79
Moulton Seas End. Linc —3C 76
Mount. Corn —2F 7
(nr. Bodmin)
Mount. Corn —3B 6
(nr. Newquay)
Mountain Ash. Rhon —2D 32
Mountain Cross. Scot —5E 129
Mountain Water. Pemb —2D 42
Mount Ambrose. Corn —4B 6
Mountbenger. Scot —2F 119
Mountblow. W Dun —2F 127
Mount Bures. Essx —2C 54
Mountfield. E Sus —3B 28
Mountgerald. High —2H 157
Mount Hawke. Corn —4B 6
Mount High. High —2A 158
Mountjoy. Corn —2C 6
Mount Lothian. Midl —4F 129
Mountnessing. Essx —1H 39
Mounton. Mon —2A 34
Mount Pleasant. Buck —2E 51
Mount Pleasant. Ches —5C 84
Mount Pleasant. Derbs —1H 73
(nr. Derby)
Mount Pleasant. Derbs —4G 73
(nr. Swadlincote)
Mount Pleasant. E Sus —4F 27
Mount Pleasant. Fife —2E 137
Mount Pleasant. Hants —3A 16
Mount Pleasant. Norf —1B 66
Mountsorrel. Leics —4C 74
Mount Stuart. Arg —4C 126
Mousehole. Corn —4B 4
Mouswald. Dum —2B 112
Mow Cop. Ches —5C 84
Mowden. Darl —3F 105
Mowhaugh. Scot —2C 120
Mowmacre Hill. Leic C —5C 74
Mowsley. Leics —2D 62
Moy. High —5B 158
Moylgrove. Pemb —1B 44
Moy Lodge. High —5G 149
Muasdale. Arg —5E 125
Muchalls. Aber —4F 153
Much Birch. Here —2A 48
Much Cowarne. Here —1B 48
Much Dewchurch. Here —2H 47
Muchelney. Som —4H 21
Muchelney Ham. Som —4H 21
Much Hadham. Herts —4E 53
Much Hoole. Lanc —2C 90
Muchlarnick. Corn —3G 7
Much Marcle. Here —2B 48
Muchrachd. High —5E 157
Much Wenlock. Shrp —5A 72
Mucking. Thur —2A 40
Muckleford. Dors —3B 14
Mucklestone. Staf —2B 72
Muckleton. Norf —2H 77
Muckleton. Shrp —3H 71
Muckley. Shrp —1A 60
Muckley Corner. Staf —5E 73
Muckton. Linc —2C 88
Mudale. High —5F 167
Muddiford. Devn —3F 19
Mudeford. Dors —3G 15
Mudford. Som —1A 14
Mudgley. Som —2H 21
Mugdock. Stir —2G 127
Mugeary. High —5D 154
Muggington. Derbs —1G 73
Muggintonlane End. Derbs —1G 73
Muggleswick. Dur —4D 114
Mugswell. Surr —5D 38
Muie. High —3D 164
Muirden. Aber —3E 160
Muirdrum. Ang —5E 145
Muiredge. Per —1E 137
Muirend. Glas —3G 127
Muirhead. Ang —5C 144
Muirhead. Fife —3E 137
Muirhead. N Lan —3H 127
Muirhouses. Falk —1D 128
Muirkirk. E Ayr —2F 117
Muir of Alford. Aber —2C 152
Muir of Fairburn. High —3G 157
Muir of Fowlis. Aber —2C 152
Muir of Ord. High —3H 157
Muir of Tarradale. High —3H 157
Muirshearlich. High —5D 148
Muirtack. Aber —5G 161
Muirton. High —2B 158
Muirton. Per —1D 136
Muirton of Ardblair. Per —4A 144
Muirtown. Per —2B 136
Muiryfold. Aber —3E 161
Muker. N Yor —5C 104
Mulbarton. Norf —5D 78
Mulben. Mor —3A 160
Mulindry. Arg —4B 124
Mulla. Shet —5F 173
Mullach Charlabhaigh. W Isl —3E 171
Mullacott. Devn —2F 19
Mullion. Corn —5D 5
Mullion Cove. Corn —5D 4
Mumbles, The. Swan —4F 31
Mumby. Linc —3E 89
Munderfield Row. Here —5A 60
Munderfield Stocks. Here —5A 60
Mundesley. Norf —2F 79
Mundford. Norf —1H 65
Mundham. Norf —1F 67
Mundon. Essx —5B 54
Munerigie. High —3E 149
Muness. Shet —1H 173
Mungasdale. High —4D 162
Mungrisdale. Cumb —1E 103
Munlochy. High —3A 158
Munsley. Here —1B 48
Munslow. Shrp —2H 59
Murchington. Devn —4G 11
Murcot. Worc —1F 49
Murcott. Oxon —4D 50
Murdishaw. Hal —2H 83
Murieston. W Lot —3D 128
Murkle. High —2D 168
Murlaggan. High —4C 148
Murra. Orkn —7B 172
Murrayfield. Edin —2F 129
Murray, The. S Lan —4H 127
Murrell Green. Hants —1F 25
Murroes. Ang —5D 144
Murrow. Cambs —5C 76
Mursley. Buck —3G 51
Murthly. Per —5H 143
Murton. Cumb —2A 104
Murton. Dur —5G 115
Murton. Nmbd —5F 131
Murton. Swan —4E 31
Murton. York —4A 100
Musbury. Devn —3F 13
Muscoates. N Yor —1A 100
Muscott. Nptn —4D 62
Musselburgh. E Lot —2G 129
Muston. Leics —2F 75
Muston. N Yor —2E 101
Mustow Green. Worc —3C 60
Muswell Hill. G Lon —2D 39
Mutehill. Dum —5D 111
Mutford. Suff —2G 67
Muthill. Per —2A 136
Mutterton. Devn —2D 12
Muxton. Telf —4B 72
Mwmbwls. Swan —4F 31
Mybster. High —3D 168
Myddfai. Carm —2A 46
Myddle. Shrp —3G 71
Mydroilyn. Cdgn —5D 56
Mylor Bridge. Corn —5C 6
Mylor Churchtown. Devn —5C 6
Mynachlog-ddu. Pemb —1F 43
Mynydd-bach. Mon —2H 33
Mynydd Isa. Flin —4E 83
Mynyddislwyn. Cphy —2E 33
Mynydd Llandegai. Gwyn —4F 81
Mynydd-y-briw. Powy —3D 70
Mynyddygarreg. Carm —5E 45
Mynytho. Gwyn —2C 68
Myrebird. Aber —4E 153
Myrelandhorn. High —3E 169
Mytchett. Surr —1G 25
Mythe, The. Glos —2D 49
Mytholmroyd. W Yor —2A 92
Myton-on-Swale. N Yor —3G 99
Mytton. Shrp —4G 71

Naast. High —5C 162
Na Buirgh. W Isl —8C 171
Naburn. York —5H 99
Nab Wood. W Yor —1B 92
Nackington. Kent —5F 41
Nacton. Suff —1F 55
Nafferton. E Yor —4E 101
Na Gearrannan. W Isl —3D 171
Nailbridge. Glos —4B 48
Nailsbourne. Som —4F 21
Nailsea. N Som —4H 33
Nailstone. Leics —5B 74
Nailsworth. Glos —2D 34
Nairn. High —3C 158
Naisberry. Hart —1B 106
Nalderswood. Surr —1D 26
Nancegollan. Corn —3D 4
Nancekuke. Corn —4A 6
Nancledra. Corn —3C 4
Nangreaves. Lanc —3G 91
Nanhyfer. Pemb —1A 44
Nannerch. Flin —4D 82
Nanpantan. Leics —4C 74
Nanpean. Corn —3D 6
Nanstallon. Corn —2E 7
Nant-ddu. Rhon —4D 46
Nanternis. Cdgn —5C 56
Nantgaredig. Carm —3E 45
Nantgarw. Rhon —3E 33
Nant Glas. Powy —4B 58
Nantglyn. Den —4C 82
Nantgwyn. Powy —3B 58
Nantlle. Gwyn —5E 81
Nantmawr. Shrp —3E 71
Nantmel. Powy —4C 58
Nantmor. Gwyn —1F 69
Nant Peris. Gwyn —5F 81
Nantwich. Ches —5A 84
Nant-y-bai. Carm —1A 46
Nant-y-Derry. Mon —5G 47
Nant-y-dugoed. Powy —4B 70
Nant-y-felin. Cnwy —3F 81
Nantyffyllon. B'End —2B 32
Nantyglo. Blae —4E 47
Nant-y-meichiaid. Powy —4D 70
Nant-y-moel. B'End —2C 32
Nant-y-Pandy. Cnwy —3F 81
Naphill. Buck —2G 37
Nappa. N Yor —4A 98
Napton on the Hill. Warw —4B 62
Narberth. Pemb —3F 43
Narberth Bridge. Pemb —3F 43
Narborough. Leics —1C 62
Narborough. Norf —4G 77
Narkurs. Corn —3H 7
Narth, The. Mon —5A 48
Narthwaite. Cumb —5A 104
Nasareth. Gwyn —1D 68
Naseby. Nptn —3D 62
Nash. Buck —2F 51
Nash. Here —4F 59
Nash. Kent —5G 41
Nash. Newp —3G 33
Nash. Shrp —3A 60
Nash Lee. Buck —5G 51
Nassington. Nptn —1H 63
Nasty. Herts —3D 52
Natcott. Devn —4C 18
Nateby. Cumb —4A 104
Nateby. Lanc —5D 96
Nately Scures. Hants —1F 25
Natland. Cumb —1E 97
Naughton. Suff —1D 54
Naunton. Glos —3G 49
Naunton. Worc —2D 49
Naunton Beauchamp. Worc —5D 60
Navenby. Linc —5G 87
Navestock Heath. Essx —1G 39
Navestock Side. Essx —1G 39
Navidale. High —2H 165
Nawton. N Yor —1A 100
Nayland. Suff —2C 54
Nazeing. Essx —5E 53
Neacroft. Hants —3G 15
Neal's Green. W Mid —2H 61
Neap House. N Lin —3B 94
Near Sawrey. Cumb —5E 103
Neasden. G Lon —2D 38
Neasham. Darl —3A 106
Neath. Neat —2A 32
Neath Abbey. Neat —3G 31
Neatishead. Norf —3F 79
Neaton. Norf —5B 78
Nebo. Cdgn —4E 57
Nebo. Cnwy —5H 81
Nebo. Gwyn —5D 81
Nebo. IOA —1D 80
Necton. Norf —5A 78
Nedd. High —5B 166
Nedderton. Nmbd —1F 115
Nedging. Suff —1D 54
Nedging Tye. Suff —1D 54
Needham. Norf —2E 67
Needham Market. Suff —5C 66
Needham Street. Suff —4G 65
Needingworth. Cambs —3C 64
Needwood. Staf —3F 73
Neen Savage. Shrp —3A 60
Neen Sollars. Shrp —3A 60
Neenton. Shrp —2A 60
Nefyn. Gwyn —1C 68
Neilston. E Ren —4F 127
Neithrop. Oxon —1C 50
Nelly Andrews Green. Powy —5E 71
Nelson. Cphy —2E 32
Nelson. Lanc —1G 91
Nelson Village. Nmbd —2F 115
Nemphlar. S Lan —5B 128
Nempnett Thrubwell. Bath —5A 34
Nene Terrace. Linc —5B 76
Nenthall. Cumb —5A 114
Nenthead. Cumb —5A 114
Nenthorn. Scot —1A 120
Nercwys. Flin —4E 83
Nereabolls. Arg —4A 124
Nerston. S Lan —4H 127
Nesbit. Nmbd —1D 121
Nesfield. N Yor —5C 98
Ness. Ches —3F 83
Nesscliffe. Shrp —4F 71
Neston. Ches —3E 83
Neston. Wilts —5D 34
Netchwood. Shrp —1A 60
Nethanfoot. S Lan —5B 128
Nether Alderley. Ches —3C 84
Netheravon. Wilts —2G 23
Nether Blainslie. Scot —5B 130
Netherbrae. Aber —3E 161
Netherbrough. Orkn —6C 172
Nether Broughton. Leics —3D 74
Netherburn. S Lan —5B 128
Nether Burrow. Lanc —2F 97
Netherbury. Dors —3H 13
Netherby. Cumb —2E 113
Nether Careston. Ang —3E 145
Nether Cerne. Dors —3B 14
Nether Compton. Dors —1A 14
Nethercote. Glos —3G 49
Nethercote. Warw —4C 62
Nethercott. Devn —3E 19
Nethercott. Oxon —3C 50
Nether Dallachy. Mor —2A 160
Nether Durdie. Per —1E 136
Nether End. Derbs —3G 85
Netherend. Glos —5A 48
Nether Exe. Devn —2C 12
Netherfield. E Sus —4B 28
Netherfield. Notts —1D 74
Nethergate. Norf —3C 78
Nethergate. N Lin —1E 87
Netherhampton. Wilts —3G 23
Nether Handley. Derbs —3B 86
Nether Haugh. S Yor —1B 86
Nether Heage. Derbs —5A 86
Nether Heyford. Nptn —5D 62
Netherhouses. Cumb —1B 96
Nether Howcleugh. Dum —3C 118
Nether Kellet. Lanc —3E 97
Nether Kinmundy. Aber —4H 161
Netherland Green. Staf —2F 73
Nether Langwith. Notts —4C 86
Netherlaw. Dum —5E 111
Netherley. Aber —4F 153
Nethermill. Dum —1B 112
Nethermills. Mor —3C 160
Nether Moor. Derbs —4A 86
Nether Padley. Derbs —3G 85
Netherplace. E Ren —4G 127
Nether Poppleton. York —4H 99
Netherseal. Derbs —4G 73
Nether Silton. N Yor —5B 106
Nether Stowey. Som —3E 21
Nether Street. Essx —4F 53
Netherstreet. Wilts —5E 35
Netherthird. E Ayr —3E 117
Netherthong. W Yor —4B 92
Netherton. Ang —3E 145
Netherton. Cumb —1B 102
Netherton. Devn —5B 12
Netherton. Hants —1B 24
Netherton. Here —3A 48
Netherton. Mers —1F 83
Netherton. N Lan —4A 128
Netherton. Nmbd —4D 121
Netherton. Per —3A 144
Netherton. Shrp —2B 60
Netherton. Stir —2G 127
Netherton. W Mid —2D 60
Netherton. W Yor —3C 92
(nr. Horbury)
Netherton. W Yor —3B 92
(nr. Huddersfield)
Netherton. Worc —1E 49
Nethertown. Cumb —4A 102
Nethertown. High —1F 169
Nethertown. Staf —4F 73
Nether Urquhart. Fife —3D 136
Nether Wallop. Hants —3B 24
Nether Wasdale. Cumb —4C 102
Nether Welton. Cumb —5E 113
Nether Whitacre. Warw —1G 61
Netherwhitton. Nmbd —5F 121
Nether Worton. Oxon —2C 50
Nethy Bridge. High —1E 151
Netley. Hants —2C 16
Netley. Shrp —5G 71
Netley Marsh. Hants —1B 16
Nettlebed. Oxon —3F 37
Nettlebridge. Som —2B 22
Nettlecombe. Dors —3A 14
Nettlecombe. IOW —5D 16
Nettleden. Herts —4A 52
Nettleham. Linc —3H 87
Nettlestead. Kent —5A 40
Nettlestead Green. Kent —5A 40
Nettlestone. IOW —3E 16
Nettlesworth. Dur —5F 115
Nettleton. Linc —4E 94
Nettleton. Wilts —4D 34
Netton. Devn —4B 8

Netton. *Wilts* —3G **23**
Neuadd. *Carm* —3H **45**
Neuadd. *Powy* —5C **70**
Neuk, The. *Aber* —4E **153**
Nevendon. *Essx* —1B **40**
Nevern. *Pemb* —1A **44**
New Abbey. *Dum* —3A **112**
New Aberdour. *Aber* —2F **161**
Newall. *W Yor* —5D **98**
New Alresford. *Hants* —3D **24**
New Alyth. *Per* —4B **144**
Newark. *Orkn* —3G **172**
Newark. *Pet* —5B **76**
Newark-on-Trent. *Notts* —5E **87**
New Arley. *Warw* —2G **61**
Newarthill. *N Lan* —4A **128**
New Ash Green. *Kent* —4H **39**
New Balderton. *Notts* —5F **87**
New Barn. *Kent* —4H **39**
New Barnetby. *N Lin* —3D **94**
Newbattle. *Midl* —3G **129**
New Bewick. *Nmbd* —2E **121**
Newbiggin. *Cumb* —2H **103**
(nr. Appleby)
Newbiggin. *Cumb* —3B **96**
(nr. Barrow-in-Furness)
Newbiggin. *Cumb* —5G **113**
(nr. Cumrew)
Newbiggin. *Cumb* —2F **103**
(nr. Penrith)
Newbiggin. *Cumb* —5B **102**
(nr. Seascale)
Newbiggin. *Dur* —5E **115**
(nr. Consett)
Newbiggin. *Dur* —2C **104**
(nr. Holwick)
Newbiggin. *Nmbd* —5C **114**
Newbiggin. *N Yor* —5C **104**
(nr. Askrigg)
Newbiggin. *N Yor* —1F **101**
(nr. Filey)
Newbiggin. *N Yor* —1B **98**
(nr. Thoralby)
Newbiggin-by-the-Sea. *Nmbd*
—1G **115**
Newbigging. *Ang* —5D **144**
(nr. Balgray)
Newbigging. *Ang* —5E **145**
(nr. Monikie)
Newbigging. *Ang* —4B **144**
(nr. Newtyle)
Newbigging. *Edin* —2E **129**
Newbigging. *S Lan* —5D **128**
Newbiggin-on-Lune. *Cumb* —4A **104**
Newbold. *Derbs* —3A **86**
Newbold. *Leics* —4B **74**
Newbold on Avon. *Warw* —3B **62**
Newbold on Stour. *Warw* —1H **49**
Newbold Pacey. *Warw* —5G **61**
Newbold Verdon. *Leics* —5B **74**
New Bolingbroke. *Linc* —5C **88**
Newborough. *Pet* —5B **76**
Newborough. *Staf* —3F **73**
Newbottle. *Nptn* —2D **50**
Newbottle. *Tyne* —4G **115**
New Boultham. *Linc* —3G **87**
Newbourne. *Suff* —1F **55**
New Brancepeth. *Dur* —5F **115**
Newbridge. *Cphy* —2F **33**
Newbridge. *Cdgn* —5E **57**
Newbridge. *Corn* —3B **4**
New Bridge. *Dum* —2G **111**
Newbridge. *Edin* —2E **129**
Newbridge. *Hants* —1A **16**
Newbridge. *IOW* —4C **16**
Newbridge. *N Yor* —1C **100**
Newbridge. *Pemb* —1D **42**
Newbridge. *Wrex* —1E **71**
Newbridge Green. *Worc* —2D **48**
Newbridge-on-Usk. *Mon* —2G **33**
Newbridge on Wye. *Powy* —5C **58**

New Brighton. *Flin* —4E **83**
New Brighton. *Hants* —2F **17**
New Brinsley. *Notts* —5B **86**
Newbrough. *Nmbd* —3B **114**
New Broughton. *Wrex* —5F **83**
New Buckenham. *Norf* —1C **66**
Newbuildings. *Devn* —2A **12**
Newburgh. *Aber* —1G **153**
Newburgh. *Fife* —2E **137**
Newburgh. *Lanc* —3C **90**
Newburn. *Tyne* —3E **115**
Newbury. *W Ber* —5C **36**
Newbury. *Wilts* —2D **22**
Newby. *Cumb* —2G **103**
Newby. *N Yor* —2G **97**
(nr. Ingleton)
Newby. *N Yor* —1E **101**
(nr. Scarborough)
Newby. *N Yor* —3C **106**
(nr. Stokesley)
Newby Bridge. *Cumb* —1C **96**
Newby Cote. *N Yor* —2G **97**
Newby East. *Cumb* —4F **113**
Newby Head. *Cumb* —2G **103**
New Byth. *Aber* —3F **161**
Newby West. *Cumb* —4E **113**
Newby Wiske. *N Yor* —1F **99**
Newcastle. *B'End* —4B **32**
Newcastle. *Mon* —4H **47**
Newcastle. *Shrp* —2E **59**
Newcastle Airport. *Tyne* —2E **115**
Newcastle Emlyn. *Carm* —1D **44**
Newcastleton. *Scot* —1F **113**
Newcastle-under-Lyme. *Staf* —1C **72**
Newcastle upon Tyne. *Tyne* —3F **115**
Newchapel. *Pemb* —1G **43**
Newchapel. *Powy* —2B **58**
Newchapel. *Staf* —5C **84**
Newchapel. *Surr* —1E **27**
New Cheriton. *Hants* —4D **24**
Newchurch. *Carm* —3D **45**
Newchurch. *Here* —5F **59**
Newchurch. *IOW* —4D **16**
Newchurch. *Kent* —2E **29**
Newchurch. *Lanc* —2G **91**
(nr. Nelson)
Newchurch. *Lanc* —2G **91**
(nr. Rawtenstall)
Newchurch. *Mon* —2H **33**
Newchurch. *Powy* —5E **58**
Newchurch. *Staf* —3F **73**
New Costessey. *Norf* —4D **78**
Newcott. *Devn* —2F **13**
New Cowper. *Cumb* —5C **112**
Newcraighall. *Edin* —2G **129**
New Crofton. *W Yor* —3D **93**
New Cross. *Cdgn* —3F **57**
New Cumnock. *E Ayr* —3F **117**
New Deer. *Aber* —4F **161**
New Denham. *Buck* —2B **38**
Newdigate. *Surr* —1C **26**
New Duston. *Nptn* —4E **62**
New Earswick. *York* —4A **100**
New Edlington. *S Yor* —1C **86**
New Elgin. *Mor* —2G **159**
New Ellerby. *E Yor* —1E **95**
Newell Green. *Brac* —4G **37**
New Eltham. *G Lon* —3F **39**
New End. *Warw* —4F **61**
New End. *Worc* —5E **61**
Newenden. *Kent* —3C **28**
New England. *Essx* —1H **53**
New England. *Pet* —5A **76**
Newent. *Glos* —3C **48**
New Ferry. *Mers* —2F **83**
Newfield. *Dur* —4F **115**
(nr. Chester-le-Street)
Newfield. *Dur* —1F **105**
(nr. Willington)
Newfound. *Hants* —1D **24**
New Fryston. *W Yor* —2E **93**
New Galloway. *Dum* —2D **110**
Newgate. *Norf* —1C **78**

Newgate. *Pemb* —2C **42**
Newgate Street. *Herts* —5D **52**
New Greens. *Herts* —5B **52**
New Grimsby. *IOS* —1A **4**
New Hainford. *Norf* —4E **78**
Newhall. *Ches* —1A **72**
Newhall. *Staf* —3G **73**
Newham. *Nmbd* —2F **121**
New Hartley. *Nmbd* —2G **115**
Newhaven. *Derbs* —4F **85**
Newhaven. *E Sus* —5F **27**
Newhaven. *Edin* —2F **129**
New Haw. *Surr* —4B **38**
New Hedges. *Pemb* —4F **43**
New Herrington. *Tyne* —4G **115**
Newhey. *G Man* —3H **91**
New Holkham. *Norf* —2A **78**
New Holland. *N Lin* —2D **94**
Newholm. *N Yor* —3F **107**
New Horton Grange. *Nmbd* —2F **115**
New Houghton. *Derbs* —4C **86**
New Houghton. *Norf* —3G **77**
Newhouse. *N Lan* —3A **128**
New Houses. *N Yor* —2H **97**
New Hutton. *Cumb* —5G **103**
New Hythe. *Kent* —5B **40**
Newick. *E Sus* —3F **27**
Newingreen. *Kent* —2F **29**
Newington. *Edin* —2F **129**
Newington. *Kent* —4C **40**
(nr. Folkestone)
Newington. *Kent* —2F **29**
(nr. Sittingbourne)
Newington. *Notts* —1D **86**
Newington. *Oxon* —2E **36**
Newington Bagpath. *Glos* —2D **34**
New Inn. *Carm* —2E **45**
New Inn. *Mon* —5H **47**
New Inn. *N Yor* —2H **97**
New Inn. *Torf* —2G **33**
New Invention. *Shrp* —3E **59**
New Kelso. *High* —4B **156**
New Lanark. *S Lan* —5B **128**
Newland. *Glos* —5A **48**
Newland. *Hull* —1D **94**
Newland. *N Yor* —2G **93**
Newland. *Som* —3B **20**
Newland. *Worc* —1C **48**
Newlandrig. *Midl* —3G **129**
Newlands. *Cumb* —1E **103**
Newlands. *Essx* —2C **40**
Newlands. *High* —4B **158**
Newlands. *Nmbd* —4D **115**
Newlands. *Notts* —4C **86**
Newlands. *Staf* —3E **73**
Newlands of Geise. *High* —2C **168**
Newlands of Tynet. *Mor* —2A **160**
New Lane. *Lanc* —3C **90**
New Lane End. *Warr* —1A **84**
New Langholm. *Dum* —1E **113**
New Leake. *Linc* —5D **88**
New Leeds. *Aber* —3G **161**
New Longton. *Lanc* —2D **90**
Newlot. *Orkn* —6E **172**
New Luce. *Dum* —3G **109**
Newlyn. *Corn* —4B **4**
Newmachar. *Aber* —2F **153**
Newmains. *N Lan* —4B **128**
New Mains of Ury. *Aber* —5F **153**
New Malden. *G Lon* —4D **38**
Newman's Green. *Suff* —1B **54**
Newmarket. *Suff* —4F **65**
Newmarket. *W Isl* —4G **171**
New Marske. *Red C* —2D **106**
New Marton. *Shrp* —2F **71**
New Mill. *Aber* —4E **160**
New Mill. *Corn* —3B **4**
New Mill. *Herts* —4H **51**
Newmill. *Mor* —3B **160**
New Mill. *W Yor* —4B **92**
New Mill. *Wilts* —5G **35**
Newmillerdam. *W Yor* —3D **92**
New Mills. *Corn* —3D **6**

New Mills. *Derbs* —2E **85**
Newmills. *Fife* —1D **128**
Newmills. *High* —2A **158**
New Mills. *Mon* —5A **48**
New Mills. *Powy* —5C **70**
Newmilm. *Per* —5A **144**
Newmilns. *E Ayr* —1E **117**
New Milton. *Hants* —3H **15**
New Mistley. *Essx* —2E **54**
New Moat. *Pemb* —2E **43**
Newmore. *High* —3H **157**
(nr. Dingwall)
Newmore. *High* —1A **158**
(nr. Invergordon)
Newnham. *Cambs* —5D **64**
Newnham. *Glos* —4B **48**
Newnham. *Hants* —1F **25**
Newnham. *Herts* —2C **52**
Newnham. *Kent* —5D **40**
Newnham. *Nptn* —5C **62**
Newnham. *Warw* —4F **61**
Newnham Bridge. *Worc* —4A **60**
New Ollerton. *Notts* —4D **86**
New Oscott. *W Mid* —1F **61**
Newpark. *Fife* —2G **137**
New Park. *N Yor* —4E **98**
New Pitsligo. *Aber* —3F **161**
New Polzeath. *Corn* —1D **6**
Newport. *Corn* —4D **10**
Newport. *Devn* —3F **19**
Newport. *E Yor* —1B **94**
Newport. *Essx* —2F **53**
Newport. *Glos* —2B **34**
Newport. *High* —1H **165**
Newport. *IOW* —4D **16**
Newport. *Norf* —4H **79**
Newport. *Pemb* —1E **43**
Newport. *Som* —4G **21**
Newport. *Telf* —4B **72**
Newport-on-Tay. *Fife* —1G **137**
Newport Pagnell. *Mil* —1G **51**
Newpound Common. *W Sus* —3B **26**
New Prestwick. *S Ayr* —2C **116**
New Quay. *Cdgn* —5C **56**
Newquay. *Corn* —2C **6**
Newquay Cornwall (St Mawgan)
Airport. *Corn* —2C **6**
New Rackheath. *Norf* —4E **79**
New Radnor. *Powy* —4E **58**
New Rent. *Cumb* —1F **103**
New Ridley. *Nmbd* —4D **114**
New Romney. *Kent* —3E **29**
New Rossington. *S Yor* —1D **86**
New Row. *Cdgn* —3G **57**
New Row. *Lanc* —1E **91**
New Row. *N Yor* —3D **106**
New Sauchie. *Clac* —4A **136**
Newsbank. *Ches* —4C **84**
New Scone. *Per* —1D **136**
Newseat. *Aber* —5E **160**
Newsham. *Lanc* —1D **90**
Newsham. *Nmbd* —2G **115**
Newsham. *N Yor* —3E **105**
(nr. Richmond)
Newsham. *N Yor* —1F **99**
(nr. Thirsk)
New Sharlston. *W Yor* —3D **93**
Newsholme. *E Yor* —2H **93**
Newsholme. *Lanc* —4H **97**
New Shoreston. *Nmbd* —1F **121**
New Springs. *G Man* —4E **90**
Newstead. *Notts* —5C **86**
Newstead. *Scot* —1H **119**
New Stevenston. *N Lan* —3A **128**
New Street. *Here* —5F **59**
Newstreet Lane. *Shrp* —2A **72**
New Swanage. *Dors* —4F **15**
New Swannington. *Leics* —4B **74**
Newthorpe. *N Yor* —1E **93**
Newthorpe. *Notts* —1B **74**
Newton. *Arg* —4H **133**
Newton. *B'End* —4B **32**

Newton. *Cambs* —1E **53**
(nr. Cambridge)
Newton. *Cambs* —4D **76**
(nr. Wisbech)
Newton. *Ches* —4G **83**
(nr. Chester)
Newton. *Ches* —5H **83**
(nr. Tattenhall)
Newton. *Cumb* —2B **96**
Newton. *Derbs* —5B **86**
Newton. *Dum* —2U **112**
(nr. Annan)
Newton. *Dum* —5D **118**
(nr. Moffat)
Newton. *G Man* —1D **84**
Newton. *Here* —2G **47**
(nr. Ewyas Harold)
Newton. *Here* —5H **59**
(nr. Leominster)
Newton. *High* —2B **158**
(nr. Cromarty)
Newton. *High* —4B **158**
(nr. Inverness)
Newton. *High* —5C **166**
(nr. Kylestrome)
Newton. *High* —4F **169**
(nr. Wick)
Newton. *Lanc* —2E **97**
(nr. Carnforth)
Newton. *Lanc* —4G **97**
(nr. Clitheroe)
Newton. *Lanc* —1C **90**
(nr. Kirkham)
Newton. *Linc* —2H **75**
Newton. *Mers* —2E **83**
Newton. *Mor* —2F **159**
Newton. *Norf* —4H **77**
Newton. *Nptn* —2F **63**
Newton. *Nmbd* —3D **114**
Newton. *Notts* —1D **74**
Newton. *Scot* —2A **120**
Newton. *Shrp* —1B **60**
(nr. Bridgnorth)
Newton. *Shrp* —2G **71**
(nr. Wem)
Newton. *Som* —3E **20**
Newton. *S Lan* —3H **127**
(nr. Glasgow)
Newton. *S Lan* —1B **118**
(nr. Lanark)
Newton. *Staf* —3E **73**
Newton. *Suff* —1C **54**
Newton. *Swan* —4F **31**
Newton. *Warw* —3C **62**
Newton. *W Lot* —2D **129**
Newton. *Wilts* —4H **23**
Newton Abbot. *Devn* —5B **12**
Newtonairds. *Dum* —1F **111**
Newton Arlosh. *Cumb* —4D **112**
Newton Aycliffe. *Dur* —2F **105**
Newton Bewley. *Hart* —2B **106**
Newton Blossomville. *Mil* —5G **63**
Newton Bromswold. *Nptn* —4G **63**
Newton Burgoland. *Leics* —5A **74**
Newton by Toft. *Linc* —2H **87**
Newton Ferrers. *Devn* —4B **8**
Newton Flotman. *Norf* —1E **66**
Newtongarry Croft. *Aber* —5C **160**
Newtongrange. *Midl* —3G **129**
Newton Green. *Mon* —2A **34**
Newton Hall. *Dur* —5F **115**
Newton Hall. *Nmbd* —3D **114**
Newton Harcourt. *Leics* —1D **62**
Newton Heath. *G Man* —4G **91**
Newtonhill. *Aber* —4G **153**
Newtonhill. *High* —4H **157**
Newton Hill. *W Yor* —2D **92**
Newton Kyme. *N Yor* —5G **99**
Newton-le-Willows. *Mers* —1H **83**
Newton-le-Willows. *N Yor* —1E **98**
Newton Longville. *Buck* —2G **51**
Newton Mearns. *E Ren* —4G **127**

Newtonmore—North Seaton

Newtonmore. High —4B 150
Newton Morrell. N Yor —4F 105
Newton Mulgrave. N Yor —3E 107
Newton of Ardtoe. High —1A 140
Newton of Balcanquhal. Per —2D 136
Newton of Beltrees. Ren —4E 127
Newton of Falkland. Fife —3E 137
Newton of Mountblairy. Aber —3D 160
Newton of Pitcairns. Per —2C 136
Newton-on-Ouse. N Yor —3H 99
Newton-on-Rawcliffe. N Yor —5F 107
Newton on the Hill. Shrp —3G 71
Newton-on-the-Moor. Nmbd —4F 121
Newton on Trent. Linc —3F 87
Newton Poppleford. Devn —4D 12
Newton Purcell. Oxon —2E 51
Newton Regis. Warw —5G 73
Newton Reigny. Cumb —1F 103
Newton Rigg. Cumb —1F 103
Newton St Cyres. Devn —3B 12
Newton St Faith. Norf —4E 78
Newton St Loe. Bath —5C 34
Newton St Petrock. Devn —1E 11
Newton Solney. Derbs —3G 73
Newton Stacey. Hants —2C 24
Newton Stewart. Dum —3B 110
Newton Toney. Wilts —2H 23
Newton Tracey. Devn —4F 19
Newton under Roseberry. Red C —3C 106
Newton Unthank. Leics —5B 74
Newton upon Ayr. S Ayr —2C 116
Newton upon Derwent. E Yor —5B 100
Newton Valence. Hants —3F 25
Newton with Scales. Lanc —1B 90
Newtown. Aber —2E 160
Newtown. Cambs —4H 63
Newtown. Ches —1A 72
Newtown. Corn —5C 10
Newtown. Cumb —5B 112 (nr. Aspatria)
Newtown. Cumb —3G 113 (nr. Brampton)
Newtown. Cumb —2G 103 (nr. Penrith)
Newtown. Derbs —2D 85
Newtown. Devn —4A 20
Newtown. Dors —2H 13 (nr. Beaminster)
New Town. Dors —1E 15 (nr. Sixpenny Handley)
Newtown. Dum —4G 117
New Town. E Lot —2H 129
Newtown. Falk —1D 128
Newtown. Glos —5B 48 (nr. Lydney)
Newtown. Glos —2E 49 (nr. Tewkesbury)
Newtown. Hants —1D 16 (nr. Bishop's Waltham)
Newtown. Hants —1A 16 (nr. Lyndhurst)
Newtown. Hants —5C 36 (nr. Newbury)
Newtown. Hants —4B 24 (nr. Romsey)
Newtown. Hants —2C 16 (nr. Warsash)
Newtown. Hants —1E 16 (nr. Wickham)
Newtown. Here —2B 48 (nr. Ledbury)
Newtown. Here —2A 48 (nr. Little Dewchurch)
Newtown. Here —1B 48 (nr. Stretton Grandison)
Newtown. High —3F 149
Newtown. IOM —4C 108
Newtown. IOW —3C 16
Newtown. Lanc —3D 90
New Town. Lutn —3A 52
Newtown. Nmbd —4E 121 (nr. Rothbury)
Newtown. Nmbd —2E 121 (nr. Wooler)
Newtown. Pool —3F 15
Newtown. Powy —1D 58
Newtown. Rhon —2D 32
Newtown. Shrp —2G 71
Newtown. Som —1F 13
Newtown. Staf —4D 84 (nr. Biddulph)
Newtown. Staf —5D 73 (nr. Cannock)
Newtown. Staf —4E 85 (nr. Longnor)
New Town. W Yor —2E 93
Newtown. Wilts —4E 23
Newtown-in-St Martin. Corn —4E 5
Newtown Linford. Leics —4C 74
Newtown St Boswells. Scot —1H 119
New Tredegar. Cphy —5E 47
Newtyle. Ang —4B 144
New Village. E Yor —1D 94
New Village. S Yor —4F 93
New Walsoken. Cambs —5D 76
New Waltham. NE Lin —4F 95
New Wimpole. Cambs —1D 52
New Winton. E Lot —2H 129
New World. Cambs —1C 64
New Yatt. Oxon —4B 50
Newyears Green. G Lon —2B 38
New York. Linc —5B 88
New York. Tyne —2G 115
Nextend. Here —5F 59
Neyland. Pemb —4D 42
Nib Heath. Shrp —4G 71
Nicholashayne. Devn —1E 12
Nicholaston. Swan —4E 31
Nidd. N Yor —3F 99
Niddrie. Edin —2F 129
Niddry. W Lot —2D 129
Nigg. Aber C —3G 153
Nigg. High —1C 158
Nigg Ferry. High —2B 158
Nightcott. Som —4B 20
Nine Ashes. Essx —5F 53
Ninebanks. Nmbd —4A 114
Nine Elms. Swin —3G 35
Ninemile Bar. Dum —2F 111
Nine Mile Burn. Midl —4E 129
Ninfield. E Sus —4B 28
Ningwood. IOW —4C 16
Nisbet. Scot —2A 120
Nisbet Hill. Scot —4E 130
Niton. IOW —5D 16
Nitshill. E Ren —4G 127
Niwbwrch. IOA —4D 80
Noak Hill. G Lon —1G 39
Nobold. Shrp —4G 71
Nobottle. Nptn —4D 62
Nocton. Linc —4H 87
Nogdam End. Norf —5F 79
Noke. Oxon —4D 50
Nolton. Pemb —3C 42
Nolton Haven. Pemb —3C 42
No Man's Heath. Ches —1H 71
No Man's Heath. Warw —5G 73
Nomansland. Devn —1B 12
Nomansland. Wilts —1A 16
Noneley. Shrp —3G 71
Nonikiln. High —1A 158
Nonington. Kent —5G 41
Nook. Cumb —2F 113 (nr. Longtown)
Nook. Cumb —1E 97 (nr. Milnthorpe)
Noranside. Ang —2D 144
Norbreck. Bkpl —5C 96
Norbridge. Here —1C 48
Norbury. Ches —1H 71
Norbury. Derbs —1F 73
Norbury. Shrp —1F 59
Norbury. Staf —3B 72
Norby. N Yor —1G 99
Norby. Shet —6C 173
Norcross. Lanc —5C 96
Nordelph. Norf —5E 77
Norden. G Man —3G 91
Nordley. Shrp —1A 60
Norham. Nmbd —5F 131
Norland Town. W Yor —2A 92
Norley. Ches —3H 83
Norleywood. Hants —3B 16
Normanby. N Lin —3B 94
Normanby. N Yor —1B 100
Normanby. Red C —3C 106
Normanby-by-Spital. Linc —2H 87
Normanby le Wold. Linc —1A 88
Norman Cross. Cambs —1A 64
Normandy. Surr —5A 38
Norman's Bay. E Sus —5A 28
Norman's Green. Devn —2D 12
Normanton. Dby C —2H 73
Normanton. Leics —1F 75
Normanton. Linc —1G 75
Normanton. Notts —5E 86
Normanton. W Yor —2D 93
Normanton le Heath. Leics —4A 74
Normanton on Soar. Notts —3C 74
Normanton-on-the-Wolds. Notts —2D 74
Normanton on Trent. Notts —4E 87
Normoss. Lanc —1B 90
Norrington Common. Wilts —5D 35
Norris Green. Mers —1F 83
Norris Hill. Leics —4H 73
Norristhorpe. W Yor —2C 92
North Acre. Norf —1B 66
Northall. Buck —3H 51
Northallerton. N Yor —5A 106
Northam. Devn —4E 19
Northam. Sotn —1C 16
Northampton. Nptn —4E 63
North Anston. S Yor —2C 86
North Ascot. Brac —4A 38
North Aston. Oxon —3C 50
Northaw. Herts —5C 52
Northay. Som —1F 13
North Baddesley. Hants —4B 24
North Balfern. Dum —4B 110
North Ballachulish. High —2E 141
North Barrow. Som —4B 22
North Barsham. Norf —2B 78
Northbeck. Linc —1H 75
North Benfleet. Essx —2B 40
North Bersted. W Sus —5A 26
North Berwick. E Lot —1B 130
North Bitchburn. Dur —1E 105
North Blyth. Nmbd —1G 115
North Boarhunt. Hants —1E 16
North Bockhampton. Dors —3G 15
Northborough. Pet —5A 76
Northbourne. Kent —5H 41
Northbourne. Oxon —3D 36
North Bovey. Devn —4H 11
North Bradley. Wilts —1D 22
North Brentor. Devn —4E 11
North Brewham. Som —3C 22
Northbrook. Oxon —3C 50
North Brook End. Cambs —1C 52
North Buckland. Devn —2E 19
North Burlingham. Norf —4F 79
North Cadbury. Som —4B 22
North Carlton. Linc —3G 87
North Cave. E Yor —1B 94
North Cerney. Glos —5F 49
North Chailey. E Sus —3E 27
Northchapel. W Sus —3A 26
North Charford. Hants —1G 15
North Charlton. Nmbd —2F 121
North Cheriton. Som —4B 22
North Chideock. Dors —3H 13
Northchurch. Herts —5H 51
North Cliffe. E Yor —1B 94
North Clifton. Notts —3F 87
North Close. Dur —1F 105
North Cockerington. Linc —1C 88
North Coker. Som —1A 14
North Collafirth. Shet —3E 173
North Common. E Sus —3E 27
North Commonty. Aber —4F 161
North Coombe. Devn —1B 12
North Corbelly. Dum —3A 112
North Cornelly. B'End —3B 32
North Cotes. Linc —4G 95
Northcott. Devn —3D 10
Northcourt. Oxon —2D 36
North Cove. Suff —2G 67
North Cowton. N Yor —4F 105
North Craigo. Ang —2F 145
North Crawley. Mil —1H 51
North Cray. G Lon —3F 39
North Creake. Norf —2A 78
North Curry. Som —4G 21
North Dalton. E Yor —4D 100
North Deighton. N Yor —4F 99
North Dronley. Ang —5C 144
North Duffield. N Yor —1G 93
Northedge. Derbs —4A 86
North Elkington. Linc —1B 88
North Elmham. Norf —3B 78
North Elmsall. W Yor —3E 93
North End. E Yor —1F 95
North End. Essx —4G 53 (nr. Great Dunmow)
North End. Essx —2A 54 (nr. Great Yeldham)
North End. Hants —5C 36
North End. Leics —4C 74
North End. Linc —1B 76
North End. Norf —1B 66
North End. N Som —5H 33
Northend. Oxon —2F 37
North End. Port —2E 17
Northend. Warw —5A 62
North End. W Sus —5C 26
North End. Wilts —2F 35
North Erradale. High —5B 162
North Evington. Leic C —5D 74
North Fambridge. Essx —1C 40
North Fearns. High —5E 155
North Featherstone. W Yor —2E 93
North Feorline. N Ayr —3D 122
North Ferriby. E Yor —2C 94
Northfield. Aber C —3F 153
Northfield. E Yor —2D 94
Northfield. Som —3F 21
Northfield. W Mid —3E 61
Northfleet. Kent —3H 39
North Frodingham. E Yor —4F 101
Northgate. Linc —3A 76
North Gluss. Shet —4E 173
North Gorley. Hants —1G 15
North Green. Norf —2E 66
North Green. Suff —4F 67 (nr. Framlingham)
North Green. Suff —3F 67 (nr. Halesworth)
North Green. Suff —4F 67 (nr. Saxmundham)
North Greetwell. Linc —3H 87
North Grimston. N Yor —3C 100
North Halling. Medw —4B 40
North Hayling. Hants —2F 17
North Hazelrigg. Nmbd —1E 121
North Heasley. Devn —3H 19
North Heath. W Sus —3B 26
North Hill. Corn —5C 10
North Hinksey Village. Oxon —5C 50
North Holmwood. Surr —1C 26
North Huish. Devn —3D 8
North Hykeham. Linc —4G 87
Northiam. E Sus —3C 28
Northill. Beds —1B 52
Northington. Hants —3D 24
North Kelsey. Linc —4D 94
North Kelsey Moor. Linc —4D 94
North Kessock. High —4A 158
North Killingholme. N Lin —3E 95
North Kilvington. N Yor —1G 99
North Kilworth. Leics —2D 62
North Kyme. Linc —5A 88
North Lancing. W Sus —5C 26
Northlands. Linc —5C 88
Northleach. Glos —4G 49
North Lee. Buck —5G 51
North Lees. N Yor —2F 99
Northleigh. Devn —3G 19 (nr. Barnstaple)
Northleigh. Devn —3E 13 (nr. Honiton)
North Leigh. Kent —1F 29
North Leigh. Oxon —4B 50
North Leverton with Habblesthorpe. Notts —2E 87
Northlew. Devn —3F 11
North Littleton. Worc —1F 49
North Lopham. Norf —2C 66
North Luffenham. Rut —5G 75
North Marden. W Sus —1G 17
North Marston. Buck —3F 51
North Middleton. Midl —4G 129
North Middleton. Nmbd —2E 121
North Molton. Devn —4H 19
North Moor. N Yor —1D 100
Northmoor. Oxon —5C 50
Northmoor Green. Som —3G 21
North Moreton. Oxon —3D 36
Northmuir. Ang —3C 144
North Mundham. W Sus —2G 17
North Murie. Per —1E 137
North Muskham. Notts —5E 87
North Ness. Orkn —8C 172
North Newbald. E Yor —1C 94
North Newington. Oxon —2C 50
North Newnton. Wilts —1G 23
North Newton. Som —3F 21
Northney. Hants —2F 17
North Nibley. Glos —2C 34
North Oakley. Hants —1D 24
North Ockendon. G Lon —2G 39
Northolt. G Lon —2C 38
Northop. Flin —4E 83
Northop Hall. Flin —4E 83
North Ormesby. Midd —2C 106
North Ormsby. Linc —1B 88
Northorpe. Linc —4H 75 (nr. Bourne)
Northorpe. Linc —2B 76 (nr. Donington)
Northorpe. Linc —1F 87 (nr. Gainsborough)
North Otterington. N Yor —1F 99
Northover. Som —3H 21 (nr. Glastonbury)
Northover. Som —4A 22 (nr. Yeovil)
North Owersby. Linc —1H 87
Northowram. W Yor —2B 92
North Perrott. Som —2H 13
North Petherton. Som —3F 21
North Petherwin. Corn —4C 10
North Pickenham. Norf —5A 78
North Piddle. Worc —5D 60
North Poorton. Dors —3A 14
North Port. Arg —1H 133
Northport. Dors —4E 15
North Queensferry. Fife —1E 129
North Radworthy. Devn —3A 20
North Rauceby. Linc —1H 75
Northrepps. Norf —2E 79
North Rigton. N Yor —5E 99
North Rode. Ches —4C 84
North Roe. Shet —3E 173
North Ronaldsay Airport. Orkn —2G 172
North Row. Cumb —1D 102
North Runcton. Norf —4F 77
North Sannox. N Ayr —5B 126
North Scale. Cumb —3A 96
North Scarle. Linc —4F 87
North Seaton. Nmbd —1F 115

Old Wives Lees. *Kent* —5E **41**
Old Woking. *Surr* —5B **38**
Oldwood Common. *Worc* —4H **59**
Old Woodstock. *Oxon* —4C **50**
Olgrinmore. *High* —3C **168**
Oliver's Battery. *Hants* —4C **24**
Ollaberry. *Shet* —3E **173**
Ollerton. *Ches* —3B **84**
Ollerton. *Notts* —4D **86**
Ollerton. *Shrp* —3A **72**
Olmarch. *Cdgn* —5F **57**
Olmstead Green. *Cambs* —1G **53**
Olney. *Mil* —5F **63**
Olrig. *High* —2D **169**
Olton. *W Mid* —2F **61**
Olveston. *S Glo* —3B **34**
Ombersley. *Worc* —4C **60**
Ompton. *Notts* —4D **86**
Omunsgarth. *Shet* —7E **173**
Onchan. *IOM* —4D **108**
Onecote. *Staf* —5E **85**
Onehouse. *Suff* —5C **66**
Onen. *Mon* —4H **47**
Ongar Hill. *Norf* —3E **77**
Ongar Street. *Here* —4F **59**
Onibury. *Shrp* —3G **59**
Onich. *High* —2E **141**
Onllwyn. *Neat* —4B **46**
Onneley. *Shrp* —1B **72**
Onslow Green. *Essx* —4G **53**
Onslow Village. *Surr* —1A **26**
Onthank. *E Ayr* —1D **116**
Openwoodgate. *Derbs* —1A **74**
Opinan. *High* —1G **155**
  (nr. Gairloch)
Opinan. *High* —4C **162**
  (nr. Poolewe)
Orasaigh. *W Isl* —6F **171**
Orbost. *High* —4B **154**
Orby. *Linc* —4D **89**
Orchard Hill. *Devn* —4E **19**
Orchard Portman. *Som* —4F **21**
Orcheston. *Wilts* —2F **23**
Orcop. *Here* —3H **47**
Orcop Hill. *Here* —3H **47**
Ord. *High* —2E **147**
Ordhead. *Aber* —2D **152**
Ordie. *Aber* —3B **152**
Ordiquish. *Mor* —3H **159**
Ordley. *Nmbd* —4C **114**
Ordsall. *Notts* —3E **86**
Ore. *E Sus* —4C **28**
Oreham Common. *W Sus* —4D **26**
Oreton. *Shrp* —2A **60**
Orford. *Linc* —1B **88**
Orford. *Suff* —1H **55**
Orford. *Warr* —1A **84**
Organford. *Dors* —3E **15**
Orgil. *Orkn* —7B **172**
Orgreave. *Staf* —4F **73**
Oridge Street. *Glos* —3C **48**
Orlestone. *Kent* —2D **28**
Orleton. *Here* —4G **59**
Orleton. *Worc* —4A **60**
Orleton Common. *Here* —4G **59**
Orlingbury. *Nptn* —3F **63**
Ormacleit. *W Isl* —5C **170**
Ormathwaite. *Cumb* —2D **102**
Ormesby. *Midd* —3C **106**
Ormesby St Margaret. *Norf* —4G **79**
Ormesby St Michael. *Norf* —4G **79**
Ormiscaig. *High* —4C **162**
Ormiston. *E Lot* —3H **129**
Ormsaigbeg. *High* —2F **139**
Ormsaigmore. *High* —2F **139**
Ormsary. *Arg* —2F **125**
Ormsgill. *Cumb* —2A **96**
Ormskirk. *Lanc* —4C **90**
Orphir. *Orkn* —7C **172**
Orpington. *G Lon* —4F **39**
Orrell. *G Man* —4D **90**
Orrell. *Mers* —1F **83**
Orrisdale. *IOM* —2C **108**

Orsett. *Thur* —2H **39**
Orslow. *Staf* —4C **72**
Orston. *Notts* —1E **75**
Orthwaite. *Cumb* —1D **102**
Orton. *Cumb* —4H **103**
Orton. *Nptn* —3F **63**
Orton. *Staf* —1C **60**
Orton Longueville. *Pet* —1A **64**
Orton-on-the-Hill. *Leics* —5H **73**
Orton Waterville. *Pet* —1A **64**
Orton Wistow. *Pet* —1A **64**
Orwell. *Cambs* —5C **64**
Osbaldeston. *Lanc* —1E **91**
Osbaldwick. *York* —4A **100**
Osbaston. *Leics* —5B **74**
Osbaston. *Shrp* —3F **71**
Osbournby. *Linc* —2H **75**
Osclay. *High* —5E **169**
Oscroft. *Ches* —4H **83**
Ose. *High* —4C **154**
Osgathorpe. *Leics* —4B **74**
Osgodby. *Linc* —1H **87**
Osgodby. *N Yor* —1E **101**
  (nr. Scarborough)
Osgodby. *N Yor* —1G **93**
  (nr. Selby)
Oskaig. *High* —5E **155**
Oskamull. *Arg* —4F **139**
Osleston. *Derbs* —2G **73**
Osmaston. *Dby C* —2A **74**
Osmaston. *Derbs* —1G **73**
Osmington. *Dors* —4C **14**
Osmington Mills. *Dors* —4C **14**
Osmondthorpe. *W Yor* —1D **92**
Osmotherley. *N Yor* —5B **106**
Osnaburgh. *Fife* —2G **137**
Ospisdale. *High* —5E **164**
Ospringe. *Kent* —4E **40**
Ossett. *W Yor* —2C **92**
Ossington. *Notts* —4E **87**
Ostend. *Essx* —1D **40**
Ostend. *Norf* —2F **79**
Osterley. *G Lon* —3C **38**
Oswaldkirk. *N Yor* —2A **100**
Oswaldtwistle. *Lanc* —2F **91**
Oswestry. *Shrp* —3E **71**
Otby. *Linc* —1A **88**
Otford. *Kent* —5G **39**
Otham. *Kent* —5B **40**
Otherton. *Staf* —4D **72**
Othery. *Som* —3G **21**
Otley. *Suff* —5E **66**
Otley. *W Yor* —5E **98**
Otterbourne. *Hants* —4C **24**
Otterburn. *Nmbd* —5C **120**
Otterburn. *N Yor* —4A **98**
Otterburn Camp. *Nmbd* —5C **120**
Otterburn Hall. *Nmbd* —5C **120**
Otter Ferry. *Arg* —1H **125**
Otterford. *Som* —1F **13**
Otterham. *Corn* —3B **10**
Otterhampton. *Som* —2F **21**
Otterham Quay. *Kent* —4C **40**
Ottershaw. *Surr* —4B **38**
Otterspool. *Mers* —2F **83**
Otterswick. *Shet* —3G **173**
Otterton. *Devn* —4D **12**
Otterwood. *Hants* —2C **16**
Ottinge. *Kent* —1F **29**
Ottringham. *E Yor* —2F **95**
Oughterby. *Cumb* —4D **112**
Oughtershaw. *N Yor* —1A **98**
Oughterside. *Cumb* —5C **112**
Oughtibridge. *S Yor* —1H **85**
Oughtrington. *Warr* —2A **84**
Oulston. *N Yor* —2H **99**
Oulton. *Cumb* —4D **112**
Oulton. *Norf* —3D **78**
Oulton. *Staf* —3B **72**
  (nr. Gnosall Heath)
Oulton. *Staf* —2D **72**
  (nr. Stone)

Oulton. *Suff* —1H **67**
Oulton. *W Yor* —2D **92**
Oulton Broad. *Suff* —1H **67**
Oulton Street. *Norf* —3D **78**
Oundle. *Nptn* —2H **63**
Ousby. *Cumb* —1H **103**
Ousdale. *High* —1H **165**
Ousden. *Suff* —5G **65**
Ousefleet. *E Yor* —2B **94**
Ouston. *Dur* —4F **115**
Ouston. *Nmbd* —4A **114**
  (nr. Bearsbridge)
Ouston. *Nmbd* —2D **114**
  (nr. Stamfordham)
Outer Hope. *Devn* —4C **8**
Outertown. *Orkn* —6B **172**
Outgate. *Cumb* —5E **103**
Outhgill. *Cumb* —4A **104**
Outlands. *Staf* —2B **72**
Outlane. *W Yor* —3A **92**
Out Newton. *E Yor* —2G **95**
Out Rawcliffe. *Lanc* —5D **96**
Outwell. *Norf* —5E **77**
Outwick. *Hants* —1G **15**
Outwood. *Surr* —1E **27**
Outwood. *W Yor* —2D **92**
Outwood. *Worc* —3D **60**
Outwoods. *Leics* —4B **74**
Outwoods. *Staf* —4B **72**
Ouzlewell Green. *W Yor* —2D **92**
Ovenden. *W Yor* —2A **92**
Over. *Cambs* —3C **64**
Over. *Ches* —4A **84**
Over. *Glos* —4D **48**
Over. *S Glo* —3A **34**
Overbister. *Orkn* —3F **172**
Over Burrows. *Derbs* —2G **73**
Overbury. *Worc* —2E **49**
Overcombe. *Dors* —4B **14**
Over Compton. *Dors* —1A **14**
Over End. *Cambs* —1H **63**
Over Finlarg. *Ang* —4D **144**
Overgreen. *Derbs* —3H **85**
Over Green. *W Mid* —1F **61**
Over Haddon. *Derbs* —4G **85**
Over Hulton. *G Man* —4E **91**
Over Kellet. *Lanc* —2E **97**
Over Kiddington. *Oxon* —3C **50**
Overleigh. *Som* —3H **21**
Overley. *Staf* —4F **73**
Over Monnow. *Mon* —4A **48**
Over Norton. *Oxon* —3B **50**
Over Peover. *Ches* —3B **84**
Overpool. *Ches* —3F **83**
Overscaig. *High* —1B **164**
Overseal. *Derbs* —4G **73**
Over Silton. *N Yor* —5B **106**
Oversland. *Kent* —5E **41**
Overstone. *Nptn* —4F **63**
Over Stowey. *Som* —3E **21**
Overstrand. *Norf* —1E **79**
Over Stratton. *Som* —1H **13**
Over Street. *Wilts* —3F **23**
Overthorpe. *Nptn* —1C **50**
Overton. *Aber C* —2F **153**
Overton. *Ches* —3H **83**
Overton. *Hants* —2D **24**
Overton. *High* —5E **169**
Overton. *Lanc* —4D **96**
Overton. *N Yor* —4H **99**
Overton. *Shrp* —2A **60**
  (nr. Bridgnorth)
Overton. *Shrp* —3H **59**
  (nr. Ludlow)
Overton. *Swan* —4D **30**
Overton. *W Yor* —3C **92**
Overton. *Wrex* —1F **71**
Overtown. *N Lan* —4B **128**
Overtown. *Swin* —4G **35**
Over Wallop. *Hants* —3A **24**
Over Whitacre. *Warw* —1G **61**
Over Worton. *Oxon* —3C **50**
Oving. *Buck* —3F **51**

Oving. *W Sus* —5A **26**
Ovingdean. *Brig* —5E **27**
Ovingham. *Nmbd* —3D **115**
Ovington. *Dur* —3E **105**
Ovington. *Essx* —1A **54**
Ovington. *Hants* —3D **24**
Ovington. *Norf* —5B **78**
Ovington. *Nmbd* —3D **114**
Owen's Bank. *Staf* —3G **73**
Ower. *Hants* —2C **16**
  (nr. Holbury)
Ower. *Hants* —1B **16**
  (nr. Totton)
Owermoigne. *Dors* —4C **14**
Owlbury. *Shrp* —1F **59**
Owler Bar. *Derbs* —3G **85**
Owlerton. *S Yor* —2H **85**
Owlswick. *Buck* —5F **51**
Owmby. *Linc* —4D **94**
Owmby-by-Spital. *Linc* —2H **87**
Ownham. *W Ber* —4C **36**
Owrytn. *Wrex* —1F **71**
Owslebury. *Hants* —4D **24**
Owston. *Leics* —5E **75**
Owston. *S Yor* —3F **93**
Owston Ferry. *N Lin* —4B **94**
Owstwick. *E Yor* —1F **95**
Owthorne. *E Yor* —2G **95**
Owthorpe. *Notts* —2D **74**
Owton Manor. *Hart* —2B **106**
Oxborough. *Norf* —5G **77**
Oxcombe. *Linc* —3C **88**
Oxen End. *Essx* —3G **53**
Oxenhall. *Glos* —3C **48**
Oxenholme. *Cumb* —5G **103**
Oxenhope. *W Yor* —1A **92**
Oxen Park. *Cumb* —1C **96**
Oxenpill. *Som* —2H **21**
Oxenton. *Glos* —2E **49**
Oxenwood. *Wilts* —1B **24**
Oxford. *Oxon* —5D **50**
Oxgangs. *Edin* —3F **129**
Oxhey. *Herts* —1C **38**
Oxhill. *Warw* —1B **50**
Oxley. *W Mid* —5C **72**
Oxley Green. *Essx* —4C **54**
Oxley's Green. *E Sus* —3A **28**
Oxlode. *Cambs* —2D **65**
Oxnam. *Scot* —3B **120**
Oxshott. *Surr* —4C **38**
Oxspring. *S Yor* —4C **92**
Oxted. *Surr* —5E **39**
Oxton. *Mers* —2E **83**
Oxton. *N Yor* —5H **99**
Oxton. *Notts* —5D **86**
Oxton. *Scot* —4A **130**
Oxwich. *Swan* —4D **31**
Oxwich Green. *Swan* —4D **31**
Oxwick. *Norf* —3B **78**
Oykel Bridge. *High* —3A **164**
Oyne. *Aber* —1D **152**
Oystermouth. *Swan* —4F **31**

Pabail Iarach. *W Isl* —4H **171**
Pabail Uarach. *W Isl* —4H **171**
Pachesham. *Surr* —5C **38**
Packers Hill. *Dors* —1C **14**
Packington. *Leics* —4A **74**
Packmoor. *Stoke* —5C **84**
Packmores. *Warw* —4G **61**
Packwood. *W Mid* —3F **61**
Packwood Gullett. *W Mid* —3F **61**
Padanaram. *Ang* —3D **144**
Padbury. *Buck* —2F **51**
Paddington. *G Lon* —2D **38**
Paddington. *Warr* —2A **84**
Paddlesworth. *Kent* —2F **29**
Paddock. *Kent* —5D **40**
Paddockhole. *Dum* —1D **112**
Paddock Wood. *Kent* —1A **28**
Paddolgreen. *Shrp* —2H **71**
Padeswood. *Flin* —4E **83**

Padiham. *Lanc* —1F **91**
Padside. *N Yor* —4D **98**
Padson. *Devn* —3F **11**
Padstow. *Corn* —1D **6**
Padworth. *W Ber* —5E **36**
Page Bank. *Dur* —1F **105**
Pagham. *W Sus* —3G **17**
Paglesham Churchend. *Essx* —1D **40**
Paglesham Eastend. *Essx* —1D **40**
Paibeil. *W Isl* —8C **171**
Paibeil. *W Isl* —2C **170**
Paignton. *Torb* —2E **9**
Pailton. *Warw* —2B **62**
Paine's Corner. *E Sus* —3H **27**
Painleyhill. *Staf* —2E **73**
Painscastle. *Powy* —1E **47**
Painshawfield. *Nmbd* —3D **114**
Painsthorpe. *E Yor* —4C **100**
Painswick. *Glos* —5D **48**
Painter's Forstal. *Kent* —5D **40**
Painthorpe. *W Yor* —3D **92**
Pairc Shiaboist. *W Isl* —3E **171**
Paisley. *Ren* —3F **127**
Pakefield. *Suff* —1H **67**
Pakenham. *Suff* —4B **66**
Pale. *Gwyn* —2B **70**
Palehouse Common. *E Sus* —4F **27**
Palestine. *Hants* —2A **24**
Paley Street. *Wind* —4G **37**
Palgowan. *Dum* —1A **110**
Palgrave. *Suff* —3D **66**
Pallington. *Dors* —3C **14**
Palmarsh. *Kent* —2F **29**
Palmer Moor. *Derbs* —2F **73**
Palmers Cross. *W Mid* —5C **72**
Palmerstown. *V Glam* —5E **33**
Palnackie. *Dum* —4F **111**
Palnure. *Dum* —3B **110**
Palterton. *Derbs* —4B **86**
Pamber End. *Hants* —1E **24**
Pamber Green. *Hants* —1E **24**
Pamber Heath. *Hants* —5E **36**
Pamington. *Glos* —2E **49**
Pamphill. *Dors* —2E **15**
Pampisford. *Cambs* —1E **53**
Panborough. *Som* —2H **21**
Panbride. *Ang* —5E **145**
Pancakehill. *Glos* —4F **49**
Pancrasweek. *Devn* —2C **10**
Pandy. *Gwyn* —3A **70**
  (nr. Bala)
Pandy. *Gwyn* —5F **69**
  (nr. Tywyn)
Pandy. *Mon* —3G **47**
Pandy. *Powy* —5B **70**
Pandy. *Wrex* —2D **70**
Pandy Tudur. *Cnwy* —4A **82**
Panfield. *Essx* —3H **53**
Pangbourne. *W Ber* —4E **37**
Pannal. *N Yor* —4F **99**
Pannal Ash. *N Yor* —4E **99**
Pannanich. *Aber* —4A **152**
Pant. *Shrp* —3E **71**
Pant. *Wrex* —1F **71**
Pantasaph. *Flin* —3D **82**
Pant Glas. *Gwyn* —1D **68**
Pant-glas. *Shrp* —2E **71**
Pantgwyn. *Carm* —3F **45**
Pantgwyn. *Cdgn* —1C **44**
Pant-lasau. *Swan* —3F **31**
Panton. *Linc* —3A **88**
Pant-pastynog. *Den* —4C **82**
Pantperthog. *Gwyn* —5G **69**
Pant-teg. *Carm* —3E **45**
Pant-y-Caws. *Carm* —2F **43**
Pant-y-dwr. *Powy* —3B **58**
Pant-y-ffridd. *Powy* —5D **70**
Pantyffynnon. *Carm* —4G **45**
Pantygasseg. *Torf* —5F **47**
Pant-y-llyn. *Carm* —4G **45**
Pant-yr-awel. *B'End* —3C **32**
Panty Wacco. *Flin* —3D **82**
Panxworth. *Norf* —4F **79**

Papa Westray Airport. *Orkn* —2D 172
Papcastle. *Cumb* —1C 102
Papigoe. *High* —3F 169
Papil. *Shet* —8E 173
Papple. *E Lot* —2B 130
Papplewick. *Notts* —5C 86
Papworth Everard. *Cambs* —4B 64
Papworth St Agnes. *Cambs* —4B 64
Par. *Corn* —3E 7
Paramour Street. *Kent* —4G 41
Parbold. *Lanc* —3C 90
Parbrook. *Som* —3A 22
Parbrook. *W Sus* —3B 26
Parc. *Gwyn* —2A 70
Parcllyn. *Cdgn* —5B 56
Parc-Seymour. *Newp* —2H 33
Pardown. *Hants* —2D 24
Pardshaw. *Cumb* —2B 102
Parham. *Suff* —4F 67
Park. *Aber* —4E 153
Park. *Arg* —4D 140
Park. *Dum* —5B 118
Park Bottom. *Corn* —4A 6
Parkburn. *Aber* —5E 161
Park Corner. *E Sus* —2G 27
Park Corner. *Oxon* —3E 37
Parkend. *Glos* —5B 48
Park End. *Nmbd* —2B 114
Parkeston. *Essx* —2F 55
Parkfield. *Corn* —2H 7
Parkgate. *Ches* —3E 83
Parkgate. *Cumb* —5D 112
Parkgate. *Dum* —1B 112
Park Gate. *Hants* —2D 16
Parkgate. *Surr* —1D 26
Park Gate. *Worc* —3D 60
Parkhall. *W Dun* —2F 127
Parkham. *Devn* —4D 18
Parkham Ash. *Devn* —4D 18
Parkhead. *Cumb* —5E 113
Parkhead. *Glas* —3H 127
Park Hill. *Mers* —4C 90
Parkhouse. *Mon* —5H 47
Parkhurst. *IOW* —3C 16
Park Lane. *G Man* —4F 91
Park Lane. *Staf* —5C 72
Parkmill. *Swan* —4E 31
Park Mill. *W Yor* —3C 92
Parkneuk. *Aber* —1G 145
Parkside. *N Lan* —4B 128
Parkstone. *Pool* —3F 15
Park Street. *Herts* —5B 52
Park Street. *W Sus* —2C 26
Park Town. *Oxon* —5D 50
Park Village. *Nmbd* —3H 113
Parkway. *Here* —2C 48
Parley Cross. *Dors* —3F 15
Parmoor. *Buck* —3F 37
Parr. *Mers* —1H 83
Parracombe. *Devn* —2G 19
Parrog. *Pemb* —1E 43
Parsonage Green. *Essx* —4H 53
Parsonby. *Cumb* —1C 102
Parson Cross. *S Yor* —1A 86
Parson Drove. *Cambs* —5C 76
Partick. *Glas* —3G 127
Partington. *G Man* —1B 84
Partney. *Linc* —4D 88
Parton. *Cumb* —2A 102
  (nr. Whitehaven)
Parton. *Cumb* —4D 112
  (nr. Wigton)
Parton. *Dum* —2D 111
Partridge Green. *W Sus* —4C 26
Parwich. *Derbs* —5F 85
Passenham. *Nptn* —2F 51
Passfield. *Hants* —3G 25
Passingford Bridge. *Essx* —1G 39
Paston. *Norf* —2F 79
Pasturefields. *Staf* —3D 73
Patchacott. *Devn* —3E 11
Patcham. *Brig* —5E 27
Patchetts Green. *Herts* —1C 38

Patching. *W Sus* —5B 26
Patchole. *Devn* —2G 19
Patchway. *S Glo* —3B 34
Pateley Bridge. *N Yor* —3D 98
Pathe. *Som* —3G 21
Pathhead. *Aber* —2G 145
Pathhead. *E Ayr* —3F 117
Pathhead. *Fife* —4E 137
Pathhead. *Midl* —3G 129
Pathlow. *Warw* —5F 61
Path of Condie. *Per* —2C 136
Pathstruie. *Per* —2C 136
Patmore Heath. *Herts* —3E 53
Patna. *E Ayr* —3D 116
Patney. *Wilts* —1F 23
Patrick. *IOM* —3B 108
Patrick Brompton. *N Yor* —5F 105
Patrington. *E Yor* —2G 95
Patrington Haven. *E Yor* —2G 95
Patrixbourne. *Kent* —5F 41
Patterdale. *Cumb* —3E 103
Pattiesmuir. *Fife* —1D 129
Pattingham. *Staf* —1C 60
Pattishall. *Nptn* —5D 62
Pattiswick. *Essx* —3B 54
Patton Bridge. *Cumb* —5G 103
Paul. *Corn* —4B 4
Paulerspury. *Nptn* —1F 51
Paull. *E Yor* —2E 95
Paulton. *Bath* —1B 22
Pauperhaugh. *Nmbd* —5F 121
Pave Lane. *Telf* —4B 72
Pavenham. *Beds* —5G 63
Pawlett. *Som* —2G 21
Pawston. *Nmbd* —1C 120
Paxford. *Glos* —2G 49
Paxton. *Scot* —4F 131
Payhembury. *Devn* —2D 12
Paythorne. *Lanc* —4H 97
Peacehaven. *E Sus* —5F 27
Peak Dale. *Derbs* —3E 85
Peak Forest. *Derbs* —3F 85
Peak Hill. *Linc* —4B 76
Peakirk. *Pet* —5A 76
Peanmeanach. *High* —5F 147
Pearsie. *Ang* —3C 144
Peasedown St John. *Bath* —1C 22
Peaseland Green. *Norf* —4C 78
Peasemore. *W Ber* —4C 36
Peasenhall. *Suff* —4F 67
Pease Pottage. *W Sus* —2D 26
Peaslake. *Surr* —1B 26
Peasley Cross. *Mers* —1H 83
Peasmarsh. *E Sus* —3C 28
Peasmarsh. *Surr* —1A 26
Peaston. *E Lot* —3H 129
Peastonbank. *E Lot* —3H 129
Peathill. *Aber* —2G 161
Peat Inn. *Fife* —3G 137
Peatling Magna. *Leics* —1C 62
Peatling Parva. *Leics* —1C 62
Peaton. *Arg* —1D 126
Peaton. *Shrp* —2H 59
Peats Corner. *Suff* —4D 66
Pebmarsh. *Essx* —2B 54
Pebworth. *Worc* —1G 49
Pecket Well. *W Yor* —2H 91
Peckforton. *Ches* —5H 83
Peckham Bush. *Kent* —5A 40
Peckleton. *Leics* —5B 74
Pedair-ffordd. *Powy* —3D 70
Pedlinge. *Kent* —2F 29
Pedmore. *W Mid* —2D 60
Pedwell. *Som* —3H 21
Peebles. *Scot* —5F 129
Peel. *IOM* —3B 108
Peel. *Scot* —1G 119
Peel Common. *Hants* —2D 16
Peening Quarter. *Kent* —3C 28
Pegg's Green. *Leics* —4B 74
Pegsdon. *Beds* —2B 52
Pegswood. *Nmbd* —1F 115
Peinchorran. *High* —5E 155

Peinlich. *High* —3D 154
Pelaw. *Tyne* —3G 115
Pelcomb Bridge. *Pemb* —3D 42
Pelcomb Cross. *Pemb* —3D 42
Peldon. *Essx* —4C 54
Pelsall. *W Mid* —5E 73
Pelton. *Dur* —4F 115
Pelutho. *Cumb* —5C 112
Pelynt. *Corn* —3G 7
Pemberton. *Carm* —5F 45
Pembrey. *Carm* —5E 45
Pembridge. *Here* —5F 59
Pembroke. *Pemb* —4D 43
Pembroke Dock. *Pemb* —4D 42
Pembroke Ferry. *Pemb* —4D 42
Pembury. *Kent* —1H 27
Penallt. *Mon* —5A 48
Penally. *Pemb* —5F 43
Penalt. *Here* —3A 48
Penalum. *Pemb* —5F 43
Penarth. *V Glam* —4E 33
Penbeagle. *Corn* —3C 4
Penberth. *Corn* —4B 4
Pen-bont Rhydybeddau. *Cdgn* —2F 57
Penbryn. *Cdgn* —5D 56
Pencader. *Carm* —2E 45
Pen-cae. *Cdgn* —5D 56
Pencaenewydd. *Gwyn* —1D 68
Pencaerau. *Neat* —3G 31
Pencaitland. *E Lot* —3H 129
Pencarnisiog. *IOA* —3C 80
Pencarreg. *Carm* —1F 45
Pencarrow. *Corn* —4B 10
Pencelli. *Powy* —3D 46
Pen-clawdd. *Swan* —3E 31
Pencoed. *B'End* —3C 32
Pencombe. *Here* —5H 59
Pencraig. *Here* —3A 48
Pencraig. *Powy* —3C 70
Pendeen. *Corn* —3A 4
Pendeford. *Staf* —5D 72
Penderyn. *Rhon* —5C 46
Pendine. *Carm* —4G 43
Pendlebury. *G Man* —4F 91
Pendleton. *G Man* —1C 84
Pendleton. *Lanc* —1F 91
Pendock. *Worc* —2C 48
Pendoggett. *Corn* —5A 10
Pendomer. *Som* —1A 14
Pendoylan. *V Glam* —4D 32
Pendre. *B'End* —3C 32
Penegoes. *Powy* —5G 69
Penelewey. *Corn* —4C 6
Penffordd. *Pemb* —2E 43
Penffordd-Las. *Powy* —1A 58
Penfro. *Pemb* —4D 43
Pengam. *Cphy* —2E 33
Pengam. *Card* —4F 33
Penge. *G Lon* —3E 39
Pengelly. *Corn* —4A 10
Pengenffordd. *Powy* —2E 47
Pengorffwysfa. *IOA* —1D 80
Pengover Green. *Corn* —2G 7
Pengwern. *Den* —3C 82
Penhale. *Corn* —5D 5
  (nr. Mullion)
Penhale. *Corn* —3D 6
  (nr. St Austell)
Penhale Camp. *Corn* —3B 6
Penhallow. *Corn* —3B 6
Penhalvean. *Corn* —5B 6
Penhelig. *Gwyn* —1F 57
Penhill. *Swin* —3G 35
Penhow. *Newp* —2H 33
Penhurst. *E Sus* —4A 28
Peniarth. *Gwyn* —5F 69
Penicuik. *Midl* —3F 129
Peniel. *Carm* —3E 45
Penifiler. *High* —4D 155
Peninver. *Arg* —3B 122
Penisa'r Waun. *Gwyn* —4E 81
Penistone. *S Yor* —4C 92
Penketh. *Warr* —2H 83

Penkill. *S Ayr* —5B 116
Penkridge. *Staf* —4D 72
Penley. *Wrex* —2G 71
Penllech. *Gwyn* —2B 68
Penllergaer. *Swan* —3F 31
Pen-llyn. *IOA* —2C 80
Penmachno. *Cnwy* —5G 81
Penmaen. *Swan* —4E 31
Penmaenmawr. *Cnwy* —3G 81
Penmaenpool. *Gwyn* —4F 69
Penmaen Rhos. *Cnwy* —3A 82
Penmark. *V Glam* —5D 32
Penmarth. *Corn* —5B 6
Penmon. *IOA* —2F 81
Penmorfa. *Gwyn* —1E 69
Penmynydd. *IOA* —3E 81
Penn. *Buck* —1A 38
Penn. *Dors* —3G 13
Penn. *W Mid* —1C 60
Pennal. *Gwyn* —5G 69
Pennan. *Aber* —2F 161
Pennant. *Cdgn* —4E 57
Pennant. *Den* —2C 70
Pennant. *Gwyn* —3B 70
Pennant. *Powy* —1A 58
Pennant Melangell. *Powy* —3C 70
Pennar. *Pemb* —4D 42
Pennard. *Swan* —4E 31
Pennerley. *Shrp* —1F 59
Pennington. *Cumb* —2B 96
Pennington. *G Man* —1A 84
Pennington. *Hants* —3B 16
Pennorth. *Powy* —3E 46
Penn Street. *Buck* —1A 38
Pennsylvania. *Devn* —3C 12
Pennsylvania. *S Glo* —4C 34
Penny Bridge. *Cumb* —1C 96
Pennycross. *Plym* —3A 8
Pennygate. *Norf* —3F 79
Pennyghael. *Arg* —1C 132
Penny Hill. *Linc* —3C 76
Pennylands. *Lanc* —4C 90
Pennymoor. *Devn* —1B 12
Pennyvenie. *E Ayr* —4D 117
Pennywell. *Tyne* —4G 115
Penparc. *Cdgn* —1C 44
Penparcau. *Cdgn* —2E 57
Penpedairheol. *Cphy* —2E 33
Penperlleni. *Mon* —5G 47
Penpillick. *Corn* —3E 7
Penpol. *Corn* —5C 6
Penpoll. *Corn* —3F 7
Penponds. *Corn* —3D 4
Penpont. *Corn* —5A 10
Penpont. *Dum* —5H 117
Penpont. *Powy* —3C 46
Penprysg. *B'End* —3C 32
Penquit. *Devn* —3C 8
Penrherber. *Carm* —1G 43
Penrhiw. *Pemb* —1C 44
Penrhiwceiber. *Rhon* —2D 32
Pen Rhiwfawr. *Neat* —4H 45
Penrhiw-llan. *Cdgn* —1D 44
Penrhiw-pal. *Cdgn* —1D 44
Penrhos. *Gwyn* —2C 68
Penrhos. *Here* —5F 59
Penrhos. *IOA* —2B 80
Penrhos. *Mon* —4H 47
Penrhos. *Powy* —4B 46
Penrhos garnedd. *Gwyn* —3E 81
Penrhyn. *IOA* —1C 80
Penrhyn Bay. *Cnwy* —2H 81
Penrhyn-coch. *Cdgn* —2F 57
Penrhyndeudraeth. *Gwyn* —2F 69
Penrhyn Side. *Cnwy* —2H 81
Penrice. *Swan* —4D 31
Penrith. *Cumb* —2G 103
Penrose. *Corn* —1C 6
Penruddock. *Cumb* —2F 103
Penryn. *Corn* —5B 6
Pensarn. *Carm* —4E 45
Pen-sarn. *Gwyn* —3E 69
Pensax. *Worc* —4B 60

Pensby. *Mers* —2E 83
Penselwood. *Som* —3C 22
Pensford. *Bath* —5B 34
Pensham. *Worc* —1E 49
Penshaw. *Tyne* —4G 115
Penshurst. *Kent* —1G 27
Pensilva. *Corn* —2G 7
Pensnett. *W Mid* —2D 60
Penston. *E Lot* —2H 129
Penstone. *Devn* —2A 12
Pente-tafarn-y-fedw. *Cnwy* —4H 81
Pentewan. *Corn* —4E 6
Pentir. *Gwyn* —4E 81
Pentire. *Corn* —2B 6
Pentlepoir. *Pemb* —4F 43
Pentlow. *Essx* —1B 54
Pentney. *Norf* —4G 77
Penton Mewsey. *Hants* —2B 24
Pentraeth. *IOA* —3E 81
Pentre. *Powy* —1E 59
  (nr. Church Stoke)
Pentre. *Powy* —2D 58
  (nr. Kerry)
Pentre. *Powy* —2C 58
  (nr. Mochdre)
Pentre. *Rhon* —2C 32
Pentre. *Shrp* —4F 71
  (nr. Llanfyllin)
Pentre. *Wrex* —1E 71
  (nr. Rhosllanerchrugog)
Pentrebach. *Carm* —2B 46
Pentre-bach. *Cdgn* —1F 45
Pentre-bach. *Mer T* —5D 46
Pentre-bach. *Powy* —2C 46
Pentrebach. *Swan* —5G 45
Pentre Berw. *IOA* —3D 80
Pentre-bont. *Cnwy* —5G 81
Pentrecagal. *Carm* —1D 44
Pentre-celyn. *Den* —5D 82
Pentre-clawdd. *Shrp* —2E 71
Pentreclwydau. *Neat* —5B 46
Pentre-cwrt. *Carm* —2D 45
Pentre Dolau Honddu. *Powy* —1C 46
Pentre-du. *Cnwy* —5G 81
Pentre-dwr. *Neat* —3F 31
Pentrefelin. *Carm* —3F 45
Pentrefelin. *Cdgn* —1G 45
Pentrefelin. *Cnwy* —3H 81
Pentrefelin. *Gwyn* —2E 69
Pentrefoelas. *Cnwy* —5A 82
Pentre Galar. *Pemb* —1F 43
Pentregat. *Cdgn* —5C 56
Pentre Gwenlais. *Carm* —4G 45
Pentre Gwynfryn. *Gwyn* —3E 69
Pentre Halkyn. *Flin* —3E 82
Pentre Hodre. *Shrp* —3F 59
Pentre-Llanrhaeadr. *Den* —4C 82
Pentre Llifior. *Powy* —1D 58
Pentrellwyn. *IOA* —2E 81
Pentre-llwyn-llwyd. *Powy* —5B 58
Pentre-llyn-cymmer. *Cnwy* —5B 82
Pentre Meyrick. *V Glam* —4C 32
Pentre-piod. *Gwyn* —2A 70
Pentre-poeth. *Newp* —3F 33
Pentre'r Beirdd. *Powy* —4D 70
Pentre'r-felin. *Powy* —2A 46
Pentre-uchaf. *Gwyn* —2C 68
Pentrich. *Derbs* —5A 86
Pentridge. *Dors* —1F 15
Pen-twyn. *Cphy* —5F 47
  (nr. Oakdale)
Pentwyn. *Cphy* —5E 46
  (nr. Rhymney)
Pentwyn. *Card* —3F 33
Pentyrch. *Card* —3E 32
Pentywyn. *Carm* —4G 43
Penuwch. *Cdgn* —4E 57
Penwithick. *Corn* —3E 7
Penwyllt. *Powy* —4B 46
Penybanc. *Carm* —4G 45
  (nr. Ammanford)

Renfrew. *Ren* —3G 127
Renhold. *Beds* —5H 63
Renishaw. *Derbs* —3B 86
Rennington. *Nmbd* —3G 121
Renton. *W Dun* —2E 127
Renwick. *Cumb* —5H 113
Repps. *Norf* —4G 79
Repton. *Derbs* —3H 73
Resaurie. *High* —4B 158
Rescassa. *Corn* —4D 6
Rescobie. *Ang* —3E 145
Rescorla. *Corn* —3E 7
(nr. Rosevean)
Rescorla. *Corn* —4D 6
(nr. St Ewe)
Resipole. *High* —2B 140
Resolfen. *Neat* —5B 46
Resolis. *High* —2A 158
Resolven. *Neat* —5B 46
Rest and be Thankful. *Arg* —3B 134
Reston. *Scot* —3E 131
Restrop. *Wilts* —3F 35
Retford. *Notts* —2E 86
Retire. *Corn* —2E 6
Rettendon. *Essx* —1D 40
Retyn. *Corn* —3C 6
Revesby. *Linc* —4C 88
Rew. *Devn* —5D 8
Rewe. *Devn* —3C 12
Rew Street. *IOW* —3C 16
Rexon. *Devn* —4E 11
Reybridge. *Wilts* —5E 35
Reydon. *Suff* —3H 67
Reymerston. *Norf* —5C 78
Reynalton. *Pemb* —4E 43
Reynoldston. *Swan* —4D 31
Rezare. *Corn* —5D 10
Rhadyr. *Mon* —5G 47
Rhaeadr Gwy. *Powy* —4B 58
Rhandirmwyn. *Carm* —1A 46
Rhayader. *Powy* —4B 58
Rheindown. *High* —4H 157
Rhemore. *High* —3G 139
Rhenetra. *High* —3D 154
Rhewl. *Den* —1D 70
(nr. Llangollen)
Rhewl. *Den* —4D 82
(nr. Ruthin)
Rhewl. *Shrp* —2F 71
Rhewl-Mostyn. *Flin* —2D 82
Rhian. *High* —2C 164
Rhian Breck. *High* —3C 164
Rhicarn. *High* —1E 163
Rhiconich. *High* —3C 166
Rhicullen. *High* —1A 158
Rhidorroch. *High* —4F 163
Rhifail. *High* —4H 167
Rhigos. *Rhon* —5C 46
Rhilochan. *High* —3E 165
Rhiroy. *High* —5F 163
Rhitongue. *High* —3G 167
Rhiw. *Gwyn* —3B 68
Rhiwabon. *Wrex* —1F 71
Rhiwbina. *Card* —3E 33
Rhiwbryfdir. *Gwyn* —1F 69
Rhiwderin. *Newp* —3F 33
Rhiwlas. *Gwyn* —2B 70
(nr. Bala)
Rhiwlas. *Gwyn* —4E 81
(nr. Bangor)
Rhiwlas. *Powy* —2E 70
Rhodes. *G Man* —4G 91
Rhodesia. *Notts* —3C 86
Rhodes Minnis. *Kent* —1F 29
Rhodiad-y-Brenin. *Pemb* —2B 42
Rhonehouse. *Dum* —4E 111
Rhoose. *V Glam* —5D 32
Rhos. *Carm* —2D 45
Rhos. *Neat* —5H 45
Rhosaman. *Carm* —4H 45
Rhoscefnhir. *IOA* —3E 81
Rhoscolyn. *IOA* —3B 80
Rhos Common. *Powy* —4E 71

Rhoscrowther. *Pemb* —4D 42
Rhos-ddu. *Gwyn* —2B 68
Rhosdylluan. *Gwyn* —3A 70
Rhosesmor. *Flin* —4E 82
Rhos-fawr. *Gwyn* —2C 68
Rhosgadfan. *Gwyn* —5E 81
Rhosgoch. *IOA* —2D 80
Rhosgoch. *Powy* —1E 47
Rhos Haminiog. *Cdgn* —4E 57
Rhos-hill. *Pemb* —1B 44
Rhoshirwaun. *Gwyn* —3A 68
Rhoslan. *Gwyn* —1D 68
Rhoslefain. *Gwyn* —5E 69
Rhosllanerchrugog. *Wrex* —1E 71
Rhos Lligwy. *IOA* —2D 81
Rhosmaen. *Carm* —3G 45
Rhosmeirch. *IOA* —3D 81
Rhosneigr. *IOA* —3C 80
Rhos-on-Sea. *Cnwy* —2H 81
Rhossili. *Swan* —4D 30
Rhosson. *Pemb* —2B 42
Rhos, The. *Pemb* —3E 43
Rhostrenwfa. *IOA* —3D 80
Rhostryfan. *Gwyn* —5D 81
Rhostyllen. *Wrex* —1F 71
Rhoswiel. *Shrp* —2E 71
Rhosybol. *IOA* —2D 80
Rhos-y-brithdir. *Powy* —3D 70
Rhos-y-garth. *Cdgn* —3F 57
Rhos-y-gwaliau. *Gwyn* —2B 70
Rhos-y-llan. *Gwyn* —2B 68
Rhos-y-meirch. *Powy* —4E 59
Rhu. *Arg* —1D 126
Rhualit. *Den* —3C 82
Rhubodach. *Arg* —2B 126
Rhubha Stoer. *High* —1E 163
Rhuddall Heath. *Ches* —4H 83
Rhuddlan. *Cdgn* —1E 45
Rhuddlan. *Den* —3C 82
Rhue. *High* —4E 163
Rhulen. *Powy* —5D 58
Rhunahaorine. *Arg* —5F 125
Rhuthun. *Den* —5D 82
Rhuvoult. *High* —3C 166
Rhyd. *Gwyn* —1F 69
Rhydaman. *Carm* —4G 45
Rhydargaeau. *Carm* —3E 45
Rhydcymerau. *Carm* —2F 45
Rhydd. *Worc* —1D 48
Rhyd-Ddu. *Gwyn* —5E 81
Rhydding. *Neat* —3G 31
Rhydfudr. *Cdgn* —4E 57
Rhydlanfair. *Cnwy* —5H 81
Rhydlewis. *Cdgn* —1D 44
Rhydlios. *Gwyn* —2A 68
Rhydlydan. *Cnwy* —5A 82
Rhyd-meirionydd. *Cdgn* —2F 57
Rhydowen. *Cdgn* —1E 45
Rhyd-Rosser. *Cdgn* —4E 57
Rhydspence. *Powy* —1F 47
Rhydtalog. *Flin* —5E 83
Rhyd-uchaf. *Gwyn* —2B 70
Rhydwyn. *IOA* —2C 80
Rhyd-y-clafdy. *Gwyn* —2C 68
Rhydycroesau. *Shrp* —2E 71
Rhydyfelin. *Cdgn* —3E 57
Rhydyfelin. *Rhon* —3E 32
Rhyd-y-foel. *Cnwy* —3B 82
Rhyd-y-fro. *Neat* —5H 45
Rhydymain. *Gwyn* —3H 69
Rhyd-y-meirch. *Mon* —5G 47
Rhyd-y-meudwy. *Den* —5D 82
Rhydymwyn. *Flin* —4E 82
Rhyd-yr-onen. *Gwyn* —5F 69
Rhyd-y-sarn. *Gwyn* —1F 69
Rhyl. *Den* —2C 82
Rhymney. *Cphy* —5E 46
Rhymni. *Cphy* —5E 46
Rhynd. *Per* —1D 136
Rhynie. *Aber* —1B 152
Ribbesford. *Worc* —3B 60
Ribbleton. *Lanc* —1D 90
Ribby. *Lanc* —1C 90

Ribchester. *Lanc* —1E 91
Riber. *Derbs* —5H 85
Ribigill. *High* —3F 167
Riby. *Linc* —4E 95
Riccall. *N Yor* —1G 93
Riccarton. *E Ayr* —1D 116
Richards Castle. *Here* —4G 59
Richborough Port. *Kent* —4H 41
Richings Park. *Buck* —3B 38
Richmond. *G Lon* —3C 38
Richmond. *N Yor* —4E 105
Rickarton. *Aber* —5F 153
Rickerby. *Cumb* —4F 113
Rickerscote. *Staf* —3D 72
Rickford. *N Som* —1H 21
Rickham. *Devn* —5D 8
Rickinghall Superior. *Suff* —3C 66
Rickleton. *Tyne* —4F 115
Rickling. *Essx* —2E 53
Rickling Green. *Essx* —3F 53
Rickmansworth. *Herts* —1B 38
Riddings. *Derbs* —5B 86
Riddlecombe. *Devn* —1G 11
Riddlesden. *W Yor* —5C 98
Ridge. *Dors* —4E 15
Ridge. *Herts* —5C 52
Ridge. *Wilts* —3E 23
Ridgebourne. *Powy* —4C 58
Ridge Lane. *Warw* —1G 61
Ridgeway. *Derbs* —5A 86
(nr. Alfreton)
Ridgeway. *Derbs* —2B 86
(nr. Sheffield)
Ridgeway. *Staf* —5C 84
Ridgeway Cross. *Here* —1C 48
Ridgeway Moor. *Derbs* —2B 86
Ridgewell. *Essx* —1H 53
Ridgewood. *E Sus* —3F 27
Ridgmont. *Beds* —2H 51
Ridgwardine. *Shrp* —2A 72
Riding Mill. *Nmbd* —3D 114
Ridley. *Kent* —4H 39
Ridley. *Nmbd* —3A 114
Ridlington. *Norf* —2F 79
Ridlington. *Rut* —5F 75
Ridsdale. *Nmbd* —1C 114
Rieff. *High* —2D 162
Riemore Lodge. *Per* —1H 143
Rievaulx. *N Yor* —1H 99
Rift House. *Hart* —1B 106
Rigg. *Dum* —3D 112
Riggend. *N Lan* —2A 128
Rigmaden Park. *Cumb* —1F 97
Rigsby. *Linc* —3D 88
Rigside. *S Lan* —1A 118
Riley Green. *Lanc* —2E 90
Rileyhill. *Staf* —4F 73
Rilla Mill. *Corn* —5C 10
Rillington. *N Yor* —2C 100
Rimington. *Lanc* —5H 97
Rimpton. *Som* —4B 22
Rimsdale. *High* —4H 167
Rimswell. *E Yor* —2G 95
Ringasta. *Shet* —10E 173
Ringford. *Dum* —4D 111
Ringing Hill. *Leics* —4B 74
Ringinglow. *S Yor* —2G 85
Ringland. *Norf* —4D 78
Ringlestone. *Kent* —5C 40
Ringmer. *E Sus* —4F 27
Ringmore. *Devn* —4C 8
(nr. Kingsbridge)
Ringmore. *Devn* —5C 12
(nr. Teignmouth)
Ring o' Bells. *Lanc* —3C 90
Ring's End. *Cambs* —5C 76
Ringsfield. *Suff* —2G 67
Ringsfield Corner. *Suff* —2G 67
Ringshall. *Buck* —4H 51
Ringshall. *Suff* —5C 66
Ringshall Stocks. *Suff* —5C 66
Ringstead. *Norf* —1G 77
Ringstead. *Nptn* —3G 63

Ringwood. *Hants* —2G 15
Ringwould. *Kent* —1H 29
Rinmore. *Aber* —2B 152
Rinnigill. *Orkn* —8C 172
Rinsey. *Corn* —4C 4
Riof. *W Isl* —4D 171
Ripe. *E Sus* —4G 27
Ripley. *Derbs* —1B 74
Ripley. *Hants* —3G 15
Ripley. *N Yor* —3F 99
Ripley. *Surr* —5B 38
Riplingham. *E Yor* —1C 94
Riplington. *Hants* —4E 25
Ripon. *N Yor* —2F 99
Rippingale. *Linc* —3H 75
Ripple. *Kent* —1H 29
Ripple. *Worc* —2D 48
Ripponden. *W Yor* —3A 92
Rireavach. *High* —4E 163
Risabus. *Arg* —5B 124
Risbury. *Here* —5H 59
Risby. *E Yor* —1D 94
Risby. *N Lin* —3C 94
Risby. *Suff* —4G 65
Risca. *Cphy* —2F 33
Rise. *E Yor* —5F 101
Riseden. *E Sus* —2H 27
Riseden. *Kent* —2B 28
Rise End. *Derbs* —5G 85
Risegate. *Linc* —3B 76
Riseholme. *Linc* —3G 87
Riseley. *Beds* —4H 63
Riseley. *Wok* —5F 37
Rishangles. *Suff* —4D 66
Rishton. *Lanc* —1F 91
Rishworth. *W Yor* —3A 92
Risley. *Derbs* —2B 74
Risley. *Warr* —1A 84
Risplith. *N Yor* —3E 99
Rispond. *High* —2E 167
Rivar. *Wilts* —5B 36
Rivenhall. *Essx* —4B 54
Rivenhall End. *Essx* —4B 54
River. *Kent* —1G 29
River. *W Sus* —3A 26
River Bank. *Cambs* —4E 65
Riverhead. *Kent* —5G 39
Rivington. *Lanc* —3C 91
Roach Bridge. *Lanc* —2D 90
Roachill. *Devn* —4B 20
Roade. *Nptn* —5E 63
Road Green. *Norf* —1E 67
Roadhead. *Cumb* —2G 113
Roadmeetings. *S Lan* —5B 128
Roadside. *High* —2D 168
Roadside of Catterline. *Aber* —1H 145
Roadside of Kinneff. *Aber* —1H 145
Roadwater. *Som* —3D 20
Road Weedon. *Nptn* —5D 62
Roag. *High* —4B 154
Roa Island. *Cumb* —3B 96
Roath. *Card* —4E 33
Roberton. *Scot* —3G 119
Roberton. *S Lan* —2B 118
Robertsbridge. *E Sus* —3B 28
Robertstown. *Mor* —4G 159
Robertstown. *Rhon* —5C 46
Roberttown. *W Yor* —2B 92
Robeston Back. *Pemb* —3E 43
Robeston Wathen. *Pemb* —3E 43
Robeston West. *Pemb* —4C 42
Robin Hood. *Lanc* —3D 90
Robin Hood. *W Yor* —2D 92
Robinhood End. *Essx* —2H 53
Robin Hood's Bay. *N Yor* —4G 107
Roborough. *Devn* —1F 11
(nr. Great Torrington)
Roborough. *Devn* —2B 8
(nr. Plymouth)
Rob Roy's House. *Arg* —2A 134
Roby Mill. *Lanc* —4D 90
Rocester. *Staf* —2F 73
Roch. *Pemb* —2C 42

Rochdale. *G Man* —3G 91
Roche. *Corn* —2D 6
Rochester. *Medw* —4B 40
Rochester. *Nmbd* —5C 120
Rochford. *Essx* —1C 40
Rock. *Corn* —1D 6
Rock. *Nmbd* —2G 121
Rock. *W Sus* —4C 26
Rock. *Worc* —3B 60
Rockbeare. *Devn* —3D 12
Rockbourne. *Hants* —1G 15
Rockcliffe. *Cumb* —3E 113
Rockcliffe. *Dum* —4F 111
Rockcliffe Cross. *Cumb* —3E 113
Rock Ferry. *Mers* —2F 83
Rockfield. *High* —5G 165
Rockfield. *Mon* —4H 47
Rockford. *Hants* —2G 15
Rockgreen. *Shrp* —3H 59
Rockhampton. *S Glo* —2B 34
Rockhead. *Corn* —4A 10
Rockingham. *Nptn* —1F 63
Rockland All Saints. *Norf* —1B 66
Rockland St Mary. *Norf* —5F 79
Rockland St Peter. *Norf* —1B 66
Rockley. *Wilts* —4G 35
Rockwell End. *Buck* —3F 37
Rockwell Green. *Som* —1E 13
Rodborough. *Glos* —5D 48
Rodbourne. *Wilts* —3E 35
Rodd. *Here* —4F 59
Roddam. *Nmbd* —2E 121
Rodden. *Dors* —4B 14
Roddymoor. *Dur* —1E 105
Rode. *Som* —1D 22
Rode Heath. *Ches* —5C 84
Rodeheath. *Ches* —4C 84
Roden. *Telf* —4H 71
Rodenloft. *E Ayr* —2D 117
Rodhuish. *Som* —3D 20
Rodington. *Telf* —4H 71
Rodington Heath. *Telf* —4H 71
Rodley. *Glos* —4C 48
Rodmarton. *Glos* —2E 35
Rodmell. *E Sus* —5F 27
Rodmersham. *Kent* —4D 40
Rodmersham Green. *Kent* —4D 40
Rodney Stoke. *Som* —2H 21
Rodsley. *Derbs* —1G 73
Rodway. *Som* —2F 21
Rodway. *Telf* —4A 72
Rodwell. *Dors* —5B 14
Roecliffe. *N Yor* —3F 99
Roe Green. *Herts* —2D 52
Roehampton. *G Lon* —3D 38
Roffey. *W Sus* —2C 26
Rogart. *High* —3E 165
Rogate. *W Sus* —4G 25
Roger Ground. *Cumb* —5E 103
Rogerstone. *Newp* —3F 33
Roghadal. *W Isl* —9C 171
Rogiet. *Mon* —3H 33
Rogue's Alley. *Cambs* —5C 76
Roke. *Oxon* —2E 37
Rokemarsh. *Oxon* —2E 36
Roker. *Tyne* —4H 115
Rollesby. *Norf* —4G 79
Rolleston. *Leics* —5E 75
Rolleston. *Notts* —5E 87
Rolleston on Dove. *Staf* —3G 73
Rolston. *E Yor* —5G 101
Rolvenden. *Kent* —2C 28
Rolvenden Layne. *Kent* —2C 28
Romaldkirk. *Dur* —2C 104
Roman Bank. *Shrp* —1H 59
Romanby. *N Yor* —5A 106
Roman Camp. *W Lot* —2D 129
Romannobridge. *Scot* —5E 129
Romansleigh. *Devn* —4H 19
Romers Common. *Worc* —4H 59
Romesdal. *High* —3D 154
Romford. *Dors* —2F 15
Romford. *G Lon* —2G 39

Romiley—St Columb Major

Romiley. *G Man* —1D **84**
Romsey. *Hants* —4B **24**
Romsley. *Shrp* —2B **60**
Romsley. *Worc* —3D **60**
Ronague. *IOM* —4B **108**
Rookby. *Cumb* —3B **104**
Rookhope. *Dur* —5C **114**
Rooking. *Cumb* —3F **103**
Rookley. *IOW* —4D **16**
Rooks Bridge. *Som* —1G **21**
Rooksey Green. *Suff* —5B **66**
Rooks Nest. *Som* —3D **20**
Rookwood. *W Sus* —3F **17**
Roos. *E Yor* —1F **95**
Roosebeck. *Cumb* —3B **96**
Roosecote. *Cumb* —3B **96**
Rootfield. *High* —3H **157**
Rootham's Green. *Beds* —5A **64**
Rootpark. *S Lan* —4C **128**
Ropley. *Hants* —3E **25**
Ropley Dean. *Hants* —3E **25**
Ropsley. *Linc* —2G **75**
Rora. *Aber* —3H **161**
Rorandle. *Aber* —2D **152**
Rorrington. *Shrp* —5F **71**
Rose. *Corn* —3B **6**
Roseacre. *Lanc* —1C **90**
Rose Ash. *Devn* —4A **20**
Rosebank. *S Lan* —5B **128**
Rosebush. *Pemb* —2E **43**
Rosedale Abbey. *N Yor* —5E **107**
Roseden. *Nmbd* —2E **121**
Rose Green. *Essx* —3B **54**
Rose Green. *Suff* —1C **54**
Rosehall. *High* —3B **164**
Rosehearty. *Aber* —2G **161**
Rose Hill. *E Sus* —4F **27**
Rose Hill. *Lanc* —1G **91**
Rosehill. *Shrp* —2A **72**
(nr. Market Drayton)
Rosehill. *Shrp* —4G **71**
(nr. Shrewsbury)
Roseisle. *Mor* —2F **159**
Rosemarket. *Pemb* —4D **42**
Rosemarkie. *High* —3B **158**
Rosemary Lane. *Devn* —1E **13**
Rosemount. *Per* —4A **144**
Rosenannon. *Corn* —2D **6**
Roser's Cross. *E Sus* —3G **27**
Rosevean. *Corn* —3E **7**
Rosewell. *Midl* —3F **129**
Roseworth. *Stoc T* —2B **106**
Roseworthy. *Corn* —3D **4**
Rosgill. *Cumb* —3G **103**
Roshven. *High* —1B **140**
Roskhill. *High* —4B **154**
Roskorwell. *Corn* —4E **5**
Rosley. *Cumb* —5E **112**
Roslin. *Midl* —3F **129**
Rosliston. *Derbs* —4G **73**
Rosneath. *Arg* —1D **126**
Ross. *Dum* —5D **110**
Ross. *Nmbd* —1F **121**
Ross. *Per* —1G **135**
Ross. *Scot* —3F **131**
Rossendale. *Lanc* —2G **91**
Rossett. *Wrex* —5F **83**
Rossington. *S Yor* —1D **86**
Rosskeen. *High* —2A **158**
Rossland. *Ren* —2F **127**
Ross-on-Wye. *Here* —3B **48**
Roster. *High* —4E **169**
Rostherne. *Ches* —2B **84**
Rostholme. *S Yor* —4F **93**
Rosthwaite. *Cumb* —3D **102**
Roston. *Derbs* —1F **73**
Rosudgeon. *Corn* —4C **4**
Rosyth. *Fife* —1E **129**
Rothbury. *Nmbd* —4E **121**
Rotherby. *Leics* —4D **74**
Rotherfield. *E Sus* —3G **27**
Rotherfield Greys. *Oxon* —3F **37**
Rotherfield Peppard. *Oxon* —3F **37**

Rotherham. *S Yor* —1B **86**
Rotherthorpe. *Nptn* —5E **62**
Rotherwick. *Hants* —1F **25**
Rothes. *Mor* —4G **159**
Rothesay. *Arg* —3B **126**
Rothienorman. *Aber* —5E **160**
Rothiesholm. *Orkn* —5F **172**
Rothley. *Leics* —4C **74**
Rothley. *Nmbd* —1D **114**
Rothwell. *Linc* —1A **88**
Rothwell. *Nptn* —2F **63**
Rothwell. *W Yor* —2D **92**
Rothwell Haigh. *W Yor* —2D **92**
Rotsea. *E Yor* —4E **101**
Rottal. *Ang* —2C **144**
Rotten End. *Suff* —4F **67**
Rottenhill. *Aber* —3H **161**
Rotten Row. *Norf* —4C **78**
Rotten Row. *W Ber* —4D **36**
Rotten Row. *W Mid* —3F **61**
Rottingdean. *Brig* —5E **27**
Rottington. *Cumb* —3A **102**
Roud. *IOW* —4D **16**
Rougham. *Norf* —3H **77**
Rougham. *Suff* —4B **66**
Rough Close. *Staf* —2D **72**
Rough Common. *Kent* —5F **41**
Roughcote. *Staf* —1D **72**
Rough Haugh. *High* —4H **167**
Rough Hay. *Staf* —3G **73**
Roughlee. *Lanc* —5H **97**
Roughley. *W Mid* —1F **61**
Roughsike. *Cumb* —2G **113**
Roughton. *Linc* —4B **88**
Roughton. *Norf* —2E **78**
Roughton. *Shrp* —1B **60**
Roundbush Green. *Essx* —4F **53**
Roundham. *Som* —2H **13**
Roundhay. *W Yor* —1D **92**
Round Hill. *Torb* —2F **9**
Roundhurst Common. *W Sus* —2A **26**
Round Oak. *Shrp* —2F **59**
Roundstreet Common. *W Sus* —3B **26**
Roundthwaite. *Cumb* —4H **103**
Roundway. *Wilts* —5F **35**
Roundyhill. *Ang* —3C **144**
Rousdon. *Devn* —3F **13**
Rousham. *Oxon* —3C **50**
Rous Lench. *Worc* —5E **61**
Routh. *E Yor* —5E **101**
Rout's Green. *Buck* —2F **37**
Row. *Corn* —5A **10**
Row. *Cumb* —1D **96**
(nr. Kendal)
Row. *Cumb* —1H **103**
(nr. Penrith)
Rowanburn. *Dum* —2F **113**
Rowardennan. *Stir* —4C **134**
Rowarth. *Derbs* —2E **85**
Row Ash. *Hants* —1D **16**
Rowberrow. *Som* —1H **21**
Rowde. *Wilts* —5E **35**
Rowden. *Devn* —3G **11**
Rowden Hill. *Wilts* —4E **35**
Rowen. *Cnwy* —3G **81**
Rowfoot. *Nmbd* —3H **113**
Row Green. *Essx* —3H **53**
Row Heath. *Essx* —4E **55**
Rowhedge. *Essx* —3D **54**
Rowhook. *W Sus* —2C **26**
Rowington. *Warw* —4G **61**
Rowland. *Derbs* —3G **85**
Rowland's Castle. *Hants* —1F **17**
Rowlands Gill. *Tyne* —4E **115**
Rowledge. *Surr* —2G **25**
Rowley. *Dur* —5D **115**
Rowley. *E Yor* —1C **94**
Rowley. *Shrp* —5F **71**
Rowley. *Staf* —3F **73**
Rowley Hill. *W Yor* —3B **92**
Rowley Regis. *W Mid* —2D **60**
Rowstone. *Here* —3G **47**
Rowly. *Surr* —1B **26**

Rowner. *Hants* —2D **16**
Rowney Green. *Worc* —3E **61**
Rownhams. *Hants* —1B **16**
Rowrah. *Cumb* —3B **102**
Rowsham. *Buck* —4G **51**
Rowsley. *Derbs* —4G **85**
Rowstock. *Oxon* —3C **36**
Rowston. *Linc* —5H **87**
Row, The. *Lanc* —2D **96**
Rowthorne. *Derbs* —4B **86**
Rowton. *Ches* —4G **83**
Rowton. *Shrp* —2G **59**
(nr. Ludlow)
Rowton. *Shrp* —4F **71**
(nr. Shrewsbury)
Rowton. *Telf* —4A **72**
Row Town. *Surr* —4B **38**
Roxburgh. *Scot* —1B **120**
Roxby. *N Lin* —3C **94**
Roxby. *N Yor* —3E **107**
Roxton. *Beds* —5A **64**
Roxwell. *Essx* —5G **53**
Royal Leamington Spa. *Warw* —4H **61**
Royal Oak. *Darl* —2F **105**
Royal Oak. *Lanc* —4C **90**
Royal Oak. *N Yor* —2F **101**
Royal's Green. *Ches* —1A **72**
Royal Tunbridge Wells. *Kent* —2G **27**
Roybridge. *High* —5E **149**
Roydon. *Essx* —4E **53**
Roydon. *Norf* —2C **66**
(nr. Diss)
Roydon. *Norf* —3G **77**
(nr. King's Lynn)
Roydon Hamlet. *Essx* —5E **53**
Royston. *Herts* —1D **52**
Royston. *S Yor* —3D **92**
Royston Water. *Som* —1F **13**
Royton. *G Man* —4H **91**
Ruabon. *Wrex* —1F **71**
Ruaig. *Arg* —4B **138**
Ruan High Lanes. *Corn* —5D **6**
Ruan Lanihorne. *Corn* —4C **6**
Ruan Minor. *Corn* —5E **5**
Ruarach. *High* —1B **148**
Ruardean. *Glos* —4B **48**
Ruardean Hill. *Glos* —4B **48**
Ruardean Woodside. *Glos* —4B **48**
Rubery. *W Mid* —3D **61**
Ruchazie. *Glas* —3H **127**
Ruckcroft. *Cumb* —5G **113**
Ruckinge. *Kent* —2E **29**
Ruckland. *Linc* —3C **88**
Rucklers Lane. *Herts* —5A **52**
Ruckley. *Shrp* —5H **71**
Rudbaxton. *Pemb* —2D **42**
Rudby. *N Yor* —4B **106**
Ruddington. *Notts* —2C **74**
Rudford. *Glos* —3C **48**
Rudge. *Shrp* —1C **60**
Rudge. *Wilts* —1D **22**
Rudge Heath. *Shrp* —1B **60**
Rudgeway. *S Glo* —3B **34**
Rudgwick. *W Sus* —2B **26**
Rudhall. *Here* —3B **48**
Rudheath. *Ches* —3A **84**
Rudheath Woods. *Ches* —3B **84**
Rudley Green. *Essx* —5B **54**
Rudloe. *Wilts* —4D **34**
Rudry. *Cphy* —3E **33**
Rudston. *E Yor* —3E **101**
Rudyard. *Staf* —5D **84**
Rufford. *Lanc* —3C **90**
Rufforth. *York* —4H **99**
Rugby. *Warw* —3C **62**
Rugeley. *Staf* —4E **73**
Ruilick. *High* —4H **157**
Ruisaurie. *High* —4G **157**
Ruishton. *Som* —4F **21**
Ruisigearraidh. *W Isl* —1E **170**
Ruislip. *G Lon* —2B **38**
Ruislip Common. *G Lon* —2B **38**
Rumbling Bridge. *Per* —4C **136**

Rumburgh. *Suff* —2F **67**
Rumford. *Corn* —1C **6**
Rumford. *Falk* —2C **128**
Rumney. *Card* —4F **33**
Rumwell. *Som* —4E **21**
Runcorn. *Hal* —2H **83**
Runcton. *W Sus* —2G **17**
Runcton Holme. *Norf* —5F **77**
Rundlestone. *Devn* —5F **11**
Runfold. *Surr* —2G **25**
Runhall. *Norf* —5C **78**
Runham. *Norf* —4G **79**
Runnington. *Som* —4E **20**
Runshaw Moor. *Lanc* —3D **90**
Runswick. *N Yor* —3F **107**
Runtaleave. *Ang* —2B **144**
Runwell. *Essx* —1B **40**
Ruscombe. *Wok* —4F **37**
Rushall. *Here* —2B **48**
Rushall. *Norf* —2D **66**
Rushall. *W Mid* —5E **73**
Rushall. *Wilts* —1G **23**
Rushbrooke. *Suff* —4A **66**
Rushbury. *Shrp* —1H **59**
Rushden. *Herts* —2D **52**
Rushden. *Nptn* —4G **63**
Rushenden. *Kent* —3D **40**
Rushford. *Devn* —5E **11**
Rushford. *Suff* —2B **66**
Rush Green. *Herts* —3C **52**
Rushlake Green. *E Sus* —4H **27**
Rushmere. *Suff* —2G **67**
Rushmere St Andrew. *Suff* —1E **55**
Rushmoor. *Surr* —2G **25**
Rushock. *Worc* —3C **60**
Rusholme. *G Man* —1C **84**
Rushton. *Ches* —4H **83**
Rushton. *Nptn* —2F **63**
Rushton. *Shrp* —5A **72**
Rushton Spencer. *Staf* —4D **84**
Rushwick. *Worc* —5C **60**
Rushyford. *Dur* —2F **105**
Ruskie. *Stir* —3F **135**
Ruskington. *Linc* —5H **87**
Rusland. *Cumb* —1C **96**
Rusper. *W Sus* —2D **26**
Ruspidge. *Glos* —4B **48**
Russell's Water. *Oxon* —3F **37**
Russel's Green. *Suff* —3E **67**
Russ Hill. *Surr* —1D **26**
Russland. *Orkn* —6C **172**
Rusthall. *Kent* —2G **27**
Rustington. *W Sus* —5B **26**
Ruston. *N Yor* —1D **100**
Ruston Parva. *E Yor* —3E **101**
Ruswarp. *N Yor* —4F **107**
Rutherglen. *S Lan* —3H **127**
Ruthernbridge. *Corn* —2E **6**
Ruthin. *Den* —5D **82**
Ruthin. *V Glam* —4C **32**
Ruthrieston. *Aber C* —3G **153**
Ruthven. *Aber* —4C **160**
Ruthven. *Ang* —4B **144**
Ruthven. *High* —5C **158**
(nr. Inverness)
Ruthven. *High* —4B **150**
(nr. Kingussie)
Ruthvoes. *Corn* —2D **6**
Ruthwaite. *Cumb* —1D **102**
Ruthwell. *Dum* —3C **112**
Ruxton Green. *Here* —4A **48**
Ruyton-XI-Towns. *Shrp* —3F **71**
Ryal. *Nmbd* —2D **114**
Ryall. *Dors* —3H **13**
Ryall. *Worc* —1D **48**
Ryarsh. *Kent* —5A **40**
Rychraggan. *High* —5G **157**
Rydal. *Cumb* —4E **103**
Ryde. *IOW* —3D **16**
Rye. *E Sus* —3D **28**
Ryecroft Gate. *Staf* —4D **84**
Ryeford. *Here* —3B **48**
Rye Foreign. *E Sus* —3D **28**

Rye Harbour. *E Sus* —4D **28**
Ryehill. *E Yor* —2F **95**
Rye Street. *Worc* —2C **48**
Ryhall. *Rut* —4H **75**
Ryhill. *W Yor* —3D **93**
Ryhope. *Tyne* —4H **115**
Ryhope Colliery. *Tyne* —4H **115**
Rylands. *Notts* —2C **74**
Rylstone. *N Yor* —4B **98**
Ryme Intrinseca. *Dors* —1A **14**
Ryther. *N Yor* —1F **93**
Ryton. *Glos* —2C **48**
Ryton. *N Yor* —2B **100**
Ryton. *Shrp* —5B **72**
Ryton. *Tyne* —3E **115**
Ryton. *Warw* —2A **62**
Ryton-on-Dunsmore. *Warw* —3A **62**
Ryton Woodside. *Tyne* —3E **115**

S

Saasaig. *High* —3E **147**
Sabden. *Lanc* —1F **91**
Sacombe. *Herts* —4D **52**
Sacriston. *Dur* —5F **115**
Sadberge. *Darl* —3A **106**
Saddell. *Arg* —2B **122**
Saddington. *Leics* —1D **62**
Saddle Bow. *Norf* —4F **77**
Saddlescombe. *W Sus* —4D **26**
Saddleworth. *G Man* —4H **91**
Sadgill. *Cumb* —4F **103**
Saffron Walden. *Essx* —2F **53**
Sageston. *Pemb* —4E **43**
Saham Hills. *Norf* —5B **78**
Saham Toney. *Norf* —5A **78**
Saighdinis. *W Isl* —2D **170**
Saighton. *Ches* —4G **83**
Sain Dunwyd. *V Glam* —5C **32**
Sain Hilari. *V Glam* —4D **32**
St Abbs. *Scot* —3F **131**
St Agnes. *Corn* —3B **6**
St Albans. *Herts* —5B **52**
St Allen. *Corn* —3C **6**
St Andrews. *Fife* —2H **137**
St Andrews Major. *V Glam* —4E **33**
St Anne's. *Lanc* —2B **90**
St Ann's. *Dum* —5C **118**
St Ann's Chapel. *Corn* —5E **11**
St Ann's Chapel. *Devn* —4C **8**
St Anthony. *Corn* —4E **5**
(nr. Helford)
St Anthony. *Corn* —5C **6**
(nr. St Mawes)
St Arvans. *Mon* —2A **34**
St Asaph. *Den* —3C **82**
St Athan. *V Glam* —5D **32**
Sain Tathan. *V Glam* —5D **32**
St Austell. *Corn* —3E **6**
St Bartholomew's Hill. *Wilts* —4E **23**
St Bees. *Cumb* —3A **102**
St Blazey. *Corn* —3E **7**
St Blazey Gate. *Corn* —3E **7**
St Boswells. *Scot* —1A **120**
St Breock. *Corn* —1D **6**
St Breward. *Corn* —5A **10**
St Briavels. *Glos* —5A **48**
St Brides. *Pemb* —3B **42**
St Bride's Major. *V Glam* —4B **32**
St Bride's Netherwent. *Mon* —3H **33**
St Bride's-super-Ely. *V Glam* —4D **32**
St Brides Wentlooge. *Newp* —3F **33**
St Budeaux. *Plym* —3A **8**
Saintbury. *Glos* —2G **49**
St Buryan. *Corn* —4B **4**
St Catherine. *Bath* —4C **34**
St Catherines. *Arg* —3A **134**
St Clears. *Carm* —3G **43**
St Cleer. *Corn* —2G **7**
St Clement. *Corn* —4C **6**
St Clether. *Corn* —4C **10**
St Colmac. *Arg* —3B **126**
St Columb Major. *Corn* —2D **6**

St Columb Minor. *Corn* —2C **6**
St Columb Road. *Corn* —3D **6**
St Combs. *Aber* —2H **161**
St Cross. *Hants* —4C **24**
St Cross South Elmham. *Suff* —2E **67**
St Cyrus. *Aber* —2G **145**
St David's. *Pemb* —2B **42**
St David's. *Per* —1B **136**
St Day. *Corn* —4B **6**
St Dennis. *Corn* —3D **6**
St Dogmaels. *Pemh* —1B **44**
St Dominick. *Corn* —2H **7**
St Donat's. *V Glam* —5C **32**
St Edith's Marsh. *Wilts* —5E **35**
St Endellion. *Corn* —1D **6**
St Enoder. *Corn* —3C **6**
St Erme. *Corn* —4C **6**
St Erney. *Corn* —3H **7**
St Erth. *Corn* —3C **4**
St Erth Praze. *Corn* —3C **4**
St Ervan. *Corn* —1C **6**
St Eval. *Corn* —2C **6**
St Ewe. *Corn* —4D **6**
St Fagans. *Card* —4E **32**
St Fergus *Aber* —3H **161**
St Fillans. *Per* —1F **135**
St Florence. *Pemb* —4E **43**
St Gennys. *Corn* —3B **10**
St George. *Cnwy* —3B **82**
St George's. *N Som* —5G **33**
St Georges. *V Glam* —4D **32**
St Germans. *Corn* —3H **7**
St Gile's Hill. *Hants* —4C **24**
St Giles in the Wood. *Devn* —1F **11**
St Giles on the Heath. *Devn* —4D **10**
St Gluvias. *Corn* —5B **6**
St Harmon. *Powy* —3B **58**
St Helena. *Warw* —5G **73**
St Helen Auckland. *Dur* —2E **105**
St Helens. *Cumb* —1B **102**
St Helens. *E Sus* —4C **28**
St Helens. *IOW* —4E **17**
St Helens. *Mers* —1G **83**
St Hilary. *Corn* —3C **4**
St Hilary. *V Glam* —4D **32**
Saint Hill. *Devn* —2D **12**
Saint Hill. *W Sus* —2E **27**
St Illtyd. *Blae* —5F **47**
St Ippollitts. *Herts* —3B **52**
St Ishmael. *Carm* —5D **44**
St Ishmael's. *Pemb* —4C **42**
St Issey. *Corn* —1D **6**
St Ive. *Corn* —2H **7**
St Ives. *Cambs* —3C **64**
St Ives. *Corn* —2C **4**
St Ives. *Dors* —2G **15**
St James End. *Nptn* —4E **63**
St James South Elmham. *Suff* —2F **67**
St Jidgey. *Corn* —2D **6**
St John. *Corn* —3A **8**
St John's. *IOM* —3B **108**
St Johns. *Worc* —5C **60**
St John's Chapel. *Devn* —4F **19**
St John's Chapel. *Dur* —1B **104**
St John's Hall. *Dur* —1B **104**
St John's Town of Dalry. *Dum* —1D **110**
St Judes. *IOM* —2D **108**
St Just. *Corn* —5C **6**
(nr. Falmouth)
St Just. *Corn* —3A **4**
(nr. Penzance)
St Just in Roseland. *Corn* —5C **6**
St Katherines. *Aber* —5E **161**
St Keverne. *Corn* —4E **5**
St Kew. *Corn* —1D **6**
St Kew Highway. *Corn* —5A **10**
St Keyne. *Corn* —2G **7**
St Lawrence. *Corn* —2E **7**
St Lawrence. *Essx* —5C **54**
St Lawrence. *IOW* —5D **16**

St Leonards. *Buck* —5H **51**
St Leonards. *Dors* —2G **15**
St Leonards. *E Sus* —5B **28**
St Levan. *Corn* —4A **4**
St Lythans. *V Glam* —4E **32**
St Mabyn. *Corn* —5A **10**
St Madoes. *Per* —1D **136**
St Margarets. *Here* —2G **47**
St Margaret's. *Herts* —4A **52**
(nr. Hemel Hempstead)
St Margarets. *Herts* —4D **53**
(nr. Hoddesdon)
St Margaret's. *Wilts* —5G **35**
St Margaret's at Cliffe. *Kent* —1H **29**
St Margaret's Hope. *Orkn* —8D **172**
St Margaret South Elmham.
Suff —2F **67**
St Mark's. *IOM* —4C **108**
St Martin. *Corn* —4E **5**
(nr. Helston)
St Martin. *Corn* —3G **7**
(nr. Looe)
St Martins. *Per* —5A **144**
St Martin's. *Shrp* —2F **71**
St Mary Bourne. *Hants* —1C **24**
St Marychurch. *Torb* —2F **9**
St Mary Church. *V Glam* —4D **32**
St Mary Cray. *G Lon* —4F **39**
St Mary Hill. *V Glam* —4C **32**
St Mary Hoo. *Medw* —3C **40**
St Mary in the Marsh. *Kent* —3E **29**
St Mary's. *Orkn* —7D **172**
St Mary's Airport. *IOS* —1B **4**
St Mary's Bay. *Kent* —3E **29**
St Mary's Grove. *N Som* —5H **33**
St Maughan's Green. *Mon* —4H **47**
St Mawes. *Corn* —5C **6**
St Mawgan. *Corn* —2C **6**
St Mellion. *Corn* —2H **7**
St Mellons. *Card* —3F **33**
St Merryn. *Corn* —1C **6**
St Mewan. *Corn* —3D **6**
St Michael Caerhays. *Corn* —4D **6**
St Michael Penkevil. *Corn* —4C **6**
St Michaels. *Kent* —2C **28**
St Michaels. *Torb* —3E **9**
St Michaels. *Worc* —4H **59**
St Michael's on Wyre. *Lanc* —5D **96**
St Michael South Elmham. *Suff* —2F **67**
St Minver. *Corn* —1D **6**
St Monans. *Fife* —3H **137**
St Neot. *Corn* —2F **7**
St Neots. *Cambs* —4A **64**
St Newlyn East. *Corn* —3C **6**
St Nicholas. *Pemb* —1D **42**
St Nicholas. *V Glam* —4D **32**
St Nicholas at Wade. *Kent* —4G **41**
St Nicholas South Elmham. *Suff* —2F **67**
St Ninians. *Stir* —4H **135**
St Olaves. *Norf* —1G **67**
St Osyth. *Essx* —4E **54**
St Osyth Heath. *Essx* —4E **55**
St Owen's Cross. *Here* —3A **48**
St Paul's Cray. *G Lon* —4F **39**
St Paul's Walden. *Herts* —3B **52**
St Peter's. *Kent* —4H **41**
St Peter the Great. *Worc* —5C **60**
St Petrox. *Pemb* —5D **42**
St Pinnock. *Corn* —2G **7**
St Quivox. *S Ayr* —2C **116**
St Ruan. *Corn* —5E **5**
St Stephen. *Corn* —3D **6**
St Stephens. *Corn* —4D **10**
(nr. Launceston)
St Stephens. *Corn* —3A **8**
(nr. Saltash)
St Teath. *Corn* —4A **10**
St Thomas. *Devn* —3C **12**
St Thomas. *Swan* —3F **31**
St Tudy. *Corn* —5A **10**
St Twynnells. *Pemb* —5D **42**

St Veep. *Corn* —3F **7**
St Vigeans. *Ang* —4F **145**
St Wenn. *Corn* —2D **6**
St Weonards. *Here* —3H **47**
St Winnolls. *Corn* —3H **7**
St Winnow. *Corn* —3F **7**
Salcombe. *Devn* —5E **9**
Salcombe Regis. *Devn* —4E **13**
Salcott. *Essx* —4C **54**
Sale. *G Man* —1B **84**
Saleby. *Linc* —3D **88**
Sale Green. *Worc* —5D **60**
Salehurst. *E Sus* —3B **28**
Salem. *Carm* —3G **45**
Salem. *Cdgn* —2F **57**
Salem. *Gwyn* —5E **81**
Salen. *Arg* —4G **139**
Salen. *High* —2A **140**
Salesbury. *Lanc* —1E **91**
Saleway. *Worc* —5D **60**
Salford. *Beds* —2H **51**
Salford. *G Man* —1C **84**
Salford. *Oxon* —3A **50**
Salford Priors. *Warw* —5E **61**
Salfords. *Surr* —1D **27**
Salhouse. *Norf* —4F **79**
Saligo. *Arg* —3A **124**
Saline. *Fife* —4C **136**
Salisbury. *Wilts* —3G **23**
Salkeld Dykes. *Cumb* —1G **103**
Sallachan. *High* —2D **141**
Sallachy. *High* —5B **156**
(nr. Darnie)
Sallachy. *High* —3C **164**
(nr. Lairg)
Salle. *Norf* —3D **78**
Salmonby. *Linc* —3C **88**
Salmond's Muir. *Ang* —5E **145**
Salperton. *Glos* —3F **49**
Salph End. *Beds* —5H **63**
Salsburgh. *N Lan* —3B **128**
Salt. *Staf* —3D **72**
Salta. *Cumb* —5B **112**
Saltaire. *W Yor* —1B **92**
Saltash. *Corn* —3A **8**
Saltburn. *High* —2B **158**
Saltburn-by-the-Sea. *Red C* —2D **106**
Saltby. *Leics* —3F **75**
Saltcoats. *Cumb* —5B **102**
Saltcoats. *N Ayr* —5D **126**
Saltdean. *Brig* —5E **27**
Salt End. *E Yor* —2E **95**
Salter. *Lanc* —3F **97**
Salterforth. *Lanc* —5A **98**
Salters Lode. *Norf* —5E **77**
Salterswall. *Ches* —4A **84**
Saltfleet. *Linc* —1D **88**
Saltfleetby All Saints. *Linc* —1D **88**
Saltfleetby St Clements. *Linc* —1D **88**
Saltfleetby St Peter. *Linc* —2D **88**
Saltford. *Bath* —5B **34**
Salthouse. *Norf* —1C **78**
Saltmarshe. *E Yor* —2A **94**
Saltmead. *Card* —4E **33**
Saltney. *Flin* —4F **83**
Salton. *N Yor* —1B **100**
Saltrens. *Devn* —4E **19**
Saltwick. *Nmbd* —2E **115**
Saltwood. *Kent* —2F **29**
Salum. *Arg* —4B **138**
Salwarpe. *Worc* —4C **60**
Salwayash. *Dors* —3H **13**
Samalaman. *High* —1A **140**
Sambourne. *Warw* —4E **61**
Sambourne. *Wilts* —2D **22**
Sambrook. *Telf* —3B **72**
Samhla. *W Isl* —2C **170**
Samlesbury. *Lanc* —1D **90**
Samlesbury Bottoms. *Lanc* —2E **90**
Sampford Arundel. *Som* —1E **12**
Sampford Brett. *Som* —2D **20**
Sampford Courtenay. *Devn* —2G **11**

Sampford Peverell. *Devn* —1D **12**
Sampford Spiney. *Devn* —5F **11**
Samsonlane. *Orkn* —5F **172**
Samuelston. *E Lot* —2A **130**
Sanaigmore. *Arg* —2A **124**
Sancreed. *Corn* —4B **4**
Sancton. *E Yor* —1C **94**
Sand. *High* —4D **162**
Sand. *Som* —2H **21**
Sandaig. *High* —3F **147**
Sandale. *Cumb* —5D **112**
Sandal Magna. *W Yor* —3D **92**
Sandavore. *High* —5C **146**
Sanday Airport. *Orkn* —3F **172**
Sandbach. *Ches* —4B **84**
Sandbank. *Arg* —1C **126**
Sandbanks. *Pool* —4F **15**
Sandend. *Aber* —2C **160**
Sanderstead. *G Lon* —4E **39**
Sandfields. *Neat* —3G **31**
Sandford. *Cumb* —3A **104**
Sandford. *Devn* —2B **12**
Sandford. *Dors* —4E **15**
Sandford. *Hants* —2G **15**
Sandford. *IOW* —4D **16**
Sandford. *N Som* —1H **21**
Sandford. *Shrp* —3F **71**
(nr. Oswestry)
Sandford. *Shrp* —2H **71**
(nr. Whitchurch)
Sandford. *S Lan* —5A **128**
Sandfordhill. *Aber* —4H **161**
Sandford-on-Thames. *Oxon* —5D **50**
Sandford Orcas. *Dors* —4B **22**
Sandford St Martin. *Oxon* —3C **50**
Sandgate. *Kent* —2F **29**
Sandgreen. *Dum* —4C **110**
Sandhaven. *Aber* —2G **161**
Sandhead. *Dum* —4F **109**
Sandhill. *Cambs* —2E **65**
Sandhills. *Dor* —3B **14**
Sandhills. *Surr* —2A **26**
Sandhoe. *Nmbd* —3C **114**
Sand Hole. *E Yor* —1B **94**
Sandholme. *E Yor* —1B **94**
Sandholme. *Linc* —2C **76**
Sandhurst. *Brac* —5G **37**
Sandhurst. *Glos* —3D **48**
Sandhurst. *Kent* —3B **28**
Sandhurst Cross. *Kent* —3B **28**
Sandhutton. *N Yor* —1F **99**
(nr. Thirsk)
Sand Hutton. *N Yor* —4A **100**
(nr. York)
Sandiacre. *Derbs* —2B **74**
Sandilands. *Linc* —2E **89**
Sandiway. *Ches* —3A **84**
Sandleheath. *Hants* —1G **15**
Sandling. *Kent* —5B **40**
Sandlow Green. *Ches* —4B **84**
Sandness. *Shet* —6C **173**
Sandon. *Essx* —5H **53**
Sandon. *Herts* —2D **52**
Sandon. *Staf* —3D **72**
Sandonbank. *Staf* —3D **72**
Sandown. *IOW* —4D **16**
Sandplace. *Corn* —3G **7**
Sandridge. *Herts* —4B **52**
Sandridge. *Wilts* —5E **35**
Sandringham. *Norf* —3F **77**
Sandsend. *N Yor* —3F **107**
Sandside. *Cumb* —2C **96**
Sands, The. *Surr* —2G **25**
Sandtoft. *N Lin* —4H **93**
Sandway. *Kent* —5C **40**
Sandwich. *Kent* —5H **41**
Sandwick. *Cumb* —3F **103**
Sandwick. *Orkn* —6B **172**
Sandwick. *Shet* —9F **173**
Sandwith. *Cumb* —3A **102**
Sandy. *Beds* —1B **52**
Sandy. *Carm* —5E **45**
Sandy Bank. *Linc* —5B **88**

Sandycroft. *Flin* —4F **83**
Sandy Cross. *Here* —5A **60**
Sandygate. *Devn* —5B **12**
Sandygate. *IOM* —2C **108**
Sandy Haven. *Pemb* —4C **42**
Sandyhills. *Dum* —4F **111**
Sandylands. *Lanc* —3D **96**
Sandylane. *Swan* —4E **31**
Sandy Lane. *Wilts* —5E **35**
Sandypark. *Devn* —4H **11**
Sandystones. *Scot* —2H **119**
Sandyway. *Here* —3H **47**
Sangobeg. *High* —2E **167**
Sangomore. *High* —2E **166**
Sankyn's Green. *Worc* —4B **60**
Sanna. *High* —2F **139**
Sanndabhaig. *W Isl* —4G **171**
(on Lewis)
Sanndabhaig. *W Isl* —4D **170**
(on South Uist)
Sannox. *N Ayr* —5B **126**
Sanquhar. *Dum* —3G **117**
Santon. *Cumb* —4C **102**
Santon Bridge. *Cumb* —4C **102**
Santon Downham. *Suff* —2H **65**
Sapcote. *Leics* —1B **62**
Sapey Common. *Here* —4B **60**
Sapiston. *Suff* —3B **66**
Sapley. *Cambs* —3B **64**
Sapperton. *Derbs* —2F **73**
Sapperton. *Glos* —5E **49**
Sapperton. *Linc* —2H **75**
Saracen's Head. *Linc* —3C **76**
Sarclet. *High* —4F **169**
Sardis. *Carm* —5F **45**
Sardis. *Pemb* —4D **42**
(nr. Milford Haven)
Sardis. *Pemb* —4F **43**
(nr. Tenby)
Sarisbury. *Hants* —2D **16**
Sarn. *B'End* —3C **32**
Sarn. *Powy* —1E **58**
Sarnau. *Carm* —3E **45**
Sarnau. *Cdgn* —5C **56**
Sarnau. *Gwyn* —2B **70**
Sarnau. *Powy* —2D **46**
(nr. Brecon)
Sarnau. *Powy* —4E **71**
(nr. Welshpool)
Sarn Bach. *Gwyn* —3C **68**
Sarnesfield. *Here* —5F **59**
Sarn Meyllteyrn. *Gwyn* —2B **68**
Saron. *Carm* —4G **45**
(nr. Ammanford)
Saron. *Carm* —2D **45**
(nr. Newcastle Emlyn)
Saron. *Gwyn* —4E **81**
(nr. Bethel)
Saron. *Gwyn* —5D **80**
(nr. Bontnewydd)
Sarratt. *Herts* —1B **38**
Sarre. *Kent* —4G **41**
Sarsden. *Oxon* —3A **50**
Satley. *Dur* —5E **115**
Satron. *N Yor* —5C **104**
Satterleigh. *Devn* —4G **19**
Satterthwaite. *Cumb* —5E **103**
Satwell. *Oxon* —3F **37**
Sauchen. *Aber* —2D **152**
Saucher. *Per* —5A **144**
Saughall. *Ches* —3F **83**
Saughtree. *Scot* —5H **119**
Saul. *Glos* —5C **48**
Saundby. *Notts* —2E **87**
Saundersfoot. *Pemb* —4F **43**
Saunderton. *Buck* —5F **51**
Saunderton Lee. *Buck* —2G **37**
Saunton. *Devn* —3E **19**
Sausthorpe. *Linc* —4C **88**
Saval. *High* —3C **164**
Saverley Green. *Staf* —2D **72**
Sawbridge. *Warw* —4C **62**
Sawbridgeworth. *Herts* —4E **53**

Sawdon—Sheigra

Sawdon. N Yor —1D 100
Sawley. Derbs —2B 74
Sawley. Lanc —5G 97
Sawley. N Yor —3E 99
Sawston. Cambs —1E 53
Sawtry. Cambs —2A 64
Saxby. Leics —3F 75
Saxby. Linc —2H 87
Saxby All Saints. N Lin —3C 94
Saxelby. Leics —3D 74
Saxham Street. Suff —4C 66
Saxilby. Linc —3F 87
Saxlingham. Norf —2C 78
Saxlingham Green. Norf —1E 67
Saxlingham Nethergate. Norf —1E 67
Saxlingham Thorpe. Norf —1E 66
Saxmundham. Suff —4F 67
Saxondale. Notts —1D 74
Saxon Street. Cambs —5F 65
Saxtead. Suff —4E 67
Saxtead Green. Suff —4E 67
Saxthorpe. Norf —2D 78
Saxton. N Yor —1E 93
Sayers Common. W Sus —4D 26
Scackleton. N Yor —2A 100
Scadabhagh. W Isl —8D 171
Scaftworth. Notts —1D 86
Scagglethorpe. N Yor —2C 100
Scaitcliffe. Lanc —2F 91
Scalasaig. Arg —4A 132
Scalby. E Yor —2B 94
Scalby. N Yor —5H 107
Scalby Mills. N Yor —5H 107
Scaldwell. Nptn —3E 63
Scaleby. Cumb —3F 113
Scaleby Hill. Cumb —3F 113
Scale Houses. Cumb —5G 113
Scales. Cumb —2B 96 (nr. Barrow-in-Furness)
Scales. Cumb —2E 103 (nr. Keswick)
Scalford. Leics —3E 75
Scaling. Red C —3E 107
Scaling Dam. Red C —3E 107
Scalloway. Shet —8E 173
Scalpaigh. W Isl —8E 171
Scalpay House. High —1E 147
Scamblesby. Linc —3B 88
Scamodale. High —1C 140
Scampston. N Yor —2C 100
Scampton. Linc —3G 87
Scaniport. High —5A 158
Scapa. Orkn —7D 172
Scapegoat Hill. W Yor —3A 92
Scar. Orkn —3F 172
Scarasta. W Isl —8C 171
Scarborough. N Yor —1E 101
Scarcliffe. Derbs —4B 86
Scarcroft. W Yor —5F 99
Scardroy. High —3E 156
Scarfskerry. High —1E 169
Scargill. Dur —3D 104
Scarinish. Arg —4B 138
Scarisbrick. Lanc —3B 90
Scarning. Norf —4B 78
Scarrington. Notts —1E 75
Scarth Hill. Lanc —4C 90
Scartho. NE Lin —4F 95
Scarvister. Shet —7E 173
Scatwell. High —3F 157
Scaur. Dum —4F 111
Scawby. N Lin —4C 94
Scawsby. S Yor —4F 93
Scawton. N Yor —1H 99
Scayne's Hill. W Sus —3E 27
Scethrog. Powy —3E 46
Scholar Green. Ches —5C 84
Scholes. G Man —4E 90
Scholes. W Yor —2B 92 (nr. Bradford)
Scholes. W Yor —4B 92 (nr. Holmfirth)
Scholes. W Yor —1D 93 (nr. Leeds)
Scholey Hill. W Yor —2D 93
School Aycliffe. Darl —2F 105
School Green. Ches —4A 84
School Green. Essx —2H 53
Scissett. W Yor —3C 92
Scleddau. Pemb —1D 42
Scofton. Notts —2D 86
Scole. Norf —3D 66
Scolton. Pemb —2D 43
Sconser. High —5E 155
Scoonie. Fife —3F 137
Scopwick. Linc —5H 87
Scoraig. High —4E 163
Scorborough. E Yor —5E 101
Scorrier. Corn —4B 6
Scorriton. Devn —2D 8
Scorton. Lanc —5E 97
Scorton. N Yor —4F 105
Sco Ruston. Norf —3E 79
Scotby. Cumb —4F 113
Scotch Corner. N Yor —4F 105
Scotforth. Lanc —3D 97
Scot Hay. Staf —1C 72
Scothern. Linc —3H 87
Scotland End. Oxon —2B 50
Scotlandwell. Per —3D 136
Scot Lane End. G Man —4E 91
Scotsburn. High —1B 158
Scotsdike. Cumb —2E 113
Scots Gap. Nmbd —1D 114
Scotstoun. Glas —3G 127
Scotstown. High —2C 140
Scotswood. Tyne —3F 115
Scottas. High —3F 147
Scotter. Linc —4B 94
Scotterthorpe. Linc —4B 94
Scottlethorpe. Linc —3H 75
Scotton. Linc —1F 87
Scotton. N Yor —5E 105 (nr. Catterick Garrison)
Scotton. N Yor —4F 99 (nr. Harrogate)
Scottow. Norf —3E 79
Scoulton. Norf —5B 78
Scounslow Green. Staf —3E 73
Scourie. High —4B 166
Scourie More. High —4B 166
Scousburgh. Shet —10E 173
Scout Green. Cumb —4G 103
Scouthead. G Man —4H 91
Scrabster. High —1C 168
Scrafield. Linc —4C 88
Scrainwood. Nmbd —4D 121
Scrane End. Linc —1C 76
Scraptoft. Leics —5D 74
Scratby. Norf —4H 79
Scrayingham. N Yor —3B 100
Scredington. Linc —1H 75
Scremby. Linc —4D 88
Scremerston. Nmbd —5G 131
Screveton. Notts —1E 75
Scrivelsby. Linc —4B 88
Scriven. N Yor —4F 99
Scronkey. Lanc —5D 96
Scrooby. Notts —1D 86
Scropton. Derbs —2F 73
Scrub Hill. Linc —5B 88
Scruton. N Yor —5A 106
Scuggate. Cumb —2F 113
Sculcoates. Hull —1D 94
Sculthorpe. Norf —2A 78
Scunthorpe. N Lin —3B 94
Scurlage. Swan —4D 30
Sea. Som —1G 13
Seaborough. Dors —2H 13
Seabridge. Staf —1C 72
Seabrook. Kent —2F 29
Seaburn. Tyne —4H 115
Seacombe. Mers —1F 83
Seacroft. Linc —4E 89
Seacroft. W Yor —1D 92
Seadyke. Linc —2C 76
Seafield. High —5G 165
Seafield. Midl —3F 129
Seafield. S Ayr —2C 116
Seafield. W Lot —3D 128
Seaford. E Sus —5F 27
Seaforth. Mers —1F 83
Seagrave. Leics —4D 74
Seaham. Dur —5H 115
Seahouses. Nmbd —1G 121
Seal. Kent —5G 39
Sealand. Flin —4F 83
Seale. Surr —2G 25
Seamer. N Yor —1E 101 (nr. Scarborough)
Seamer. N Yor —3B 106 (nr. Stokesley)
Seamill. N Ayr —5C 126
Sea Mills. Bris —4A 34
Sea Palling. Norf —3G 79
Searby. Linc —4D 94
Seasalter. Kent —4E 41
Seascale. Cumb —4B 102
Seaside. Per —1E 137
Seater. High —1F 169
Seathorne. Linc —4E 89
Seathwaite. Cumb —3D 102 (nr. Borrowdale)
Seathwaite. Cumb —5D 102 (nr. Ulpha)
Seatle. Cumb —1C 96
Seatoller. Cumb —3D 102
Seaton. Corn —3H 7
Seaton. Cumb —1B 102
Seaton. Devn —3F 13
Seaton. Dur —5G 115
Seaton. E Yor —5F 101
Seaton. Nmbd —2G 115
Seaton. Rut —1G 63
Seaton Burn. Tyne —2F 115
Seaton Carew. Hart —2C 106
Seaton Delaval. Nmbd —2G 115
Seaton Junction. Devn —3F 13
Seaton Ross. E Yor —5B 100
Seaton Sluice. Nmbd —2G 115
Seatown. Dors —3H 13
Seatown. Mor —2C 160 (nr. Cullen)
Seatown. Mor —1G 159 (nr. Lossiemouth)
Seatown. Mor —2C 160 (nr. Portsoy)
Seave Green. N Yor —4C 106
Seaview. IOW —3E 17
Seaville. Cumb —4C 112
Seavington St Mary. Som —1H 13
Seavington St Michael. Som —1H 13
Seawick. Essx —4E 55
Sebastopol. Cphy —5E 47
Sebastopol. Torf —2F 33
Sebergham. Cumb —5E 113
Seckington. Warw —5G 73
Second Coast. High —4D 162
Sedbergh. Cumb —5H 103
Sedbury. Glos —2A 34
Sedbusk. N Yor —5B 104
Sedgeberrow. Worc —2F 49
Sedgebrook. Linc —2F 75
Sedgefield. Dur —2A 106
Sedgeford. Norf —2G 77
Sedgehill. Som —4D 22
Sedgley. W Mid —1D 60
Sedgwick. Cumb —1E 97
Sedlescombe. E Sus —4B 28
Seend. Wilts —5E 35
Seend Cleeve. Wilts —5E 35
Seer Green. Buck —1A 38
Seething. Norf —1F 67
Sefton. Mers —4B 90
Sefton Park. Mers —2F 83
Seggat. Aber —4E 161
Seghill. Nmbd —2F 115
Seifton. Shrp —2G 59
Seighford. Staf —3C 72
Seilebost. W Isl —8C 171
Seisdon. Staf —1C 60
Seisiadar. W Isl —4H 171
Selattyn. Shrp —2E 71
Selborne. Hants —3F 25
Selby. N Yor —1G 93
Selham. W Sus —3A 26
Selkirk. Scot —2G 119
Sellack. Here —3A 48
Sellafirth. Shet —2G 173
Sellindge. Kent —2E 29
Selling. Kent —5E 41
Sells Green. Wilts —5E 35
Selly Oak. W Mid —2E 61
Selmeston. E Sus —5G 27
Selsdon. G Lon —4E 39
Selsey. W Sus —3G 17
Selsfield Common. W Sus —2E 27
Selside. Cumb —5G 103
Selside. N Yor —2G 97
Selsley. Glos —5D 48
Selsted. Kent —1G 29
Selston. Notts —5B 86
Selworthy. Som —2C 20
Semer. Suff —1D 54
Semington. Wilts —5D 35
Semley. Wilts —4D 23
Send. Surr —5B 38
Send Marsh. Surr —5B 38
Senghenydd. Cphy —2E 32
Sennen. Corn —4A 4
Sennen Cove. Corn —4A 4
Sennicotts. W Sus —2G 17
Sennybridge. Powy —3C 46
Serlby. Notts —2D 86
Sessay. N Yor —2G 99
Setchey. Norf —4F 77
Setley. Hants —2B 16
Setter. Shet —3F 173
Settiscarth. Orkn —6C 172
Settle. N Yor —3H 97
Settrington. N Yor —2C 100
Seven Ash. Som —3E 21
Sevenhampton. Glos —3F 49
Sevenhampton. Swin —2H 35
Sevenoaks. Kent —5G 39
Sevenoaks Weald. Kent —5G 39
Seven Sisters. Neat —5B 46
Seven Springs. Glos —4E 49
Severn Beach. S Glo —3A 34
Severn Stoke. Worc —1D 48
Sevington. Kent —1E 29
Sewards End. Essx —2F 53
Sewardstone. Essx —1E 39
Sewell. Beds —3H 51
Sewerby. E Yor —3F 101
Seworgan. Corn —5B 6
Sewstern. Leics —3F 75
Sgallairidh. W Isl —9B 170
Sgarasta Mhor. W Isl —8C 171
Sgiogarstaigh. W Isl —1H 171
Sgreadan. Arg —4A 132
Shabbington. Buck —5E 51
Shackerley. Shrp —5C 72
Shackerstone. Leics —5A 74
Shackleford. Surr —1A 26
Shadforth. Dur —5G 115
Shadingfield. Suff —2G 67
Shadoxhurst. Kent —2D 28
Shadsworth. Bkbn —2E 91
Shadwell. Norf —2B 66
Shadwell. W Yor —1D 92
Shaftesbury. Dors —4D 22
Shafton. S Yor —3D 93
Shafton Two Gates. S Yor —3D 93
Shaggs. Dors —4D 14
Shakesfield. Glos —2B 48
Shalbourne. Wilts —5B 36
Shalcombe. IOW —4B 16
Shalden. Hants —2E 25
Shaldon. Devn —5C 12
Shalfleet. IOW —4C 16
Shalford. Essx —3H 53
Shalford. Surr —1B 26
Shalford Green. Essx —3H 53
Shallochpark. S Ayr —5A 116
Shallowford. Devn —2H 19
Shallowford. Staf —3C 72
Shalmsford Street. Kent —5E 41
Shalstone. Buck —2E 51
Shamley Green. Surr —1B 26
Shandon. Arg —1D 126
Shandwick. High —1C 158
Shangton. Leics —1E 62
Shankhouse. Nmbd —2F 115
Shanklin. IOW —4D 16
Shannochie. N Ayr —3D 122
Shap. Cumb —3G 103
Shapwick. Dors —2E 15
Shapwick. Som —3H 21
Sharcott. Wilts —1G 23
Shardlow. Derbs —2B 74
Shareshill. Staf —5D 72
Sharlston. W Yor —3D 93
Sharlston Common. W Yor —3D 93
Sharnal Street. Medw —3B 40
Sharnbrook. Beds —5G 63
Sharneyford. Lanc —2G 91
Sharnford. Leics —1B 62
Sharnhill Green. Dors —2C 14
Sharow. N Yor —2F 99
Sharpe Green. Lanc —1D 90
Sharpenhoe. Beds —2A 52
Sharperton. Nmbd —4D 120
Sharpness. Glos —5B 48
Sharp Street. Norf —3F 79
Sharpthorne. W Sus —2E 27
Sharrington. Norf —2C 78
Shatterford. Worc —2B 60
Shatton. Derbs —2F 85
Shaugh Prior. Devn —2B 8
Shavington. Ches —5B 84
Shaw. G Man —4H 91
Shaw. W Ber —5C 36
Shaw. Wilts —5D 35
Shawbirch. Telf —4A 72
Shawbury. Shrp —3H 71
Shawdon Hall. Nmbd —3E 121
Shawell. Leics —2C 62
Shawford. Hants —4C 24
Shawforth. Lanc —2G 91
Shaw Green. Lanc —3D 90
Shawhead. Dum —2F 111
Shaw Mills. N Yor —3E 99
Shawwood. E Ayr —2E 117
Shearington. Dum —3B 112
Shearsby. Leics —1D 62
Shearston. Som —3F 21
Shebbear. Devn —2E 11
Shebdon. Staf —3B 72
Shebster. High —2C 168
Shedfield. Hants —1D 16
Shedog. N Ayr —2D 122
Sheen. Staf —4F 85
Sheepbridge. Derbs —3A 86
Sheep Hill. Dur —4E 115
Sheepscar. W Yor —1D 92
Sheepscombe. Glos —4D 49
Sheepstor. Devn —2B 8
Sheepwash. Devn —2E 11
Sheepwash. Nmbd —1F 115
Sheepway. N Som —4H 33
Sheepy Magna. Leics —5H 73
Sheepy Parva. Leics —5H 73
Sheering. Essx —4F 53
Sheerness. Kent —3D 40
Sheerwater. Surr —4B 38
Sheet. Hants —4F 25
Sheffield. S Yor —2H 85
Sheffield Bottom. W Ber —5E 37
Sheffield City Airport. S Yor —2B 86
Sheffield Green. E Sus —3F 27
Shefford. Beds —2B 52
Shefford Woodlands. W Ber —4B 36
Sheigra. High —2B 166

Sheinton—Skelmanthorpe

Sheinton. *Shrp* —5A **72**
Shelderton. *Shrp* —3G **59**
Sheldon. *Derbs* —4F **85**
Sheldon. *Devn* —2E **12**
Sheldon. *W Mid* —2F **61**
Sheldwich. *Kent* —5E **40**
Sheldwich Lees. *Kent* —5E **40**
Shelf. *W Yor* —2B **92**
Shelfanger. *Norf* —2D **66**
Shelfield. *Warw* —4F **61**
Shelfield. *W Mid* —5E **73**
Shelford. *Notts* —1D **74**
Shelford. *Warw* —2B **62**
Shell. *Worc* —5D **60**
Shelley. *Suff* —2D **54**
Shelley. *W Yor* —3C **92**
Shell Green. *Hal* —2H **83**
Shellingford. *Oxon* —2B **36**
Shellow Bowells. *Essx* —5G **53**
Shelsley Beauchamp. *Worc* —4B **60**
Shelsley Walsh. *Worc* —4B **60**
Shelthorpe. *Leics* —4C **74**
Shelton. *Beds* —4H **63**
Shelton. *Norf* —1E **67**
Shelton. *Notts* —1E **75**
Shelton. *Shrp* —4G **71**
Shelton Green. *Norf* —1E **67**
Shelton Lock. *Dby C* —2A **74**
Shelve. *Shrp* —1F **59**
Shelwick. *Here* —1A **48**
Shelwick Green. *Here* —1A **48**
Shenfield. *Essx* —1H **39**
Shenington. *Oxon* —1B **50**
Shenley. *Herts* —5B **52**
Shenley Brook End. *Mil* —2G **51**
Shenleybury. *Herts* —5B **52**
Shenley Church End. *Mil* —2G **51**
Shenmore. *Here* —2G **47**
Shennanton. *Dum* —3A **110**
Shenstone. *Staf* —5F **73**
Shenstone. *Worc* —3C **60**
Shenstone Woodend. *Staf* —5F **73**
Shenton. *Leics* —5A **74**
Shenval. *Mor* —1G **151**
Shepeau Stow. *Linc* —4C **76**
Shephall. *Herts* —3C **52**
Shepherd's Bush. *G Lon* —2D **38**
Shepherds Gate. *Norf* —4E **77**
Shepherd's Green. *Oxon* —3F **37**
Shepherd's Port. *Norf* —2F **77**
Shepherdswell. *Kent* —1G **29**
Shepley. *W Yor* —4B **92**
Sheppardstown. *High* —4D **169**
Shepperdine. *S Glo* —2B **34**
Shepperton. *Surr* —4B **38**
Shepreth. *Cambs* —1D **53**
Shepshed. *Leics* —4B **74**
Shepton Beauchamp. *Som* —1H **13**
Shepton Mallet. *Som* —2B **22**
Shepton Montague. *Som* —3B **22**
Shepway. *Kent* —5B **40**
Sheraton. *Dur* —1B **106**
Sherborne. *Bath* —1A **22**
Sherborne. *Dors* —1B **14**
Sherborne. *Glos* —4G **49**
Sherborne Causeway. *Dors* —4D **22**
Sherborne St John. *Hants* —1E **24**
Sherbourne. *Warw* —4G **61**
Sherburn. *Dur* —5G **115**
Sherburn. *N Yor* —2D **100**
Sherburn Hill. *Dur* —5G **115**
Sherburn in Elmet. *N Yor* —1E **93**
Shere. *Surr* —1B **26**
Shereford. *Norf* —3A **78**
Sherfield English. *Hants* —4A **24**
Sherfield on Loddon. *Hants* —1E **25**
Sherford. *Devn* —4D **9**
Sherford. *Dors* —3E **15**
Sheriffhales. *Shrp* —4B **72**
Sheriff Hutton. *N Yor* —3A **100**
Sheriffston. *Mor* —2G **159**
Sheringham. *Norf* —1D **78**
Sherington. *Mil* —1G **51**
Shermanbury. *W Sus* —4D **26**
Shernal Green. *Worc* —4D **60**
Shernborne. *Norf* —2G **77**
Sherrington. *Wilts* —3E **23**
Sherston. *Wilts* —3D **34**
Sherwood. *Not C* —1C **74**
Sherwood Green. *Devn* —4F **19**
Shettleston. *Glas* —3H **127**
Shevington. *G Man* —4D **90**
Shevington Moor. *G Man* —3D **90**
Shevington Vale. *G Man* —4D **90**
Sheviock. *Corn* —3H **7**
Shiel Bridge. *High* —2B **148**
Shieldaig. *High* —1H **155**
(nr. Charlestown)
Shieldaig. *High* —3H **155**
(nr. Loch Shieldaig)
Shieldhill. *Dum* —1B **112**
Shieldhill. *Falk* —2B **128**
Shieldhill. *S Lan* —5D **128**
Shieldmuir. *N Lan* —4A **128**
Shielfoot. *High* —2A **140**
Shielhill. *Aber* —3H **161**
Shielhill. *Ang* —3D **144**
Shifnal. *Shrp* —5B **72**
Shilbottle. *Nmbd* —4F **121**
Shilbottle Grange. *Nmbd* —4G **121**
Shildon. *Dur* —2F **105**
Shillford. *E Ren* —4F **127**
Shillingford. *Devn* —4C **20**
Shillingford. *Oxon* —2D **36**
Shillingford St George. *Devn* —4C **12**
Shillingstone. *Dors* —1D **14**
Shillington. *Beds* —2B **52**
Shillmoor. *Nmbd* —4C **120**
Shilton. *Oxon* —5A **50**
Shilton. *Warw* —2B **62**
Shilvinghampton. *Dors* —4B **14**
Shilvington. *Nmbd* —1E **115**
Shimpling. *Norf* —2D **66**
Shimpling. *Suff* —5A **66**
Shimpling Street. *Suff* —5A **66**
Shincliffe. *Dur* —5F **115**
Shiney Row. *Tyne* —4G **115**
Shinfield. *Wok* —5F **37**
Shingay. *Cambs* —1D **52**
Shingham. *Norf* —5G **77**
Shingle Street. *Suff* —1G **55**
Shinner's Bridge. *Devn* —2D **9**
Shinness. *High* —2C **164**
Shipbourne. *Kent* —5G **39**
Shipdham. *Norf* —5B **78**
Shipham. *Som* —1H **21**
Shiphay. *Torb* —2E **9**
Shiplake. *Oxon* —4F **37**
Shipley. *Derbs* —1B **74**
Shipley. *Nmbd* —3F **121**
Shipley. *Shrp* —1C **60**
Shipley. *W Sus* —3C **26**
Shipley. *W Yor* —1B **92**
Shipley Bridge. *Surr* —1E **27**
Shipmeadow. *Suff* —1F **67**
Shippon. *Oxon* —2C **36**
Shipston on Stour. *Warw* —1A **50**
Shipton. *Buck* —3F **51**
Shipton. *Glos* —4F **49**
Shipton. *N Yor* —4H **99**
Shipton. *Shrp* —1H **59**
Shipton Bellinger. *Hants* —2H **23**
Shipton Gorge. *Dors* —3H **13**
Shipton Green. *W Sus* —3G **17**
Shipton Moyne. *Glos* —3D **35**
Shipton-on-Cherwell. *Oxon* —4C **50**
Shiptonthorpe. *E Yor* —5C **100**
Shipton-under-Wychwood. *Oxon* —4A **50**
Shirburn. *Oxon* —2E **37**
Shirdley Hill. *Lanc* —3B **90**
Shire. *Cumb* —1H **103**
Shirebrook. *Derbs* —4C **86**
Shiregreen. *S Yor* —1A **86**
Shirehampton. *Bris* —4A **34**
Shiremoor. *Tyne* —2G **115**
Shirenewton. *Mon* —2H **33**
Shireoaks. *Notts* —2C **86**
Shires Mill. *Fife* —1D **128**
Shirkoak. *Kent* —2D **28**
Shirland. *Derbs* —5A **86**
Shirley. *Derbs* —1G **73**
Shirley. *Sotn* —1C **16**
Shirley. *W Mid* —3F **61**
Shirleywich. *Staf* —3D **73**
Shirl Heath. *Here* —5G **59**
Shirrell Heath. *Hants* —1D **16**
Shirwell. *Devn* —3F **19**
Shiskine. *N Ayr* —3D **122**
Shobdon. *Here* —4F **59**
Shobnall. *Staf* —3G **73**
Shobrooke. *Devn* —2B **12**
Shoby. *Leics* —3D **74**
Shocklach. *Ches* —1G **71**
Shoeburyness. *S'end* —2D **40**
Sholden. *Kent* —5H **41**
Sholing. *Sotn* —1C **16**
Sholver. *G Man* —4H **91**
Shoot Hill. *Shrp* —4G **71**
Shop. *Corn* —1C **10**
(nr. Bude)
Shop. *Corn* —1C **6**
(nr. Padstow)
Shop. *Devn* —1D **11**
Shopford. *Cumb* —2G **113**
Shop Street. *Suff* —4E **66**
Shoreditch. *G Lon* —2E **39**
Shoreditch. *Som* —4F **21**
Shoreham. *Kent* —4G **39**
Shoreham-by-Sea. *W Sus* —5D **26**
Shoresdean. *Nmbd* —5F **131**
Shoreswood. *Nmbd* —5F **131**
Shore, The. *Fife* —2E **137**
Shorncote. *Glos* —2F **35**
Shorne. *Kent* —3A **40**
Shorne Ridgeway. *Kent* —3A **40**
Shortacombe. *Devn* —4F **11**
Shortbridge. *E Sus* —3F **27**
Shortgate. *E Sus* —4F **27**
Short Green. *Norf* —2C **66**
Shorthampton. *Oxon* —3B **50**
Short Heath. *Leics* —4H **73**
Short Heath. *W Mid* —1E **61**
(nr. Erdington)
Short Heath. *W Mid* —5D **73**
(nr. Wednesfield)
Shortlanesend. *Corn* —4C **6**
Shorton. *Torb* —2E **9**
Shortstown. *Beds* —1A **52**
Shortwood. *S Glo* —4B **34**
Shorwell. *IOW* —4C **16**
Shoscombe. *Bath* —1C **22**
Shotesham. *Norf* —1E **67**
Shotgate. *Essx* —1B **40**
Shotley. *Suff* —2F **55**
Shotley Bridge. *Dur* —4D **115**
Shotleyfield. *Nmbd* —4D **114**
Shotley Gate. *Suff* —2F **55**
Shottenden. *Kent* —5E **41**
Shottermill. *Surr* —3G **25**
Shottery. *Warw* —5F **61**
Shotteswell. *Warw* —1C **50**
Shottisham. *Suff* —1G **55**
Shottle. *Derbs* —1H **73**
Shotton. *Dur* —1B **106**
(nr. Peterlee)
Shotton. *Dur* —2A **106**
(nr. Sedgefield)
Shotton. *Flin* —4E **83**
Shotton. *Nmbd* —2F **115**
(nr. Morpeth)
Shotton. *Nmbd* —1C **120**
(nr. Town Yetholm)
Shotton Colliery. *Dur* —5G **115**
Shotts. *N Lan* —3B **128**
Shotwick. *Ches* —3F **83**
Shouldham. *Norf* —5F **77**
Shouldham Thorpe. *Norf* —5F **77**
Shoulton. *Worc* —5C **60**
Shrawardine. *Shrp* —4F **71**
Shrawley. *Worc* —4C **60**
Shreding Green. *Buck* —2B **38**
Shrewley. *Warw* —4G **61**
Shrewsbury. *Shrp* —4G **71**
Shrewton. *Wilts* —2F **23**
Shripney. *W Sus* —5A **26**
Shrivenham. *Oxon* —3H **35**
Shropham. *Norf* —1B **66**
Shroton. *Dors* —1D **14**
Shrub End. *Essx* —3C **54**
Shucknall. *Here* —1A **48**
Shudy Camps. *Cambs* —1G **53**
Shulista. *High* —1D **154**
Shurdington. *Glos* —4E **49**
Shurlock Row. *Wind* —4G **37**
Shurrery. *High* —3C **168**
Shurton. *Som* —2F **21**
Shustoke. *Warw* —1G **61**
Shute. *Devn* —3F **13**
(nr. Axminster)
Shute. *Devn* —2B **12**
(nr. Crediton)
Shutford. *Oxon* —1B **50**
Shut Heath. *Staf* —3C **72**
Shuthonger. *Glos* —2D **49**
Shutlanehead. *Staf* —1C **72**
Shutlanger. *Nptn* —1F **51**
Shutt Green. *Staf* —5C **72**
Shuttington. *Warw* —5G **73**
Shuttlewood. *Derbs* —3B **86**
Shuttleworth. *G Man* —3G **91**
Siabost. *W Isl* —3E **171**
Siabost bho Dheas. *W Isl* —3E **171**
Siabost bho Thuath. *W Isl* —3E **171**
Siadar. *W Isl* —2F **171**
Siadar Uarach. *W Isl* —2F **171**
Sibbaldbie. *Dum* —1C **112**
Sibbertoft. *Nptn* —2D **62**
Sibdon Carwood. *Shrp* —2G **59**
Sibertswold. *Kent* —1G **29**
Sibford Ferris. *Oxon* —2B **50**
Sibford Gower. *Oxon* —2B **50**
Sible Hedingham. *Essx* —2A **54**
Sibsey. *Linc* —5C **88**
Sibsey Fen Side. *Linc* —5C **88**
Sibson. *Cambs* —1H **63**
Sibson. *Leics* —5A **74**
Sibster. *High* —3F **169**
Sibthorpe. *Notts* —1E **75**
Sibton. *Suff* —4F **67**
Sicklesmere. *Suff* —4A **66**
Sicklinghall. *N Yor* —5F **99**
Sid. *Devn* —4E **13**
Sidbury. *Devn* —3E **13**
Sidbury. *Shrp* —2A **60**
Sidcot. *N Som* —1H **21**
Sidcup. *G Lon* —3F **39**
Siddick. *Cumb* —1B **102**
Siddington. *Ches* —3C **84**
Siddington. *Glos* —2F **35**
Side of the Moor. *G Man* —3F **91**
Sidestrand. *Norf* —2E **79**
Sidford. *Devn* —3E **13**
Sidlesham. *W Sus* —3G **17**
Sidley. *E Sus* —5B **28**
Sidlowbridge. *Surr* —1D **26**
Sidmouth. *Devn* —4E **13**
Sigford. *Devn* —5A **12**
Sigglesthorne. *E Yor* —5F **101**
Sighthill. *Edin* —2E **129**
Sigingstone. *V Glam* —4C **32**
Signet. *Oxon* —4H **49**
Silchester. *Hants* —5E **37**
Sileby. *Leics* —4D **74**
Silecroft. *Cumb* —1A **96**
Silfield. *Norf* —1D **66**
Silian. *Cdgn* —5E **57**
Silkstone. *S Yor* —4C **92**
Silkstone Common. *S Yor* —4C **92**
Silksworth. *Tyne* —4G **115**
Silk Willoughby. *Linc* —1H **75**
Silloth. *Cumb* —4C **112**
Sills. *Nmbd* —4C **120**
Sillyearn. *Mor* —3C **160**
Silpho. *N Yor* —5G **107**
Silsden. *W Yor* —5C **98**
Silsoe. *Beds* —2A **52**
Silverbank. *Aber* —4E **152**
Silverburn. *Midl* —3F **129**
Silverdale. *Lanc* —2D **96**
Silverdale. *Staf* —1C **72**
Silverdale Green. *Lanc* —2D **96**
Silver End. *Essx* —4B **54**
Silver End. *W Mid* —2D **60**
Silvergate. *Norf* —3D **78**
Silverhillocks. *Aber* —2E **161**
Silverley's Green. *Suff* —3E **67**
Silverstone. *Nptn* —1E **51**
Silverton. *Devn* —2C **12**
Silverton. *W Dun* —2F **127**
Silvington. *Shrp* —3A **60**
Simm's Cross. *Hal* —2H **83**
Simm's Lane End. *Mers* —1H **83**
Simonburn. *Nmbd* —2B **114**
Simonsbath. *Som* —3A **20**
Simonstone. *Lanc* —1F **91**
Simprim. *Scot* —5E **131**
Simpson. *Pemb* —3C **42**
Simpson Cross. *Pemb* —3C **42**
Sinclairston. *E Ayr* —3D **116**
Sinclairtown. *Fife* —4E **137**
Sinderby. *N Yor* —1F **99**
Sinderhope. *Nmbd* —4B **114**
Sindlesham. *Wok* —5F **37**
Sinfin. *Dby C* —2A **74**
Singleborough. *Buck* —2F **51**
Singleton. *Kent* —1D **28**
Singleton. *Lanc* —1B **90**
Singleton. *W Sus* —1G **17**
Singlewell. *Kent* —3A **40**
Sinkhurst Green. *Kent* —1C **28**
Sinnahard. *Aber* —2B **152**
Sinnington. *N Yor* —1B **100**
Sinton Green. *Worc* —4C **60**
Sipson. *G Lon* —3B **38**
Sirhowy. *Blae* —4E **47**
Sissinghurst. *Kent* —2B **28**
Siston. *S Glo* —4B **34**
Sithney. *Corn* —4D **4**
Sittingbourne. *Kent* —4D **40**
Six Ashes. *Staf* —2B **60**
Six Bells. *Blae* —5F **47**
Six Hills. *Leics* —3D **74**
Sixhills. *Linc* —2A **88**
Six Mile Bottom. *Cambs* —5E **65**
Sixpenny Handley. *Dors* —1E **15**
Sizewell. *Suff* —4G **67**
Skail. *High* —4H **167**
Skaills. *Orkn* —7E **172**
Skares. *E Ayr* —3E **117**
Skateraw. *E Lot* —2D **130**
Skaw. *Shet* —5G **173**
Skeabost. *High* —4D **154**
Skeeby. *N Yor* —4E **105**
Skeffington. *Leics* —5E **75**
Skeffling. *E Yor* —3G **95**
Skegby. *Notts* —4B **86**
(nr. Mansfield)
Skegby. *Notts* —4E **87**
(nr. Tuxford)
Skegness. *Linc* —4E **89**
Skelberry. *Shet* —10E **173**
(nr. Boddam)
Skelberry. *Shet* —3E **173**
(nr. Housetter)
Skelbo. *High* —4E **165**
Skelbo Street. *High* —4E **165**
Skelbrooke. *S Yor* —3F **93**
Skeldyke. *Linc* —2C **76**
Skelfhill. *Scot* —4G **119**
Skellingthorpe. *Linc* —3G **87**
Skellister. *Shet* —6F **173**
Skellorn Green. *Ches* —2D **84**
Skellow. *S Yor* —3F **93**
Skelmanthorpe. *W Yor* —3C **92**

Skelmersdale—Southleigh

Skelmersdale. Lanc —4C 90
Skelmorlie. N Ayr —3C 126
Skelpick. High —3H 167
Skelton. Cumb —1F 103
Skelton. E Yor —2A 94
Skelton. N Yor —4D 105
(nr. Richmond)
Skelton. N Yor —3F 99
(nr. Ripon)
Skelton. Red C —3D 106
Skelton. York —4H 99
Skelton Green. Red C —3D 106
Skelwick. Orkn —3D 172
Skelwith Bridge. Cumb —4E 103
Skendleby. Linc —4D 88
Skendleby Psalter. Linc —3D 88
Skenfrith. Mon —3H 47
Skerne. E Yor —4E 101
Skeroblingarry. Arg —3B 122
Skerray. High —2G 167
Skerray. High —2G 167
Skerricha. High —3C 166
Skerton. Lanc —3D 96
Sketchley. Leics —1B 62
Sketty. Swan —3F 31
Skewen. Neat —3G 31
Skewsby. N Yor —2A 100
Skeyton. Norf —3E 79
Skeyton Corner. Norf —3E 79
Skiall. High —2C 168
Skidbrooke. Linc —1D 88
Skidbrooke North End. Linc —1D 88
Skidby. E Yor —1D 94
Skilgate. Som —4C 20
Skillington. Linc —3F 75
Skinburness. Cumb —4C 112
Skinflats. Falk —1C 128
Skinidin. High —4B 154
Skinnet. High —2F 167
Skinningrove. Red C —2E 107
Skipness. Arg —4G 125
Skippool. Lanc —5C 96
Skiprigg. Cumb —5E 113
Skipsea. E Yor —4F 101
Skipsea Brough. E Yor —4F 101
Skipton. N Yor —4B 98
Skipton-on-Swale. N Yor —2F 99
Skipwith. N Yor —1G 93
Skirbeck. Linc —1C 76
Skirbeck Quarter. Linc —1C 76
Skirlaugh. E Yor —1E 95
Skirling. Scot —1C 118
Skirmett. Buck —2F 37
Skirpenbeck. E Yor —4B 100
Skirwith. Cumb —1H 103
Skirwith. N Yor —2G 97
Skirza. High —2F 169
Skitby. Cumb —3F 113
Skitham. Lanc —5D 96
Skittle Green. Buck —5F 51
Skulamus. High —1E 147
Skullomie. High —2G 167
Skyborry Green. Shrp —3E 59
Skye Green. Essx —3B 54
Skye of Curr. High —1D 151
Slack. W Yor —2H 91
Slackhall. Derbs —2E 85
Slack Head. Cumb —2D 97
Slackhead. Mor —2B 160
Slackholme End. Linc —3E 89
Slacks of Cairnbanno. Aber —4F 161
Slack, The. Dur —2E 105
Slad. Glos —5D 48
Slade. Devn —2F 19
Slade. Swan —4D 31
Slade End. Oxon —2D 36
Slade Field. Cambs —2C 64
Slade Green. G Lon —3G 39
Slade Heath. Staf —5D 72
Slade Hooton. S Yor —2C 86
Sladesbridge. Corn —5A 10
Slade, The. W Ber —5D 36
Slaggyford. Nmbd —4H 113
Slaidburn. Lanc —4G 97
Slaid Hill. W Yor —5F 99
Slaithwaite. W Yor —3A 92
Slaley. Derbs —5G 85
Slaley. Nmbd —4C 114
Slamannan. Falk —2B 128
Slapton. Buck —3H 51
Slapton. Devn —4E 9
Slapton. Nptn —1E 51
Slattock. G Man —4G 91
Slaugham. W Sus —3D 26
Slaughterford. Wilts —4D 34
Slawston. Leics —1E 63
Sleaford. Hants —3G 25
Sleaford. Linc —1H 75
Sleagill. Cumb —3G 103
Sleap. Shrp —3G 71
Sledmere. E Yor —3D 100
Sleightholme. Dur —3C 104
Sleights. N Yor —4F 107
Slepe. Dors —3E 15
Slickly. High —2E 169
Sliddery. N Ayr —3D 122
Sligachan. High —1C 146
Slimbridge. Glos —5C 48
Slindon. Staf —2C 72
Slindon. W Sus —5A 26
Slinfold. W Sus —2C 26
Slingsby. N Yor —2A 100
Slip End. Herts —4A 52
Slipton. Nptn —3G 63
Slitting Mill. Staf —4E 73
Slochd. High —1C 150
Slockavullin. Arg —4F 133
Sloley. Norf —3E 79
Sloncombe. Devn —4H 11
Sloothby. Linc —3D 89
Slough. Slo —3A 38
Slough Green. Som —4F 21
Slough Green. W Sus —3D 27
Sluggan. High —1C 150
Slyne. Lanc —3D 97
Smailholm. Scot —1A 120
Smallbridge. G Man —3H 91
Smallbrook. Devn —3B 12
Smallburgh. Norf —3F 79
Smallburn. E Ayr —2F 117
Smalldale. Derbs —3E 85
Small Dole. W Sus —4D 26
Smalley. Derbs —1B 74
Smallfield. Surr —1E 27
Small Heath. W Mid —2F 61
Smallholm. Dum —2C 112
Small Hythe. Kent —2C 28
Smallrice. Staf —2D 72
Smallridge. Devn —2G 13
Smallwood Hey. Lanc —5C 96
Smallworth. Norf —2C 66
Smannell. Hants —2B 24
Smardale. Cumb —4A 104
Smarden. Kent —1C 28
Smarden Bell. Kent —1C 28
Smart's Hill. Kent —1G 27
Smeatharpe. Devn —1F 13
Smeeth. Kent —2E 29
Smeeth, The. Norf —4E 77
Smeeton Westerby. Leics —1D 62
Smeircleit. W Isl —7C 170
Smerral. High —5D 169
Smestow. Staf —1C 60
Smethwick. W Mid —2E 61
Smirisary. High —1A 140
Smisby. Derbs —4H 73
Smitham Hill. Bath —1A 22
Smith End Green. Worc —5B 60
Smithfield. Cumb —3F 113
Smith Green. Lanc —4D 97
Smithies, The. Shrp —1A 60
Smithincott. Devn —1D 12
Smith's Green. Essx —3F 53
Smithstown. High —1G 155
Smithton. High —4B 158
Smithwood Green. Suff —5B 66
Smithy Bridge. G Man —3H 91
Smithy Green. Ches —3B 84
Smithy Lane Ends. Lanc —3C 90
Smockington. Warw —2B 62
Smyth's Green. Essx —4C 54
Snaigow House. Per —4H 143
Snailbeach. Shrp —5F 71
Snailwell. Cambs —4F 65
Snainton. N Yor —1D 100
Snaith. E Yor —2G 93
Snape. N Yor —1E 99
Snape. Suff —5F 67
Snape Green. Lanc —3B 90
Snarestone. Leics —5H 73
Snarford. Linc —2H 87
Snargate. Kent —3D 28
Snave. Kent —3E 28
Sneachill. Worc —5D 60
Snead. Powy —1F 59
Snead Common. Worc —4B 60
Sneaton. N Yor —4F 107
Sneatonthorpe. N Yor —4G 107
Snelland. Linc —2H 87
Snelston. Derbs —1F 73
Snetterton. Norf —1B 66
Snettisham. Norf —2F 77
Snibston. Leics —4B 74
Snig's End. Glos —3C 48
Sniseabhal. W Isl —6C 170
Snitter. Nmbd —4E 121
Snitterby. Linc —1G 87
Snitterfield. Warw —5G 61
Snitton. Shrp —3H 59
Snodhill. Here —1G 47
Snodland. Kent —4A 40
Snods Edge. Nmbd —4D 114
Snowshill. Glos —2F 49
Snow Street. Norf —2C 66
Snydale. W Yor —3E 93
Soake. Hants —1E 17
Soar. Carm —3G 45
Soar. Gwyn —2F 69
Soar. Powy —2C 46
Soberton. Hants —1E 16
Soberton Heath. Hants —1E 16
Sockbridge. Cumb —2F 103
Sockburn. Darl —4A 106
Sodom. Den —3C 82
Soham. Cambs —3E 65
Soham Cotes. Cambs —3E 65
Solas. W Isl —1D 170
Soldon Cross. Devn —1D 10
Soldridge. Hants —3E 25
Solent Breezes. Hants —2D 16
Sole Street. Kent —4A 40
(nr. Meopham)
Sole Street. Kent —1E 29
(nr. Waltham)
Solihull. W Mid —3F 61
Sollers Dilwyn. Here —5G 59
Sollers Hope. Here —2B 48
Sollom. Lanc —3C 90
Solva. Pemb —2B 42
Somerby. Leics —4E 75
Somerby. Linc —4D 94
Somercotes. Derbs —5B 86
Somerford. Dors —3G 15
Somerford. Staf —5C 72
Somerford Keynes. Glos —2F 35
Somerley. W Sus —3G 17
Somerleyton. Suff —1G 67
Somersal Herbert. Derbs —2F 73
Somersby. Linc —3C 88
Somersham. Cambs —3C 64
Somersham. Suff —1D 54
Somerton. Oxon —3C 50
Somerton. Som —4H 21
Somerton. Suff —5H 65
Sompting. W Sus —5C 26
Sonning. Wok —4F 37
Sonning Common. Oxon —3F 37
Sookholme. Notts —4C 86
Sopley. Hants —3G 15
Sopworth. Wilts —3D 34
Sorbie. Dum —5B 110
Sordale. High —2D 168
Sorisdale. Arg —2D 138
Sorn. E Ayr —2E 117
Sornhill. E Ayr —1E 117
Sortat. High —2E 169
Sotby. Linc —3B 88
Sots Hole. Linc —4A 88
Sotterley. Suff —2G 67
Soudley. Shrp —1G 59
(nr. Church Stretton)
Soudley. Shrp —3B 72
(nr. Market Drayton)
Soughton. Flin —4E 83
Soulbury. Buck —3G 51
Soulby. Cumb —3A 104
(nr. Appleby)
Soulby. Cumb —2F 103
(nr. Penrith)
Souldern. Oxon —2D 50
Souldrop. Beds —4G 63
Sound. Shet —7F 173
Soundwell. S Glo —4B 34
Sourhope. Scot —2C 120
Sourin. Orkn —4D 172
Sourton. Devn —3F 11
Soutergate. Cumb —1B 96
South Acre. Norf —4H 77
Southall. G Lon —3C 38
South Allington. Devn —5D 9
South Alloa. Falk —4A 136
Southam. Glos —3E 49
Southam. Warw —4B 62
South Ambersham. W Sus —3A 26
Southampton. Sotn —1C 16
Southampton Airport. Hants —1C 16
Southannan. N Ayr —4D 126
South Anston. S Yor —2C 86
South Ascot. Wind —4A 38
South Baddesley. Hants —3B 16
South Balfern. Dum —4B 110
South Ballachulish. High —3E 141
South Bank. Red C —2C 106
South Barrow. Som —4B 22
South Beach. Nmbd —2G 115
South Benfleet. Essx —2B 40
South Bents. Tyne —3H 115
South Bersted. W Sus —5A 26
Southborough. Kent —1G 27
Southbourne. Bour —3G 15
Southbourne. W Sus —2F 17
South Brent. Devn —2D 8
South Brewham. Som —3C 22
South Broomage. Falk —1B 128
South Broomhill. Nmbd —5G 121
Southburgh. Norf —5B 78
South Burlingham. Norf —5F 79
Southburn. E Yor —4D 101
South Cadbury. Som —4B 22
South Carlton. Linc —3G 87
South Cave. E Yor —1C 94
South Cerney. Glos —2F 35
South Chard. Som —2G 13
South Charlton. Nmbd —2F 121
South Cheriton. Som —4B 22
South Church. Dur —2F 105
Southchurch. S'end —2D 40
South Cleatlam. Dur —3E 105
South Cliffe. E Yor —1B 94
South Clifton. Notts —3F 87
South Clunes. High —4H 157
South Cockerington. Linc —2C 88
South Common. E Sus —4E 27
South Cornelly. B'End —3B 32
Southcott. Devn —1E 11
(nr. Great Torrington)
Southcott. Devn —3F 11
(nr. Okehampton)
Southcott. Wilts —1G 23
Southcourt. Buck —4G 51
South Cove. Suff —2G 67
South Creagan. Arg —4D 141
South Creake. Norf —2A 78
South Crosland. W Yor —3B 92
South Croxton. Leics —4D 74
South Dalton. E Yor —5D 100
South Darenth. Kent —4G 39
Southdean. Scot —4A 120
Southdown. Bath —5C 34
South Duffield. N Yor —1G 93
Southease. E Sus —5F 27
South Elkington. Linc —2B 88
South Elmsall. W Yor —3E 93
Southend. Arg —5A 122
South End. Cumb —3B 96
Southend. Glos —2C 34
South End. N Lin —2E 94
South End. W Ber —4D 36
Southend (London) Airport. Essx —2C 40
Southend-on-Sea. S'end —2C 40
Southerfield. Cumb —5C 112
Southerly. Devn —4F 11
Southernden. Kent —1C 28
Southerndown. V Glam —4B 32
Southerness. Dum —4A 112
South Erradale. High —1G 155
Southerton. Devn —3D 12
Southery. Norf —1F 65
Southey Green. Essx —2A 54
South Fambridge. Essx —1C 40
South Fawley. W Ber —3B 36
South Feorline. N Ayr —3D 122
South Ferriby. N Lin —2C 94
South Field. E Yor —2D 94
Southfleet. Kent —3H 39
South Garvan. High —1D 141
Southgate. Cdgn —2E 57
Southgate. G Lon —1E 39
Southgate. Norf —3D 78
(nr. Aylsham)
Southgate. Norf —2F 77
(nr. Dersingham)
Southgate. Norf —2A 78
(nr. Fakenham)
Southgate. Swan —4E 31
South Godstone. Surr —1E 27
South Gorley. Hants —1G 15
South Green. Essx —1A 40
(nr. Billericay)
South Green. Essx —4D 54
(nr. Colchester)
South Green. Kent —4C 40
South Hanningfield. Essx —1B 40
South Harting. W Sus —1F 17
South Hayling. Hants —3F 17
South Hazelrigg. Nmbd —1E 121
South Heath. Buck —5H 51
South Heath. Essx —4E 54
South Heighton. E Sus —5F 27
South Hetton. Dur —5G 115
South Hiendley. W Yor —3D 93
South Hill. Corn —5D 10
South Hill. Som —4H 21
South Hinksey. Oxon —5D 50
South Hole. Devn —4C 18
South Holme. N Yor —2B 100
South Holmwood. Surr —1C 26
South Hornchurch. G Lon —2G 39
South Huish. Devn —4C 8
South Hykeham. Linc —4G 87
South Hylton. Tyne —4G 115
Southill. Beds —1B 52
Southington. Hants —2D 24
South Kelsey. Linc —1H 87
South Kessock. High —4A 158
South Killingholme. N Lin —3E 95
South Kilvington. N Yor —1G 99
South Kilworth. Leics —2D 62
South Kirkby. W Yor —3E 93
South Kirton. Aber —3E 153
South Kyme. Linc —1A 76
South Lancing. W Sus —5C 26
South Ledaig. Arg —5D 140
Southleigh. Devn —3F 13

South Leigh—Stapleford

South Leigh. Oxon —5B 50
South Leverton. Notts —2E 87
South Limmerhaugh. E Ayr —2F 117
South Littleton. Worc —1F 49
South Lopham. Norf —2C 66
South Luffenham. Rut —5G 75
South Malling. E Sus —4F 27
South Marston. Swin —3G 35
South Middleton. Nmbd —2E 121
South Milford. N Yor —1E 93
South Milton. Devn —4D 8
South Mimms. Herts —5C 52
Southminster. Essx —1D 40
South Molton. Devn —4H 19
South Moor. Dur —4E 115
Southmoor. Oxon —2B 36
South Moreton. Oxon —3D 36
South Mundham. W Sus —2G 17
South Muskham. Notts —5E 87
South Newbald. E Yor —1C 94
South Newington. Oxon —2C 50
South Newsham. Nmbd —2G 115
South Newton. N Ayr —4H 125
South Newton. Wilts —3F 23
South Normanton. Derbs —5B 86
South Norwood. G Lon —4E 39
South Nutfield. Surr —1E 27
South Ockendon. Thur —2G 39
Southoe. Cambs —4A 64
Southolt. Suff —4D 66
South Ormsby. Linc —3C 88
Southorpe. Pet —5H 75
South Otterington. N Yor —1F 99
South Owersby. Linc —1H 87
Southowram. W Yor —2B 92
South Oxhey. Herts —1C 38
South Perrott. Dors —2H 13
South Petherton. Som —1H 13
South Petherwin. Corn —4D 10
South Pickenham. Norf —5A 78
South Pool. Devn —4D 9
South Port. Arg —1H 133
Southport. Mers —3B 90
South Queensferry. Edin —2E 129
South Radworthy. Devn —3A 20
South Rauceby. Linc —1H 75
South Raynham. Norf —3A 78
Southrepps. Norf —2E 79
South Reston. Linc —2D 88
Southrey. Linc —4A 88
Southrop. Glos —5G 49
Southrope. Hants —2E 25
South Runcton. Norf —5F 77
South Scarle. Notts —4F 87
Southsea. Port —3E 17
South Shields. Tyne —3G 115
South Shore. Bkpl —1B 90
Southside. Orkn —5E 172
South Somercotes. Linc —1D 88
South Stainley. N Yor —3F 99
South Stainmore. Cumb —3B 104
South Stifford. Thur —3G 39
Southstoke. Bath —5C 34
South Stoke. Oxon —3D 36
South Stoke. W Sus —4B 26
South Street. E Sus —4E 27
South Street. Kent —5E 41
(nr. Faversham)
South Street. Kent —4F 41
(nr. Whitstable)
South Tawton. Devn —3G 11
South Thoresby. Linc —3D 88
South Tidworth. Wilts —2H 23
South Town. Devn —4C 12
South Town. Hants —3E 25
Southtown. Norf —5H 79
Southtown. Orkn —8D 172
Southwaite. Cumb —5F 113
South Walsham. Norf —4F 79
South Warnborough. Hants —2F 25
Southwater. W Sus —3C 26
Southwater Street. W Sus —3C 26
Southway. Som —2A 22
South Weald. Essx —1G 39
South Weirs. Hants —2A 16
Southwell. Dors —5B 14
Southwell. Notts —5D 86
South Weston. Oxon —2F 37
South Wheatley. Corn —3C 10
South Wheatley. Notts —2E 87
Southwick. Hants —2E 17
Southwick. Nptn —1H 63
Southwick. Tyne —4G 115
Southwick. W Sus —5D 26
Southwick. Wilts —1D 22
South Widcombe. Bath —1A 22
South Wigston. Leics —1C 62
South Willingham. Linc —2A 88
South Wingfield. Derbs —5A 86
South Witham. Linc —4G 75
Southwold. Suff —3H 67
South Wonston. Hants —3C 24
Southwood. Norf —5F 79
Southwood. Som —3A 22
South Woodham Ferrers. Essx —1C 40
South Wootton. Norf —3F 77
South Wraxall. Wilts —5D 34
South Zeal. Devn —3G 11
Soval Lodge. W Isl —5F 171
Sowerby. N Yor —1G 99
Sowerby. W Yor —2A 92
Sowerby Bridge. W Yor —2A 92
Sowerby Row. Cumb —5E 113
Sower Carr. Lanc —5C 96
Sowley Green. Suff —5G 65
Sowood. W Yor —3A 92
Sowton. Devn —3C 12
Soyal. High —4C 164
Soyland Town. W Yor —2A 92
Spacey Houses. N Yor —4F 99
Spa Common. Norf —2E 79
Spalding. Linc —3B 76
Spaldington. E Yor —1A 94
Spaldwick. Cambs —3A 64
Spalford. Notts —4F 87
Spanby. Linc —2H 75
Sparham. Norf —4C 78
Sparhamhill. Norf —4C 78
Spark Bridge. Cumb —1C 96
Sparket. Cumb —2F 103
Sparkford. Som —4B 22
Sparkwell. Devn —3B 8
Sparrow Green. Norf —4B 78
Sparrowpit. Derbs —2E 85
Sparrow's Green. E Sus —2H 27
Sparsholt. Hants —3C 24
Sparsholt. Oxon —3B 36
Spartylea. Nmbd —5B 114
Spath. Staf —2E 73
Spaunton. N Yor —1B 100
Spaxton. Som —3F 21
Spean Bridge. High —5E 149
Spear Hill. W Sus —4C 26
Speen. Buck —2G 37
Speen. W Ber —5C 36
Speeton. N Yor —2F 101
Speke. Mers —2G 83
Speldhurst. Kent —1G 27
Spellbrook. Herts —4E 53
Spelsbury. Oxon —3B 50
Spencers Wood. Wok —5F 37
Spennithorne. N Yor —1D 98
Spennymoor. Dur —1F 105
Spernall. Warw —4E 61
Spetchley. Worc —5C 60
Spetisbury. Dors —2E 15
Spexhall. Suff —2F 67
Speybank. High —3C 150
Spey Bay. Mor —2A 160
Speybridge. High —1E 151
Speyview. Mor —4G 159
Spilsby. Linc —4C 88
Spindlestone. Nmbd —1F 121
Spinkhill. Derbs —3B 86
Spinney Hills. Leic C —5D 74
Spinningdale. High —5D 164
Spital. Mers —2F 83
Spitalhill. Derbs —1F 73
Spital in the Street. Linc —2G 87
Spithurst. E Sus —4F 27
Spittal. Dum —4A 110
Spittal. E Lot —2A 130
Spittal. High —3D 168
Spittal. Nmbd —4G 131
Spittal. Pemb —2D 43
Spittalfield. Per —4A 144
Spittal of Glenmuick. Aber —5H 151
Spittal of Glenshee. Per —1A 144
Spittal-on-Rule. Scot —3H 119
Spixworth. Norf —4E 79
Splatt. Corn —4C 10
Spofforth. N Yor —4F 99
Spondon. Dby C —2B 74
Spon End. W Mid —3H 61
Spooner Row. Norf —1C 66
Sporle. Norf —4H 77
Spott. E Lot —2C 130
Spratton. Nptn —3E 62
Spreakley. Surr —2G 25
Spreyton. Devn —3H 11
Spridlington. Linc —2H 87
Springburn. Glas —3H 127
Springfield. Dum —3E 113
Springfield. Fife —2F 137
Springfield. High —2A 158
Springfield. W Mid —2E 61
Springhill. Staf —5D 73
Springholm. Dum —3F 111
Springside. N Ayr —1C 116
Springthorpe. Linc —2F 87
Spring Vale. IOW —3E 16
Spring Valley. IOM —4C 108
Springwell. Tyne —4F 115
Sproatley. E Yor —1E 95
Sproston Green. Ches —4B 84
Sprotbrough. S Yor —4F 93
Sproughton. Suff —1E 54
Sprouston. Scot —1B 120
Sprowston. Norf —4E 79
Sproxton. Leics —3F 75
Sproxton. N Yor —1A 100
Sprunston. Cumb —5F 113
Spurstow. Ches —5H 83
Squires Gate. Lanc —1B 90
Sraid Ruadh. Arg —4A 138
Srannda. W Isl —9C 171
Sronphadruig Lodge. Per —1E 142
Sruth Mor. W Isl —2E 170
Stableford. Shrp —1B 60
Stackhouse. N Yor —3H 97
Stackpole. Pemb —5D 43
Stackpole Elidor. Pemb —5D 43
Stacksford. Norf —1C 66
Stacksteads. Lanc —2G 91
Staddiscombe. Plym —3B 8
Staddlethorpe. E Yor —2B 94
Staddon. Devn —2D 10
Staden. Derbs —3E 85
Stadhampton. Oxon —2E 36
Stadhlaigearraidh. W Isl —5C 170
Staffield. Cumb —5G 113
Staffin. High —2D 155
Stafford. Staf —3D 72
Stafford Park. Telf —5B 72
Stagden Cross. Essx —4G 53
Stagsden. Beds —1H 51
Stag's Head. Devn —4G 19
Stainburn. Cumb —2B 102
Stainburn. N Yor —5E 99
Stainby. Linc —3G 75
Staincliffe. W Yor —2C 92
Staincross. S Yor —3D 92
Staindrop. Dur —2E 105
Staines. Surr —3B 38
Stainfield. Linc —3H 75
(nr. Bourne)
Stainfield. Linc —3A 88
(nr. Lincoln)
Stainforth. N Yor —3H 97
Stainforth. S Yor —3G 93
Staining. Lanc —1B 90
Stainland. W Yor —3A 92
Stainsacre. N Yor —4G 107
Stainton. Cumb —4E 113
(nr. Carlisle)
Stainton. Cumb —1E 97
(nr. Kendal)
Stainton. Cumb —2F 103
(nr. Penrith)
Stainton. Dur —3D 104
Stainton. Midd —3B 106
Stainton. N Yor —5E 105
Stainton. S Yor —1C 86
Stainton by Langworth. Linc —3H 87
Staintondale. N Yor —5G 107
Stainton le Vale. Linc —1A 88
Stainton with Adgarley. Cumb —2B 96
Stair. Cumb —2D 102
Stair. E Ayr —2D 116
Staithes. N Yor —3E 107
Stakeford. Nmbd —1F 115
Stake Pool. Lanc —5D 96
Stakes. Hants —2E 17
Stalbridge. Dors —1C 14
Stalbridge Weston. Dors —1C 14
Stalham. Norf —3F 79
Stalham Green. Norf —3F 79
Stalisfield Green. Kent —5D 40
Stallen. Dors —1B 14
Stallingborough. NE Lin —3F 95
Stalling Busk. N Yor —1B 98
Stallington. Staf —1D 72
Stalmine. Lanc —5C 96
Stalybridge. G Man —1D 84
Stambourne. Essx —2H 53
Stamford. Linc —5H 75
Stamford. Nmbd —3G 121
Stamford Bridge. Ches —4G 83
Stamford Bridge. E Yor —4B 100
Stamfordham. Nmbd —2D 115
Stamperland. E Ren —4G 127
Stanah. Lanc —5C 96
Stanborough. Herts —4C 52
Stanbridge. Beds —3H 51
Stanbridge. Dors —2F 15
Stanbury. W Yor —1A 92
Stand. N Lan —3A 128
Standburn. Falk —2C 128
Standeford. Staf —5D 72
Standen. Kent —1C 28
Standen Street. Kent —2C 28
Standerwick. Som —1D 22
Standford. Hants —3G 25
Standford Bridge. Telf —3B 72
Standingstone. Cumb —1B 102
(nr. Maryport)
Standingstone. Cumb —5D 112
(nr. Wigton)
Standish. Glos —5D 48
Standish. G Man —3D 90
Standish Lower Ground. G Man —4D 90
Standlake. Oxon —5C 50
Standon. Hants —4C 24
Standon. Herts —3D 53
Standon. Staf —2C 72
Standon Green End. Herts —4D 52
Standwell Green. Suff —3D 66
Stane. N Lan —3B 128
Stanecastle. N Ayr —1C 116
Stanfield. Norf —3B 78
Stanford. Beds —1B 52
Stanford. Kent —2F 29
Stanford Bishop. Here —5A 60
Stanford Bridge. Worc —4B 60
Stanford Dingley. W Ber —4D 36
Stanford in the Vale. Oxon —2B 36
Stanford-le-Hope. Thur —2A 40
Stanford on Avon. Nptn —3C 62
Stanford on Soar. Notts —3C 74
Stanford on Teme. Worc —4B 60
Stanford Rivers. Essx —5F 53
Stanfree. Derbs —3B 86
Stanghow. Red C —3D 107
Stanground. Pet —1B 64
Stanhoe. Norf —2H 77
Stanhope. Dur —1C 104
Stanhope. Scot —1D 118
Stanion. Nptn —2G 63
Stanley. Derbs —1B 74
Stanley. Dur —4F 115
Stanley. Per —5A 144
Stanley. Shrp —2B 60
Stanley. Staf —5D 84
Stanley. W Yor —2D 93
Stanley Common. Derbs —1B 74
Stanley Crook. Dur —1E 105
Stanley Hill. Here —1B 48
Stanlow. Ches —3G 83
Stanmer. Brig —5E 27
Stanmore. G Lon —1C 38
Stanmore. Hants —4C 24
Stanmore. W Ber —4C 36
Stannersburn. Nmbd —1A 114
Stanningfield. Suff —5A 66
Stannington. Nmbd —2F 115
Stannington. S Yor —2H 85
Stansbatch. Here —4F 59
Stansfield. Suff —5G 65
Stanshope. Staf —5F 85
Stanstead. Suff —1B 54
Stanstead Abbotts. Herts —4D 53
Stansted. Kent —4H 39
Stansted (London) Airport. Essx —3F 53
Stansted Mountfitchet. Essx —3F 53
Stanthorne. Ches —4A 84
Stanton. Derbs —4G 73
Stanton. Glos —2F 49
Stanton. Nmbd —5F 121
Stanton. Staf —1F 73
Stanton. Suff —3B 66
Stanton by Bridge. Derbs —3A 74
Stanton by Dale. Derbs —2B 74
Stanton Chare. Suff —3B 66
Stanton Drew. Bath —5A 34
Stanton Fitzwarren. Swin —2G 35
Stanton Harcourt. Oxon —5C 50
Stanton Hill. Notts —4B 86
Stanton in Peak. Derbs —4G 85
Stanton Lacy. Shrp —3G 59
Stanton Long. Shrp —1H 59
Stanton-on-the-Wolds. Notts —2D 74
Stanton Prior. Bath —5B 34
Stanton St Bernard. Wilts —5F 35
Stanton St John. Oxon —5D 50
Stanton St Quintin. Wilts —4E 35
Stanton Street. Suff —4B 66
Stanton under Bardon. Leics —4B 74
Stanton upon Hine Heath. Shrp —3H 71
Stanton Wick. Bath —5B 34
Stanwardine in the Fields. Shrp —3G 71
Stanwardine in the Wood. Shrp —3G 71
Stanway. Essx —3C 54
Stanway. Glos —2F 49
Stanwell. Surr —3B 38
Stanwell Moor. Surr —3B 38
Stanwick. Nptn —3G 63
Staoinebrig. W Isl —5C 170
Stape. N Yor —5E 107
Stapehill. Dors —2F 15
Stapeley. Ches —1A 72
Stapenhill. Staf —3G 73
Staple. Kent —5G 41
Staple Cross. Devn —4D 20
Staplecross. E Sus —3B 28
Staplefield. W Sus —3D 27
Staple Fitzpaine. Som —1F 13
Stapleford. Cambs —5D 64
Stapleford. Herts —4D 52
Stapleford. Leics —4F 75

Stowting—Swincliffe

Stowting. Kent —1F 29
Stowupland. Suff —5C 66
Straad. Arg —3B 126
Strachan. Aber —4D 152
Stradbroke. Suff —3E 67
Stradbrook. Wilts —1E 23
Stradishall. Suff —5G 65
Stradsett. Norf —5F 77
Stragglethorpe. Linc —5G 87
Stragglethorpe. Notts —2D 74
Straid. S Ayr —5A 116
Straight Soley. Wilts —4B 36
Straiton. S Ayr —4C 116
Straiton. W Lot —3F 129
Straloch. Per —2H 143
Stramshall. Staf —2E 73
Strang. IOM —4C 108
Strangford. Here —3A 48
Stranraer. Dum —3F 109
Strata Florida. Cdgn —4G 57
Stratfield Mortimer. W Ber —5E 37
Stratfield Saye. Hants —5E 37
Stratfield Turgis. Hants —1E 25
Stratford. Worc —2D 49
Stratford St Andrew. Suff —4F 67
Stratford St Mary. Suff —2D 54
Stratford sub Castle. Wilts —3G 23
Stratford Tony. Wilts —4F 23
Stratford-upon-Avon. Warw —5G 61
Strath. High —1G 155
Strathan. High —4B 148
(nr. Fort William)
Strathan. High —1E 163
(nr. Lochinver)
Strathan. High —2F 167
(nr. Tongue)
Strathan Skerray. High —2G 167
Strathaven. S Lan —5A 128
Strathblane. Stir —2G 127
Strathcanaird. High —3F 163
Strathcarron. High —4B 156
Strathcoil. Arg —5A 140
Strathdon. Aber —2A 152
Strathkinness. Fife —2G 137
Strathmashie House. High —4H 149
Strathmiglo. Fife —2E 136
Strathmore Lodge. High —4D 168
Strathpeffer. High —3G 157
Strathrannoch. High —1F 157
Strathtay. Per —3G 143
Strathvaich Lodge. High —1F 157
Strathwhillan. N Ayr —2E 123
Strathy. High —1A 158
(nr. Invergordon)
Strathy. High —2A 168
(nr. Melvich)
Strathyre. Stir —2E 135
Stratton. Corn —2C 10
Stratton. Dors —3B 14
Stratton. Glos —5F 49
Stratton Audley. Oxon —3E 50
Stratton-on-the-Fosse. Som —1B 22
Stratton St Margaret. Swin —3G 35
Stratton St Michael. Norf —1E 66
Stratton Strawless. Norf —3E 78
Stravithie. Fife —2H 137
Stream. Som —3D 20
Streat. E Sus —4E 27
Streatham. G Lon —3D 39
Streatley. Beds —3A 52
Streatley. W Ber —3D 36
Street. Corn —3C 10
Street. Lanc —4E 97
Street. N Yor —4E 107
Street. Som —2G 13
(nr. Chard)
Street. Som —3H 21
(nr. Glastonbury)
Street Dinas. Shrp —2F 71
Street End. W Sus —3G 17
Street Gate. Tyne —4F 115
Streethay. Staf —4F 73
Streethouse. W Yor —3D 93
Streetlam. N Yor —5A 106
Street Lane. Derbs —1A 74
Streetly. W Mid —1E 61
Streetly End. Cambs —1G 53
Street on the Fosse. Som —3B 22
Strefford. Shrp —2G 59
Strelley. Notts —1C 74
Strensall. York —3A 100
Strensall Camp. York —4A 100
Stretcholt. Som —2F 21
Strete. Devn —4E 9
Stretford. G Man —1C 84
Stretford. Here —5H 59
Strethall. Essx —2E 53
Stretham. Cambs —3E 65
Stretton. Ches —5G 83
Stretton. Derbs —4A 86
Stretton. Rut —4G 75
Stretton. Staf —4C 72
(nr. Brewood)
Stretton. Staf —3G 73
(nr. Burton upon Trent)
Stretton. Warr —2A 84
Stretton en le Field. Leics —4H 73
Stretton Grandison. Here —1B 48
Stretton Heath. Shrp —4F 71
Stretton-on-Dunsmore. Warw —3B 62
Stretton on Fosse. Warw —2H 49
Stretton Sugwas. Here —1H 47
Stretton under Fosse. Warw —2B 62
Stretton Westwood. Shrp —1H 59
Strichen. Aber —3G 161
Strines. G Man —2D 84
Stringston. Som —2E 21
Strixton. Nptn —4G 63
Stroanfreggan. Dum —5F 117
Stroat. Glos —2A 34
Stromeferry. High —5A 156
Stromemore. High —5A 156
Stromness. Orkn —7B 172
Stronachie. Per —3C 136
Stronachlachar. Stir —2D 134
Stronchreggan. High —1E 141
Strone. Arg —1C 126
Strone. High —1H 149
(nr. Drumnadrochit)
Strone. High —4B 150
(nr. Kingussie)
Stronenaba. High —5E 148
Stronmilchan. Arg —1A 134
Stronsay Airport. Orkn —5F 172
Strontian. High —2C 140
Strood. Kent —2C 28
Strood. Medw —4B 40
Strood Green. Surr —1D 26
Strood Green. W Sus —3B 26
(nr. Billingshurst)
Strood Green. W Sus —2C 26
(nr. Horsham)
Strothers Dale. Nmbd —4C 114
Stroud. Glos —5D 48
Stroud. Hants —4F 25
Stroud Green. Essx —1C 40
Stroxton. Linc —2G 75
Struan. High —5C 154
Struan. Per —2F 143
Struanmore. High —5C 154
Strubby. Linc —2D 88
Strugg's Hill. Linc —2B 76
Strumpshaw. Norf —5F 79
Strutherhill. S Lan —4A 128
Struy. High —5F 157
Stryd. IOA —2B 80
Stryt-issa. Wrex —1E 71
Stuartfield. Aber —4G 161
Stubbington. Hants —2D 16
Stubbins. Lanc —3F 91
Stubble Green. Cumb —5B 102
Stubb's Cross. Kent —2D 28
Stubbs Green. Norf —1F 67
Stubhampton. Dors —1E 15
Stub Place. Cumb —5B 102
Stubton. Linc —1F 75
Stubwood. Staf —2E 73
Stuckton. Hants —1G 15
Studham. Beds —4A 52
Studland. Dors —4F 15
Studley. Warw —4E 61
Studley. Wilts —4E 35
Studley Roger. N Yor —2E 99
Stuntney. Cambs —3E 65
Stunts Green. E Sus —4H 27
Sturbridge. Staf —2C 72
Sturgate. Linc —2F 87
Sturmer. Essx —1G 53
Sturminster Common. Dors —1C 14
Sturminster Marshall. Dors —2E 15
Sturminster Newton. Dors —1C 14
Sturry. Kent —4F 41
Sturton. N Lin —4C 94
Sturton by Stow. Linc —2F 87
Sturton le Steeple. Notts —2E 87
Stuston. Suff —3D 66
Stutton. N Yor —5G 99
Stutton. Suff —2E 55
Styal. Ches —2C 84
Stydd. Lanc —1E 91
Styrrup. Notts —1D 86
Suainebost. W Isl —1H 171
Suardail. W Isl —4G 171
Succoth. Aber —5B 160
Succoth. Arg —3B 134
Suckley. Worc —5B 60
Suckley Knowl. Worc —5B 60
Sudborough. Nptn —2G 63
Sudbourne. Suff —5G 67
Sudbrook. Linc —1G 75
Sudbrook. Mon —3A 34
Sudbrooke. Linc —3H 87
Sudbury. Derbs —2F 73
Sudbury. Suff —1B 54
Sudgrove. Glos —5E 49
Suffield. Norf —2E 79
Suffield. N Yor —5G 107
Sugnall. Staf —2B 72
Sugwas Pool. Here —1H 47
Suisnish. High —5E 155
Sulaisiadar. W Isl —4H 171
Sulby. IOM —2C 108
Sulgrave. Nptn —1D 50
Sulham. W Ber —4E 37
Sulhamstead. W Ber —5E 37
Sulishaderbeg. High —4D 154
Sullington. W Sus —4B 26
Sullom. Shet —4E 173
Sully. V Glam —5E 33
Sumburgh. Shet —10F 173
Sumburgh Airport. Shet —10E 173
Summer Bridge. N Yor —3E 98
Summercourt. Corn —3C 6
Summerfield. Norf —2G 77
Summergangs. Hull —1E 95
Summerhill. Aber C —3G 153
Summerhill. Pemb —4F 43
Summer Hill. W Mid —1D 60
Summerhouse. Darl —3F 105
Summersdale. W Sus —2G 17
Summerseat. G Man —3F 91
Summit. G Man —3H 91
Sunbury. Surr —4C 38
Sunderland. Cumb —1C 102
Sunderland. Lanc —4D 96
Sunderland. Tyne —4G 115
Sunderland Bridge. Dur —1F 105
Sundon Park. Lutn —3A 52
Sundridge. Kent —5F 39
Sunk Island. E Yor —3F 95
Sunningdale. Wind —4A 38
Sunninghill. Wind —4A 38
Sunningwell. Oxon —5C 50
Sunniside. Dur —1E 105
Sunniside. Tyne —4F 115
Sunny Bank. Cumb —5D 102
Sunny Hill. Dby C —2H 73
Sunnyhurst. Bkbn —2E 91
Sunnylaw. Stir —4G 135
Sunnymead. Oxon —5D 50
Sunnyside. S Yor —1B 86
Sunnyside. W Sus —2E 27
Sunton. Wilts —1H 23
Surbiton. G Lon —4C 38
Surby. IOM —4B 108
Surfleet. Linc —3B 76
Surfleet Seas End. Linc —3B 76
Surlingham. Norf —5F 79
Surrex. Essx —3B 54
Sustead. Norf —2D 78
Susworth. Linc —4B 94
Sutcombe. Devn —1D 10
Suton. Norf —1C 66
Sutors of Cromarty. High —2C 158
Sutterby. Linc —3C 88
Sutterton. Linc —2B 76
Sutterton Dowdyke. Linc —2B 76
Sutton. Beds —1C 52
Sutton. Buck —3B 38
Sutton. Cambs —3D 64
Sutton. E Sus —5F 27
Sutton. G Lon —4D 38
Sutton. Kent —1H 29
Sutton. Norf —3F 79
Sutton. Notts —2E 75
(nr. Bingham)
Sutton. Notts —2D 86
(nr. East Retford)
Sutton. Oxon —5C 50
Sutton. Pemb —3D 42
Sutton. Pet —1H 63
Sutton. Shrp —2B 60
(nr. Bridgnorth)
Sutton. Shrp —2A 72
(nr. Market Drayton)
Sutton. Shrp —3F 71
(nr. Oswestry)
Sutton. Shrp —4H 71
(nr. Shrewsbury)
Sutton. Som —3B 22
Sutton. S Yor —3F 93
Sutton. Staf —3B 72
Sutton. Suff —1G 55
Sutton. W Sus —4A 26
Sutton. Worc —4A 60
Sutton Abinger. Surr —1C 26
Sutton at Hone. Kent —4G 39
Sutton Bassett. Nptn —1E 63
Sutton Benger. Wilts —4E 35
Sutton Bingham. Som —1A 14
Sutton Bonington. Notts —3C 74
Sutton Bridge. Linc —3D 76
Sutton Cheney. Leics —5B 74
Sutton Coldfield. W Mid —1F 61
Sutton Corner. Linc —3D 76
Sutton Courtenay. Oxon —2D 36
Sutton Crosses. Linc —3D 76
Sutton Gault. Cambs —3D 64
Sutton Grange. N Yor —2E 99
Sutton Green. Surr —5B 38
Sutton Howgrave. N Yor —2F 99
Sutton in Ashfield. Notts —5C 86
Sutton-in-Craven. N Yor —5C 98
Sutton Ings. Hull —1E 94
Sutton in the Elms. Leics —1C 62
Sutton Lane Ends. Ches —3D 84
Sutton Leach. Mers —1H 83
Sutton Maddock. Shrp —5B 72
Sutton Mallet. Som —3G 21
Sutton Mandeville. Wilts —4E 23
Sutton Montis. Som —4B 22
Sutton-on-Hull. Hull —1E 94
Sutton on Sea. Linc —2E 89
Sutton-on-the-Forest. N Yor —3H 99
Sutton on the Hill. Derbs —2G 73
Sutton on Trent. Notts —4E 87
Sutton Poyntz. Dors —4C 14
Sutton St Edmund. Linc —4C 76
Sutton St Edmund's Common. Linc —5C 76
Sutton St James. Linc —4C 76
Sutton St Michael. Here —1A 48
Sutton St Nicholas. Here —1A 48
Sutton Scarsdale. Derbs —4B 86
Sutton Scotney. Hants —3C 24
Sutton-under-Brailes. Warw —2B 50
Sutton-under-Whitestonecliffe. N Yor —1G 99
Sutton upon Derwent. E Yor —5B 100
Sutton Valence. Kent —1C 28
Sutton Veny. Wilts —2E 23
Sutton Waldron. Dors —1D 14
Sutton Weaver. Ches —3H 83
Swaby. Linc —3C 88
Swadlincote. Derbs —4G 73
Swaffham. Norf —5H 77
Swaffham Bulbeck. Cambs —4E 65
Swaffham Prior. Cambs —4E 65
Swafield. Norf —2E 79
Swainby. N Yor —4B 106
Swainshill. Here —1H 47
Swainsthorpe. Norf —5E 78
Swainswick. Bath —5C 34
Swalcliffe. Oxon —2B 50
Swalecliffe. Kent —4F 41
Swallow. Linc —4E 95
Swallow Beck. Linc —4G 87
Swallowcliffe. Wilts —4E 23
Swallowfield. Wok —5F 37
Swallownest. S Yor —2B 86
Swampton. Hants —1C 24
Swanage. Dors —5F 15
Swanbourne. Buck —3G 51
Swanbridge. V Glam —5E 33
Swan Green. Ches —3B 84
Swanland. E Yor —2C 94
Swanley. Kent —4G 39
Swanmore. Hants —1D 16
Swannington. Leics —4B 74
Swannington. Norf —4D 78
Swanpool. Linc —4G 87
Swanscombe. Kent —3G 39
Swansea. Swan —3F 31
Swansmoor. Staf —3E 73
Swan Street. Essx —3B 54
Swanton Abbot. Norf —3E 79
Swanton Morley. Norf —4C 78
Swanton Novers. Norf —2C 78
Swanton Street. Kent —5C 40
Swanwick. Derbs —5B 86
Swanwick. Hants —2D 16
Swanwick Green. Ches —1H 71
Swarby. Linc —1H 75
Swardeston. Norf —5E 78
Swarkestone. Derbs —3A 74
Swarland. Nmbd —4F 121
Swarland Estate. Nmbd —4F 121
Swarraton. Hants —3D 24
Swartha. W Yor —5C 98
Swarthmoor. Cumb —2B 96
Swaton. Linc —2A 76
Swavesey. Cambs —4C 64
Sway. Hants —3A 16
Swayfield. Linc —3G 75
Swaythling. Sotn —1C 16
Sweet Green. Worc —4A 60
Sweetham. Devn —3B 12
Sweetholme. Cumb —3G 103
Sweets. Corn —3B 10
Sweetshouse. Corn —2E 7
Swefling. Suff —4F 67
Swell. Som —4G 21
Swepstone. Leics —4A 74
Swerford. Oxon —2B 50
Swettenham. Ches —4C 84
Swetton. N Yor —2D 98
Swffryd. Cphy —2F 33
Swiftsden. E Sus —3B 28
Swilland. Suff —5D 66
Swillington. W Yor —1D 93
Swimbridge. Devn —4G 19
Swimbridge Newland. Devn —3G 19
Swinbrook. Oxon —4A 50
Swincliffe. N Yor —4E 99
Swincliffe. W Yor —2C 92

Swinderby—Thomas Chapel

Swinderby. Linc —4F 87
Swindon. Glos —3E 49
Swindon. Nmbd —5D 121
Swindon. Staf —1C 60
Swindon. Swin —3G 35
Swine. E Yor —1E 95
Swinefleet. E Yor —2A 94
Swineshead. Beds —4H 63
Swineshead. Linc —1B 76
Swineshead Bridge. Linc —1B 76
Swiney. High —5E 169
Swinford. Leics —3C 62
Swinford. Oxon —5C 50
Swingate. Notts —1C 74
Swingbrow. Cambs —2C 64
Swingfield Minnis. Kent —1G 29
Swingfield Street. Kent —1G 29
Swingleton Green. Suff —1C 54
Swinhill. S Lan —5A 128
Swinhoe. Nmbd —2G 121
Swinhope. Linc —1B 88
Swinithwaite. N Yor —1C 98
Swinmore Common. Here —1B 48
Swinscoe. Staf —1F 73
Swinside Hall. Scot —3B 120
Swinstead. Linc —3H 75
Swinton. G Man —4F 91
Swinton. N Yor —2B 100
(nr. Malton)
Swinton. N Yor —2E 98
(nr. Masham)
Swinton. Scot —5E 131
Swinton. S Yor —1B 86
Swithland. Leics —4C 74
Swordale. High —2H 157
Swordly. High —2H 167
Sworton Heath. Ches —2A 84
Swyddffynnon. Cdgn —4F 57
Swyffrd. Cphy —2F 33
Swynnerton. Staf —2C 72
Swyre. Dors —4A 14
Sycharth. Powy —3E 70
Sychdyn. Flin —4E 83
Sychnant. Powy —3B 58
Sychtyn. Powy —5B 70
Syde. Glos —4E 49
Sydenham. G Lon —3E 39
Sydenham. Oxon —5F 51
Sydenham. Som —3G 21
Sydenham Damerel. Devn —5E 11
Syderstone. Norf —2H 77
Sydling St Nicholas. Dors —3B 14
Sydmonton. Hants —1C 24
Sydney. Ches —5B 84
Syerston. Notts —1E 75
Syke. G Man —3G 91
Sykehouse. S Yor —3G 93
Sykes. Lanc —4F 97
Syleham. Suff —3E 66
Sylen. Carm —5F 45
Sylfaen. Powy —5D 70
Symbister. Shet —5G 173
Symington. S Ayr —1C 116
Symington. S Lan —1B 118
Symondsbury. Dors —3H 13
Symonds Yat. Here —4A 48
Synod Inn. Cdgn —5D 56
Syre. High —4G 167
Syreford. Glos —3F 49
Syresham. Nptn —1E 51
Syston. Leics —4D 74
Syston. Linc —1G 75
Sytchampton. Worc —4C 60
Sywell. Nptn —4F 63

Tabost. W Isl —6F 171
(nr. Cearsiadar)
Tabost. W Isl —1H 171
(nr. Suainebost)
Tachbrook Mallory. Warw —4H 61
Tackley. Oxon —3C 50
Tacleit. W Isl —4D 171

Tacolneston. Norf —1D 66
Tadcaster. N Yor —5G 99
Taddington. Derbs —3F 85
Taddington. Glos —2F 49
Taddiport. Devn —1E 11
Tadley. Hants —5E 36
Tadlow. Cambs —1C 52
Tadmarton. Oxon —2B 50
Tadwick. Bath —4C 34
Tadworth. Surr —5D 38
Tafarnaubach. Cphy —4E 46
Tafarn-y-bwlch. Pemb —1E 43
Tafarn-y-Gelyn. Den —4D 82
Taff's Well. Card —3E 33
Tafolwern. Powy —5A 70
Taibach. Neat —3A 32
Tai-bach. Powy —3D 70
Taigh a Ghearraidh. W Isl —1C 170
Tain. High —5E 165
(nr. Invergordon)
Tain. High —2E 169
(nr. Thurso)
Tai-Nant. Wrex —1E 71
Taï'n Lon. Gwyn —5D 80
Tairbeart. W Isl —8D 171
Tairgwaith. Neat —4H 45
Takeley. Essx —3F 53
Takeley Street. Essx —3F 53
Talachddu. Powy —2D 46
Talacre. Flin —2D 82
Talardd. Gwyn —3A 70
Talaton. Devn —3D 12
Talbenny. Pemb —3C 42
Talbot Green. Rhon —3D 32
Taleford. Devn —3D 12
Talerddig. Powy —5B 70
Talgarreg. Cdgn —5D 56
Talgarth. Powy —2E 47
Talisker. High —5C 154
Talke. Staf —5C 84
Talkin. Cumb —4G 113
Talladale. High —1B 156
Talla Linnfoots. Scot —2D 118
Tallaminnock. S Ayr —5D 116
Tallarn Green. Wrex —1G 71
Tallentire. Cumb —1C 102
Talley. Carm —2G 45
Tallington. Linc —5H 75
Talmine. High —2F 167
Talog. Carm —2H 43
Talsarn. Carm —3A 46
Talsarn. Cdgn —5E 57
Talsarnau. Gwyn —2F 69
Talskiddy. Corn —2D 6
Talwrn. IOA —3D 81
Talwrn. Wrex —1E 71
Tal-y-bont. Cdgn —2F 57
Tal-y-Bont. Cnwy —4G 81
Tal-y-bont. Gwyn —3F 81
(nr. Bangor)
Tal-y-bont. Gwyn —3E 69
(nr. Barmouth)
Talybont-on-Usk. Powy —3E 46
Tal-y-cafn. Cnwy —3G 81
Tal-y-coed. Mon —4H 47
Tal-y-llyn. Gwyn —5G 69
Talyllyn. Powy —3E 46
Talysarn. Gwyn —5D 81
Tal-y-waenydd. Gwyn —1F 69
Talywain. Torf —5F 47
Talywern. Powy —5H 69
Tamerton Foliot. Plym —2A 8
Tamworth. Staf —5G 73
Tamworth Green. Linc —1C 76
Tandlehill. Ren —3F 127
Tandridge. Surr —5E 39
Tanerdy. Carm —3E 45
Tanfield. Dur —4E 115
Tanfield Lea. Dur —4E 115
Tangasdale. W Isl —8B 170
Tang Hall. York —4A 100
Tangiers. Pemb —3D 42
Tangley. Hants —1B 24

Tangmere. W Sus —5A 26
Tangwick. Shet —4D 173
Tankerness. Orkn —7E 172
Tankersley. S Yor —1H 85
Tankerton. Kent —4F 41
Tan-lan. Cnwy —4G 81
Tan-lan. Gwyn —1F 69
Tannach. High —4F 169
Tannadice. Ang —3D 145
Tanners Green. Worc —3E 61
Tannington. Suff —4E 67
Tannochside. N Lan —3A 128
Tan Office Green. Suff —5G 65
Tansley. Derbs —5H 85
Tansley Knoll. Derbs —4H 85
Tansor. Nptn —1H 63
Tantobie. Dur —4E 115
Tanton. N Yor —3C 106
Tanvats. Linc —4A 88
Tanworth-in-Arden. Warw —3F 61
Tan-y-bwlch. Gwyn —1F 69
Tan-y-fron. Cnwy —4B 82
Tanyfron. Wrex —5E 83
Tan-y-goes. Cdgn —1C 44
Tanygrisiau. Gwyn —1F 69
Tan-y-pistyll. Powy —3C 70
Tan-yr-allt. Den —2C 82
Taobh a Chaolais. W Isl —7C 170
Taobh a Deas Loch Aineort.
                        W Isl —6C 170
Taobh a Ghlinne. W Isl —6F 171
Taobh Tuath. W Isl —9B 171
Taplow. Buck —2A 38
Tapton. Derbs —3A 86
Tarbert. Arg —1E 125
(on Jura)
Tarbert. Arg —3G 125
(on Knapdale)
Tarbert. W Isl —8D 171
Tarbet. Arg —3C 134
Tarbet. High —4F 147
(nr. Mallaig)
Tarbet. High —4B 166
(nr. Scourie)
Tarbock Green. Mers —2G 83
Tarbolton. S Ayr —2D 116
Tarbrax. S Lan —4D 128
Tardebigge. Worc —4E 61
Tarfside. Ang —1D 145
Tarland. Aber —3B 152
Tarleton. Lanc —2C 90
Tarlogie. High —5E 165
Tarlscough. Lanc —3C 90
Tarlton. Glos —2E 35
Tarnbrook. Lanc —4E 97
Tarnock. Som —1G 21
Tarns. Cumb —5C 112
Tarporley. Ches —4H 83
Tarpots. Essx —2B 40
Tarr. Som —3E 20
Tarrant Crawford. Dors —2E 15
Tarrant Gunville. Dors —1E 15
Tarrant Hinton. Dors —1E 15
Tarrant Keyneston. Dors —2E 15
Tarrant Launceston. Dors —2E 15
Tarrant Monkton. Dors —2E 15
Tarrant Rawston. Dors —2E 15
Tarrant Rushton. Dors —2E 15
Tarrel. High —5F 165
Tarring Neville. E Sus —5F 27
Tarrington. Here —1B 48
Tarsappie. Per —1D 136
Tarskavaig. High —3D 147
Tarves. Aber —5F 161
Tarvie. High —3G 157
Tarvin. Ches —4G 83
Tasburgh. Norf —1E 66
Tasley. Shrp —1A 60
Taston. Oxon —3B 50
Tatenhill. Staf —3G 73
Tathall End. Mil —1G 51
Tatham. Lanc —3F 97
Tathwell. Linc —2C 88

Tatling End. Buck —2B 38
Tatsfield. Surr —5F 39
Tattenhall. Ches —5G 83
Tatterford. Norf —3A 78
Tattersett. Norf —2H 77
Tattershall. Linc —5B 88
Tattershall Bridge. Linc —5A 88
Tattershall Thorpe. Linc —5B 88
Tattingstone. Suff —2E 55
Tattingstone White Horse. Suff
                        —2E 55
Tattle Bank. Warw —4F 61
Tatworth. Som —2G 13
Taunton. Som —4F 21
Taverham. Norf —4D 78
Taverners Green. Essx —4F 53
Tavernspite. Pemb —3F 43
Tavistock. Devn —5E 11
Tavool House. Arg —1B 132
Taw Green. Devn —3G 11
Tawstock. Devn —4F 19
Taxal. Derbs —2E 85
Tayinloan. Arg —5E 125
Taynish. Arg —1F 125
Taynton. Glos —3C 48
Taynton. Oxon —4H 49
Taynuilt. Arg —5E 141
Tayport. Fife —1G 137
Tayvallich. Arg —1F 125
Tealby. Linc —1A 88
Tealing. Ang —5D 144
Teangue. High —3E 147
Tebay. Cumb —4H 103
Tebworth. Beds —3H 51
Tedburn St Mary. Devn —3B 12
Teddington. Glos —2E 49
Teddington. G Lon —3C 38
Tedsmore. Shrp —3F 71
Tedstone Delamere. Here —5A 60
Tedstone Wafer. Here —5A 60
Teeside. Stoc T —2C 106
Teesport. Red C —2C 106
Teesside. Stoc T —2C 106
Teesside Airport. Stoc T —3A 106
Teeton. Nptn —3D 62
Teffont Evias. Wilts —3E 23
Teffont Magna. Wilts —3E 23
Tegryn. Pemb —1G 43
Teigh. Rut —4F 75
Teigncombe. Devn —4G 11
Teigngrace. Devn —5B 12
Teignmouth. Devn —5C 12
Telford. Telf —4A 72
Telham. E Sus —4B 28
Tellisford. Som —1D 22
Telscombe. E Sus —5F 27
Telscombe Cliffs. E Sus —5E 27
Tempar. Per —3D 142
Templand. Dum —1B 112
Temple. Corn —5B 10
Temple. Glas —3G 127
Temple. Midl —4G 129
Temple Balsall. W Mid —3G 61
Temple Bar. Carm —4F 45
Temple Bar. Cdgn —5E 57
Temple Cloud. Bath —1B 22
Templecombe. Som —4C 22
Temple Ewell. Kent —1G 29
Temple Grafton. Warw —5F 61
Temple Guiting. Glos —3F 49
Templehall. Fife —4E 137
Temple Hirst. N Yor —2G 93
Temple Normanton. Derbs —4B 86
Temple Sowerby. Cumb —2H 103
Templeton. Devn —1B 12
Templeton. Pemb —3F 43
Templeton. W Ber —5B 36
Templetown. Dur —5E 115
Tempsford. Beds —5A 64
Tenandry. Per —2G 143
Tenbury Wells. Worc —4H 59
Tenby. Pemb —4F 43
Tendring. Essx —3E 55

Tendring Green. Essx —3E 55
Ten Mile Bank. Norf —1F 65
Tenterden. Kent —2C 28
Terfyn. Cnwy —3B 82
Terling. Essx —4A 54
Ternhill. Shrp —2A 72
Terregles. Dum —2G 111
Terrick. Buck —5G 51
Terrington. N Yor —2A 100
Terrington St Clement. Norf —3E 77
Terrington St John. Norf —4E 77
Terry's Green. Warw —3F 61
Teston. Kent —5B 40
Testwood. Hants —1B 16
Tetbury. Glos —2D 35
Tetbury Upton. Glos —2D 35
Tetchill. Shrp —2F 71
Tetcott. Devn —3D 10
Tetford. Linc —3C 88
Tetney. Linc —4G 95
Tetney Lock. Linc —4G 95
Tetsworth. Oxon —5E 51
Tettenhall. W Mid —1C 60
Teversal. Notts —4B 86
Teversham. Cambs —5D 65
Teviothead. Scot —4G 119
Tewel. Aber —5F 153
Tewin. Herts —4C 52
Tewkesbury. Glos —2D 49
Teynham. Kent —4D 40
Teynham Street. Kent —4D 40
Thackthwaite. Cumb —2F 103
Thakeham. W Sus —4C 26
Thame. Oxon —5F 51
Thames Ditton. Surr —4C 38
Thames Haven. Thur —2B 40
Thamesmead. G Lon —3F 39
Thamesport. Medw —3C 40
Thanington Without. Kent —5F 41
Thankerton. S Lan —1B 118
Tharston. Norf —1D 66
Thatcham. W Ber —5D 36
Thatto Heath. Mers —1H 83
Thaxted. Essx —2G 53
Theakston. N Yor —1F 99
Thealby. N Lin —3B 94
Theale. Som —2H 21
Theale. W Ber —4E 37
Thearne. E Yor —1D 94
Theberton. Suff —4G 67
Theddingworth. Leics —2D 62
Theddlethorpe All Saints. Linc
                        —2D 88
Theddlethorpe St Helen. Linc —2D 89
Thelbridge Barton. Devn —1A 12
Thelnetham. Suff —3C 66
Thelveton. Norf —2D 66
Thelwall. Warr —2A 84
Themelthorpe. Norf —3C 78
Thenford. Nptn —1D 50
Therfield. Herts —2D 52
Thetford. Linc —4A 76
Thetford. Norf —2A 66
Thethwaite. Cumb —5E 113
Theydon Bois. Essx —1F 39
Thick Hollins. W Yor —4B 92
Thickwood. Wilts —4D 34
Thimbleby. Linc —3B 88
Thimbleby. N Yor —5B 106
Thingwall. Mers —2F 83
Thirlby. N Yor —1G 99
Thirlestane. Scot —5B 130
Thirn. N Yor —1E 98
Thirsk. N Yor —1G 99
Thirtleby. E Yor —1E 95
Thistleton. Lanc —1C 90
Thistleton. Rut —4G 75
Thistley Green. Suff —3F 65
Thixendale. N Yor —3C 100
Thockrington. Nmbd —2C 114
Tholomas Drove. Cambs —5D 76
Tholthorpe. N Yor —3G 99
Thomas Chapel. Pemb —4F 43

Toddington. *Beds* —3A **52**
Toddington. *Glos* —2F **49**
Todenham. *Glos* —2H **49**
Todhills. *Cumb* —3E **113**
Todmorden. *W Yor* —2H **91**
Todwick. *S Yor* —2B **86**
Toft. *Cambs* —5C **64**
Toft. *Linc* —4H **75**
Toft Hill. *Dur* —2E **105**
Toft Monks. *Norf* —1G **67**
Toft next Newton. *Linc* —2H **87**
Toftrees. *Norf* —3A **78**
Tofts. *High* —2F **169**
Toftwood. *Norf* —4B **78**
Togston. *Nmbd* —4G **121**
Tokavaig. *High* —2E **147**
Tokers Green. *Oxon* —4F **37**
Tolastadh a Chaolais. *W Isl* —4D **171**
Tolladine. *Worc* —5C **60**
Tolland. *Som* —3E **20**
Tollard Farnham. *Dors* —1E **15**
Tollard Royal. *Wilts* —1E **15**
Toll Bar. *S Yor* —4F **93**
Toller Fratrum. *Dors* —3A **14**
Toller Porcorum. *Dors* —3A **14**
Tollerton. *N Yor* —3H **99**
Tollerton. *Notts* —2D **74**
Toller Whelme. *Dors* —2A **14**
Tollesbury. *Essx* —4C **54**
Tolleshunt D'Arcy. *Essx* —4C **54**
Tolleshunt Knights. *Essx* —4C **54**
Tolleshunt Major. *Essx* —4C **54**
Tollie. *High* —3H **157**
Tollie Farm. *High* —1A **156**
Tolm. *W Isl* —4G **171**
Tolpuddle. *Dors* —3C **14**
Tolstadh bho Thuath. *W Isl* —3H **171**
Tolworth. *G Lon* —4C **38**
Tomachlaggan. *Mor* —1F **151**
Tomaknock. *Per* —1A **136**
Tomatin. *High* —1C **150**
Tombuidhe. *Arg* —3H **133**
Tomdoun. *High* —3D **148**
Tomich. *High* —1F **149**
 (nr. Cannich)
Tomich. *High* —1A **158**
 (nr. Invergordon)
Tomich. *High* —3D **164**
 (nr. Lairg)
Tomintoul. *Mor* —2F **151**
Tomnavoulin. *Mor* —1G **151**
Tomsleibhe. *Arg* —5A **140**
Ton. *Mon* —2G **33**
Tonbridge. *Kent* —1G **27**
Tondu. *B'End* —3B **32**
Tonedale. *Som* —4E **21**
Tonfanau. *Gwyn* —5E **69**
Tong. *Shrp* —5B **72**
Tonge. *Leics* —3B **74**
Tong Forge. *Shrp* —5B **72**
Tongham. *Surr* —2G **25**
Tongland. *Dum* —4D **111**
Tong Norton. *Shrp* —5B **72**
Tongue. *High* —3F **167**
Tongwynlais. *Card* —3E **33**
Tonmawr. *Neat* —2B **32**
Tonna. *Neat* —2A **32**
Tonnau. *Neat* —2A **32**
Ton-Pentre. *Rhon* —2C **32**
Tonwell. *Herts* —4D **52**
Tonypandy. *Rhon* —2C **32**
Tonyrefail. *Rhon* —3D **32**
Toot Baldon. *Oxon* —5D **50**
Toot Hill. *Essx* —5F **53**
Toot Hill. *Hants* —1B **16**
Topcliffe. *N Yor* —2G **99**
Topcliffe. *W Yor* —2C **92**
Topcroft. *Norf* —1E **67**
Topcroft Street. *Norf* —1E **67**
Toppesfield. *Essx* —2H **53**
Toppings. *G Man* —3F **91**
Toprow. *Norf* —1D **66**
Topsham. *Devn* —4C **12**

Torbay. *Devn* —2F **9**
Torbeg. *N Ayr* —3C **122**
Torbothie. *N Lan* —3B **128**
Torbryan. *Devn* —2E **9**
Torcross. *Devn* —4E **9**
Tore. *High* —3A **158**
Torgyle. *High* —2F **149**
Torinturk. *Arg* —3G **125**
Torksey. *Linc* —3F **87**
Torlum. *W Isl* —3C **170**
Torlundy. *High* —1F **141**
Tormarton. *S Glo* —4C **34**
Tormitchell. *S Ayr* —5B **116**
Tormore. *High* —3E **147**
Tormore. *N Ayr* —2C **122**
Tornagrain. *High* —4B **158**
Tornaveen. *Aber* —3D **152**
Torness. *High* —1H **149**
Toronto. *Dur* —1E **105**
Torpenhow. *Cumb* —1D **102**
Torphichen. *W Lot* —2C **128**
Torphins. *Aber* —3D **152**
Torpoint. *Corn* —3A **8**
Torquay. *Torb* —2F **9**
Torr. *Devn* —3B **8**
Torra. *Arg* —4B **124**
Torran. *High* —4E **155**
Torrance. *E Dun* —2H **127**
Torrans. *Arg* —1B **132**
Torranyard. *E Ayr* —5E **127**
Torre. *Torb* —2E **9**
Torridon. *High* —3B **156**
Torrin. *High* —1D **147**
Torrisdale. *Arg* —2B **122**
Torrisdale. *High* —2G **167**
Torrish. *High* —2G **165**
Torrisholme. *Lanc* —3D **96**
Torroble. *High* —3C **164**
Torroy. *High* —4C **164**
Tor Royal. *Devn* —5G **11**
Torry. *Aber* C —3G **153**
Torryburn. *Fife* —1D **128**
Torthorwald. *Dum* —2B **112**
Tortington. *W Sus* —5B **26**
Tortworth. *S Glo* —2C **34**
Torvaig. *High* —4D **155**
Torver. *Cumb* —5D **102**
Torwood. *Falk* —1B **128**
Torworth. *Notts* —2D **86**
Toscaig. *High* —5G **155**
Toseland. *Cambs* —4B **64**
Tosside. *Lanc* —4G **97**
Tostock. *Suff* —4B **66**
Totaig. *High* —3B **154**
Totardor. *High* —5C **154**
Tote. *High* —4D **154**
Totegan. *High* —2A **168**
Tothill. *Linc* —2D **88**
Totland. *IOW* —4B **16**
Totley. *S Yor* —3H **85**
Totnell. *Dors* —2B **14**
Totnes. *Devn* —2E **9**
Toton. *Derbs* —2B **74**
Totronald. *Arg* —3C **138**
Totscore. *High* —2C **154**
Tottenham. *G Lon* —1E **39**
Tottenhill. *Norf* —4F **77**
Tottenhill Row. *Norf* —4F **77**
Totteridge. *G Lon* —1D **38**
Totternhoe. *Beds* —3H **51**
Tottington. *G Man* —3F **91**
Totton. *Hants* —1B **16**
Touchenend. *Wind* —4G **37**
Touches. *Som* —2B **13**
Toulvaddie. *High* —5F **165**
Towans, The. *Corn* —3C **4**
Toward. *Arg* —3C **126**
Towcester. *Nptn* —1E **51**
Towednack. *Corn* —3B **4**
Tower End. *Norf* —4F **77**
Towerhill. *Norf* —2B **12**
Tower Hill. *Mers* —4C **90**
Tower Hill. *W Sus* —3C **26**

Towersey. *Oxon* —5F **51**
Towie. *Aber* —2B **152**
Towiemore. *Mor* —4A **160**
Tow Law. *Dur* —1E **105**
Town End. *Cambs* —1D **64**
Town End. *Cumb* —4F **103**
 (nr. Ambleside)
Town End. *Cumb* —2H **103**
 (nr. Appleby)
Town End. *Cumb* —1D **96**
 (nr. Lindale)
Town End. *Cumb* —1C **96**
 (nr. Newby Bridge)
Town End. *Mers* —2G **83**
Townend. *W Dun* —2F **127**
Townfield. *Dur* —5C **114**
Towngate. *Cumb* —5G **113**
Towngate. *Linc* —4A **76**
Town Green. *Lanc* —4B **90**
Town Head. *Cumb* —4E **103**
 (nr. Grasmere)
Town Head. *Cumb* —3H **103**
 (nr. Great Asby)
Townhead. *Cumb* —1G **103**
 (nr. Lazonby)
Townhead. *Cumb* —1B **102**
 (nr. Maryport)
Townhead. *Cumb* —1H **103**
 (nr. Ousby)
Townhead. *Dum* —5D **111**
Townhead of Greenlaw. *Dum* —3E **111**
Townhill. *Fife* —1E **129**
Townhill. *Swan* —3F **31**
Town Kelloe. *Dur* —1A **106**
Town Littleworth. *E Sus* —4F **27**
Town Row. *E Sus* —2G **27**
Towns End. *Hants* —1D **24**
Townsend. *Herts* —5B **52**
Townshend. *Corn* —3C **4**
Town Street. *Suff* —2G **65**
Town Yetholm.*Scot* —2C **120**
Towthorpe. *E Yor* —3C **100**
Towthorpe. *York* —4A **100**
Towton. *N Yor* —1E **93**
Towyn. *Cnwy* —3B **82**
Toxteth. *Mers* —2F **83**
Toynton All Saints. *Linc* —4C **88**
Toynton Fen Side. *Linc* —4C **88**
Toynton St Peter. *Linc* —4D **88**
Toy's Hill. *Kent* —5F **39**
Trabboch. *E Ayr* —2D **116**
Traboe. *Corn* —4E **5**
Tradespark. *High* —3C **158**
Trafford Park. *G Man* —1B **84**
Trallong. *Powy* —3C **46**
Tranent. *E Lot* —2H **129**
Tranmere. *Mers* —2F **83**
Trantlebeg. *High* —3A **168**
Tranwell. *Nmbd* —1E **115**
Trapp. *Carm* —4G **45**
Traquair. *Scot* —1F **119**
Trash Green. *W Ber* —5E **37**
Trawden. *Lanc* —1H **91**
Trawscoed. *Powy* —2D **46**
Trawsfynydd. *Gwyn* —2G **69**
Trawsgoed. *Cdgn* —3F **57**
Treaddow. *Here* —3A **48**
Trealaw. *Rhon* —2D **32**
Treales. *Lanc* —1C **90**
Trearddur. *IOA* —3B **80**
Treaslane. *High* —3C **154**
Treator. *Corn* —1D **6**
Trebanog. *Rhon* —2D **32**
Trebanos. *Neat* —5H **45**
Trebarber. *Corn* —2C **6**
Trebartha. *Corn* —5C **10**
Trebarwith. *Corn* —4A **10**
Trebetherick. *Corn* —1D **6**
Treborough. *Som* —3D **20**
Trebudannon. *Corn* —2C **6**
Trebullett. *Corn* —5D **10**
Treburley. *Corn* —5D **10**

Treburrick. *Corn* —1C **6**
Trebyan. *Corn* —2E **7**
Trecastle. *Powy* —3B **46**
Trecenydd. *Cphy* —3E **33**
Trecott. *Devn* —2G **11**
Trecwn. *Pemb* —1D **42**
Trecynon. *Rhon* —5C **46**
Tredaule. *Corn* —4C **10**
Tredegar. *Blae* —5E **47**
Trederwen. *Powy* —4E **71**
Tredington. *Glos* —3E **49**
Tredington. *Warw* —1A **50**
Tredinnick. *Corn* —2F **7**
 (nr. Bodmin)
Tredinnick. *Corn* —3G **7**
 (nr. Looe)
Tredinnick. *Corn* —1D **6**
 (nr. Padstow)
Tredogan. *V Glam* —5D **32**
Tredomen. *Powy* —2E **46**
Tredunnock. *Mon* —2G **33**
Tredustan. *Powy* —2E **47**
Treen. *Corn* —4A **4**
 (nr. Land's End)
Treen. *Corn* —3B **4**
 (nr. St Ives)
Treeton. *S Yor* —2B **86**
Trefaldwyn. *Powy* —1E **58**
Trefasser. *Pemb* —1C **42**
Trefdraeth. *IOA* —3D **80**
Trefdraeth. *Pemb* —1E **43**
Trefecca. *Powy* —2E **47**
Trefechan. *Mer T* —5D **46**
Trefeglwys. *Powy* —1B **58**
Trefeitha. *Powy* —2E **46**
Trefenter. *Cdgn* —4F **57**
Treffgarne. *Pemb* —2D **42**
Treffynnon. *Flin* —3D **82**
Treffynnon. *Pemb* —2C **42**
Trefil. *Blae* —4E **46**
Trefilan. *Cdgn* —5E **57**
Trefin. *Pemb* —1C **42**
Treflach. *Shrp* —3E **71**
Trefnant. *Den* —3C **82**
Trefonen. *Shrp* —3E **71**
Trefor. *Gwyn* —1C **68**
Trefor. *IOA* —3C **80**
Treforest. *Rhon* —3D **32**
Trefrew. *Corn* —4B **10**
Trefriw. *Cnwy* —4G **81**
Tref-y-Clawdd. *Powy* —3E **59**
Trefynwy. *Mon* —4A **48**
Tregada. *Corn* —4D **10**
Tregadillett. *Corn* —4D **10**
Tregare. *Mon* —4H **47**
Tregarne. *Corn* —4E **5**
Tregaron. *Cdgn* —5F **57**
Tregarth. *Gwyn* —4F **81**
Tregear. *Corn* —3C **6**
Tregeare. *Corn* —4C **10**
Tregeiriog. *Wrex* —2D **70**
Tregele. *IOA* —1C **80**
Tregiskey. *Corn* —4E **6**
Tregole. *Corn* —3B **10**
Tregolwyn. *V Glam* —4C **32**
Tregonetha. *Corn* —2D **6**
Tregonhawke. *Corn* —3A **8**
Tregony. *Corn* —4D **6**
Tregoodwell. *Corn* —4B **10**
Tregorrick. *Corn* —3E **6**
Tregoss. *Corn* —2D **6**
Tregowris. *Corn* —4E **5**
Tregoyd. *Powy* —2E **47**
Tregrehan Mills. *Corn* —3E **7**
Tre-groes. *Cdgn* —1E **45**
Tregullon. *Corn* —2E **7**
Tregurrian. *Corn* —2C **6**
Tregynon. *Powy* —1C **58**
Trehafod. *Rhon* —2D **32**
Trehan. *Corn* —3A **8**
Treharris. *Mer T* —2E **32**
Treherbert. *Rhon* —2C **32**
Trehunist. *Corn* —2H **7**

Trekenner. *Corn* —5D **10**
Trekenning. *Corn* —2D **6**
Treknow. *Corn* —4A **10**
Trelales. *B'end* —3B **32**
Trelan. *Corn* —5E **5**
Trelash. *Corn* —3B **10**
Trelassick. *Corn* —3C **6**
Trelawnyd. *Flin* —3C **82**
Trelech. *Carm* —1G **43**
Treleddyd-fawr. *Pemb* —2B **42**
Trelewis. *Mer T* —2E **32**
Treligga. *Corn* —4A **10**
Trelights. *Corn* —1D **6**
Trelill. *Corn* —5A **10**
Trelissick. *Corn* —5C **6**
Trelleck. *Mon* —5A **48**
Trelleck Grange. *Mon* —5H **47**
Trelogan. *Flin* —2D **82**
Trelystan. *Powy* —5E **71**
Tremadog. *Gwyn* —1E **69**
Tremail. *Corn* —4B **10**
Tremain. *Cdgn* —1C **44**
Tremaine. *Corn* —4C **10**
Tremar. *Corn* —2G **7**
Trematon. *Corn* —3H **7**
Tremeirchion. *Den* —3C **82**
Tremore. *Corn* —2E **6**
Tremorfa. *Card* —4F **33**
Trenance. *Corn* —5D **4**
 (nr. Helston)
Trenance. *Corn* —2C **6**
 (nr. Newquay)
Trenance. *Corn* —1D **6**
 (nr. Padstow)
Trenarren. *Corn* —4E **7**
Trench. *Telf* —4A **72**
Trencreek. *Corn* —2C **6**
Trendeal. *Corn* —3C **6**
Trenear. *Corn* —5A **6**
Treneglos. *Corn* —4C **10**
Trenewan. *Corn* —3F **7**
Trengune. *Corn* —3B **10**
Trent. *Dors* —1A **14**
Trentham. *Stoke* —1C **72**
Trentishoe. *Devn* —2G **19**
Trentlock. *Derbs* —2B **74**
Treoes. *V Glam* —4C **32**
Treorchy. *Rhon* —2C **32**
Treorci. *Rhon* —2C **32**
Tre'r-ddol. *Cdgn* —1F **57**
Tre'r Llai. *Powy* —5E **71**
Trerulefoot. *Corn* —3H **7**
Tresaith. *Cdgn* —5B **56**
Trescott. *Staf* —1C **60**
Trescowe. *Corn* —3C **4**
Tresham. *Glos* —2C **34**
Tresigin. *V Glam* —4C **32**
Tresillian. *Corn* —4C **6**
Tresimwn. *V Glam* —4D **32**
Tresinney. *Corn* —4B **10**
Treskillard. *Corn* —5A **6**
Treskinnick Cross. *Corn* —3C **10**
Tresmeer. *Corn* —4C **10**
Tresparrett. *Corn* —3B **10**
Tresparrett Posts. *Corn* —3B **10**
Tressady. *High* —3D **164**
Tressait. *Per* —2F **143**
Tresta. *Shet* —6E **173**
Treswell. *Notts* —3E **87**
Treswithian. *Corn* —2D **4**
Tre Taliesin. *Cdgn* —1F **57**
Trethomas. *Cphy* —3E **33**
Trethosa. *Corn* —3D **6**
Trethurgy. *Corn* —3E **7**
Tretio. *Pemb* —2B **42**
Tretire. *Here* —3A **48**
Tretower. *Powy* —3E **47**
Treuddyn. *Flin* —5E **83**
Trevadlock. *Corn* —5C **10**
Trevalga. *Corn* —3A **10**
Trevalyn. *Wrex* —5F **83**
Trevance. *Corn* —1D **6**
Trevanger. *Corn* —1D **6**

Uplees—Walcot Green

Uplees. Kent —4D 40
Uploders. Dors —3A 14
Uplowman. Devn —1D 12
Uplyme. Devn —3G 13
Up Marden. W Sus —1F 17
Upminster. G Lon —2G 39
Up Nately. Hants —1E 25
Upottery. Devn —2F 13
Uppat. High —3F 165
Upper Affcot. Shrp —2G 59
Upper Arley. Worc —2B 60
Upper Armley. W Yor —1C 92
Upper Arncott. Oxon —4E 50
Upper Astrop. Nptn —2D 50
Upper Badcall. High —4B 166
Upper Bangor. Gwyn —3E 81
Upper Basildon. W Ber —4D 36
Upper Batley. W Yor —2C 92
Upper Beeding. W Sus —4C 26
Upper Benefield. Nptn —2G 63
Upper Bentley. Worc —4D 61
Upper Bighouse. High —3A 168
Upper Boddam. Aber —5D 160
Upper Boddington. Nptn —5B 62
Upper Booth. Derbs —2F 85
Upper Borth. Cdgn —2F 57
Upper Boyndlie. Aber —2G 161
Upper Brailes. Warw —2B 50
Upper Breakish. High —1E 147
Upper Breinton. Here —1H 47
Upper Broadheath. Worc —5C 60
Upper Broughton. Notts —3D 74
Upper Brynamman. Carm —4H 45
Upper Bucklebury. W Ber —5D 36
Upper Bullington. Hants —2C 24
Upper Burgate. Hants —1G 15
Upper Caldecote. Beds —1B 52
Upper Canterton. Hants —1A 16
Upper Catesby. Nptn —5C 62
Upper Chapel. Powy —1D 46
Upper Cheddon. Som —4F 21
Upper Chicksgrove. Wilts —4E 23
Upper Church Village. Rhon —3D 32
Upper Chute. Wilts —1A 24
Upper Clatford. Hants —2B 24
Upper Coberley. Glos —4E 49
Upper Coedcae. Torf —5F 47
Upper Cokeham. W Sus —5C 26
Upper Common. Hants —2E 25
Upper Cound. Shrp —5H 71
Upper Cudworth. S Yor —4D 93
Upper Cumberworth. W Yor —4C 92
Upper Cuttlehill. Aber —4B 160
Upper Cwmbran. Torf —2F 33
Upper Dallachy. Mor —2A 160
Upper Dean. Beds —4H 63
Upper Dean. Devn —2D 8
Upper Denby. W Yor —4C 92
Upper Derraid. High —5E 159
Upper Diabaig. High —2H 155
Upper Dicker. E Sus —5G 27
Upper Dinchope. Shrp —2G 59
Upper Dochcarty. High —2H 157
Upper Dounreay. High —2B 168
Upper Dovercourt. Essx —2F 55
Upper Dunsforth. N Yor —3G 99
Upper Dunsley. Herts —4H 51
Upper Eastern Green. W Mid —3G 61
Upper Elkstone. Staf —5E 85
Upper Ellastone. Staf —1F 73
Upper End. Derbs —3E 85
Upper Enham. Hants —2B 24
Upper Farringdon. Hants —3F 25
Upper Framilode. Glos —4C 48
Upper Froyle. Hants —2F 25
Upper Gills. High —1F 169
Upper Glenfintaig. High —5E 149
Upper Godney. Som —2H 21
Upper Gravenhurst. Beds —2B 52
Upper Green. Essx —2E 53
Upper Green. W Ber —5B 36
Upper Green. W Yor —2C 92
Upper Grove Common. Here —3A 48
Upper Hackney. Derbs —4G 85
Upper Hale. Surr —2G 25
Upper Halliford. Surr —4B 38
Upper Halling. Medw —4A 40
Upper Hambleton. Rut —5G 75
Upper Hardwick. Here —5G 59
Upper Hartfield. E Sus —2F 27
Upper Haugh. S Yor —1B 86
Upper Hayton. Shrp —2H 59
Upper Heath. Shrp —2H 59
Upper Hellesdon. Norf —4E 79
Upper Helmsley. N Yor —4A 100
Upper Hengoed. Shrp —2E 71
Upper Hergest. Here —5E 59
Upper Heyford. Nptn —5D 62
Upper Heyford. Oxon —3C 50
Upper Hill. Here —5G 59
Upper Hindhope. Scot —4B 120
Upper Hopton. W Yor —3B 92
Upper Horsebridge. E Sus —4C 28
Upper Howsell. Worc —1C 48
Upper Hulme. Staf —4E 85
Upper Inglesham. Swin —2H 35
Upper Kilcott. S Glo —3C 34
Upper Killay. Swan —3E 31
Upper Kirkton. Aber —5E 161
Upper Kirkton. N Ayr —4C 126
Upper Knockando. Mor —4F 159
Upper Knockchoilum. High —2G 149
Upper Lambourn. W Ber —3B 36
Upper Langford. N Som —1H 21
Upper Langwith. Derbs —4C 86
Upper Largo. Fife —3G 137
Upper Latheron. High —5D 169
Upper Layham. Suff —1D 54
Upper Leigh. Staf —2E 73
Upper Lenie. High —1H 149
Upper Lochton. Aber —4D 152
Upper Longdon. Staf —4E 73
Upper Longwood. Shrp —5A 72
Upper Lybster. High —5E 169
Upper Lydbrook. Glos —4B 48
Upper Lye. Here —4F 59
Upper Maes-coed. Here —2G 47
Uppermill. G Man —4H 91
Upper Millichope. Shrp —2H 59
Upper Milovaig. High —4A 154
Upper Minety. Wilts —2F 35
Upper Mitton. Worc —3C 60
Upper Nash. Pemb —4E 43
Upper Netchwood. Shrp —1A 60
Upper Nobut. Staf —2E 73
Upper North Dean. Buck —2G 37
Upper Norwood. W Sus —4A 26
Upper Nyland. Dors —4C 22
Upper Oddington. Glos —3H 49
Upper Ollach. High —5E 155
Upper Outwoods. Staf —3G 73
Upper Padley. Derbs —3G 85
Upper Pennington. Hants —3B 16
Upper Poppleton. York —4H 99
Upper Quinton. Warw —1G 49
Upper Rochford. Worc —4A 60
Upper Rusko. Dum —3C 110
Upper Sandaig. High —2F 147
Upper Sanday. Orkn —7E 172
Upper Sapey. Here —4A 60
Upper Seagry. Wilts —3E 35
Upper Shelton. Beds —1H 51
Upper Sheringham. Norf —1D 78
Upper Skelmorlie. N Ayr —3C 126
Upper Slaughter. Glos —3G 49
Upper Sonachan. Arg —1H 133
Upper Soudley. Glos —4B 48
Upper Staploe. Beds —5A 64
Upper Stoke. Norf —5E 79
Upper Stondon. Beds —2B 52
Upper Stowe. Nptn —5D 62
Upper Street. Hants —1G 15
Upper Street. Norf —4F 79
(nr. Horning)
Upper Street. Norf —4F 79
(nr. Hoveton)
Upper Street. Suff —2E 55
Upper Strensham. Worc —2E 49
Upper Studley. Wilts —1D 22
Upper Sundon. Beds —3A 52
Upper Swell. Glos —3G 49
Upper Tankersley. S Yor —1H 85
Upper Tean. Staf —2E 73
Upperthong. W Yor —4B 92
Upperthorpe. N Lin —4A 94
Upper Thurnham. Lanc —4D 96
Upper Tillyrie. Per —3D 136
Upperton. W Sus —3A 26
Upper Tooting. G Lon —3D 38
Uppertown. Derbs —4H 85
(nr. Ashover)
Upper Town. Derbs —5G 85
(nr. Bonsall)
Upper Town. Derbs —5G 85
(nr. Hognaston)
Upper Town. Here —1A 48
Uppertown. High —1F 169
Upper Town. N Som —5A 34
Uppertown. Nmbd —2B 114
Uppertown. Orkn —8D 172
Upper Tysoe. Warw —1B 50
Upper Upham. Wilts —4H 35
Upper Upnor. Medw —3B 40
Upper Urquhart. Fife —3D 136
Upper Wardington. Oxon —1C 50
Upper Weald. Mil —2F 51
Upper Weedon. Nptn —5D 62
Upper Wellingham. E Sus —4F 27
Upper Whiston. S Yor —2B 86
Upper Wield. Hants —3E 25
Upper Winchendon. Buck —4F 51
Upperwood. Derbs —5G 85
Upper Woodford. Wilts —3G 23
Upper Wootton. Hants —1D 24
Upper Wraxall. Wilts —4D 34
Upper Wyche. Here —1C 48
Uppincott. Devn —2B 12
Uppingham. Rut —1F 63
Uppington. Shrp —5H 71
Upsall. N Yor —1G 99
Upsettlington. Scot —5E 131
Upshire. Essx —5E 53
Up Somborne. Hants —3B 24
Upstreet. Kent —4G 41
Up Sydling. Dors —2B 14
Upthorpe. Suff —3B 66
Upton. Buck —4F 51
Upton. Cambs —3A 64
Upton. Ches —4G 83
Upton. Corn —2C 10
(nr. Bude)
Upton. Corn —5C 10
(nr. Liskeard)
Upton. Cumb —1E 102
Upton. Devn —2D 12
(nr. Honiton)
Upton. Devn —4D 8
(nr. Kingsbridge)
Upton. Dors —3E 15
(nr. Poole)
Upton. Dors —4C 14
(nr. Weymouth)
Upton. E Yor —4F 101
Upton. Hants —1B 24
(nr. Andover)
Upton. Hants —1B 16
(nr. Southampton)
Upton. IOW —3D 16
Upton. Leics —1A 62
Upton. Linc —2F 87
Upton. Mers —2E 83
Upton. Norf —4F 79
Upton. Nptn —4E 62
Upton. Notts —3E 87
(nr. East Retford)
Upton. Notts —5E 87
(nr. Southwell)
Upton. Oxon —3D 36
Upton. Pemb —4E 43
Upton. Pet —5A 76
Upton. Slo —3A 38
Upton. Som —4H 21
(nr. Somerton)
Upton. Som —4C 20
(nr. Wiveliscombe)
Upton. Warw —5F 61
Upton. W Yor —3E 93
Upton. Wilts —3D 22
Upton Bishop. Here —3B 48
Upton Cheyney. S Glo —5B 34
Upton Cressett. Shrp —1A 60
Upton Crews. Here —3B 48
Upton Cross. Corn —5C 10
Upton End. Beds —2B 52
Upton Grey. Hants —2E 25
Upton Heath. Ches —4G 83
Upton Hellions. Devn —2B 12
Upton Lovell. Wilts —2E 23
Upton Magna. Shrp —4H 71
Upton Noble. Som —3C 22
Upton Pyne. Devn —3C 12
Upton St Leonards. Glos —4D 48
Upton Scudamore. Wilts —2D 22
Upton Snodsbury. Worc —5D 60
Upton upon Severn. Worc —1D 48
Upton Warren. Worc —4D 60
Upwaltham. W Sus —4A 26
Upware. Cambs —3E 65
Upwell. Cambs —5D 77
Upwey. Dors —4B 14
Upwick Green. Herts —3E 53
Upwood. Cambs —2B 64
Urafirth. Shet —4E 173
Uragaig. Arg —3A 132
Urchany. High —4C 158
Urchfont. Wilts —1F 23
Urdimarsh. Here —1A 48
Ure. Shet —4D 173
Ure Bank. N Yor —2F 99
Urgha. W Isl —8D 171
Urlay Nook. Stoc T —3B 106
Urmston. G Man —1B 84
Urquhart. Mor —2G 159
Urra. N Yor —4C 106
Urray. High —3H 157
Usan. Ang —3G 145
Ushaw Moor. Dur —5F 115
Usk. Mon —5G 47
Usselby. Linc —1H 87
Usworth. Tyne —4G 115
Uton. Devn —3B 12
Utterby. Linc —1C 88
Uttoxeter. Staf —2E 73
Uwchmynydd. Gwyn —3A 68
Uxbridge. G Lon —2B 38
Uyeasound. Shet —1G 173
Uzmaston. Pemb —3D 42

Valley. IOA —3B 80
Valley End. Surr —4A 38
Valley Truckle. Corn —4B 10
Valtos. High —2E 155
Van. Powy —2B 58
Vange. Essx —2B 40
Varteg. Torf —5F 47
Vatten. High —4B 154
Vaul. Arg —4B 138
Vauld, The. Here —1A 48
Vaynol. Gwyn —3E 81
Vaynor. Mer T —4D 46
Veensgarth. Shet —7F 173
Velindre. Powy —2E 47
Vellow. Som —3D 20
Velly. Devn —4C 18
Venhay. Devn —1A 12
Venn. Devn —4D 8
Venngreen. Devn —1D 11
Vennington. Shrp —5F 71
Venn Ottery. Devn —3D 12
Venn's Green. Here —1A 48
Venny Tedburn. Devn —3B 12
Venterdon. Corn —5D 10
Ventnor. IOW —5D 16
Vernham Dean. Hants —1B 24
Vernham Street. Hants —1B 24
Vernolds Common. Shrp —2G 59
Verwood. Dors —2F 15
Veryan. Corn —5D 6
Veryan Green. Corn —4D 6
Vicarage. Devn —4F 13
Vickerstown. Cumb —3A 96
Victoria. Corn —2D 6
Vidlin. Shet —5F 173
Viewpark. N Lan —3A 128
Vigo. W Mid —5E 73
Vigo Village. Kent —4H 39
Vinehall Street. E Sus —3B 28
Vine's Cross. E Sus —4G 27
Viney Hill. Glos —5B 48
Virginia Water. Surr —4A 38
Virginstow. Devn —3D 11
Vobster. Som —2C 22
Voe. Shet —5F 173
Vole. Som —2G 21
Vowchurch. Here —2G 47
Vulcan Village. Warr —1H 83

Wackerfield. Dur —2E 105
Wacton. Norf —1D 66
Wadborough. Worc —1E 49
Waddesdon. Buck —4F 51
Waddeton. Devn —3E 9
Waddicar. Mers —1F 83
Waddingham. Linc —1G 87
Waddington. Lanc —5G 97
Waddington. Linc —4G 87
Waddon. Devn —5B 12
Wadebridge. Corn —1D 6
Wadeford. Som —1G 13
Wadenhoe. Nptn —2H 63
Wadesmill. Herts —4D 52
Wadhurst. E Sus —2H 27
Wadshelf. Derbs —3H 85
Wadsley. S Yor —1H 85
Wadsley Bridge. S Yor —1H 85
Wadswick. Wilts —5D 34
Wadwick. Hants —1C 24
Wadworth. S Yor —1C 86
Waen. Den —4C 82
(nr. Bodfari)
Waen. Den —4D 82
(nr. Llandyrnog)
Waen. Den —4B 82
(nr. Nantglyn)
Waen. Powy —1B 58
Waen Fach. Powy —4E 70
Waen Goleugoed. Den —3C 82
Wag. High —1H 165
Wainfleet All Saints. Linc —5D 89
Wainfleet Bank. Linc —5D 88
Wainfleet St Mary. Linc —5D 89
Wainhouse Corner. Corn —3B 10
Wainscott. Medw —3B 40
Wainstalls. W Yor —2A 92
Waitby. Cumb —4A 104
Waithe. Linc —4F 95
Wakefield. W Yor —2D 92
Wakerley. Nptn —1G 63
Wakes Colne. Essx —3B 54
Walberswick. Suff —3G 67
Walberton. W Sus —5A 26
Walbottle. Tyne —3E 115
Walby. Cumb —3F 113
Walcombe. Som —2A 22
Walcot. Linc —2H 75
Walcot. N Lin —2B 94
Walcot. Swin —3G 35
Walcot. Telf —4H 71
Walcot. Warw —5F 61
Walcote. Leics —2C 62
Walcot Green. Norf —2D 66

Walcott. *Linc* —5A 88
Walcott. *Norf* —2F 79
Walden. *N Yor* —1C 98
Walden Head. *N Yor* —1B 98
Walden Stubbs. *N Yor* —3F 93
Walderslade. *Medw* —4B 40
Walderton. *W Sus* —1F 17
Walditch. *Dors* —3H 13
Waldley. *Derbs* —2F 73
Waldridge. *Dur* —4F 115
Waldringfield. *Suff* —1F 55
Waldron. *E Sus* —4G 27
Wales. *S Yor* —2B 86
Walesby. *Linc* —1A 88
Walesby. *Notts* —3D 86
Walford. *Here* —3F 59
  (nr. Leintwardine)
Walford. *Here* —3A 48
  (nr. Ross-on-Wye)
Walford. *Shrp* —3G 71
Walford. *Staf* —2C 72
Walford Heath. *Shrp* —4G 71
Walgherton. *Ches* —1A 72
Walgrave. *Nptn* —3F 63
Walhampton. *Hants* —3B 16
Walkden. *G Man* —4F 91
Walker. *Tyne* —3F 115
Walkerburn. *Scot* —1F 119
Walker Fold. *Lanc* —5F 97
Walkeringham. *Notts* —1E 87
Walkerith. *Linc* —1E 87
Walkern. *Herts* —3C 52
Walker's Green. *Here* —1A 48
Walkerton. *Fife* —3E 127
Walkerville. *N Yor* —5F 105
Walkford. *Dors* —3H 15
Walkhampton. *Devn* —2B 8
Walkington. *E Yor* —1C 94
Walkley. *S Yor* —2H 85
Walk Mill. *Lanc* —1G 91
Wall. *Corn* —3D 4
Wall. *Nmbd* —3C 114
Wall. *Staf* —5F 73
Wallaceton. *Dum* —1F 111
Wallacetown. *S Ayr* —2C 116
  (nr. Ayr)
Wallacetown. *S Ayr* —4B 116
  (nr. Dailly)
Wallands Park. *E Sus* —4F 27
Wallasey. *Mers* —1F 83
Wallaston Green. *Pemb* —4D 42
Wallbrook. *W Mid* —1D 60
Wallcrouch. *E Sus* —2A 28
Wall End. *Cumb* —1B 96
Wallend. *Medw* —3C 40
Wall Heath. *W Mid* —2C 60
Wallingford. *Oxon* —3E 36
Wallington. *G Lon* —4D 39
Wallington. *Hants* —2D 16
Wallington. *Herts* —2C 52
Wallis. *Pemb* —2E 43
Wallisdown. *Pool* —3F 15
Walliswood. *Surr* —2C 26
Wall Nook. *Dur* —5F 115
Walls. *Shet* —7D 173
Wallsend. *Tyne* —3G 115
Wallsworth. *Glos* —3D 48
Wall under Heywood. *Shrp* —1H 59
Wallyford. *E Lot* —2G 129
Walmer. *Kent* —5H 41
Walmer Bridge. *Lanc* —2C 90
Walmersley. *G Man* —3G 91
Walmley. *W Mid* —1F 61
Walnut Grove. *Per* —1D 136
Walpole. *Suff* —3F 67
Walpole Cross Keys. *Norf* —4E 77
Walpole Gate. *Norf* —4E 77
Walpole Highway. *Norf* —4E 77
Walpolelane. *Suff* —3F 67
Walpole Marsh. *Norf* —4D 77
Walpole St Andrew. *Norf* —4E 77
Walpole St Peter. *Norf* —4E 77
Walsall. *W Mid* —1E 61

Walsall Wood. *W Mid* —5E 73
Walsden. *W Yor* —2H 91
Walsgrave on Sowe. *W Mid* —2A 62
Walsham le Willows. *Suff* —3C 66
Walshaw. *G Man* —3F 91
Walshford. *N Yor* —4G 99
Walsoken. *Cambs* —4D 76
Walston. *S Lan* —5D 128
Walsworth. *Herts* —2B 52
Walterston. *V Glam* —4D 32
Walterstone. *Here* —3G 47
Waltham. *Kent* —1F 29
Waltham. *NE Lin* —4F 95
Waltham Abbey. *Essx* —5D 53
Waltham Chase. *Hants* —1D 16
Waltham Cross. *Herts* —5D 52
Waltham on the Wolds. *Leics* —3F 75
Waltham St Lawrence. *Wind* —4G 37
Waltham's Cross. *Essx* —2G 53
Walthamstow. *G Lon* —2E 39
Walton. *Cumb* —3G 113
Walton. *Derbs* —4A 86
Walton. *Leics* —2C 62
Walton. *Mers* —1F 83
Walton. *Mil* —2G 51
Walton. *Pet* —5A 76
Walton. *Powy* —5E 59
Walton. *Som* —3H 21
Walton. *Staf* —3C 72
  (nr. Eccleshall)
Walton. *Staf* —2C 72
  (nr. Stone)
Walton. *Suff* —2F 55
Walton. *Telf* —4H 71
Walton. *Warw* —5G 61
Walton. *W Yor* —3D 92
  (nr. Wakefield)
Walton. *W Yor* —5G 99
  (nr. Wetherby)
Walton Cardiff. *Glos* —2E 49
Walton East. *Pemb* —2E 43
Walton Elm. *Dors* —1C 14
Walton Highway. *Norf* —4D 76
Walton-in-Gordano. *N Som* —4H 33
Walton-le-Dale. *Lanc* —2D 90
Walton-on-Thames. *Surr* —4C 38
Walton-on-the-Hill. *Staf* —3D 72
Walton on the Hill. *Surr* —5D 38
Walton-on-the-Naze. *Essx* —3F 55
Walton on the Wolds. *Leics*
  —4C 74
Walton-on-Trent. *Derbs* —4G 73
Walton Park. *N Som* —4H 33
Walton West. *Pemb* —3C 42
Walwick. *Nmbd* —2C 114
Walworth. *Darl* —3F 105
Walworth Gate. *Darl* —2F 105
Walwyn's Castle. *Pemb* —3C 42
Wambrook. *Som* —2F 13
Wampool. *Cumb* —4D 112
Wanborough. *Surr* —1A 26
Wanborough. *Swin* —3H 35
Wandel. *S Lan* —2B 118
Wandsworth. *G Lon* —3D 38
Wangford. *Suff* —2G 65
  (nr. Lakenheath)
Wangford. *Suff* —3G 67
  (nr. Southwold)
Wanlip. *Leics* —4C 74
Wanlockhead. *Dum* —3A 118
Wannock. *E Sus* —5G 27
Wansford. *Cambs* —1H 63
Wansford. *E Yor* —4E 101
Wanshurst Green. *Kent* —1B 28
Wanstead. *G Lon* —2F 39
Wanstrow. *Som* —2C 22
Wanswell. *Glos* —5B 48
Wantage. *Oxon* —3B 36
Wapley. *S Glo* —4C 34
Wappenbury. *Warw* —4A 62
Wappenham. *Nptn* —1E 51
Warbleton. *E Sus* —4H 27
Warblington. *Hants* —2F 17

Warborough. *Devn* —3F 9
Warborough. *Oxon* —2D 36
Warboys. *Cambs* —2C 64
Warbreck. *Bkpl* —1B 90
Warbstow. *Corn* —3C 10
Warburton. *G Man* —2A 84
Warcop. *Cumb* —3A 104
Warden. *Kent* —3E 40
Warden. *Nmbd* —3C 114
Ward End. *W Mid* —2F 61
Ward Green. *Suff* —4C 66
Ward Green Cross. *Lanc* —5F 97
Wardhedges. *Beds* —2A 52
Wardhouse. *Aber* —5C 160
Wardington. *Oxon* —1C 50
Wardle. *Ches* —5A 84
Wardle. *G Man* —3H 91
Wardley. *Rut* —5F 75
Wardley. *W Sus* —4G 25
Wardlow. *Derbs* —3F 85
Wardsend. *Ches* —2D 84
Wardy Hill. *Cambs* —2D 64
Ware. *Herts* —4D 52
Ware. *Kent* —4G 41
Wareham. *Dors* —4E 15
Warehorne. *Kent* —2D 28
Warenford. *Nmbd* —2F 121
Waren Mill. *Nmbd* —1F 121
Warenton. *Nmbd* —1F 121
Wareside. *Herts* —4D 53
Waresley. *Cambs* —5B 64
Waresley. *Worc* —4C 60
Warfield. *Brac* —4G 37
Warfleet. *Devn* —3E 9
Wargate. *Linc* —2B 76
Wargrave. *Wok* —4F 37
Warham. *Norf* —1B 78
Wark. *Nmbd* —1C 120
  (nr. Coldstream)
Wark. *Nmbd* —2B 114
  (nr. Hexham)
Warkleigh. *Devn* —4G 19
Warkton. *Nptn* —3F 63
Warkworth. *Nptn* —1C 50
Warkworth. *Nmbd* —4G 121
Warlaby. *N Yor* —5A 106
Warland. *W Yor* —2H 91
Warleggan. *Corn* —2F 7
Warlingham. *Surr* —5E 39
Warmanbie. *Dum* —3C 112
Warmfield. *W Yor* —2D 92
Warmingham. *Ches* —4B 84
Warminghurst. *W Sus* —4C 26
Warmington. *Nptn* —1H 63
Warmington. *Warw* —1C 50
Warminster. *Wilts* —2D 23
Warmley. *S Glo* —4B 34
Warmsworth. *S Yor* —4F 93
Warmwell. *Dors* —4C 14
Warndon. *Worc* —5C 60
Warners End. *Herts* —5A 52
Warnford. *Hants* —4E 24
Warnham. *W Sus* —2C 26
Warningcamp. *W Sus* —5B 26
Warninglid. *W Sus* —3D 26
Warren. *Ches* —3C 84
Warren. *Pemb* —5D 42
Warrenby. *Red C* —2C 106
Warren Corner. *Hants* —2G 25
  (nr. Aldershot)
Warren Corner. *Hants* —4F 25
  (nr. Petersfield)
Warren Row. *Wind* —3G 37
Warren Street. *Kent* —5D 40
Warrington. *Mil* —5F 63
Warrington. *Warr* —2A 84
Warsash. *Hants* —2C 16
Warse. *High* —1F 169
Warslow. *Staf* —5E 85
Warsop Vale. *Notts* —4C 86
Warter. *E Yor* —4C 100
Warthermarske. *N Yor* —2E 98
Warthill. *N Yor* —4A 100

Wartling. *E Sus* —5A 28
Wartnaby. *Leics* —3E 74
Warton. *Lanc* —2D 97
  (nr. Carnforth)
Warton. *Lanc* —2C 90
  (nr. Freckleton)
Warton. *Nmbd* —4E 121
Warton. *Warw* —5G 73
Warwick. *Cumb* —4F 113
Warwick. *Warw* —4G 61
Warwick Bridge. *Cumb* —4F 113
Warwick Wold. *Surr* —5E 39
Wasbister. *Orkn* —4C 172
Wasdale Head. *Cumb* —4C 102
Wash. *Derbs* —2E 85
Washaway. *Corn* —2E 7
Washbourne. *Devn* —3E 9
Washbrook. *Suff* —1E 54
Wash Common. *W Ber* —5C 36
Washerwall. *Staf* —1D 72
Washfield. *Devn* —1C 12
Washfold. *N Yor* —4D 104
Washford. *Som* —2D 20
Washford Pyne. *Devn* —1B 12
Washingborough. *Linc* —3H 87
Washington. *Tyne* —4G 115
Washington. *W Sus* —4C 26
Washington Village. *Tyne* —4G 115
Waskerley. *Dur* —5D 114
Wasperton. *Warw* —5G 61
Wasp Green. *Surr* —1E 27
Wasps Nest. *Linc* —4H 87
Wass. *N Yor* —2H 99
Watchet. *Som* —2D 20
Watchfield. *Oxon* —2H 35
Watchgate. *Cumb* —5G 103
Watchhill. *Cumb* —5C 112
Watcombe. *Torb* —2F 9
Watendlath. *Cumb* —3D 102
Water. *Devn* —4A 12
Water. *Lanc* —2G 91
Waterbeach. *Cambs* —4D 65
Waterbeach. *W Sus* —2G 17
Waterbeck. *Dum* —2D 112
Waterditch. *Hants* —3G 15
Water End. *Beds* —2A 52
Water End. *E Yor* —1A 94
Water End. *Herts* —5C 52
  (nr. Hatfield)
Water End. *Herts* —4A 52
  (nr. Hemel Hempstead)
Waterfall. *Staf* —5E 85
Waterfoot. *E Ren* —4G 127
Waterfoot. *Lanc* —2G 91
Waterford. *Herts* —4D 52
Water Fryston. *W Yor* —2E 93
Waterhead. *Cumb* —4E 103
Waterhead. *E Ayr* —3E 117
Waterhead. *S Ayr* —5C 116
Waterheads. *Scot* —4F 129
Waterhouses. *Dur* —5E 115
Waterhouses. *Staf* —5E 85
Wateringbury. *Kent* —5A 40
Waterlane. *Glos* —5E 49
Waterlip. *Som* —2B 22
Waterloo. *Cphy* —3E 33
Waterloo. *Corn* —5B 10
Waterloo. *Derbs* —4B 86
Waterloo. *Here* —1G 47
Waterloo. *High* —1E 147
Waterloo. *Mers* —1F 83
Waterloo. *Norf* —4E 78
Waterloo. *N Lan* —4B 128
Waterloo. *Pemb* —4D 42
Waterloo. *Per* —5H 143
Waterloo. *Pool* —3F 15
Waterloo. *Shrp* —2G 71
Waterlooville. *Hants* —2E 17
Watermillock. *Cumb* —2F 103
Water Newton. *Cambs* —1A 64
Water Orton. *Warw* —1F 61
Waterperry. *Oxon* —5E 51

Waterrow. *Som* —4D 20
Watersfield. *W Sus* —4B 26
Waterside. *Buck* —5H 51
Waterside. *Cambs* —3F 65
Waterside. *Cumb* —5D 112
Waterside. *E Ayr* —4D 116
  (nr. Ayr)
Waterside. *E Ayr* —5F 127
  (nr. Kilmarnock)
Waterside. *E Dun* —2H 127
Waterstein. *High* —4A 154
Waterstock. *Oxon* —5E 51
Waterston. *Pemb* —4D 42
Water Stratford. *Buck* —2E 51
Waters Upton. *Telf* —4A 72
Water Yeat. *Cumb* —1B 96
Watford. *Herts* —1B 38
Watford. *Nptn* —4D 62
Wath. *Cumb* —4H 103
Wath. *N Yor* —3D 98
  (nr. Pateley Bridge)
Wath. *N Yor* —2F 99
  (nr. Ripon)
Wath Brow. *Cumb* —3B 102
Wath upon Dearne. *S Yor* —1B 86
Watlington. *Norf* —4F 77
Watlington. *Oxon* —2E 37
Watten. *High* —3E 169
Wattisfield. *Suff* —3C 66
Wattisham. *Suff* —5C 66
Wattlesborough Heath. *Shrp* —4F 71
Watton. *Dors* —3H 13
Watton. *E Yor* —5E 101
Watton. *Norf* —5B 78
Watton at Stone. *Herts* —4C 52
Wattston. *N Lan* —2A 128
Wattstown. *Rhon* —2D 32
Wattsville. *Cphy* —2F 33
Wauldby. *E Yor* —2C 94
Waulkmill. *Aber* —4D 152
Waun. *Powy* —4E 71
Waunarlwydd. *Swan* —3F 31
Waun Fawr. *Cdgn* —2E 57
Waungilwen. *Carm* —1H 43
Waunlwyd. *Blae* —5E 47
Waun-y-Clyn. *Carm* —5E 45
Wavendon. *Mil* —2H 51
Waverbridge. *Cumb* —5D 112
Waverley. *Surr* —2G 25
Waverton. *Ches* —4G 83
Waverton. *Cumb* —5D 112
Wavertree. *Mers* —2F 83
Wawne. *E Yor* —1D 94
Waxham. *Norf* —3G 79
Waxholme. *E Yor* —2G 95
Wayford. *Som* —2H 13
Way Head. *Cambs* —2D 65
Waytown. *Dors* —3H 13
Way Village. *Devn* —1B 12
Wdig. *Pemb* —1D 42
Wealdstone. *G Lon* —1C 38
Weardley. *W Yor* —5E 99
Weare. *Som* —1H 21
Weare Giffard. *Devn* —4E 19
Wearhead. *Dur* —1B 104
Wearne. *Som* —4H 21
Weasdale. *Cumb* —4H 103
Weasenham All Saints. *Norf* —3H 77
Weasenham St Peter. *Norf* —3A 78
Weaverham. *Ches* —3A 84
Weaverthorpe. *N Yor* —2D 100
Webheath. *Worc* —4E 61
Webton. *Here* —2H 47
Wedderlairs. *Aber* —5F 161
Weddington. *Warw* —1A 62
Wedhampton. *Wilts* —1F 23
Wedmore. *Som* —2H 21
Wednesbury. *W Mid* —1D 61
Wednesfield. *W Mid* —5D 72
Weecar. *Notts* —4F 87
Weedon. *Buck* —4G 51
Weedon Bec. *Nptn* —5D 62

Weedon Lois—Westleigh

Weedon Lois. Nptn —1E 50
Weeford. Staf —5F 73
Week. Devn —4F 19
(nr. Barnstaple)
Week. Devn —2G 11
(nr. Okehampton)
Week. Devn —1H 11
(nr. South Molton)
Week. Devn —2D 9
(nr. Totnes)
Week. Som —3C 20
Weeke. Devn —2A 12
Weeke. Hants —3C 24
Week Green. Corn —3C 10
Weekley. Nptn —2F 63
Week St Mary. Corn —3C 10
Weel. E Yor —1D 94
Weeley. Essx —3E 55
Weeley Heath. Essx —3E 55
Weem. Per —4F 143
Weeping Cross. Staf —3D 72
Weethly. Warw —5E 61
Weeting. Norf —2G 65
Weeton. E Yor —2G 95
Weeton. Lanc —1B 90
Weeton. N Yor —5E 99
Weetwood Hall. Nmbd —2E 121
Weir. Lanc —2G 91
Welbeck Abbey. Notts —3C 86
Welborne. Norf —4C 78
Welbourn. Linc —5G 87
Welburn. N Yor —1A 100
(nr. Kirkbymoorside)
Welburn. N Yor —3B 100
(nr. Malton)
Welbury. N Yor —4A 106
Welby. Linc —2G 75
Welches Dam. Cambs —2D 64
Welcombe. Devn —1C 10
Weld Bank. Lanc —3D 90
Weldon. Nptn —2G 63
Weldon. Nmbd —5F 121
Welford. Nptn —2D 62
Welford. W Ber —4C 36
Welford-on-Avon. Warw —5F 61
Welham. Leics —1E 63
Welham. Notts —2E 87
Welham Green. Herts —5C 52
Well. Hants —2F 25
Well. Linc —3D 88
Well. N Yor —1E 99
Welland. Worc —1C 48
Wellbank. Ang —5D 144
Well Bottom. Dors —1E 15
Welldale. Dum —3C 112
Wellesbourne. Warw —5G 61
Well Hill. Kent —4F 39
Wellhouse. W Ber —4D 36
Welling. G Lon —3F 39
Wellingborough. Nptn —4F 63
Wellingham. Norf —3A 78
Wellingore. Linc —5G 87
Wellington. Cumb —4B 102
Wellington. Here —1H 47
Wellington. Som —4E 21
Wellington. Telf —4A 72
Wellington Heath. Here —1C 48
Wellow. Bath —1C 22
Wellow. IOW —4B 16
Wellow. Notts —4D 86
Wellpond Green. Herts —3E 53
Wells. Som —2A 22
Wellsborough. Leics —5A 74
Wells Green. Ches —5A 84
Wells-next-the-Sea. Norf —1B 78
Wells of Ythan. Aber —5D 160
Wellswood. Torb —2F 9
Wellwood. Fife —1D 129
Welney. Norf —1E 65
Welsford. Devn —4C 18
Welshampton. Shrp —2G 71
Welsh End. Shrp —2H 71
Welsh Frankton. Shrp —2F 71
Welsh Hook. Pemb —2D 42
Welsh Newton. Here —4H 47
Welsh Newton Common. Here —4A 48
Welshpool. Powy —5E 70
Welsh St Donats. V Glam —4D 32
Welton. Bath —1B 22
Welton. Cumb —5E 113
Welton. E Yor —2C 94
Welton. Linc —3H 87
Welton. Nptn —4C 62
Welton Hill. Linc —2H 87
Welton le Marsh. Linc —4D 88
Welton le Wold. Linc —2B 88
Welwick. E Yor —2G 95
Welwyn. Herts —4C 52
Welwyn Garden City. Herts —4C 52
Wem. Shrp —3H 71
Wembdon. Som —3F 21
Wembley. G Lon —2C 38
Wembury. Devn —4B 8
Wembworthy. Devn —2G 11
Wemyss Bay. Inv —2C 126
Wenallt. Cdgn —3F 57
Wenallt. Gwyn —1B 70
Wendens Ambo. Essx —2F 53
Wending. Norf —4B 78
Wendlebury. Oxon —4D 50
Wendover. Buck —5G 51
Wendron. Corn —5A 6
Wendy. Cambs —1D 52
Wenhaston. Suff —3G 67
Wennington. Cambs —3B 64
Wennington. G Lon —2G 39
Wennington. Lanc —2F 97
Wensley. Derbs —4G 85
Wensley. N Yor —1C 98
Wentbridge. W Yor —3E 93
Wentfordbridge. Corn —5A 10
Wentnor. Shrp —1F 59
Wentworth. Cambs —3D 65
Wentworth. S Yor —1A 86
Wenvoe. V Glam —4E 32
Weobley. Here —5G 59
Weobley Marsh. Here —5G 59
Wepham. W Sus —5B 26
Wereham. Norf —5F 77
Wergs. W Mid —5C 72
Wern. Gwyn —1E 69
Wern. Powy —4E 46
(nr. Brecon)
Wern. Powy —4E 71
(nr. Guilsfield)
Wern. Powy —4B 70
(nr. Llangadfon)
Wern. Powy —3E 71
(nr. Llanymynech)
Wernffrwd. Swan —3E 31
Wernyrheolydd. Mon —4G 47
Werrington. Corn —4D 10
Werrington. Pet —5A 76
Werrington. Staf —1D 72
Wervin. Ches —3G 83
Wesham. Lanc —1C 90
Wessington. Derbs —5A 86
West Aberthaw. V Glam —5D 32
West Acre. Norf —4G 77
West Allerdean. Nmbd —5F 131
West Alvington. Devn —4D 8
West Amesbury. Wilts —2G 23
West Anstey. Devn —4B 20
West Appleton. N Yor —5F 105
West Arthurlie. E Ren —4F 127
West Ashby. Linc —3B 88
West Ashling. W Sus —2G 17
West Ashton. Wilts —1D 23
West Auckland. Dur —2E 105
West Ayton. N Yor —1D 101
West Bagborough. Som —3E 21
West Bank. Hal —2H 83
West Barkwith. Linc —2A 88
West Barnby. N Yor —3F 107
West Barns. E Lot —2C 130
West Barsham. Norf —2B 78
West Bay. Dors —3H 13
West Beckham. Norf —1D 78
West Bennan. N Ayr —3D 123
Westbere. Kent —4F 41
West Bergholt. Essx —3C 54
West Bexington. Dors —4A 14
West Bilney. Norf —4G 77
West Blackdene. Dur —1B 104
West Blatchington. Brig —5D 27
Westborough. Linc —1F 75
Westbourne. Bour —3F 15
Westbourne. W Sus —2F 17
West Bowling. W Yor —1B 92
West Brabourne. Kent —1E 29
West Bradford. Lanc —5G 97
West Bradley. Som —3A 22
West Bretton. W Yor —3C 92
West Bridgford. Notts —2C 74
West Briggs. Norf —4F 77
West Bromwich. W Mid —1D 60
Westbrook. Here —1F 47
Westbrook. Kent —3H 41
Westbrook. Wilts —5E 35
West Buckland. Devn —3G 19
West Buckland. Som —4E 21
West Burnside. Aber —1G 145
West Burrafirth. Shet —6D 173
West Burton. N Yor —1C 98
West Burton. W Sus —4A 26
Westbury. Buck —2E 50
Westbury. Shrp —5F 71
Westbury. Wilts —1D 22
Westbury Leigh. Wilts —2D 22
Westbury-on-Severn. Glos —4C 48
Westbury on Trym. Bris —4A 34
Westbury-sub-Mendip. Som —2A 22
West Butsfield. Dur —5E 115
West Butterwick. N Lin —4B 94
Westby. Linc —3G 75
West Byfleet. Surr —4B 38
West Caister. Norf —4H 79
West Calder. W Lot —3D 128
West Camel. Som —4A 22
West Carr. N Lin —4H 93
West Chaldon. Dors —4C 14
West Challow. Oxon —3B 36
West Charleton. Devn —4D 8
West Chelborough. Dors —2A 14
West Chevington. Nmbd —5G 121
West Chiltington. W Sus —4B 26
West Chiltington Common. W Sus —4B 26
West Chinnock. Som —1H 13
West Chisenbury. Wilts —1G 23
West Clandon. Surr —5B 38
Westcliff. IOW —5D 16
West Cliffe. Kent —1H 29
Westcliffe-on-Sea. S'end —2C 40
West Clyne. High —3F 165
West Coker. Dors —1A 14
Westcombe. Som —3B 22
(nr. Evercreech)
Westcombe. Som —4H 21
(nr. Somerton)
West Common. Linc —3G 87
West Compton. Dors —3A 14
West Compton. Som —2A 22
West Cornforth. Dur —1A 106
Westcot. Oxon —3B 36
Westcote. Glos —3H 49
Westcott. Buck —4F 51
Westcott. Devn —2D 12
Westcott. Surr —1C 26
Westcott Barton. Oxon —3C 50
West Cowick. E Yor —2G 93
West Cranmore. Som —2B 22
West Croftmore. High —2D 150
West Cross. Swan —4F 31
West Cullerley. Aber —3E 153
West Culvennan. Dum —3H 109
West Curry. Corn —3C 10
West Curthwaite. Cumb —5E 113
Westdean. E Sus —5G 27
West Dean. W Sus —1G 17
West Dean. Wilts —4A 24
West Deeping. Linc —5A 76
West Derby. Mers —1F 83
West Dereham. Norf —5F 77
West Down. Devn —2F 19
Westdowns. Corn —4A 10
West Drayton. G Lon —3B 38
West Drayton. Notts —3E 86
West Dunnet. High —1E 169
West Ella. E Yor —2D 94
West End. Beds —5G 63
West End. Cambs —1D 64
West End. Dors —2E 15
West End. E Yor —3E 101
(nr. Kilham)
West End. E Yor —1E 95
(nr. Preston)
West End. E Yor —1C 94
(nr. South Cove)
West End. E Yor —4F 101
(nr. Ulrome)
West End. G Lon —2D 39
West End. Hants —1C 16
West End. Herts —5C 52
West End. Kent —4F 41
West End. Linc —1C 76
West End. Norf —4G 79
West End. N Som —5H 33
West End. N Yor —4D 98
West End. S Glo —3C 34
West End. S Lan —5C 128
West End. Surr —4A 38
West End. Wilts —4E 23
West End. Wind —4G 37
West End. Worc —2F 49
West End Green. Hants —5E 37
Westenhanger. Kent —2F 29
Wester Aberchalder. High —2H 149
Wester Balgedie. Per —3D 136
Wester Brae. High —2A 158
Wester Culbeuchly. Aber —2D 160
Westerdale. High —3D 168
Westerdale. N Yor —4D 106
Wester Dechmont. W Lot —2D 128
Wester Fearn. High —5D 164
Westerfield. Suff —1E 55
Wester Galcantray. High —4C 158
Westergate. W Sus —5A 26
Wester Gruinards. High —4C 164
Westerham. Kent —5F 39
Westerleigh. S Glo —4B 34
Westerloch. High —3F 169
Wester Mandally. High —3E 149
Wester Parkgate. Dum —1B 112
Wester Rarichie. High —1C 158
Westerton. Ang —3F 145
Westerton. Dur —1F 105
Westerton. W Sus —2G 17
Westerwick. Shet —7D 173
West Farleigh. Kent —5B 40
West Farndon. Nptn —5C 62
West Felton. Shrp —3F 71
Westfield. Cumb —2A 102
Westfield. E Sus —4C 28
Westfield. High —2C 168
Westfield. Norf —5B 78
Westfield. N Lan —2A 128
Westfield. W Lot —2C 128
Westfields. Dors —2C 14
Westfields of Rattray. Per —4A 144
West Firle. E Sus —5F 27
West Fleetham. Nmbd —2F 121
West Garforth. W Yor —1D 93
Westgate. Dur —1C 104
Westgate. Norf —1B 78
Westgate. N Lin —4A 94
Westgate on Sea. Kent —3H 41
West Ginge. Oxon —3C 36
West Grafton. Wilts —5H 35
West Green. Hants —1F 25
West Grimstead. Wilts —4H 23
West Grinstead. W Sus —3C 26
West Haddlesey. N Yor —2F 93
West Haddon. Nptn —3D 62
West Hagbourne. Oxon —3D 36
West Hagley. Worc —2C 60
West Hall. Cumb —3G 113
Westhall. Suff —2G 67
West Hallam. Derbs —1B 74
Westhall Terrace. Ang —5D 144
West Halton. N Lin —2C 94
Westham. Dors —5B 14
Westham. E Sus —5H 27
West Ham. G Lon —2E 39
Westham. Som —2H 21
Westhampnett. W Sus —2G 17
West Handley. Derbs —3A 86
West Hanney. Oxon —2C 36
West Hanningfield. Essx —1B 40
West Hardwick. W Yor —3E 93
West Harnham. Wilts —4G 23
West Harptree. Bath —1A 22
West Harting. W Sus —4F 25
West Harton. Tyne —3G 115
West Hatch. Som —4F 21
Westhay. Som —2H 21
Westhead. Lanc —4C 90
West Head. Norf —5E 77
West Heath. Hants —1D 24
(nr. Basingstoke)
West Heath. Hants —1G 25
(nr. Farnborough)
West Helmsdale. High —2H 165
West Hendred. Oxon —3C 36
West Heslerton. N Yor —2D 100
West Hewish. N Som —5G 33
Westhide. Here —1A 48
Westhill. Aber —3F 153
West Hill. Devn —3D 12
West Hill. E Yor —3F 101
Westhill. High —4B 158
West Hill. N Som —4H 33
West Hill. W Sus —2E 27
West Hoathly. W Sus —2E 27
West Holme. Dors —4D 15
Westhope. Here —5G 59
Westhope. Shrp —2G 59
West Horndon. Essx —2H 39
Westhorp. Nptn —5C 62
Westhorpe. Linc —2B 76
Westhorpe. Suff —4C 66
West Horrington. Som —2A 22
West Horsley. Surr —5B 38
West Horton. Nmbd —1E 121
West Hougham. Kent —1G 29
Westhoughton. G Man —4E 91
Westhouse. N Yor —2F 97
West Howe. Bour —3F 15
Westhumble. Surr —5C 38
West Huntspill. Som —2G 21
West Hyde. Herts —1B 38
West Hynish. Arg —4A 138
West Hythe. Kent —2F 29
West Ilsley. W Ber —3C 36
West Itchenor. W Sus —2F 17
West Keal. Linc —4C 88
West Kennett. Wilts —5G 35
West Kilbride. N Ayr —5D 126
West Kingsdown. Kent —4G 39
West Kington. Wilts —4D 34
West Kirby. Mers —2E 82
West Knapton. N Yor —2C 100
West Knighton. Dors —4C 14
West Knoyle. Wilts —3D 22
Westlake. Devn —3C 8
West Lambrook. Som —1H 13
West Langdon. Kent —1H 29
West Langwell. High —3D 164
West Lavington. W Sus —4G 25
West Lavington. Wilts —1F 23
West Layton. N Yor —3E 105
West Leake. Notts —3C 74
West Learmouth. Nmbd —1C 120
Westleigh. Devn —4E 19
(nr. Bideford)

Whiteley Village—Winterborne Houghton

Whiteley Village. Surr—4B 38
Whitemans Green. W Sus—3E 27
White Mill. Carm—3E 45
Whitemire. Mor—3D 159
Whitemoor. Corn—3D 6
Whitenap. Hants—4B 24
Whiteness. Shet—7F 173
White Notley. Essx—4A 54
Whiteoak Green. Oxon—4B 50
Whiteparish. Wilts—4H 23
White Pit. Linc—3C 88
Whiterashes. Aber—1F 153
White Rocks. Here—3H 47
White Roding. Essx—4F 53
Whiterow. High—4F 169
Whiterow. Mor—3E 159
Whiteshill. Glos—5D 48
Whiteside. Nmbd—3A 114
Whiteside. W Lot—3C 128
Whitesmith. E Sus—4G 27
Whitestaunton. Som—1F 13
Whitestone. Aber—4D 152
Whitestone. Devn—3B 12
White Stone. Here—1A 48
Whitestones. Aber—3F 161
Whitestreet Green. Suff—2C 54
Whitewall Corner. N Yor—2B 100
White Waltham. Wind—4G 37
Whiteway. Glos—4E 49
Whitewell. Lanc—5F 97
Whiteworks. Devn—5G 11
Whitewreath. Mor—3G 159
Whitfield. D'dee—5D 144
Whitfield. Kent—1H 29
Whitfield. Nptn—2E 50
Whitfield. Nmbd—4A 114
Whitfield. S Glo—2B 34
Whitford. Devn—3F 13
Whitford. Flin—3D 82
Whitgift. E Yor—2B 94
Whitgreave. Staf—3C 72
Whithorn. Dum—5B 110
Whiting Bay. N Ayr—3E 123
Whitington. Norf—1G 65
Whitkirk. W Yor—1D 92
Whitland. Carm—3G 43
Whitleigh. Plym—2A 8
Whitletts. S Ayr—2C 116
Whitley. N Yor—2F 93
Whitley. Wilts—5D 35
Whitley Bay. Tyne—2G 115
Whitley Chapel. Nmbd—4C 114
Whitley Heath. Staf—3C 72
Whitley Lower. W Yor—3C 92
Whitley Thorpe. N Yor—2F 93
Whitlock's End. W Mid—3F 61
Whitminster. Glos—5C 48
Whitmore. Dors—2F 15
Whitmore. Staf—1C 72
Whitnage. Devn—1D 12
Whitnash. Warw—4H 61
Whitney. Here—1F 47
Whitrigg. Cumb—4D 112
(nr. Kirkbride)
Whitrigg. Cumb—1D 102
(nr. Torpenhow)
Whitsbury. Hants—1G 15
Whitsome. Scot—4E 131
Whitson. Newp—3G 33
Whitstable. Kent—4F 41
Whitstone. Corn—3C 10
Whittingham. Nmbd—3E 121
Whittingslow. Shrp—2G 59
Whittington. Derbs—3B 86
Whittington. Glos—3F 49
Whittington. Lanc—2F 97
Whittington. Shrp—2F 71
Whittington. Staf—2C 60
(nr. Kinver)
Whittington. Staf—5F 73
(nr. Lichfield)
Whittington. Warw—1G 61
Whittington. Worc—5C 60
Whittington Barracks. Staf—5F 73
Whittlebury. Nptn—1E 51
Whittleford. Warw—1H 61
Whittle-le-Woods. Lanc—2D 90
Whittlesey. Cambs—1B 64
Whittlesford. Cambs—1E 53
Whittlestone Head. Bkbn—3F 91
Whitton. N Lin—2C 94
Whitton. Nmbd—4E 121
Whitton. Powy—4E 59
Whitton. Scot—2B 120
Whitton. Shrp—3H 59
Whitton. Stoc T—2A 106
Whittonditch. Wilts—4A 36
Whittonstall. Nmbd—4D 114
Whitway. Hants—1C 24
Whitwell. Derbs—3C 86
Whitwell. Herts—3B 52
Whitwell. IOW—5D 16
Whitwell. N Yor—5F 105
Whitwell. Rut—5G 75
Whitwell-on-the-Hill. N Yor—3B 100
Whitwick. Leics—4B 74
Whitwood. W Yor—2E 93
Whitworth. Lanc—3G 91
Whixall. Shrp—2H 71
Whixley. N Yor—4G 99
Whoberley. W Mid—3G 61
Whorlton. Dur—3E 105
Whorlton. N Yor—4B 106
Whygate. Nmbd—2A 114
Whyle. Here—4H 59
Whyteleafe. Surr—5E 39
Wibdon. Glos—2A 34
Wibtoft. Warw—2B 62
Wichenford. Worc—4B 60
Wichling. Kent—5D 40
Wick. Bour—3G 15
Wick. High—3F 169
Wick. Som—2F 21
(nr. Bridgwater)
Wick. Som—1G 21
(nr. Burnham-on-Sea)
Wick. Som—4H 21
(nr. Somerton)
Wick. S Glo—4C 34
Wick. V Glam—4C 32
Wick. W Sus—5B 26
Wick. Wilts—4G 23
Wick. Worc—1E 49
Wicken. Cambs—3E 65
Wicken. Nptn—2F 51
Wicken Bonhunt. Essx—2E 53
Wickenby. Linc—2H 87
Wickersley. S Yor—1B 86
Wicker Street Green. Suff—1C 54
Wickford. Essx—1B 40
Wickham. Hants—1D 16
Wickham. W Ber—4B 36
Wickham Bishops. Essx—4B 54
Wickhambreaux. Kent—5G 41
Wickhambrook. Suff—5G 65
Wickhamford. Worc—1F 49
Wickham Green. Suff—4C 66
Wickham Heath. W Ber—5C 36
Wickham Market. Suff—5E 67
Wickhampton. Norf—5G 79
Wickham St Paul. Essx—2B 54
Wickham Skeith. Suff—4C 66
Wickham Street. Suff—4C 66
Wick Hill. Wok—5F 37
Wicklewood. Norf—5C 78
Wickmere. Norf—2D 78
Wick St Lawrence. N Som—5G 33
Wickwar. S Glo—3C 34
Widdington. Essx—2F 53
Widdrington. Nmbd—5G 121
Widdrington Station. Nmbd—5G 121
Widecombe in the Moor. Devn—5H 11
Widegates. Corn—3G 7
Widemouth Bay. Corn—2C 10
Wide Open. Tyne—2F 115
Widewall. Orkn—8D 172
Widford. Essx—5G 53
Widford. Herts—4E 53
Widham. Wilts—3F 35
Widmer End. Buck—2G 37
Widmerpool. Notts—3D 74
Widnes. Hal—2H 83
Widworthy. Devn—3F 13
Wigan. G Man—4D 90
Wigbeth. Dors—2F 15
Wiggaton. Devn—3E 12
Wiggenhall St Germans. Norf—4E 77
Wiggenhall St Mary Magdalen. Norf—4E 77
Wiggenhall St Mary the Virgin. Norf—4E 77
Wiggenhall St Peter. Norf—4F 77
Wiggens Green. Essx—1G 53
Wigginton. Herts—4H 51
Wigginton. Oxon—2B 50
Wigginton. Staf—5G 73
Wigginton. York—4H 99
Wigglesworth. N Yor—4H 97
Wiggonby. Cumb—4D 112
Wiggonholt. W Sus—4B 26
Wighill. N Yor—5G 99
Wighton. Norf—1B 78
Wightwick. W Mid—1C 60
Wigley. Hants—1B 16
Wigmore. Here—4G 59
Wigmore. Medw—4C 40
Wigsley. Notts—3F 87
Wigsthorpe. Nptn—2H 63
Wigston. Leics—1D 62
Wigtoft. Linc—2B 76
Wigton. Cumb—5D 112
Wigtown. Dum—4B 110
Wigtwizzle. S Yor—1G 85
Wike. W Yor—5F 99
Wilbarston. Nptn—2F 63
Wilberfoss. E Yor—4B 100
Wilburton. Cambs—3D 65
Wilby. Norf—1C 66
Wilby. Nptn—4F 63
Wilby. Suff—3E 67
Wilcot. Wilts—5G 35
Wilcott. Shrp—4F 71
Wilcove. Corn—3A 8
Wildboarclough. Ches—4D 85
Wilden. Beds—5H 63
Wilden. Worc—3C 60
Wildern. Hants—1C 16
Wilderspool. Warr—2A 84
Wilde Street. Suff—3G 65
Wildhern. Hants—1B 24
Wildmanbridge. S Lan—4B 128
Wildmoor. Worc—3D 60
Wildsworth. Linc—1F 87
Wildwood. Staf—3D 72
Wilford. Not C—2C 74
Wilkesley. Ches—1A 72
Wilkhaven. High—5G 165
Wilkieston. W Lot—3E 129
Wilksby. Linc—4B 88
Willand. Devn—1D 12
Willaston. Ches—5A 84
(nr. Crewe)
Willaston. Ches—3F 83
(nr. Neston)
Willaston. IOM—4C 108
Willen. Mil—1G 51
Willenhall. W Mid—3A 62
(nr. Coventry)
Willenhall. W Mid—1D 60
(nr. Wolverhampton)
Willerby. E Yor—1D 94
Willerby. N Yor—2E 101
Willersey. Glos—2G 49
Willersley. Here—1G 47
Willesborough. Kent—1E 28
Willesborough Lees. Kent—1E 29
Willesden. G Lon—2D 38
Willesley. Wilts—3D 34
Willett. Som—3E 20
Willey. Shrp—1A 60
Willey. Warw—2B 62
Willey Green. Surr—5A 38
Williamscot. Oxon—1C 50
Willian. Herts—2C 52
Willingale. Essx—5F 53
Willingdon. E Sus—5G 27
Willingham. Cambs—3D 64
Willingham by Stow. Linc—2F 87
Willingham Green. Cambs—5F 65
Willington. Beds—1B 52
Willington. Derbs—3G 73
Willington. Dur—1E 105
Willington. Tyne—3G 115
Willington. Warw—2A 50
Willington Corner. Ches—4H 83
Willisham Tye. Suff—5C 66
Willitoft. E Yor—1H 93
Williton. Som—2D 20
Willoughbridge. Staf—1B 72
Willoughby. Linc—3D 89
Willoughby. Warw—4C 62
Willoughby on the Wolds. Notts—3D 74
Willoughby Waterleys. Leics—1C 62
Willoughton. Linc—1G 87
Willow Green. Worc—5B 60
Willows Green. Essx—4H 53
Willsbridge. S Glo—4B 34
Willslock. Staf—2E 73
Willsworthy. Devn—4F 11
Wilmcote. Warw—5F 61
Wilmington. Bath—5B 34
Wilmington. Devn—3F 13
Wilmington. E Sus—5G 27
Wilmington. Kent—3G 39
Wilmslow. Ches—2C 84
Wilnecote. Staf—5G 73
Wilney Green. Norf—2C 66
Wilpshire. Lanc—1E 91
Wilsden. W Yor—1A 92
Wilsford. Linc—1H 75
Wilsford. Wilts—3G 23
(nr. Amesbury)
Wilsford. Wilts—1G 23
(nr. Devizes)
Wilsill. N Yor—3D 98
Wilsley Green. Kent—2B 28
Wilson. Here—3A 48
Wilson. Leics—3B 74
Wilsontown. S Lan—4C 128
Wilstead. Beds—1A 52
Wilsthorpe. E Yor—3F 101
Wilsthorpe. Linc—4H 75
Wilstone. Herts—4H 51
Wilton. Cumb—3B 102
Wilton. N Yor—1C 100
Wilton. Red C—3C 106
Wilton. Scot—3H 119
Wilton. Wilts—5A 36
(nr. Marlborough)
Wilton. Wilts—3F 23
(nr. Salisbury)
Wimbish. Essx—2F 53
Wimbish Green. Essx—2G 53
Wimblebury. Staf—4E 73
Wimbledon. G Lon—3D 38
Wimblington. Cambs—1D 64
Wimborne Minster. Dors—2F 15
Wimborne St Giles. Dors—1F 15
Wimbotsham. Norf—5F 77
Wimpstone. Warw—1H 49
Wincanton. Som—4C 22
Winceby. Linc—4C 88
Wincham. Ches—3A 84
Winchburgh. W Lot—2D 129
Winchcombe. Glos—3F 49
Winchelsea. E Sus—4D 28
Winchelsea Beach. E Sus—4D 28
Winchester. Hants—4C 24
Winchet Hill. Kent—1B 28
Winchfield. Hants—1F 25
Winchmore Hill. Buck—1A 38
Winchmore Hill. G Lon—1E 39
Wincle. Ches—4D 84
Windermere. Cumb—5F 103
Winderton. Warw—1B 50
Windhill. High—4H 157
Windle Hill. Ches—3F 83
Windlesham. Surr—4A 38
Windley. Derbs—1H 73
Windmill. Derbs—3F 85
Windmill Hill. E Sus—4H 27
Windmill Hill. Som—1G 13
Windrush. Glos—4G 49
Windsor. Wind—3A 38
Windsor Green. Suff—5A 66
Windyedge. Aber—4G 153
Windygates. Fife—3F 137
Windyharbour. Ches—3C 84
Windyknowe. W Lot—3C 128
Wineham. W Sus—3D 26
Winestead. E Yor—2G 95
Winfarthing. Norf—2D 66
Winford. IOW—4D 16
Winford. N Som—5A 34
Winforton. Here—1F 47
Winfrith Newburgh. Dors—4D 14
Wing. Buck—3G 51
Wing. Rut—5F 75
Wingate. Dur—1A 106
Wingates. G Man—4E 91
Wingates. Nmbd—5F 121
Wingerworth. Derbs—4A 86
Wingfield. Beds—3A 52
Wingfield. Suff—3E 67
Wingfield. Wilts—1D 22
Wingfield Park. Derbs—5A 86
Wingham. Kent—5G 41
Wingmore. Kent—1F 29
Wingrave. Buck—4G 51
Winkburn. Notts—5E 86
Winkfield. Brac—3A 38
Winkfield Row. Brac—4G 37
Winkhill. Staf—5E 85
Winklebury. Hants—1E 24
Winkleigh. Devn—2G 11
Winksley. N Yor—2E 99
Winkton. Dors—3G 15
Winlaton. Tyne—3E 115
Winlaton Mill. Tyne—3E 115
Winless. High—3F 169
Winmarleigh. Lanc—5D 96
Winnal Common. Here—2H 47
Winnard's Perch. Corn—2D 6
Winnersh. Wok—4F 37
Winnington. Ches—3A 84
Winnington. Staf—2B 72
Winnothdale. Staf—1E 73
Winscales. Cumb—2B 102
Winscombe. N Som—1H 21
Winsford. Ches—4A 84
Winsford. Som—3C 20
Winsham. Devn—3F 19
Winsham. Som—2G 13
Winshill. Staf—3G 73
Winsh-wen. Swan—3F 31
Winskill. Cumb—1G 103
Winslade. Hants—2E 25
Winsley. Wilts—5D 34
Winslow. Buck—3F 51
Winson. Glos—5F 49
Winson Green. W Mid—2E 61
Winsor. Hants—1B 16
Winster. Cumb—5F 103
Winster. Derbs—4G 85
Winston. Dur—3E 105
Winston. Suff—4D 66
Winstone. Glos—5E 49
Winswell. Devn—1E 11
Winterborne Clenston. Dors—2D 14
Winterborne Herringston. Dors—4B 14
Winterborne Houghton. Dors—2D 14

Wootton—Zouch

Wootton. *Shrp* —3F 71
(nr. Oswestry)
Wootton. *Staf* —3C 72
(nr. Eccleshall)
Wootton. *Staf* —1F 73
(nr. Ellastone)
Wootton Bassett. *Wilts* —3F 35
Wootton Bridge. *IOW* —3D 16
Wootton Common. *IOW* —3D 16
Wootton Courtenay. *Som* —2C 20
Wootton Fitzpaine. *Dors* —3G 13
Wootton Rivers. *Wilts* —5G 35
Woottons. *Staf* —2E 73
Wootton St Lawrence. *Hants* —1D 24
Wootton Wawen. *Warw* —4F 61
Worcester. *Worc* —5C 60
Worcester Park. *G Lon* —4D 38
Wordsley. *W Mid* —2C 60
Worfield. *Shrp* —1B 60
Workhouse Green. *Suff* —2C 54
Workington. *Cumb* —2A 102
Worksop. *Notts* —3C 86
Worlaby. *N Lin* —3D 94
Worlds End. *Hants* —1E 17
Worldsend. *Shrp* —1G 59
World's End. *W Ber* —4C 36
Worlds End. *W Mid* —2F 61
World's End. *W Sus* —4E 27
Worle. *N Som* —5G 33
Worleston. *Ches* —5A 84
Worley. *Glos* —2D 34
Worlingham. *Suff* —1G 67
Worlingham. *Suff* —3F 65
Worlingworth. *Suff* —4E 67
Wormbridge. *Here* —2H 47
Wormegay. *Norf* —4F 77
Wormelow Tump. *Here* —2H 47
Wormhill. *Derbs* —3F 85
Wormiehills. *Ang* —5F 145
Wormingford. *Essx* —2C 54
Worminghall. *Buck* —5E 51
Wormington. *Glos* —2F 49
Worminster. *Som* —2A 22
Wormit. *Fife* —1F 137
Wormleighton. *Warw* —5B 62
Wormley. *Herts* —5D 52
Wormley. *Surr* —2A 26
Wormshill. *Kent* —5C 40
Wormsley. *Here* —1H 47
Worplesdon. *Surr* —5A 38
Worrall. *S Yor* —1H 85
Worsbrough. *S Yor* —4D 92
Worsley. *G Man* —4F 91
Worstead. *Norf* —3F 79
Worsthorne. *Lanc* —1G 91
Worston. *Lanc* —5G 97
Worth. *Kent* —5H 41
Worth. *W Sus* —2E 27
Wortham. *Suff* —3C 66
Worthen. *Shrp* —5F 71
Worthenbury. *Wrex* —1G 71
Worthing. *Norf* —4B 78
Worthing. *W Sus* —5C 26
Worthington. *Leics* —3B 74
Worth Matravers. *Dors* —5E 15
Worting. *Hants* —1E 24
Wortley. *Glos* —2C 34
Wortley. *S Yor* —1H 85
Wortley. *W Yor* —1C 92
Worton. *N Yor* —5C 104
Worton. *Wilts* —1E 23
Wortwell. *Norf* —2E 67
Wotherton. *Shrp* —5E 71

Wothorpe. *Nptn* —5H 75
Wotter. *Devn* —2B 8
Wotton. *Glos* —4D 48
Wotton. *Surr* —1C 26
Wotton-under-Edge. *Glos* —2C 34
Wotton Underwood. *Buck* —4E 51
Wouldham. *Kent* —4B 40
Wrabness. *Essx* —2E 55
Wrafton. *Devn* —3E 19
Wragby. *Linc* —3A 88
Wragby. *W Yor* —3E 93
Wramplingham. *Norf* —5D 78
Wrangbrook. *W Yor* —3E 93
Wrangle. *Linc* —5D 88
Wrangle Lowgate. *Linc* —5D 88
Wrangway. *Som* —1E 13
Wrantage. *Som* —4G 21
Wrawby. *N Lin* —4D 94
Wraxall. *Dors* —2A 14
Wraxall. *N Som* —4H 33
Wraxall. *Som* —3B 22
Wray. *Lanc* —3F 97
Wrayland. *Devn* —4A 12
Wraysbury. *Wind* —3B 38
Wrayton. *Lanc* —2F 97
Wrea Green. *Lanc* —1B 90
Wreay. *Cumb* —5F 113
(nr. Carlisle)
Wreay. *Cumb* —2F 103
(nr. Penrith)
Wrecclesham. *Surr* —2G 25
Wrecsam. *Wrex* —5F 83
Wrekenton. *Tyne* —4F 115
Wrelton. *N Yor* —1B 100
Wrenbury. *Ches* —1H 71
Wreningham. *Norf* —1D 66
Wrentham. *Suff* —2G 67
Wrenthorpe. *W Yor* —2D 92
Wrentnall. *Shrp* —5G 71
Wressle. *E Yor* —1H 93
Wressle. *N Lin* —4C 94
Wrestlingworth. *Beds* —1C 52
Wretham. *Norf* —1B 66
Wretton. *Norf* —5F 77
Wrexham. *Wrex* —5F 83
Wrexham Industrial Estate. *Wrex*
—1F 71
Wrickton. *Shrp* —2A 60
Wrightington Bar. *Lanc* —3D 90
Wright's Green. *Essx* —4F 53
Wrinehill. *Staf* —1B 72
Wrington. *N Som* —5H 33
Writtle. *Essx* —5G 53
Wrockwardine. *Telf* —4A 72
Wroot. *N Lin* —4H 93
Wrotham. *Kent* —5H 39
Wrotham Heath. *Kent* —5H 39
Wroughton. *Swin* —3G 35
Wroxall. *IOW* —5D 16
Wroxall. *Warw* —3G 61
Wroxeter. *Shrp* —5H 71
Wroxham. *Norf* —4F 79
Wroxton. *Oxon* —1C 50
Wyaston. *Derbs* —1F 73
Wyatt's Green. *Essx* —1G 39
Wybers Wood. *NE Lin* —4F 95
Wyberton. *Linc* —1C 76
Wyboston. *Beds* —5A 64
Wybunbury. *Ches* —1A 72
Wychbold. *Worc* —4D 60
Wych Cross. *E Sus* —2F 27
Wychnor. *Staf* —4F 73
Wychnor Bridges. *Staf* —4F 73

Wyck. *Hants* —3F 25
Wyck Hill. *Glos* —3G 49
Wyck Rissington. *Glos* —3G 49
Wycliffe. *Dur* —3E 105
Wycombe Marsh. *Buck* —2G 37
Wyddial. *Herts* —2D 52
Wye. *Kent* —1E 29
Wyesham. *Mon* —4A 48
Wyfold Grange. *Oxon* —3E 37
Wyfordby. *Leics* —4E 75
Wyke. *Devn* —2B 12
Wyke. *Dors* —4C 22
Wyke. *Shrp* —5A 72
Wyke. *Surr* —5A 38
Wyke. *W Yor* —2B 92
Wyke Champflower. *Som* —3B 22
Wykeham. *Linc* —3B 76
Wykeham. *N Yor* —2C 100
(nr. Malton)
Wykeham. *N Yor* —1D 100
(nr. Scarborough)
Wyken. *Shrp* —1B 60
Wyken. *W Mid* —2A 62
Wyke Regis. *Dors* —5B 14
Wyke, The. *Shrp* —5B 72
Wykey. *Shrp* —3F 71
Wykin. *Leics* —1B 62
Wylam. *Nmbd* —3E 115
Wylde Green. *W Mid* —1F 61
Wylye. *Wilts* —3F 23
Wymering. *Port* —2E 17
Wymeswold. *Leics* —3D 74
Wymington. *Beds* —4G 63
Wymondham. *Leics* —4F 75
Wymondham. *Norf* —5D 78
Wyndham. *B'End* —2C 32
Wynford Eagle. *Dors* —3A 14
Wyre Piddle. *Worc* —1E 49
Wysall. *Notts* —3D 74
Wyson. *Here* —4H 59
Wythall. *Worc* —3E 61
Wytham. *Oxon* —5C 50
Wythburn. *Cumb* —3E 103
Wythenshawe. *G Man* —2C 84
Wythop Mill. *Cumb* —2C 102
Wyton. *Cambs* —3B 64
Wyton. *E Yor* —1E 95
Wyverstone. *Suff* —4C 66
Wyverstone Street. *Suff* —4C 66
Wyville. *Linc* —3F 75
Wyvis Lodge. *High* —1G 157

Y

Yaddlethorpe. *N Lin* —4B 94
Yafford. *IOW* —4C 16
Yafforth. *N Yor* —5A 106
Yalberton. *Torb* —3E 9
Yalding. *Kent* —5A 40
Yanley. *N Som* —5A 34
Yanwath. *Cumb* —2G 103
Yanworth. *Glos* —4F 49
Yapham. *E Yor* —4B 100
Yapton. *W Sus* —5A 26
Yarburgh. *Linc* —1C 88
Yarcombe. *Devn* —2F 13
Yarde. *Som* —3D 20
Yardley. *W Mid* —2F 61
Yardley Gobion. *Nptn* —1F 51
Yardley Hastings. *Nptn* —5F 63
Yardley Wood. *W Mid* —2F 61
Yardro. *Powy* —5E 58
Yarhampton. *Worc* —4B 60
Yarkhill. *Here* —1B 48

Yarlet. *Staf* —3D 72
Yarley. *Som* —2A 22
Yarlington. *Som* —4B 22
Yarm. *Stoc T* —3B 106
Yarmouth. *IOW* —4B 16
Yarnbrook. *Wilts* —1D 22
Yarnfield. *Staf* —2C 72
Yarnscombe. *Devn* —4F 19
Yarnton. *Oxon* —4C 50
Yarpole. *Here* —4G 59
Yarrow. *Nmbd* —1A 114
Yarrow. *Scot* —2F 119
Yarrow. *Som* —2G 21
Yarrow Feus. *Scot* —2F 119
Yarrow Ford. *Scot* —1G 119
Yarsop. *Here* —1H 47
Yarwell. *Nptn* —1H 63
Yate. *S Glo* —3C 34
Yateley. *Hants* —5G 37
Yatesbury. *Wilts* —4F 35
Yattendon. *W Ber* —4D 36
Yatton. *Here* —4G 59
(nr. Leominster)
Yatton. *Here* —2B 48
(nr. Ross-on-Wye)
Yatton. *N Som* —5H 33
Yatton Keynell. *Wilts* —4D 34
Yaverland. *IOW* —4E 16
Yawl. *Devn* —3G 13
Yaxham. *Norf* —4C 78
Yaxley. *Cambs* —1A 64
Yaxley. *Suff* —3D 66
Yazor. *Here* —1H 47
Y Bala. *Gwyn* —2B 70
Y Bont-Faen. *V Glam* —4C 32
Y Dref. *Gwyn* —2D 69
Y Drenewydd. *Powy* —1D 58
Yeading. *G Lon* —2C 38
Yeadon. *W Yor* —5E 98
Yealand Conyers. *Lanc* —2E 97
Yealand Redmayne. *Lanc* —2E 97
Yealmpton. *Devn* —3B 8
Yearby. *Red C* —2D 106
Yearngill. *Cumb* —5C 112
Yearsett. *Here* —5B 60
Yearsley. *N Yor* —2H 99
Yeaton. *Shrp* —4G 71
Yeaveley. *Derbs* —1F 73
Yeavering. *Nmbd* —1D 120
Yedingham. *N Yor* —2C 100
Yelden. *Beds* —4H 63
Yeldersley Hollies. *Derbs* —1G 73
Yelford. *Oxon* —5B 50
Yelland. *Devn* —3E 19
Yelling. *Cambs* —4B 64
Yelsted. *Kent* —4C 40
Yelvertoft. *Nptn* —3C 62
Yelverton. *Devn* —2B 8
Yelverton. *Norf* —5E 79
Yenston. *Som* —4C 22
Yeoford. *Devn* —3A 12
Yeolmbridge. *Corn* —4D 10
Yeo Mill. *Devn* —4B 20
Yeovil. *Som* —1A 14
Yeovil Marsh. *Som* —1A 14
Yeovilton. *Som* —4A 22
Yerbeston. *Pemb* —4E 43
Yetlington. *Nmbd* —4E 121
Yetminster. *Dors* —1A 14
Yett. *N Lan* —4A 128
Yett. *S Ayr* —2D 116
Yettington. *Devn* —4D 12
Yetts o' Muckhart. *Clac* —3C 136

Y Felinheli. *Gwyn* —4E 81
Y Fenni. *Mon* —4G 47
Y Ferwig. *Cdgn* —1B 44
Y Fflint. *Flin* —3E 83
Y Ffor. *Gwyn* —2C 68
Y Gelli Gandryll. *Powy* —1F 47
Yieldshields. *S Lan* —4B 128
Yiewsley. *G Lon* —2B 38
Yinstay. *Orkn* —6E 172
Ynysboeth. *Rhon* —2D 32
Ynysddu. *Cphy* —2E 33
Ynysforgan. *Swan* —3F 31
Ynyshir. *Rhon* —2D 32
Ynyslas. *Cdgn* —1F 57
Ynysmaerdy. *Neat* —5G 31
Ynysmaerdy. *Rhon* —3D 32
Ynysmeudwy. *Neat* —5H 45
Ynystawe. *Swan* —5G 45
Ynyswen. *Powy* —4B 46
Ynys-wen. *Rhon* —2C 32
Ynys y Barri. *V Glam* —5E 32
Ynysybwl. *Rhon* —2D 32
Yockenthwaite. *N Yor* —2B 98
Yockleton. *Shrp* —4G 71
Yokefleet. *E Yor* —2B 94
Yoker. *Glas* —3G 127
Yonder Bognie. *Aber* —4D 160
York. *York* —4A 100
Yorkletts. *Kent* —4E 41
Yorkley. *Glos* —5B 48
Yorton. *Shrp* —3H 71
Yorton Heath. *Shrp* —3H 71
Youlgreave. *Derbs* —4G 85
Youlthorpe. *E Yor* —4B 100
Youlton. *N Yor* —3G 99
Young's End. *Essx* —4H 53
Young Wood. *Linc* —3A 88
Yoxall. *Staf* —4F 73
Yoxford. *Suff* —4F 67
Yr Hob. *Flin* —5F 83
Y Rhws. *V Glam* —5D 32
Yr Wyddgrug. *Flin* —4E 83
Ysbyty Cynfyn. *Cdgn* —3G 57
Ysbyty Ifan. *Cnwy* —1H 69
Ysbyty Ystwyth. *Cdgn* —3G 57
Ysceifiog. *Flin* —3D 82
Yspitty. *Carm* —3E 31
Ystalyfera. *Neat* —5A 46
Ystrad. *Rhon* —2C 32
Ystrad Aeron. *Cdgn* —5E 57
Ystradfellte. *Powy* —4C 46
Ystradffin. *Carm* —1A 46
Ystradgynlais. *Powy* —4A 46
Ystradmeurig. *Cdgn* —4G 57
Ystrad Mynach. *Cphy* —2E 33
Ystradowen. *Neat* —4A 46
Ystradowen. *V Glam* —4D 32
Ystumtuen. *Cdgn* —3G 57
Ythanbank. *Aber* —5G 161
Ythanwells. *Aber* —5D 160
Y Trallwng. *Powy* —5E 70
Y Waun. *Wrex* —2E 71

Z

Zeal Monachorum. *Devn* —2H 11
Zeals. *Wilts* —3C 22
Zelah. *Corn* —3C 6
Zennor. *Corn* —3B 4
Zouch. *Notts* —3C 74